Communications in Computer and Information Science 1047

Commenced Publication in 2007
Founding and Former Series Editors:
Phoebe Chen, Alfredo Cuzzocrea, Xiaoyong Du, Orhun Kara, Ting Liu,
Krishna M. Sivalingam, Dominik Ślęzak, Takashi Washio, and Xiaokang Yang

More information about this series at http://www.springer.com/series/7899

Fernando De La Prieta ·
Alfonso González-Briones ·
Pawel Pawleski · Davide Calvaresi ·
Elena Del Val · Fernando Lopes ·
Vicente Julian · Eneko Osaba ·
Ramón Sánchez-Iborra (Eds.)

Highlights of Practical Applications of Survivable Agents and Multi-Agent Systems

The PAAMS Collection

International Workshops of PAAMS 2019
Ávila, Spain, June 26–28, 2019
Proceedings

Springer

Editors
Fernando De La Prieta (iD)
University of Salamanca
Salamanca, Spain

Pawel Pawleski
Poznań University of Technology
Poznan, Poland

Elena Del Val
Polytechnic University of Valencia
Valencia, Spain

Vicente Julian
Polytechnic University of Valencia
Valencia, Spain

Ramón Sánchez-Iborra
University of Murcia
Murcia, Spain

Alfonso González-Briones
University of Salamanca
Salamanca, Spain

Davide Calvaresi
HES-SO Valais Wallis
Sierre, Switzerland

Fernando Lopes
National Laboratory for Energy and Geology
Amadora, Portugal

Eneko Osaba
Tecnalia Research & Innovation
Derio, Spain

ISSN 1865-0929   ISSN 1865-0937   (electronic)
Communications in Computer and Information Science
ISBN 978-3-030-24298-5   ISBN 978-3-030-24299-2   (eBook)
https://doi.org/10.1007/978-3-030-24299-2

This Springer imprint is published by the registered company Springer Nature Switzerland AG
The registered company address is: Gewerbestrasse 11, 6330 Cham, Switzerland

Preface

The PAAMS Workshops complemented the regular program with new or emerging trends of particular interest connected to multi-agent systems. PAAMS, the International Conference on Practical Applications of Agents and Multi-Agent Systems, is an evolution of the International Workshop on Practical Applications of Agents and Multi-Agent Systems. PAAMS is an international yearly tribune for presenting, discussing, and disseminating the latest developments and the most important outcomes related to real-world applications. It provides a unique opportunity to bring multi-disciplinary experts, academics, and practitioners together to exchange their experience in the development of agents and multi-agent systems.

This volume presents the papers that were accepted in the workshops during the 2019 edition of PAAMS: Workshop on Agent-based Solutions for Manufacturing and Supply Chain (AMSC), Second International Workshop on Blockchain Technology for Multi-agent Systems (BTC4MAS), Workshop on MAS for Complex Networks and Social Computation (CNSC), Workshop on Multi-agent-Based Applications for Energy Markets, Smart Grids, and Sustainable Energy Systems (MASGES), Workshop on Smart Cities and Intelligent Agents (SCIA), and Workshop on Swarm Intelligence and Swarm Robotics (SISR). This volume also contains the accepted papers to the Special Session on Software Agents and Virtualization for Internet of Things (SAVIoTS). Finally, the articles sent to the Doctoral Consortium track are also included. Each paper submitted to PAAMS went through a stringent peer review by three members of the international committee of each track. From the 47 submissions received, 34 were selected for presentation at the conference.

We would like to thank all the contributing authors, the members of the Program Committee, the sponsors (IEEE Systems Man and Cybernetics Society Spain Section Chapter and the IEEE Spain Section (Technical Co-Sponsor), IBM, Indra, Viewnext, Global exchange, AEPIA, AFIA, APPIA, PU, CNRS and AIR institute. We thank the funding supporting with the project *"Intelligent and sustainable mobility supported by multi-agent systems and edge computing"* (Id. RTI2018-095390-B-C32) and, also the Organizing Committee for their hard and highly valuable work. Their work contributed to the success of the PAAMS 2019 event.

Thanks for your help – PAAMS 2019 would not exist without your contribution.

June 2019

Fernando De la Prieta
Alfonso González-Briones
Pawel Pawleski
Davide Calvaresi
Elena Del Val
Fernando Lopes
Vicente Julian
Eneko Osaba
Ramón Sánchez-Iborra

Contents

Workshop on Swarm Intelligence and Swarm Robotics (SISR)

**Special Session on Software Agents and Virtualizacion for Internet
of Things (SAVIoTS)**

Doctoral Consortium

Workshop on Agent-Based Solutions for Manufacturing and Supply Chain (AMSC)

Workshop on Agent-Based Solutions for Manufacturing and Supply Chain (AMSC)

The AMSC 2019 workshop was a forum to share ideas, projects, research results, applications, and experiences associated with agent-based solutions for various issues in manufacturing and supply chains. This workshop was held in Avila (Spain) as the part of International Conference on Practical Applications of Agents and Multi-Agent Systems 2019 (PAAMS 2019).

The supply chain concept includes many aspects such as inventory management, places to stock goods, flow of materials throughout the chain, means of transport for goods, and many others. A second important aspect is one of production, with many emerging issues, such as: resource allocation, production planning, production scheduling and control, materials flow etc. Currently, many method and solutions for this area have been defined; however, further improvements are still sought. The aim of the AMSC workshop is to provide a platform for discussions on the new multi-agent solutions that may be successfully applied for improvement of manufacturing operations and supply chain management. Both theoretical and practical approaches in the area are welcome.

Organization

Organizing Committee

Patrycja Hoffa-Dabrowska   Poznan University of Technology, Poland
Pawel Pawlewski   Poznan University of Technology, Poland
Paulina Golinska-Dawson   Poznan University of Technology, Poland

Program Committee

Zbigniew J. Pasek   IMSE/University of Windsor, Canada
Paul-Eric Dossou   ICAM Vendee, France
Grzegorz Bocewicz   Koszalin University of Technology, Poland
Paweł Sitek   Kielce University of technology, Poland
Izabela E. Nielsen   Aalborg University, Denmark
Peter Nielsen   Aalborg University, Denmark
Allen Greenwood   Mississippi State University, USA

Implementation Techniques to Parallelize Agent-Based Graph Analysis

Collin Gordon[✉][iD], Utku Mert, Matthew Sell[iD], and Munehiro Fukuda[iD]

Computing and Software Systems, University of Washington,
Bothell, WA 98011, USA
colntrev@gmail.com, utkumert@gmail.com, {mrsell,mfukuda}@uw.edu
http://depts.washington.edu/dslab

Abstract. The current trend for parallelizing scalable graph analysis is to use major big-data tools such as MapReduce, Spark/GraphX, and Storm. Each programming framework uses graph analysis strategies based on either (1) message passing among graph vertices or (2) screening of graph edges. The former keeps exchanging messages among all neighboring vertices until all of them fall into a stable state and thus no more messages are generated. The latter examines the connectivity of edges to find particular network shapes, (e.g., counting the number of triangles). Although these two approaches are well established as conventional graph solutions, the underlying algorithms may not be clear enough to keep track of how vertices, edges, and messages are processed in parallel. Contrary to these conventional approaches, agent-based graph analysis drives agents over a graph, which allows programmers to code their solutions from the drivers seat view. However, there are performance drawbacks, mainly resulting from agent management overheads, that make it impractical to use agents. The Multi-Agent Spatial Simulation (MASS) library uses reactive agents, small enough to spawn, move, and get terminated quickly. By implementing two optimization techniques in MASS: agent population control and asynchronous agent migration, we have facilitated agent-based graph analysis. This paper presents these two techniques, demonstrates agents intuitive programmability, and their competitive execution performance.

Keywords: Agent-based models · Parallelization · Graph analysis

1 Introduction

Scalable graph analysis has substantial applications in industry. For instance, page ranking, connected components, and triangle counting are typical analysis social network services use to rank web sites, find friendship clusters, and compute closeness among users. As the services maintain numerous web sites and network users in a data center – in most cases over cluster systems, a spontaneous solution is to pursue the graph scalability with major big-data tools

© Springer Nature Switzerland AG 2019
F. De la Prieta et al. (Eds.): PAAMS 2019 Workshops, CCIS 1047, pp. 3–14, 2019.
https://doi.org/10.1007/978-3-030-24299-2_1

such as Hadoop/MapReduce[1], Spark/GraphX[2], and Storm[3]. In fact, GraphX facilitates all the above three social-network algorithms as its built-in functions.

Although these tools provided users with their unique parallel-programming framework, their graph analyses are all based on either (1) message passing among graph vertices or (2) screening of graph edges. The former keeps exchanging messages among all neighboring vertices until all of them fall into a stable state and thus no more messages are generated. An example is breadth-first search (BFS) in MapReduce [11] where messages are diffused over a graph. The latter examines the connectivity of edges to find a particular network shape. An example is triangle counting in Spark [14] where all edges are screened to find which of them constitute triangles.

These two approaches, (which we respectively call vertex- and edge-oriented approaches in the following discussions), are well established as conventional graph solutions, however programmers cannot always understand the underlying algorithm behaviors intuitively. For instance, triangle counting in [14] needs to enumerate edges emanating from each vertex, to choose only pairs that can create a triad, (i.e., those connecting three vertices in a series of edges), to check if they have another edge to connect their two end vertices, thus creating a triangle, and to get rid of redundant triangles. Easy to say but hard to code.

Contrary to the conventional vertex- and edge-oriented approaches is to walk agents over a graph. Agents are computing entities or objects with navigational autonomy. Using agents, programmers can code a graph application as if they are driving a car, (i.e., an agent) over the graph. We will call this agent-based approach below. Back to triangle counting, all we need is to let an agent start at each graph vertex and move its clones along each emanating edge three times, which can find triangles if the agents can drive back to their original vertex in three hops. The idea of agent-based approach is not brand new [3,9,15]. However, their execution performance was not competitive to the conventional approaches, due to their heavy-weight agent implementation, using processes or threads whose instantiation, termination, and migration overheads kill parallel performance.

We have strived to address such agent management overheads, using the concept of reactive agents that are very small objects carrying only a few rules to react to their environments or the other agents. We implemented this concept in the Multi-Agent Spatial Simulation (MASS) library. Yet, we have encountered two implementation problems inherent to graph problems: (1) the agent population rapidly grows as agents are cloned over a graph, which quickly consumes physical memory and (2) synchronization among a massive number of agents is no longer negligible, which deteriorates parallel performance.

To practicalize agent-based graph analysis, this paper presents two optimization techniques: agent population control and asynchronous agent migration, and demonstrates agents intuitive programmability and performance competitiveness

---

[1] https://hadoop.apache.org/docs/r1.2.1/mapred_tutorial.html.
[2] https://spark.apache.org/graphx/.
[3] http://storm.apache.org/.

in two graph problems: BFS and triangle counting. In the following, Sect. 2 compares vertex, edge, and agent-oriented approaches in graph analysis; Sect. 3 briefs the MASS library and discusses our performance optimization to run graph programs with agents; Sect. 4 evaluates our performance optimization techniques; and Sect. 5 summarizes our contribution.

2 Parallel Graph Analysis

This section looks at three different approaches to graph analysis: (1) vertex-oriented, (2) edge-oriented, and (3) agent-oriented approach below.

2.1 Vertex-Oriented Approach

This approach solves a graph problem by repetitively exchanging information among neighboring graph vertices until all vertices eventually fall into a stable state that emits no more new information. Its parallelization is based on the use of either message passing or data sharing among neighboring vertices.

Pregel [13] is based on message passing where each vertex updates its state with *compute( )* and diffuses its status change to neighbors with *sendMessageTo( )*, which further invokes their *compute( )*. Upon no more messages, all vertices call *voteToHalt( )* that declares a finish of the current graph execution. Pregel was originally implemented in C++ for the Google cluster architecture and thereafter was made available as GraphX running on top of Spark.

On the other hand, GraphLab [12] implements data sharing among neighboring vertices that can asynchronously access not only their local but adjacent vertices' state in its *update( )* function. Such simultaneous updates across neighboring vertices cause race conditions. Therefore, GraphLab enforces the so-called sequential consistency on modifications of a vertex, its edges, and all its neighbors. GraphLab was parallelized in C++ using Amazon EC2 and now available in Python as Turi.

MapReduce [11] invokes *map( )* for diffusing each vertexs status change to neighboring vertices and *reduce( )* for collecting such status changes from the neighbors. Therefore, map/reduce invocations must be repeated until a given network state becomes stable.

The vertex-oriented approach benefits BFS and page ranking that are based on information diffusion, whereas it needs additional operations to collect a solution: retrieve a shortest path after BFS or sort pages in their rank values. For this purpose, GraphLab prepares a sync mechanism to aggregate, merge, and format results across all vertices.

2.2 Edge-Oriented Approach

In this approach, rather than using a specific graph tool, users develop their graph application as a text-processing program that reads a list of all graph edges and that repetitively narrows candidate edges by examining their connectivity and eventually identifies sub-graphs, (e.g., triangles) in the graph. As mentioned in Sect. 1, triangle counting with Spark [14] is a typical example that enumerates all edges, narrows them down to triads, identifies those creating triangles, and removes duplicates.

The edge-oriented approach takes advantage of existing big-data tools such as MapReduce and Spark that favor text processing, so that they do not have to construct an actual graph in memory. The main drawback is a semantic gap between what users conceive of as a graph solution, (e.g., traversing a graph to count triangles) and what the actual code would be, (i.e., text-processing code). Users may also have difficulty in tracing the actual edge processing.

2.3 Agent-Oriented Approach

We define the agent-oriented approach as the one that dispatches and walks computing entities, (i.e., agents) over a graph to analyze its shape or to collect its information. This approach allows programmers to code their graph applications from the viewpoint of a drivers seat. For instance, triangle counting can be viewed as walking agents along graph edges three times to find triangles. Users can also have agents carry computing results with them back to users, which is in contrast to the vertex-oriented approach that needs to retrieve results from a graph independently after the computation, (e.g., a retrieval of the shortest path from a graph after completing BFS). As far as a graph is maintained in memory, users can dispatch one agent after another, each executing a different graph algorithm. Therefore, the agent-oriented approach could facilitate intuitive programming and reuse the same graph data. As a matter of fact, there have been several endeavors to implement this approach to graph analysis.

Among several thread-migration libraries, Olden [15] gives its threads navigational autonomy to traverse a distributed tree. It enables a user program to construct a tree over multiple computing nodes and to recursively clone threads along the tree links to different sub trees. Node information traversed is relayed as a return value from child threads to its parent.

Wave [3] describes its mobile agents in a unique script language so that they can construct any graph topologies over distributed computing nodes as well as move or clone themselves along graph edges. UCI Messengers generalized Waves idea as its navigational language [6] and permitted agents to invoke C-native functions at each graph node for speed-up purposes [2].

Among parallel simulation platforms for agent-based models (ABMs), Repast- HPC [1] provides agents with a distributed simulation space that is constructed over a cluster system. It distinguishes multi-dimensional discrete or contiguous spaces as well as any user-defined topologies of graphs. Thus, RepastHPC could serves as a platform to solve graph problems.

However, none of these frameworks are successful in achieving the speed-up of graph analysis with multiple computing nodes, due to the thread migration overheads in Olden, the interpretive nature in Wave and UCI Messengers, and the explosive growth of agent population in RepastHPC if agents are cloned over a graph. These backgrounds motivated us to facilitate a scalable execution platform for the agent-based graph analysis.

3 Framework for Agent-Based Graph Analysis

The multi-agent spatial simulation (MASS) library is the one we implemented in Java [4], in C++ [16], and CUDA [10] for parallelizing ABM simulation over a cluster system or on a GPU machine. This section overviews the MASS programming framework, explains its features for scalable computation in general, and discusses optimization techniques we used to pursue scalable graph analysis.

3.1 MASS Programming Framework

MASS originally intended to parallelize micro-simulation of a massive number of agents that interact with each other through their distributed simulation space. Focusing on this agent-space interaction, MASS distinguishes two key classes: *Places* and *Agents*. *Places* is a distributed multi-dimensional array. Each array element, named *place* and addressed with platform-independent index, maintains its environmental values, updates them with its local methods, and exchanges them with other elements. *Agents* is a collection of computing entities. Each entity, named *agent*, carries its own variables, autonomously moves from one place to another, interacts with the current *place* it resides, and thus achieves indirect communication with other *agents*.

Listing 1.1 shows the MASS programming framework. The main function is considered as a simulation scenario that starts and ends a use of parallel machines (lines 3 and 9); instantiates a user-derived *Places* array over the machines (line 4); populates *Agents* on it (line 5); invokes their methods in parallel with *callAll* (line 7); initiates *Places* inter-element communication with *exchangeAll* (line 6); and commits each agents next behavior with *manageAll* (line 8) that clones, terminates, or moves the calling *agents*.

Listing 1.1. MASS programming framework

```
 1 public class GraphProg {
 2   public static void main( String[] args ) {
 3     MASS.init( );
 4     Places graph = new Places( MyGraph.getClass().getName(), ... );
 5     Agents agents = new Agents( MyAgents.getClass().getName(), graph, ... );
 6     graph.exchangeAll( MyGraph.communicate_ );
 7     agents.callAll( MyAgents.update_ );
 8     agents.manageAll( );
 9     MASS.finish( );
10   }
11 }
```

3.2   Applying MASS to Graph Problems

While these features were designed for parallel ABM simulation, they are applicable to parallel graph analysis with the following strategies:

- Maintaining a graph in an adjacency list where each list item is represented as a place that includes the corresponding vertex information as well as a list of edges, each emanating to a different neighboring vertex, thus to the corresponding place.
- Mimicking data diffusion along graph edges with invoking *Places.exchange-All( )* that exchanges data among neighboring places.
- Simulating agents edge traverse by invoking *Agents.manageAll( )* that clones and moves agents from one place to another, based on the adjacency list.

Of most important in graph analysis is to support its fine granularity of each vertex computation that is in general limited to only a few state updates. The MASS implementation to support ABM micro-simulation satisfies this requirement in most cases:

- **Parallel method invocation:** Since Places and Agents are dynamically loaded to memory, (using reflection in Java, dlopen in C/C++, and cudaMemalloc/Memcpy in CUDA), symbol resolutions are inevitable overheads to invoke their functions. To alleviate them, *Places/Agents.callAll( )* receives an integer ID of a given function to invoke, from which each place or agent identifies the corresponding function. Needless to say, all user-derived *Places* and *Agents* have to register all function IDs as integer constants a priori, which will be a factor to hurt the MASS programmability.
- **Agent instantiation:** MASS agents are objects only with survival and navigational autonomy, which is closer to RepastHPC [1] rather than conventional mobile or cognitive agents [5] that are instantiated as an independent process or thread. To implement their lightweight duplication and migration, MASS agents are based on weak migration that does not carry their stack values and therefore needs to resume their computation from the top of a given function every time they move to a different place.
- **Direct socket communication:** Contrary to conventional cluster-based ABM simulators [1,8] that use MPI as their communication platforms, MASS spawns remote processes with JSCH or libssh2 and thereafter creates a complete socket network among them, so that agent migration is performed directly without any middleware overheads.

Despite these implementation techniques, we still found three obstacles that should be addressed in order to apply agents to graph analysis: (1) none of the parallel ABM simulators including MASS consider parallel file reading, without which the main program behaves as a focal point of data distribution to all cluster computing nodes; (2) agents will repeatedly clone themselves as they encounter multiple edges emanating from the current vertex they reside, which quickly consumes physical memory; and (3) agents move from one vertex to another synchronously regardless of the actual necessity of inter-agent synchronization, which increases communication overheads.

Regarding problem 1, most parallel ABM simulators are based on MPI where the main program at rank 0 handles all I/O unless users write their simulations using MPI/IO explicitly. We resolved this problem by implementing HDFS-based parallel I/O in MASS [17] so that all cluster nodes can read a graph structure into their memory in parallel.

Problems 2 and 3 are resulted from a mismatch between ABM simulation and graph analysis in their nature. Although ABM simulation needs to follows agents intention on when to clone themselves, graph analysis does not have to spawn new agents as need. In BFS, some agents can explore more of graph edges while the other can wait until the entire agent population can stay below the size of physical memory. Similarly, ABM simulation needs to synchronously advance its logical clock over a cluster system (otherwise it must implement optimistic synchronization), whereas graph analysis does not care which agents explore a given graph first.

Therefore, we focus on two keys to agent-based graph analysis: agent population control and asynchronous agent migration. In the following, we explain their implementation in the MASS library.

3.3 Optimization Techniques

Agent Population Control. In MASS, any changes of agent population occur in *Agents.manageAll( )* that examines each agent status to spawn offspring, terminate it, and move it to the destination place. Therefore, *manageAll( )* can suspend new offspring when the agent population grows beyond a given threshold as well as resume these suspended agents when the population drops down. For this purpose, *Agents.manageAll( )* uses the following techniques:

1. **Agent serialization:** uses Kryo[4] to converts new offspring into byte streams, (which, we empirically found, take only 0.3% of the original agent size). Then, *manageAll( )* puts these streams into a FIFO queue of suspended agents.
2. **Agent deserialization:** dequeues suspended agents from the FIFO and deserializes them to start their execution.

A MASS user can specify the maximum cap (abbreviated as *maxCap*) of agent population in *MASS.init(maxCap)*, so that *maxCap* triggers *Agents.manageAll( )* to carry out the above two optimizations.

Asynchronous Migration. Although *Agents.callAll( )* intends to change all agent states, agent migration is not committed immediately but postponed to the following *Agents.manageAll( )* invocation. This originally intended to prevent too many fine-grain agents from migrating over computing nodes individually and continuously. However, each invocation of *callAll( )* and *manageAll( )* needs to be

---
[4] https://www.baeldung.com/kryo.

initiated from the master to all worker computing nodes, which still suffers from repetitive master-worker communication. To even mitigate such communication overheads, we took the following optimizations:

1. **Combining Agents.callAll( ) and manageAll( ) in one function, (i.e., doAll( )):**
   assumes that most agents schedule their migration repetitively in graph problems, and thus reduces master-worker communication between *callAll( )* and *manageAll( )*.
2. **Repeating doAll( ) a user-specified number of times:**
   even reduces master-worker synchronization between function invocations as well as initiates agent migration only when they really need to move.

Agents.doAll(function, args[], nItrs) implemented these optimizations by allowing agents to repeat an *nItrs* number of *function* calls, each involving agent migration.

4 Evaluation

We compared MASS with MapReduce and Spark in both programmability and execution performance. Our programmability metrics were total lines of code (LoC), lines of boilerplate code, and number of instances created. Boilerplate code refers to the lines of code in the *main()* function dedicated to setting the parallel environment. Number of instances created is the number of classes or RDDs created for the duration of the program. Since MapReduce generates a mapper and reducer class for each line in a text file, we reduced the number of instances to reflect only the job class and the mapper and reducer class used in each job.

For performance, measurements were done using the University of Washington, Bothell's general purpose Linux cluster consisting of 16 Dell Optiplex 710 desktops, each with an Intel i7-3770 Quad-Core CPU at 3.40 GHz and 16 GB RAM. MASS and Spark were evaluated on clusters consisting of 1, 2, 4, and 8 nodes while MapReduce was only runnable on one node [7].

4.1 Programmability

BFS. Table 1 shows the comparison of programmability between the three frameworks discussed in this paper. The most compact was Spark while MASS has the most lines of source code. However, it can be seen by the boilerplate and agent-only columns that indeed most of the code in MASS is spent setting up a graph as a distributed adjacency list made from places. The actual agent behavior was coded in 97 lines. MapReduce is the worst performer in terms of boilerplate code.

Table 1. BFS programmability table

Framework	LoC in boilerplate	LoC in total (Agents only)	Number of instances
MASS	7	306 (97)	4
Spark	6	126	5
MapReduce	55	228	8

Triangle Counting. In Table 2 we once again see that Spark is the best overall winner. However, MASS and MapReduce have around the same amount of source code. Once again, MASS spends more time constructing a graph with places, (i.e., in 135 liens) while the agent behavior need a little more code than Spark (133 versus 122 lines). By contrast, MapReduce spends the most lines of code setting up the parallel environment.

Table 2. Triangle counting programmability table

Framework	LoC in boilerplate	LoC in total (Agents only)	Number of instances
MASS	5	268 (133)	6
Spark	6	122	6
MapReduce	44	269	10

The overall focus on boilerplate in MapReduce is evidence of its emphasis on the map and reduce paradigm. As the above tables show, the paradigm is so strict that it requires specific boilerplate to implement. This strictness also affects the algorithm as it has to be tailored to the paradigm which makes implementation more difficult. In contrast, both Spark and MASS seek to free the programmer from the parallel environment and focus on an increased ability to express the algorithm in a more comprehensible manner.

4.2   Execution Performance

BFS. Single-node performance of Spark, MASS, and MapReduce showed that MapReduce was the fastest (see Table 3). This result is likely due to the input layout to the MapReduce program. The map and reduce paradigm shines when put in situations where inputs are easily divided into key-value pairs and the implementation of BFS used followed this scheme very closely. MASS and Spark

Table 3. Single-node execution performance (in seconds)

Applications	MASS Pop control	MASS Pop + DoAll	Spark [7]	MapReduce
BFS	28.24	27.92	25.44	10.13
Triangle counting	7.91	7.56	49.74	4,217,000.00

were equal with each other, but slower than MapReduce. This is likely due to the lack of an ability to distribute the data structures well enough to make the overhead of setting them up worthwhile.

In the multi-node performance of BFS, Spark out performs MASS. This is due to the agent overhead as evidenced by the improvement in performance between the MASS with population control and the MASS with *doAll()*. It can be seen from Fig. 2 that using the asynchronous migration is an average of 1.33 times faster than going without. However, the slow performance of MASS over multiple nodes may be due to another complexity: places. This algorithm shows the complexity of expressing graph nodes as places since places are represented in a grid, the graph will not use every place meaning that while places are evenly distributed across computing nodes, the graph may not be resulting in an uneven use of CPU resources (Fig. 1).

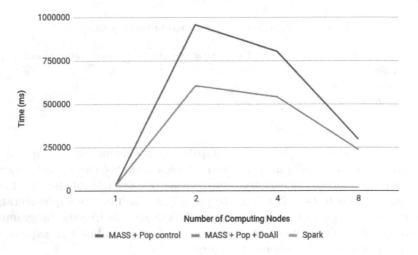

Fig. 1. BFS multi-node performance (Spark data from [7])

Triangle Counting. MapReduce was far too slow in the single-node measure of triangle counting (see Table 3 again), due to the format of the input. One of the detractions from using a strict paradigm for parallelization means that not only does the algorithm have to be altered to fit the paradigm, but the input data may have to be as well. This is the case for triangle counting with MapReduce. Additionally, this implementation required the configuration of three MapReduce jobs which meant that additional CPU resources were being used for object instantiation rather than algorithm calculations.

The multi-node performance of triangle counting shows MASS outperforming Spark. This is due to MASS not needing to remove duplicates. Additionally, the MASS algorithm benefits from limited agent spawning and migration as the agents have a more concrete stopping point which reduces travel compared to the BFS algorithm. Once again, the addition of *doAll()* asynchronous migration adds an average performance improvement of 2.7 times over MASS without it.

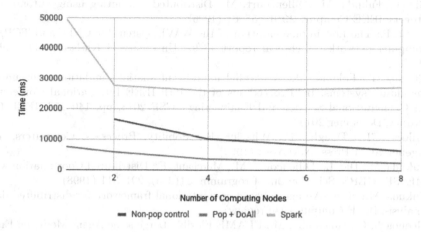

Fig. 2. Triangle counting multi-node performance (Spark data from [7]). Note that MASS with non-population control exhasuted a single node memory and thus could not perform in a reasonable time range.

5   Conclusions

Focusing on an agent-based approach to graph analysis, we developed agent population control and asynchronous migration techniques. They intended to overcome the execution drawbacks of walking agents over a graph, which explosively spawn agents as encountering new branches and which thus increase their migration. Our three findings are: (1) graph constructions with distributed array need a substantial number of LoC, (2) the agent-based approach with our optimization techniques performed much better in triangle counting than Spark and MapReduce, whereas (3) it did not yet perform well in BFS due to its repetitive and imbalanced agent dissemination over a cluster. From these facts, we will automate graph constructions over distributed memory and examine other graph algorithms to clarify what types of graph problems can take advantage of agents for their parallelization.

Acknowledgments. The cluster system used for this research was donated by Fluke Corporation. Two of the authors were supported by the UWB Computing & Software System Division's research assistantship. We would also like to thank Mr. Sinchai DeLong, the divisional senior computer specialist for all his technical supports.

References

1. Argonne National Laboratory: Repast for High Performance Computing. https://repast.gifhub.io/repast_hpc.html
2. Bic, L., Fukuda, M., Dillencourt, M.: Distributed computing using autonomous objects. IEEE Comput. **29**(8), 55–61 (1996)
3. Borst, P.: The first implementation of the WAVE system for UNIX and TCP/IP computer networks. Technical report 18/92, University of Karlsruhe, December 1992
4. Chuang, T., Fukuda, M.: A parallel multi-agent spatial simulation environment for cluster systems. In: Proceedings of the 16th IEEE International Conference on Computational Science and Engineering - CSE 2013, pp. 140–153. IEEE CS, Sydney, December 2013
5. Milojicic, D., Douglis, F., Wheeler, R.: Mobility: Processes, Computers, and Agents. ACM Press, New York (1999)
6. Fukuda, M., Bic, L., Dillencourt, M., Merchant, F.: Distributed Coordination with MESSENGERS. Sci. Comput. Programm. **31**(2–3), 291–311 (1998)
7. Fukuda, M., et al.: An agent-based computational framework for distributed data analysis. IEEE Computer (in review)
8. Geenough, C., Holcombe, M.: FLAME Flexible Large-scale Agent Modeling Environment. http://www.flame.ac.uk
9. Jenks, S., Gaudiot, J.: Nomadic threads: a migrating multithreaded approach to remote memory accesses in multiprocessors. In: Proceedings of the 5th International Conference on Parallel Architectures and Compilation Techniques, pp. 2–11 (1996)
10. Kosiachenko, L., Hart, N., Fukuda, M.: MASS CUDA: a general GPU parallelization framework for agent-based models. In: Proceedings of the 18th International Conference on Autonomous Agents and Multiagent Systems. International Foundation for AAMAS, Montreal, Canada, May 2019, to appear
11. Lin, J., Dyer, C.: Parallel breadth-first search. In: Data-Intensive Text Processing with MapReduce, Chap. 5.2. Morgan & Claypool (2010)
12. Low, Y., Gonzalez, J., Kyrola, A., Bickson, D., Guestrin, C., Hellerstein, J.M.: Distributed GraphLab: a framework fro machine learning and data mining in the cloud. In: Proceedings of the 38th International Conference on Very Large Data Bases, vol. 5, no. 8, pp. 716–727. VLDB Endowment, Istanbul, August 2012
13. Malewicz, G., et al.: Pregel: a system for large-scale graph processing. In: Proceedings of SIGMOD 2010, pp. 135–145. ACM, Indianapolis, June 2010
14. Parsian, M.: Finding, counting, and listing all triangles in large graphs. In: Data Algorithms - Recipes for Scaling up with Hadoop and Spark, chap. 16. O'Reilly (2015)
15. Rogers, A., et al.: Supporting dyanmic data structures on distributed-memory machines. ACM Trans. Programm. Lang. Syst. **17**(2), 233–263 (1995)
16. Shih, C., Yang, C., Fukuda, M.: Benchmarking the agent descriptivity of parallel multi-agent simulators. In: Bajo, J., et al. (eds.) PAAMS 2018. CCIS, vol. 887, pp. 480–492. Springer, Cham (2018). https://doi.org/10.1007/978-3-319-94779-2_41
17. Shih, Y.M., Gordon, C., Fukuda, M., van de Ven, J., Freksa, C.: Translation of string-and-pin-based shortest path construction into data-scalable agent-based computational models. In: Proceedings of the 2018 Winter Simulation Conference, pp. 881–892. IEEE, Gothenburg, December 2018

Simulation Modeling of Milk-Run Internal Logistics System – Case Study

Kamila Kluska[✉], Patrycja Hoffa-Dabrowska,
and Anna Zwolankiewicz

Faculty of Engineering Management, Poznan University of Technology,
Strzelecka 11, 60-965 Poznan, Poland
{kamila.kluska, patrycja.hoffa-dabrowska,
anna.zwolankiewicz}@put.poznan.pl

Abstract. The article describes the implementation of the methodology of simulation modeling of the milk-run system in a theoretical company. The article describes the hybrid approach in creating simulation models. It presents the basic steps of methodology, tools supporting the process of building a simulation model and analyzing internal logistics system. The goal of the study is to verify the methodology and outline the direction of its development. The final part of the article presents the directions in developing simulation tools for advanced ergonomic analysis.

Keywords: Simulation · Milk-run · Logistics · Agent-based simulation

1 Introduction

The research focuses on designing an in-plant milk-run system in the production area in a theoretical company. Authors have developed the project in automotive company, but did not get the permission for using the simulation model of real production system and describe it in articles. They inspired with the data concerning real process for building their own simulation model of production system, which has different layout, similar type and time of operations. Designed concept could be applied in real situation.

The production system consists of four production lines, which are manufacturing the same model of the metal seat. Single seat is assembled from 25 different types of parts. One production line consists of 8 workstations, operated by 6 robots, 4 production employees and 2 logistics employees transporting semi-finished products between workstations. The production process includes 11 operations.

Researchers decided to design and implement the internal logistics system, based on the milk-run concept, in order to verify created methodology. The most important motives for implementation of the milk-run system are economic benefits resulting from:

- lower cost of purchasing and maintaining modes of internal transport system,
- significant reduction of total distance covered by means of transport, due to considerable capacity of single logistic train and consolidation of transport, loading and unloading of materials, finished products and returnable packaging in one run,

F. De la Prieta et al. (Eds.): PAAMS 2019 Workshops, CCIS 1047, pp. 15–26, 2019.
https://doi.org/10.1007/978-3-030-24299-2_2

- reduction of stock levels,
- minimization of employment in the internal logistics area, and thus reduction of labor costs,
- reduction of the area occupied by transport routes,
- improvement of work safety.

To embrace this challenge the methodology of agent-based simulation modeling is used. The proposed methodology consists of 6 basic steps and uses the tools build in MS Excel, LogABS program (created on the base of FlexSim simulation software) and CSP (Constraint Solving Problem) solver [13]. The goal of the research is the initial implementation of a developed methodology in order to verify it and create automatically generated mechanisms for analysis of a milk-run system. The study includes preparation of all necessary data for simulation modeling of the milk-run system.

Verification of this methodology consists of determining in the simulation model if the designed solution guarantees collision-free, non-blocking execution of intralogistics processes and timely delivery of components to all workstations in the production area. The most important for the solution evaluation is the reliability of deliveries. Reliability of deliveries, in this case, means no deficiency of production parts in any of the workstations in the examined period, taking into account the defined constraints and assumptions.

In this project below mentioned assumptions were made:

- the trolleys have unlimited capacity,
- all operations in the system have constant duration (stochastics will be added in next step of methodology verification and development),
- there are two logistics trains, that consist respectively of two and three trolleys,
- between deliveries operators get time to rest and recharge the battery of tuggers,
- warehouse consist of two buffers – one for containers with finished goods, one for empty containers.

Following constrains have also been taken into consideration:

- the tugger and trolleys have limited speeds,
- single logistic train can use only one milk-run stop (it means that supermarket can serve only one logistic train at time),
- to every workstation has been assigned one milk-run stop,
- when one logistic train is passing through a single sector of logistics network, the other train cannot use the same sector,
- the logistics network consists only from one-way roads.

The methodology is applicable only for systems with stable frequencies of demand and relatively stable volumes of orders. It is not applicable for distribution centers and factories with high level of internal logistics automation. The implementation of milk-run system also requires work standardization and access to data concerning production system.

The goal of the publication is to provide an example of the implementation of authors' methodology for agent-based modeling of milk-run systems.

This paper is organized as follows. Section 2 presents the literature review. Section 3 describes the basic steps of methodology for simulation modeling of milk-run systems. Section 4 describes the tools for analysis of a milk-run system. Section 5 provides conclusions and further research.

2 Literature Review

Milk-run is one of the most efficient approaches used in order to improve logistics operations [8, 18]. The concept of this approach is to deliver or/and collect goods from different suppliers by one single truck in specified period time [8]. It derives from the dairy industry, in which milkman delivered bottles with milk to customers, and collected empty bottles in the same transportation cycle. The milkman had a designed route which he followed [2].

The general idea of the milk-run approach is to optimize the delivery route and also a quantity of trucks, by combining the deliveries to different customers (points), thus reducing transportation costs. Other important aspect is the inventory size – materials are delivered in exact and already defined amount, satisfying demand for a determined time period. This approach minimalizes inventory costs. The amount of delivered goods in one transport cycle depends on used replenishment method. In milk-run two replenishment method can be defined: time-fixed and event-triggered [2]. Methods of replenishment in the milk-run system:

(1) time-fixed – in which goods are delivered in the same time interval; the goods amount can be constant (in the case of continuous, reproducible production/orders) or variable (in case of changing production/orders), the order size for every period has to be defined;

(2) event-triggered – in which goods are delivered when their stocks fall below a defined level; at this concept the number of delivered goods is constant.

Originally, the milk-run concept was used for external transport and later it was adopted to internal (in-plant) transport. Milk-run approach can be successfully applied in number of industries, e.g. automotive, manufacturing, food distribution, military, consumer electronics as well as electro-mechanical [1, 2, 18].

In the literature different ways to design the logistic system based on a milk-run approach can be distinguished. The literature review of milk run and logistics system in automotive industry is presented in Brar and Saini article [1]. Milk-run as an external transportation system is described in Wang et al. article [18]. They present the Discrete Firefly Algorithm for route optimization. The objective was to minimize transportation costs through optimization of the delivery routes. The aspect of the route optimization in external transport system is described also by Huang et al. [6]. Another approach to a milk-run as an external transportation system is presented by Kitamura and Okamoto [8]. They describe the automated route planning framework using Linear Temporal Logic (LTL).

Another approach in designing the logistics system based on a milk-run concept is by using the simulation. Chee et al. [2] focus on using the simulation tool for analyzing the kanban system in an electronic assembly industry in Malaysia. Kilic et al. [7]

describe the use of simulation for modeling the in-plant milk-run distribution system. They present two models (concerning the determination time periods assignment problem for (1) one and (2) multiple routed vehicles), which were coded in the GAMS optimization program. Vieira et al. [19] describe the use of the simulation tool for modeling picking operations in a warehouse based on a milk-run system in the Bosch Car Multimedia Portugal. Another area for modeling a milk-run system is the assembly line. Korytkowski and Karkoszka [10] in their work focus on the interaction between the milk-run operator and 10 workstations on assembly lines. Moreover in their work, they have taken into account various disturbances in the production area and presented their influence on the analyzed system. The internal material supply using the milk-run system is presented also in Staab et al. article [16]. In their designed in-plant milk-run system they took into account the disturbances. They focused on modeling the traffic and the road system in order to supply 3 lines. Moreover, they present the dependencies between the logistics trains. Čujan in his article [3] presents the simulation of an automated internal milk-run logistics system.

Describing the modeling and simulation aspects in the logistics area, it is essential to mention about DES (Discrete-Event Simulation) and ABS (Agent-Based Simulation) approaches. DES is used for well-known processes, in which the uncertainty is defined by statistical distributions. In DES approach, the continuous processes are presented in a non-continuous way, i.e. defining the moment of occurrence of an event, which changes the state of the system (i.e. start or stop operation; change the object's attribute). DES approach is ideally suited to model the production aspects.

In case of modeling a complex system like a logistics system, which includes the individual autonomous entities, their behavior and correlation, ABS approach is the most suitable. ABS focuses on individual elements, their autonomous behavior, interdependencies between agents, and also between the agent and the environment in which it is located [11]. The ABS assumes, that agents communicate with each other and cooperate [11], which makes this approach perfect for modeling logistics processes, including milk-run processes. Agent systems are most useful when the decision units are distracted or various methods of decision-making are used [17].To model the production system with milk-run transportation system, the combination of DES and ABS is necessary (the hybrid approach). Hoffa-Dabrowska and Kluska showed the popularity of the topic of agents in logistics and also presented the use of ABS in logistics and intralogistics in their article [5].

3   Agent-Based Modeling of Milk-Run System

3.1   Hybrid Approach in Building Simulation Model

Greenwood et al. [4] set the framework that points out the issues that should be taken into consideration when modeling simulation of the milk-run system, from which he defines the primary physical elements, salient operational activities, and principal decision variables. He highlights the following flows in such systems: transport of containers with parts for the production process, transport of finished products to the warehouse, movement of work-in-progress materials between workstations, and transport of empty containers to the warehouse (reverse logistics). To the mentioned flows it is worth to add the flow of the information. These flows are typical also for external logistics systems e.g. supply chain. All defined issues in a framework and all flows are implemented in methodology.

Milk-run system is gaining popularity in various industries across Europe, but it is challenging when designing internal logistics system. Verification of the milk-run concept is very important, but creating a simulation model with such a system is time-consuming as it needs to model production and internal-logistics processes. Therefore the methodology and semi-automated tools supporting the design of milk-run a system have to be created.

The methodology of milk-run system modeling uses Agent-Based-Simulation approach, while modeling of production system uses DES approach. The simulation model of a production process is base for modeling of the milk-run system, so in order to build the whole system the hybrid approach is necessary. ABS enables to perform decision processes by objects in the model. The logistics train operator and the train parts (tugger and trolleys) must be able to communicate due to the need for synchronized movement and to react to the presence of other modes of transport passing nearby (to avoid collisions). The logic of work of logistics train operator has to enable the loading, transportation, and unloading of a defined number of individual containers in proper sequence to right addresses, taking into account restrictions related with the way of carrying and moving containers. The logistics train operator is an agent, which decides when to initialize the movement of logistics train, which route to use in order to achieve all destinations, which containers from what trolley to use, where containers should be delivered, to which workstation and how. He also performs the reverse logistics activities – he is able to check if any empty containers are at workstation and takes them to logistics train. The tugger receives the messages from logistics train operator and manage the work of trolleys. The trolleys cooperates in order to enable the synchronized movement. The role of agents in the approach is crucial, as it enables to model the behavior of logistics train operator, tuggers and trolleys, maintaining the complexity of the coordination activities among multiple objects.

3.2   Methodology of Building Simulation Model

Proposed methodology is the original result of the author's research work.
It consists of six stages:

- Production process analysis
- Building a simulation model of the production process
- Simulation experiment of the production system work
- Determination of delivery route and its schedule
- Modeling of an internal logistics system
- Validation and verification of the simulation model

Production Process Analysis

The analysis of the production process enables to collect the data in order to build the simulation model of the production system. It includes preparation of the production area layout, BOM, assembly diagram, the list of materials transported in the system in the PFEP table (Plan For Every Part) [12]. All containers should be defined in the container base.

Building a Simulation Model of Production Process

The simulation model of the production process (including all buffers and resources) has to be built on the layout of production space in order to determine the location of every object. The method for building an interactive layout and topography definition is described by Pawlewski [14].

An important step is to write the logic of the work of production employees and the relations between them. The best way to program operator logic is the use of script language, which is part of LogABS program. This language is described by Pawlewski [15].

After preparation of the production system in the simulation model, user should build a warehouse and supermarket with buffers for containers, which will feed the logistics train. The final stage is to design the transport routes for operators and modes of transport. This task includes building stops for logistics train near workstations.

The result of these activities is a simulation model of the production system with defined paths, presented in Fig. 1.

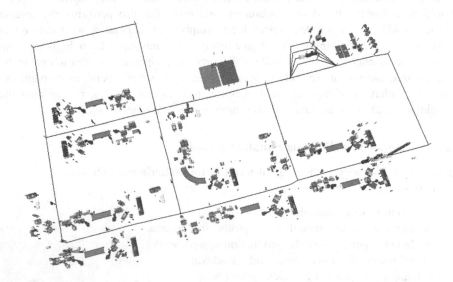

Fig. 1. The simulation model of whole production system (Source: own study based simulation model)

Simulation Experiment of the Production System Work

The experiment in the simulation model of the production system enables to collect data for CSP solver. First activity is to determine the duration of experiment. It should take into account what duration will be applicable, to finally evaluate the quality of the logistics system.

After the simulation experiment, it is possible to collect information from individual workstations about the demand for a defined number of containers with parts.

As mentioned the production system consists of four production lines.

Determination of Delivery Route and Schedule

The simulation experiment performed in the simulation model of the production process is the main source of data for CSP solver. The data includes:

- the travel time for every sector of a path of a transport network,
- the assignment of milk-run stops to workstations,
- the moments and size of demand at individual addresses,
- the parameters of logistics train.

The CSP solver processes data, performs the calculation procedure and generates a matrix with data about orders, moments of allocation transport orders to the logistics train operator (the points in time, when logistics train operator activates the movement of logistics train and starts to fulfill the order), as well as routes for logistics trains ensuring their collision-free and non-blocking traffic (presented at Fig. 2).

ID_Path	From	To	NrOfPoints	L1	L2
Path_00	MR	Supermarket	1	MRStop_05	
Path_01	Supermarket	L2_Wks_90100	2	MRStop_06	MRStop_08
Path_02	L2_Wks_90100	L2_Wks_10	2	MRStop_05	MRStop_06
Path_03	L2_Wks_20	L2_Wks_5070	1	MRStop_07	
Path_04	L2_Wks_6080	L3_Wks_10	1	MRStop_10	
Path_05	L3_Wks_10	L3_Wks_20	1	MRStop_11	
Path_06	L3_Wks_5070	L3_Wks_90100	1	MRStop_12	
Path_07	L3_Wks_90100	L3_Wks_6080	1	MRStop_13	
Path_08	L3_Wks_6080	Warehouse	1	MRStop_09	
Path_09	Supermarket	L4_Wks_10	2	MRStop_06	MRStop_14

Fig. 2. The database of routes for logistics trains (Source: own study based simulation model)

The data stated above are processed to a list of tasks for a logistics train operator. The program also generates the list of tasks for the manipulator, that manages the work of operators. The management process depends on activation of milk-run operators and assignment of transport orders to them in the desired time. The part of the list of orders is presented in Fig. 3.

What	How many	Source	Destination	Warehouse	OrderNR	TypeOfAct	MaxLoads	TrainNR	TrailerNR	ShelfNR	Route
C019	0	Supermarket_SDW	L2_Wks_90100	Warehouse	1	3	1	1	1	1	Path_01
C020	0	Supermarket_SDW	L2_Wks_90100	Warehouse	1	3	1	1	1	1	0
C021	2	Supermarket_SDW	L2_Wks_90100	Warehouse	1	3	1	1	1	1	0
C022	2	Supermarket_SDW	L2_Wks_90100	Warehouse	1	3	1	1	1	1	0
C001	1	Supermarket_SDW	L2_Wks_10	Warehouse	1	3	1	1	2	1	Path_02
C002	5	Supermarket_SDW	L2_Wks_10	Warehouse	1	3	1	1	1	1	0
C003	0	Supermarket_SDW	L2_Wks_10	Warehouse	1	3	1	1	1	1	0
C004	0	Supermarket_SDW	L2_Wks_10	Warehouse	1	3	1	1	1	1	0
C005	0	Supermarket_SDW	L2_Wks_10	Warehouse	1	3	1	1	2	1	0
C006	1	Supermarket_SDW	L2_Wks_10	Warehouse	1	3	1	1	1	1	0
C010	1	Supermarket_SDW	L2_Wks_20	Warehouse	1	3	1	1	1	1	0

Fig. 3. The list of orders designated in simulation model (Source: own study with use simulation model)

Modeling of an Internal Logistics System

Based on orders data, the simulation model automatically generates the logic of logistics-train operator work. Next important step is composition of logistic trains in the tables. Selection of number and types of trolleys depends on the number, types, and special requirements of containers designated in defined orders. A user can prepare and use the base of an available fleet of vehicles. It is also possible to define constraints in capacity and movement of modes of transport. A user can designate the composition of logistics trains for orders with use MR Calculator described by Kluska [9].

Designed parts of the milk-run system are generated automatically in the simulation model, together with logic of logistics-train operator work, taking into account all data defined in tables.

It enables to activate the work of logistics trains. The screens from work of milk-run system, where an operator of logistic train loads the containers from Supermarket, and then deliver the containers to a workstation, are presented in Fig. 4. On the left side of figure the process of grabbing containers from supermarket and moving them to trolleys by logistics train operator is presented. The right side of figure presents the process of unloading containers from trolley and transport to location at workstation, by logistics train operator.

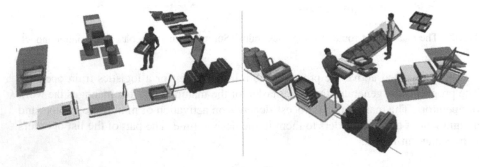

Fig. 4. The processes of loading containers with parts from supermarket and unloading containers at workstation in simulation model (Source: own study, based simulation model)

Validation and Verification of the Simulation Model

Next step is to conduct a simulation experiment. The screenshot from the simulation is presented in Fig. 5.

The results of the simulation experiment are presented in automatically generated charts, that allow to analyze and evaluate work of the system. Those results set up base for the decision whether to accept existing system or look for different organization of the internal transport system.

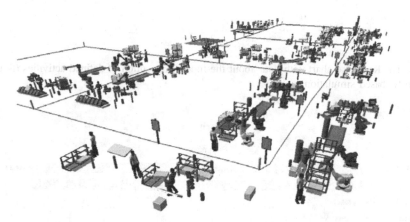

Fig. 5. The screen from simulation experiment (Source: own study based simulation mode)

4   Modelling Results

The mechanisms for generating results of simulation experiment includes:

- Yamazumi and value-added analysis, where depending on individual preferences of user it is possible to divide performed activities by four groups: (1) VA (value-added activities), (2) NVA (activities, that do not create a value), (3) NVAA (activities, that do not create a value, but user can try to reduce the time of their execution), (4) Rework.
- Analysis of the timelines of deliveries based on RepTime chart, where the user can measure the time of any activity or set of activities. An exemplary chart is presented in Fig. 6. The RepTime charts enable to group the activities performed by production employees and check if they are waiting for delivery of parts. It is strong base for confirming if the solution is meeting the criterion of reliability.
- 3d visualization of movement of milk-run objects,
- ergonomic aspects of the work of the operators of the internal transport system and production employees, e.g. the total weight (in grams) of transported goods or total distance traveled by operators (Fig. 7).

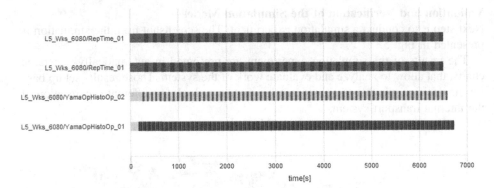

Fig. 6. The RepTime chart with data about the time of execution of defined activities (Source: own study, based simulation model)

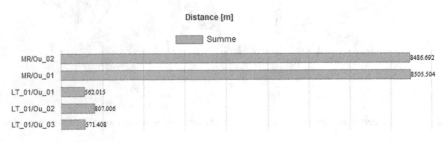

Fig. 7. The chart with total distance travelled by operators (Source: own study based simulation model)

The ergonomic analysis could also use the NIOSH method, which is used to determine the maximum weight of goods that can be transported by a human, taking into account position of his body at the workplace. It would be a significant step in improving work of logistics train operators. By calculating the maximum mass that employee can lift, the system is able to inform a user whether operator is overloaded, which can result in negative health effects. This type of analysis can bring many benefits, both for the employee and the employer, such as reduced sickness absence, greater job satisfaction, higher productivity, fewer occupational diseases related to the work of the operator.

5 Conclusions and Further Research

The article presents a milk-run simulation model based on methodology with use agent-based modeling approach. The goal of the study was to verify the methodology by checking, if the designed solution guarantees collision-free, non-blocking execution of intralogistics processes and timely delivery of components to all workstations at the production area.

The article presents and describes six stages of building a simulation model ending with validation and model verification. The most important for evaluation are RepTime charts, which enables to check if the production employees were waiting for deliveries in a defined time period. RepTime charts were prepared for each production line. Based on results the researchers agreed that solution meets all defined requirements.

The charts with distance traveled by the milk-run operator should distinguish the distance traveled in logistics train and distance traveled by the operator on his feet, because in the current version the results are unreliable. It is necessary to reduce the total weight transported by operators during one shift by, e.g. increasing the number of logistics trains. The methodology needs a more detailed analysis of the ergonomic aspect of the logistic operator's work, as well as adding the stochastics to system.

Acknowledgements. The work was carried out as part of the 11/140/DSMK/4160 project, "Methodology for design and simulation modeling of milk-run internal logistics systems", financed by Faculty of Engineering Management, Poznan University of Technology.

References

1. Brar, G.S., Saini, G.: Milk run logistics: literature review and directions. In: Proceedings of the World Congress on Engineering 2011, WCE 2011, London, U.K., 6–8 July 2011, vol. I (2011). ISSN 2078-0966 (Online)
2. Chee, S.L., Chong, M.Y., Chin, J.F.: Milk-run kanban system for raw printed circuit board withdrawal to surface-mounted equipment. J. Ind. Eng. Manag. **5**(2), 382–405 (2013)
3. Čujan, Z.: Simulation of production lines supply within internal logistics systems. Open Eng. **6**(1), 470–475 (2016)
4. Greenwood, A.G., Kluska, K., Pawlewski, P.: A multi-level framework for simulating milk-run, in-plant logistics operations. In: Bajo, J., et al. (eds.) PAAMS 2017. CCIS, vol. 722, pp. 209–220. Springer, Cham (2017). https://doi.org/10.1007/978-3-319-60285-1_18
5. Hoffa-Dabrowska, P., Kluska, K.: Agents in logistics and supply chain. In: Bajo, J., et al. (eds.) PAAMS 2018. CCIS, vol. 887, pp. 161–171. Springer, Cham (2018). https://doi.org/10.1007/978-3-319-94779-2_15
6. Huang, M., Yang, J., Ma, T., Li, X., Wang, T.: The modeling of milk-run vehicle routing problem based on improved C-W algorithm that joined time window. Transp. Res. Procedia **25**, 716–728 (2017)
7. Kilic, H.S., Durmusoglu, M.B., Baskak, M.: Classification and modeling for in-plant milk-run distribution systems. Int. J. Adv. Manuf. Technol. **62**(9–12), 1135–1146 (2012)
8. Kitamura, T., Okamoto, K.: Automated route planning for milk-run transport logistics using model checking. In: 2012 Third International Conference on Networking and Computing, pp. 240–246 (2012). https://doi.org/10.1109/icnc.2012.44
9. Kluska, K.: Determination of the optimal number of trailers for milk-run intralogistics system. In: Pawlewski, P., Hoffa-Dabrowska, P., Golinska-Dawson, P., Werner-Lewandowska, K. (eds.) FlexSim in Academe: Teaching and Research. ECOPROD, pp. 101–113. Springer, Cham (2019). https://doi.org/10.1007/978-3-030-04519-7_8
10. Korytkowski, P., Karkoszka, R.: Simulation-based efficiency analysis of an in-plant milk-run operator under disturbances. Int. J. Adv. Manuf. Technol. **82**(5–8), 827–837 (2016)
11. Macal, C.M., North, M.J.: Introductory tutorial: agent-based modeling and simulation. In: Winter Simulation Conference, pp. 362–376 (2013)

12. Pawlewski, P.: Using PFEP for simulation modeling of production systems. In: 28th International Conference on Flexible Automation and Intelligent Manufacturing (FAIM 2018), Columbus, OH, USA, 11–14 June 2018 (2018). Procedia Manuf. **17**, 811–818 (2018)
13. Pawlewski, P., Anholcer, M.: Using CSP solvers as alternative to simulation optimization engines. In: Pawlewski, P., Hoffa-Dabrowska, P., Golinska-Dawson, P., Werner-Lewandowska, K. (eds.) FlexSim in Academe: Teaching and Research. ECOPROD, pp. 131–143. Springer, Cham (2019). https://doi.org/10.1007/978-3-030-04519-7_10
14. Pawlewski, P.: Interactive layout in the redesign of intralogistics systems. In: Burduk, A., Chlebus, E., Nowakowski, T., Tubis, A. (eds.) ISPEM 2018. AISC, vol. 835, pp. 462–473. Springer, Cham (2019). https://doi.org/10.1007/978-3-319-97490-3_45
15. Pawlewski, P.: Script language to describe agent's behaviors. In: Bajo, J., et al. (eds.) PAAMS 2018. CCIS, vol. 887, pp. 137–148. Springer, Cham (2018). https://doi.org/10.1007/978-3-319-94779-2_13
16. Staab, T., Klenk, E., Günthner, W.A.: Simulating dynamic dependencies and blockages in in-plant milk-run traffic systems. In: Proceedings 27th European Conference on Modelling and Simulation, pp. 622–628 (2013). https://doi.org/10.7148/2013-0622
17. Stanek, S., Pańkowska, M.B., Żytniewski, M.K.: Realizacja agentów oprogramowania z wykorzystaniem środowiska JAVA. In: Porębska-Miąc, T., Sroka, H. (eds.) Systemy Wspomagania Organizacji SWO 2005. Akademia Ekonomiczna, Katowice (2005)
18. Wang, X., He, M., Jiang, H.: A discrete firefly algorithm for routing optimization of milk-run. In: 5th International Conference on Advanced Design and Manufacturing Engineering (ICADME 2015), pp. 1538–1543 (2015)
19. Vieira, A., Dias, L.S., Pereira, G.B., Oliveira, J.A., Carvalho, M.S., Martins, P.: 3D micro simulation of milkruns and pickers in warehouses using SIMIO. In: Modelling and Simulation 2014 - European Simulation and Modelling Conference, ESM 2014, pp. 261–269 (2014)

Hybrid Approach for Simulation Modeling of the Milk-Run Systems with Ergonomic Analysis

Kamila Kluska[✉] and Anna Zwolankiewicz

Faculty of Engineering Management, Poznan University of Technology,
Strzelecka 11, 60-965 Poznan, Poland
{kamila.kluska,anna.zwolankiewicz}@put.poznan.pl

Abstract. The article describes the methodology of simulation modeling of milk-run systems supplemented with an ergonomic analysis. In the literature analysis, the authors define what is the milk-run system, describes the benefits of implementation milk-run as an internal transport system, and explain the use of DES and ABS approaches to modeling. The article describes the tools used in the hybrid simulation modeling of the milk-run system and various stages of its application. The authors describe the ergonomic analysis of logistics employees work as the direction for further development of methodology. The last part of the article describes the necessity of developing tools for advanced ergonomic analyses and exemplary methods, which could be implemented. One selected method, that allowed to determine the maximum weight of the goods transported by the operator is also described.

Keywords: Simulation · Milk-run · Logistics · Ergonomic

1 Introduction

The research focuses on internal transport systems organized according to milk-run concept. Milk-run is a logistics system, in which the mode of transport is a logistics train that stops in specified places (milk-run stops) in order to deliver goods to various destinations during a single run. It can consist of a changeable number of various types of trolleys. It depends on the type of containers with goods and available fleet in the factory.

Logistics train can work automatically or it can be served by an operator. Its goal is to load a desired number of specified containers from a supermarket, arrange it in a proper way at trolleys, and deliver it to defined milk-run stops in the defined order, moving on a precisely defined delivery route, taking into account the desired time of deliveries. It can be based on a fixed schedule, where the quantity of containers in deliveries is variable, or on a fixed quantity of containers in deliveries, but a random time of deliveries. It is time-consuming challenge to take into account all listed conditions and many constraints.

However, milk-run approach becomes more and more popular. Its main advantage over, for example, AGV or forklifts, results from economic and operational benefits.

F. De la Prieta et al. (Eds.): PAAMS 2019 Workshops, CCIS 1047, pp. 27–38, 2019.
https://doi.org/10.1007/978-3-030-24299-2_3

Due to the growing popularity of the milk-run system, necessity for tools supporting the design and verification of such system has emerged in a relatively short time. The need for a methodology that allows supporting the design and management of this system, through a fast, semi-automated (ultimately fully automated) generation of a simulation model. Proposed modeling approach relies on DES and Agent-Based-Simulation, as it allows to model the production process and introduce intelligence to objects in the model. These objects (the train operator, as well as the manipulator managing its work) have their own logic, which allows their autonomous, independent operation and implementation of various decision-making processes. Decision-making processes allow following events in the system and automatically adjusting the behavior to the needs of the system in order to ensure timely delivery of components in the system in exactly right amount.

The designing such simulation tool is possible due to the cyclical processes taking place in both production and logistics processes. The tool uses the LogABS simulation module built in FlexSim simulation software and CSP solver described by Pawlewski and Anholcer [11].

These tools are used in the methodology described in the paper. The methodology includes semi-automatic generation of milk-run system and basic ergonomic analyzes of the logistics operator's work. Due to the growing awareness in the field of safety and ergonomics of work, researchers decided to design original mechanisms for automatic generation of ergonomic analysis of the logistics train operator work.

The goal of the publication is to provide the methodology of agent-based modeling of milk-run systems and aspects for ergonomic analysis of the logistics train operator. Such analysis is base for developing tools in methodology for verification of designed concepts from the train operator's point of view, his safety and work efficiency.

This paper is organized as follows. Section 2 presents the literature review. Section 3 describes the basics steps of methodology for simulation modeling of milk-run systems. Section 4 describes the results of the study about the analysis of ergonomic aspects of the logistics train operator. Section 5 provides conclusions and further research.

2   Literature Review

Initially, logistics trains were only used as an external means of transport in order to connect many suppliers. Klenk and Galka [8], and BusinessDictionary [3] define milk-run as internal logistics systems, where the logistics train is used to transport materials to various points in the factory during a single journey.

Milk-run enables the consolidation of transport, loading and unloading of materials, finished products and returnable packaging [4]. It is possible during one journey of a single logistics train, which can transport many loads of different types of goods at the same time. It also enables to operate with a number of workstations during one journey and minimize empty runs [16]. Additional benefits include a reduction in the level of stocks [16], minimization of employment in the area of internal logistics, reduction of labor costs, significant reduction of total distance covered by means of transport [19], and thus economic benefits through far-reaching savings. The milk-run system also allows to increase the efficiency of an internal transport system, improve loading rates of means of transport [16], reduce the area required for the transport system in the factory [7], by significantly reducing the area occupied by transport routes, improving work safety.

Milk-Run has to be adjusted to the production process, take into account all architectural and organizational constraints, make use of data concerning the frequency of demand at every production cell, parts, containers, resources, and transport network in a company, and many others mentioned below.

To take into account data, constraints, physical actions of vehicles and operators, logistics activities, strategic-level planning, and decision variables, paper propose to use a methodology based on a hybrid modeling approach that includes both discrete-event (DES) and agent-based simulation (ABS).

DES simulation has been the most popular approach for the simulation of manufacturing and logistics processes for decades. This is used for simulation of queuing systems, with variability represented through stochastic distributions [15].

ABS is an approach for simulation modeling of the system through the use of autonomously working system components (also referred to as agents), communication capabilities [9]. Macal and North [10] defines agent-based systems as "a computational framework for simulating dynamic processes that involve autonomous agents. An autonomous agent acts on its own without external direction in response to situations the agent encounters during the simulation."

The methodology of simulation modeling of milk-run systems uses DES approach in modeling production system and transportation routes. However, the milk-run system allows using agent-based modeling, as a more intuitive approach.

The new aspect proposed by this methodology is an analysis of ergonomics aspects in the milk-run system. The priority task in ergonomics is to treat human as the most important element in the work process.

Ergonomic analysis of milk-run systems focuses on technical and organizational factors of the work environment. These are: the position of the body at work, the pace of work, breaks at work, working methods, instructions, data, and supervision.

Detailed ergonomic analysis of the above factors will enable obtaining the advantages resulting from the introduction of ergonomic quality to the work environment, which are, e.g.:

- greater work efficiency,
- reduction of work negative health impact, resulting in fewer days off due to illness,
- augmentation of work quality,
- rising job security and the occurrence of fewer occupational diseases,
- greater readiness and motivation to work [17].

Designing systems without taking into account ergonomic aspects may involve losses due to poor ergonomic quality. They can be divided into three categories, which are presented in the Table 1 below:

Table 1. Three categories of losses due to poor ergonomic quality (based on [5])

Direct economic losses	Indirect economic losses	Moral losses
It is possible to estimate their size. For example, the production of defective products caused by employee fatigue, or the wrong conditions of material parameters in the work environment	It is not possible to estimate its size in a simple way. These include, for example, deterioration of health or lack of care for devices that the employee uses at the workplace	It is not possible to estimate their size from an economic point of view. These are, for example, the lack of motivation to work

Of course, each of the employer introducing the new system to the company is primarily focused on eliminating losses. Every implementation of the Milk-Run system is connected with many advantages mentioned in the first part of the article, while the improvement of this system with ergonomic aspects may bring surprisingly positive results. Performing ergonomic analysis in logistic systems is therefore as important as introducing other improvements, as it allows to focus on the aspect of human in the work environment, and thus brings far-reaching, positive effects, not only for the employee but also for the employer.

Grosse et al. [6] performed systematic literature review about evolution of works that incorporate human factors into decision support models for production and logistics.

Polka-Sopinska et al. [13] describes guidelines for the assessment of energy expenditure for logistics train operator, which operates the logistics train at factory. She also describes the process of determining effective energy expenditure with use of the G. Lehmann's estimation method and MWE-1 energy expenditure meter [14]. Mentioned methods are not applicable in analyses in simulation technology. The MWE-1 energy expenditure meter requires from the employee to wear the mask during entire work shift. The first method is quite inaccurate, because it base on observation of the employee during working day.

Authors did not find the article which describes the NIOSH analysis in simulation model of milk-run system or any automatically generated ergonomic analysis for logistics train operator.

3 Methodology of Simulation Modeling of Milk-Run Systems Based on Hybrid Modeling Approach

The methodology uses a set of tools, that:

- designate a list of transport orders,
- determines the required number and composition of trains, taking into account the fleet owned by the company,
- designates the required number of train operators and their allocation to trains, as well as the moments of the implementation of each of the orders by operators,

- defines the routes of trains moving within a transportation network, ensuring their unobstructed and collision-free run,
- includes disturbances occurring in the production system, time of loading and unloading of each container, limitations of trolleys and logistic tuggers, restrictions, logistic parameters, availability of listed resources and moments in which demand for containers appears in the system,
- enables the implementation of reverse logistics,
- allows conducting simulation experiments in order to verify and improve the concepts based on automatically generated results,
- enables observation of the system's in 3D and preparation of visualizations.

The methodology consists of six stages:

1. Production process analysis
2. Building a simulation model of the production process
3. Simulation experiment of the production system work
4. Determination of delivery route and schedule
5. Modeling of an internal logistics system
6. Validation and verification of the simulation model

3.1   Production Process Analysis

The analysis of the main process, i.e. the production area as a basis for the design of the milk-run system, require the preparation of a layout with the arrangement of work-stations in space, the location of the supermarket and the warehouse, as well as all architectural restrictions. This stage includes the adjustment of the production system for the implementation of the new internal logistics system and the collection of data. These tasks include standardizing the work of production workers and preparing a formalized description of their work in the form of a list of activities and a Gantt chart that determines the duration of the operations.

Necessary is leveling of production (Heijunka), designation of the production schedule and the time cycle of production units. For the proper design of the internal logistics system, it is necessary to define relations between the materials and containers transported in the system, taking into account their size and capacity. If the materials or containers have special requirements for transport, it should be clearly defined.

The list of materials transported in the system should be prepared based on the BOM and assembly diagram. All materials should be described is the PFEP table (Plan For Every Part – [12]). All containers should be defined in container database.

3.2   Building a Simulation Model of the Production Process

The simulation model of the production process (with all specific characteristics and disruptions) is necessary to develop a reliable project of the internal transport system and verify it.

The first step is to determine the place, number, and size of workplaces based on the layout of the production space. Then, the level of modeling detail is increased by mapping resources and buffers at each station. The next step is to write the logic of the work of production employees and the relations between them.

It is necessary to build a warehouse with the space for finished products and empty containers, as well as a supermarket that will provide containers for the logistics train. The final stage is to design the delivery network based on the available space and location of the stations. This task includes building a network of transport routes and logistic stops in the simulation model. It is also necessary to choose a method of delivering containers to workstations in order to adapt the infrastructure.

The result of these activities is a simulation model of the production system with defined delivery routes.

3.3   Simulation Experiment of the Production System Work

Using the simulation model of the production system, it is possible to conduct a simulation experiment in order to verify it and to collect data relevant to the design of the internal logistics system.

In order to collect useful data, it is necessary to determine the duration of the experiment. It should be taken into account what time will be applicable to finally determine whether the logistics system is well designed.

After setting the experiment duration, it is possible to carry out simulation and collect information about the demand for containers at individual workstations. The exemplary simulation experiment is presented in Fig. 1.

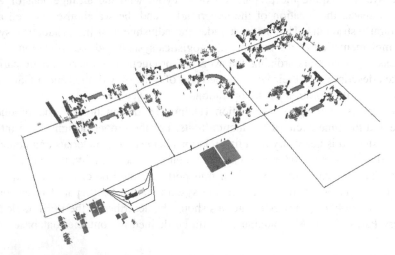

Fig. 1. Exemplary simulation model of production system (source: own study based on simulation model)

3.4 Determination of Delivery Route and Schedule

In order to determine the timetable and delivery routes, it is necessary to define all activities performed during each delivery and their execution times. Then, the information about the production system and logistics operations are processed by an external operating CSP solver.

CSP solver generates a list of orders, moments of work initiation of logistic trains, as well as routes for logistic trains ensuring their collision-free and non-blocking movement.

3.5 Modeling of an Internal Logistics System

The data generated in the previous step is implemented in the simulation model. Logistic trains are characterized in the tables in a simulation program. Modeler can use the database with available fleet of vehicles, taking into account the constraints about the allocation of individual containers to trailers and its capacity.

Designed trains are automatically generated in the simulation model altogether with necessary number of the train operators and logic of their work, including the order of performing activities during the implementation of each transport order, type of activities, number of containers for transport, addresses for deliveries and maximum number of defined types containers which logistics train operator can load and transport together.

The result of this stage is the simulation model of the production system with the milk-run system.

3.6 Validation and Verification of the Simulation Model

Validation and verification of the milk-run system built in the simulation model is an extremely important stage of the methodology. In order to verify the work of simulation model, it is important to conduct a simulation experiment. The aim of the simulation experiment is to generate charts allowing analyze the timeliness of deliveries, collision-free and unobstructed work of logistics trains, as well as ergonomic aspects of the operators work within the internal transport system. The operation of logistics train is presented in Fig. 2.

Fig. 2. The milk-run system in simulation model (Source: own study based on simulation model)

Currently, available mechanisms enable analysis of the total distance traveled by the operator, total, maximum, and minimum weight of loads transported by the operator, delivery delays, Value-Added distribution, and also Yamazumi analysis.

The results of the analysis are the basis for making a decision to accept or search for other variants of the internal transport system organization. An exemplary chart with analysis of time of each activity (the purple part of the chart) and the time of individually set up fragments of the operator's work is presented at the Fig. 3 below.

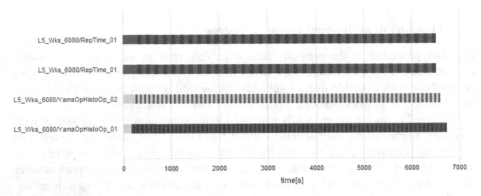

Fig. 3. The milk-run system in simulation model (Source: own study based on simulation model) (Color figure online)

4 Ergonomic Analyses of Logistics Train Operator

Ergonomic analyses are important not only for the Milk-Run system but also for each system in which one of the components is a human. It is (not only from the point of view of ergonomics) the most important link allowing the system to thrive. The efficient operation of the logistics network, is as important as providing the right conditions for working with this system. The Milk-Run system enables to obtain many benefits for the employee, including the reduction of hazards typical for warehouse transport system using forklifts.

During the design of the operation, the method of work should be properly defined, i.e. the systematized way of performing activities by the employee. The work method should be characterized by features such as:

- priority of employees safety,
- direct contact with other employees,
- the schema to repeatable activities,
- lack of presence of machines forcing the pace of work,
- the employee can choose periods of work and rest according to their own work capacity,
- work movements performed in accordance with the rules of movement ergonomics [18].

Therefore, understanding the importance of ergonomic analyses and knowledge of factors that make up for the correct design of working methods, one can focus on the methods that could be used to implement ergonomic elements for Milk-Run simulations. Although transport by logistics trains is associated with the reduction of workload associated with the transfer of materials, this transfer still occurs. The simulation usually does not take into account elements such as the weight of the object being moved, the way it is carried and the detailed way that the worker has to overcome by moving the element from point A to point B. Manual transport work is often the cause of many health problems, diseases caused by the way of work.

It is important, therefore, that the work process is designed to show the correct methods of moving objects, taking into account their mass and the distance. There are several methods that allow assessing stress of the musculoskeletal system during manual transport work:

– the LMM method of indicators relevant to lifting, holding and handling,
– NIOSH method for calculating the recommended weight of lifted elements,
– OWAS method for determining static loads,
– OCRA method to determine loads of upper limbs,
– REBA method for rapid overall assessment of the entire body load,
– RULA method for quick assessment of upper limb load,
– questionnaire methods that allow an employee to judge subjective feelings of pain related to work performed in individual parts of the body [2].

The proposed method which is implemented in the simulation system is NIOSH, as it is directly related to the weight of the transported goods. This method allows calculating the value of the weight of the lifting element, which does not involve an increase in the risk of discomfort of the musculoskeletal system. This is the so-called recommended limit value W. This value is determined for specific sets of operating conditions that are related to manual transport work. The NIOSH formula is used when two-handed, symmetrical or asymmetrical transfer operations occur. The NIOSH equation is presented below:

$$W = 23 \cdot K_H \cdot K_V \cdot K_F \cdot K_D \cdot K_A \cdot K_C [kg] \qquad (1)$$

Where:

- K_H - horizontal distance coefficient
- K_V - vertical distance coefficient
- K_F - frequency coefficient
- K_D - vertical displacement coefficient
- K_A - asymmetry coefficient
- K_C - grip's ease coefficient
- W_{max} = 23 kg

The Fig. 4 shows the individual symbols assigned to the above coefficients, where:

- H - the distance of the hand level from the midpoint between the ankle joint blocks,
- V - the vertical distance of hands from the floor,

- D - vertical displacement distance,
- A - asymmetry angle, angular displacement of the weight in relation to the sagittal plane,
- C - ease of grip.

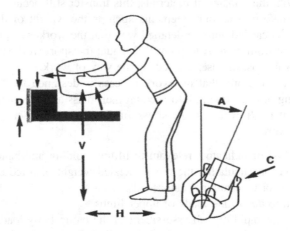

Fig. 4. Explanation of the symbolism of the NIOSH method, Source: [1]

The implementation of NIOSH analysis in the simulation can bring positive effects not only for the employee but also for the employer. Due to the possibility of calculating the maximum weight of the lifted item in the simulation program, the employee can avoid excessive overloads, what will increase efficiency, reduce the number of sick leave, and the number of occupational diseases related to manual transportation.

5 Conclusions and Further Research

The article presents a methodology of simulation modeling of milk-run internal logistics systems and describes ergonomic analyses for milk-run systems. The analysis of exemplary ergonomic methods allows determining the maximum workload of an employee in a real working environment. The NIOSH method allows determining the employee load factor during the transportation of containers. The designation of load factor at every stage of the logistic train operator's work allows for signaling exceeding the maximum value of this factor. This type of information enables to search for solutions, which minimize the employee overload. An example of such a solution is placing a given type of containers on the easily accessible shelf of a train.

After the NIOSH coefficient, it is still necessary to analyze:

- the distance traveled by an employee during transferring loads,
- the distance traveled by an employee without loads,
- what is the maximum weight of transported goods,

The NIOSH method is the basis for the development of analytical methods. The challenge is the adaptation of existing methods or the development of a new method allowing the implementation of ergonomic analysis for milk-run simulation. The NIOSH tool in simulation should enable to define all necessary parameters of operator and containers. The value of factor calculated at the most important activities performed by logistics train operator should be presented at the end of simulation experiment, and each exceeding of the maximum value should be marked.

The implementation of ergonomic analysis enables to increase the efficiency of work, better use of existing resources in the work environment.

Acknowledgements. The work was carried out as part of the 11/140/DSMK/4160 project, "Methodology for design and simulation modeling of milk-run internal logistics systems", financed by Faculty of Engineering Management, Poznan University of Technology.

References

1. Bartnicka, J.: Projektowanie systemów antropotechnicznych. Metody analizy i oceny układów antropotechnicznych (2015). http://dydaktyka.polsl.pl/ROZ5/jbartnicka/Dokumenty/Dydakt yka/Projektowanie%20system%C3%B3w%20antropotechnicznych/Wyk%C5%82ady/PSA _metody.pdf
2. Bukała, W.: Ergonomiczne warunki pracy, p. 108. Wydawnictwa Szkolne i Pedagogiczne, Warszawa (2015)
3. BusinessDisctionary.com2017.   WebFinance,   Inc.,   31   January   2017.   www. businessdictionary.com/definitions/milk-run.html
4. Brar, G.S., Saini G.: Milk run logistics: literature review and directions. In: Proceedings of the World Congress on Engineering, WCE 2011, vol. I, pp. 797–801 (2011)
5. Górska, E., Tytyk, E.: Ergonomia w projektowaniu stanowisk pracy. Podstawy teoretyczne, pp. 15–16. Oficyna Wydawnicza Politechniki Warszawskiej, Warszawa (1998)
6. Grosse, E.H., Calzavara, M., Glock, C.H., Sgarbossa, F.: Incorporating human factors into decision support models for production and logistics: current state of research. IFAC-PapersOnLine, **50**(1), 6900–6905 (2017)
7. Karagul, H., Albayrakoglu, M. M.: Selecting a third-party logistics provider for an automotive company: an analytic hierarchy process model (2007)
8. Klenk, E., Galka, S.: Analysis of parameters influencing in-plant milk-run design for production supply. In: 12th International Material Handling Research Colloquium, Technische Universität München (2012)
9. Macal, C.M., North, M.J., Introductory tutorial: agent-based modeling and simulation. In: Winter Simulation Conference, pp. 6–20 (2014)
10. North, M.J., Macal, C.M.: Managing Business Complexity: Discovering Strategic Solutions with Agent-Based Modeling and Simulation. Oxford University Press, New York (2007)
11. Pawlewski, P., Anholcer, M.: Using CSP solvers as alternative to simulation optimization engines. In: Pawlewski, P., Hoffa-Dabrowska, P., Golinska-Dawson, P., Werner-Lewand-owska, K. (eds.) FlexSim in Academe: Teaching and Research. ECOPROD, pp. 131–143. Springer, Cham (2019). https://doi.org/10.1007/978-3-030-04519-7_10
12. Pawlewski, P.: Using PFEP for simulation modeling of production systems. In: 28th International Conference on Flexible Automation and Intelligent Manufacturing (FAIM 2018), Columbus, OH, USA, 11–14 June 2018 (2018). Procedia Manuf. **17**, 811–818 (2018)

13. Polak-Sopinska, A., Wrobel-Lachowska, M., Wisniewski, Z., Jalmuzna, I.: Physical work intensity of in-plant milk run operator. Part I - guidelines for assessment. In: Karwowski, W., Trzcielinski, S., Mrugalska, B., Di Nicolantonio, M., Rossi, E. (eds.) AHFE 2018. AISC, vol. 793, pp. 66–76. Springer, Cham (2019). https://doi.org/10.1007/978-3-319-94196-7_7

14. Polak-Sopinska, A.: Physical work intensity of in-plant milk run operator. Part II – case study. In: Karwowski, W., Trzcielinski, S., Mrugalska, B., Di Nicolantonio, M., Rossi, E. (eds.) AHFE 2018. AISC, vol. 793, pp. 77–89. Springer, Cham (2019). https://doi.org/10.1007/978-3-319-94196-7_8

15. Siebers, P.O., Macal, C.M., Garnett, J., Buxton, D., Pidd, M.: Discrete-event simulation is dead, long live agent-based simulation! J. Simul. 4(3), 204–210 (2010)

16. Nemoto, T., Hayashi, K., Hashimoto, M.: Milk-run logistics by Japanese automobile manufacturers in Thailand. Procedia Soc. Behav. Sci. 2(3), 5980–5989 (2010)

17. Tytyk, E.: Bezpieczeństwo i higiena pracy, ergonomia i ochrona własności intelektualnej, p. 64. Wydawnictwo Politechniki Poznańskiej, Poznań (2017)

18. Tytyk, E.: Ergonomia w technice, p. 28. Wydawnictwo Politechniki Poznańskiej, Poznań (2011)

19. Zhenlai, Y., Yang, J.: Development and application of milk-run distribution systems in the express industry based on saving algorithm. Math. Probl. Eng. 2014(536459), 1–6 (2014)

The Supply Chain Network Integration

Nuno Trindade Magessi[1,2(✉)] and Luis Antunes[1,2]

[1] Faculdade de Ciências, Universidade de Lisboa, Lisbon, Portugal
nmagessi@campus.ul.pt, xarax@ciencias.ulisboa.pt
[2] BioISI – Biosystems and Integrative Sciences Institute, Lisbon, Portugal

Abstract. Supply Chain Network (SCN) is one of the most important elements of Logistic nowadays. One of the aspects, which is not covered very well in literature, is the one concerned to the mechanisms behind the connections that are established among players. In this work it was analysed the impact of the variation in the probabilities in being a member of a network, the relation of players with risk and respective effect on the SCN, the individualism versus collaborative approach of players and the problem solving effect. For that, it was developed a multi-agent based system. The obtained results demonstrate that experienced members prefer to establish links with other experienced members or repeated partners when the SCN are built for important businesses. The results also show the critical role of companies' risk aversion conceiving a SCN.

Keywords: Supply Chain Network · Multi-agent based system

1 Introduction

Supply Chain Management is considered as all activities related to the management of an interconnected business network involved on the final provision of product packages, but also services [1]. The management of the supply chain, incorporates all the movement and storage of raw material, the work in inventory process and the finished products, from the point of origin to the point of consumption.

One of the issues is to know how and with whom the business network should be constituted. The idea behind the selection is to build mechanisms and a team assembly with the goal of determining the collaboration among network [2].

Normally, literature brings more emphasis to another type of criteria like quality of raw materials that were delivered, time-to-delivery and costs. This aspect reveals the continuous prevalence of parameters more directly related to the financial conditions and structure of companies.

The selected economic agents are integrated in a supply chain networks that adds value to the initial companies, supporting them and evaluating their performance. This article has the goal to understand how the mechanisms by which supply chain self-assemble, determining the structure of these collaboration networks. In this sense, it is proposed a multi-agent model for the self-assembly of the supply chain network, which has its basis in three parameters: network size, the proportion of new members in new productions and the tendency of incumbents to repeat previous collaborations.

© Springer Nature Switzerland AG 2019
F. De la Prieta et al. (Eds.): PAAMS 2019 Workshops, CCIS 1047, pp. 39–49, 2019.
https://doi.org/10.1007/978-3-030-24299-2_4

This work is organized as follows. In the next part, it is presented a review of important advances occurred in the supply chain management. Section 3 describes the developed model using a multi-agent based systems methodology. On Sect. 4 is where the obtained output results are revealed. After this section, it is discussed the obtained results and the contribution they supply for this field of knowledge. Finally, on section six, conclusions are presented and explained, focusing on the future work to be developed.

2 Advances in Supply Chain Management (SCM)

The Council of Supply Chain Management (CSCM) defines Supply Chain Management as the planning and management of all activities related to the internal and inter-organisational logistic. It is centred on the coordination and collaboration existent among all supply chain partners. These partners could be suppliers, service providers and customers who have the objective of creating net value to the SCM [3]. A net value created through the construction of a competitive infra-structure which allows the leverage of worldwide logistic by synchronising supply with demand and evaluating global performance According with this definition, the planning of involved agents assumes an important core role on supply management [4].

2.1 Supply Chain Networking

Supply Chain Networking is the core of this article and it is important to review some of the most relevant progresses done in this field of Logistic. Supply Chain Network (SCN) is considered a development from the basic supply chain. This is possible, taking in consideration the exponential advances that are occurring in technology. Advances which have been allowing organizations to transform rudimentary supply chain structures into a more complex structure. These new structures are characterised by the existence of a high degree of interdependence and connectivity among companies that participate on it and constitutes a supply management network [5].

As it was described before, companies have the tendency to focus even more on their core business, letting the other part of their business to be bought in the market. For this reason, companies are becoming members of a larger network of organizations. Instead, a supply chain networking is normally used to highlight the complexity of interactions that emerge from companies, looking for an opportunity to add value. This contemplates the flux of materials but more important, the flux of information, that are critical nowadays [4, 6]. Supply chain networks gives the capacity to their members to become more global and have access to a multiple types of resources [7]. The built of networks is sustained in structures that obey five key areas: external suppliers, production and distribution centers, demand zones and transportation assets [7].

All the companies must acquire the capability to make or buy the components they need to build a supply chain network. It means that they need to avoid a position of a passive member in the supply chain and start working on an active position. Of course, it could be argued, that everything depends of the bargaining power they have in the future supply chain.

It is the collection of physical locations, transportation vehicles and supporting systems through which the products and services firm markets are managed and ultimately delivered. Global Standards are now making it possible to automate these Supply Chain Networks in a real time manner making them more efficient than the simple supply chain of the past.

One of the important points when we want to build a supply chain network is the design of its architecture [8]. The design of a supply chain network must be considered an important strategic issue, according to these authors. The architecture must be designed in such away, that the reduction of costs must be guaranteed in the entire supply chain [8]. For these authors, the majority of experts on this field of knowledge expect that 80% of the supply chain costs are influenced by the location of the involved facilities and the flows of materials and products between them [8]. For this reason, it is always relevant to model the network. Basically, it is developed a mathematical model on the design stage in order to "optimize the supply chain network" [8].

The importance is so high, that companies have been investing in tools and resources to develop a better design for SCN. Consequently, we can deduce that "taxation regulations, the risk of new entrants into their industry and the availability of resources, has resulted in more complex network designs" [9].

When we design a SCN, we must take into account all the facilities, means of production, products and transportation assets owned by the organisation or those not owned by the organisation but which immediately support the supply chain operations and product flow [10]. Therefore, a SCN design should be considered as the combination of nodes with the capability and capacity, connected by lanes to help products move between facilities [10].

In literature, there are multiple forms to design a SCN considering the capability, capacity and product flow. All of them are interdependent without chances for a single optimal SCN design. So designing a SCN there is, with no doubt, a permanently trade-off among responsiveness, risk tolerance and efficiency [10, 11].

The environmental impacts of goods at the end of their line brought to the spotlight the concept of "reverse supply chain network design". This particular network design follows the inverse logic of a supply chain. It is a supply chain that causes some issues on the logistic operations like recycling [12]. For [13], companies with competencies and experience, in both forward and reverse supply chain processes, were noticed with more prone to success. Through this, some companies can achieve a "closed-loop system" [12, 14].

Risk is also considered a key factor on SCN. Normally it is recommended to do a risk analysis before creating a SCN. The main cause is the fact that, designing a supply chain network can cut costs within a company. We must not forget to highlight that a supply chain is not static but rather a continually improving model, looking for adaptation. A key point in designing the Supply Chain Network is to guarantee the versatility of the network and if it is enough to cover future uncertainties [7]. Obviously, there is always inherent uncertainty about the future behaviour of the partners and if they match. A supply chain network risk analysis can be conducted by using information available to mitigate these risks and the future of business environment.

In literature, there are some uncertainties associated with supply chain networks. They fall within two categories: endogenous uncertainty and exogenous uncertainty

[11, 15]. When classified as endogenous, an uncertainty has the source of its risk within the supply chain network itself [11, 15]. In the case of an uncertainty being classified exogenous, the source of risk is external to the supply chain network [11, 15]. Exogenous uncertainties can be further categorised as ongoing risks such as economic volatility. There is a 'continuous risk'. 'Discrete' events refer to infrequent events that could disrupt the supply chain process, such as natural disasters [11, 15]. Making the distinction between these types of uncertainty, any company can decide the best approach to risk management. A company has a very limited ability to prevent exogenous uncertainty. The risk to the supply chain network can be minimised by being well prepared for potential events. Endogenous uncertainty can be somewhat mitigated by taking precautions, such as regular communication between an organisation and its supplier [11, 15].

3 Supply Chain Networking Model

The Supply Chain Networking Model (SCN) is a multi-agent model built under Netlogo software [16] referent to an illustration of collaborative networks, with the main objective of analysing how the behaviour of companies in assembling supply chains for specific short term projects of production can give rise to a variety of large-scale business network structures. In fact, the model reflects the dimension for each supply chain and the consequent complexity that was established among the companies. The model is an adaptation of the team assembly model [2, 17]. The rules of the model are based in specific features that come from the theoretical contents of logistic and more precisely the network management of supply chain in a small production project (e.g. the deliver of Nespresso small packages of coffee to the clients).

Many of the general features that we can find in the supply chain networks of logistic companies can be captured by the SCN model with some simple parameters.

3.1 SCN Model Parameters

The SCN Model is composed by a set of parameters that characterises some aspects of supply chain management. The model is split on the parameters who affect all the type of companies:

1. Supply Chain Size: the number of companies (agents) in a newly supply chain network.
2. Max-Downtime: the number of steps a company will remain in the market without belonging to any supply chain, before it retires.
3. p: the probability of a company outside the supply chain (new member) and with less resources and capabilities of being chosen to become a member of a new supply chain project.
4. ς: the probability of a new supply chain being assembled with the inclusion of a previous company (experienced member) which has collaborated in one of the last supply chains generated before, given that the supply chain has, at least, one company.

5. δ: the probability of a company (agent) being individualist and do not participate in a network. This company does not want to participate in any supply chain and prefers to act alone in the competition. Of course, $(1 - δ)$ gives the probability of a company being collaborative and committed to be part of a supply chain. It means that these agents, try to add value by doing networking.
6. υ: the probability of a company (agent) being uncertainty avoidant, concerning the supply chain that will be constituted. Of course $(1 - υ)$ makes an agent as non-averse to uncertainty.
7. φ: the probability of an agent being a problem solver in the supply chain. In the same way $(1 - φ)$ causes an agent to not be a problem solver for a supply chain that will be constituted. Normally, all these probabilities come from a logistic regression model by using probit algorithm.

The combination of these parameters permits researcher to build a distinctive model which capture the relations among the different types of agents and different links established respectively.

3.2 Explaining SCN Model

The majority of the general features and types of connections could be found in the networks established among the companies which become members of the supply chain created. These general features can be captured by the Supply Chain Network Model with two simple parameters: the proportion of new members participating in a supply chain and the propensity for past companies to work again with one another [2]. However, this model goes a step further and it was added more parameters in order to check out what is the impact of the propensity to accept risks in SCN and the role that agents have on the network.

At each tick, a new company member is assembled to the supply chain or leaves it. Supply chain members are either inexperienced partners without reputation in the market (companies who have not previously participated in any type of supply chains) or are established companies with credentials in participating on supply chains. Typically, these are experienced players, who have already participated on a supply chain project. Each member is chosen sequentially. The ρ slider, gives the probability that an outsider will be an inexperienced supply chain member. If the new member is not an experienced player, then with a probability given by the ς slider, an experienced member will be chosen at random from the pool of previous network members, which has already collaborated on a supply chain before. Otherwise, a new member will just be randomly chosen from all experienced members. When a supply chain is created, all the members are linked to one another. If an agent does not participate in a new supply chain for a prolonged period of time, the agent and her links are removed from the network.

The agents in a newly "assembled supply chain" has the blue colour if they are new members and yellow if they are experienced members. Smaller grey circles represent those that are not currently collaborating. Links indicate members' experience at their most recent time of collaboration. For example, blue links between agents indicate that two agents collaborated as new members [2]. Green and yellow links correspond to one-time new member - experienced member and experienced member - experienced member collaborations, respectively. Finally, red links indicate that agents have collaborated with one another multiple times [2, 17].

Blue	Two new members
Green	A new member and an experienced member
Red	Repeated partners
Yellow	Two experienced members that have not previously collaborated with one another

The model counts the number of links established in the collaboration among the supply chain over time. The model also outputs the percentage of agents in a giant component. This output variable gives us the extension of complexity that a SCN could have. It plots the percentage of agents belonging to the largest supply chain, over time.

On the other hand, the average supply chain size gives the size of isolated supply chains as a fraction of the total number of companies. If we analyse the dynamism of plots, we can observe important features of the supply chain, like the distribution of link types or the connectivity of the supply chains varying over time.

The SCN model catches from one hand the distribution type of the connections among supply chain members. An overabundance of new member-new member (blue) links might indicate that the supply chain is not taking advantage of experienced players. On the other hand, a multitude of repeated networking (red) and experienced member-experienced member (yellow) links may indicate a lack of diversity in ideas or experiences.

From the other hand is the overall connectivity of the supply chain networking. We can also see the different emergent topologies in the display. New collaborations or synergies among supply chains naturally tend to the center of the display. Supply chains with few connections to new collaborations naturally "float" to the edges of the market (world). New members always start in the center of the world. Experienced members, who are chosen at random basis, may be located in any part of the screen. Thus, collaborations amongst new members and or distant supply chain components tend toward the center, and disconnected clusters are repelled from the centered.

Finally, we have to notice that the structure of supply chains in the model can change dramatically over time. Initially, only new supply chains are generated, the collaborative field has not existed long enough for members to retire. However, after a period of time (Max-Downtime), inactive companies begin to retire from the market, and the number of companies becomes relatively stable – the emergent effects of ρ and ς become more apparent in this equilibrium stage. To note also, in the end of the growth stage is often marked by a drop in the connectivity of the supply chains.

4   Output Results

The results reported in this section were obtained conducting the described experiments using version 5.0.4 of the NetLogo framework [16]. NetLogo is a programmable modelling environment for simulating natural and social phenomena. It is particularly well suited for modelling complex systems and developing them over time.

At this stage of research, the main goal is strictly committed for the scope of this article. In this section, I will only hint the obtained results and present the respective analysis. The simulations contemplated firstly an analysis of the variations on probabilities in a supply chain network about a new member being included or experienced members being included. Secondly, there is the comparison between individualist and collaborative approaches. Third is the relation of companies with risk. Fourth is the profile they have about solving problems given by the variation of respective parameter. For this exercise, it was simulated 300 times/assemblies for supply chain networks.

4.1 Variations in Constitution of Supply Chain Networks

First of all, it was simulated a variation on the probability of new members without experience in SCN and respective impact in terms of established connections.

As we can see, a decrease in the probability (10%) of experienced members to be included on supply chain network and consequently an increase of new members without experience to be part of SCN, provokes a creation of a small supply chain networks disperse in the market, where the majority of the partners are composed by new and few members. The SCN achieves 336 connections during the simulation. There is no tendency to obtain large SCN and the average in supply chain is close to the initial supply chain size (See Fig. 1).

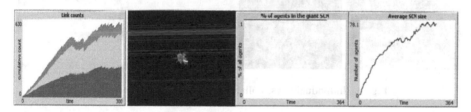

Fig. 1. Decrease of experienced members in deterrence of new members.

Other situation is an increase on the probability of experienced members being part of the SCN in deterrence of new members. As we can see, the number of connections has a large increase on SCN. Basically, the connections are made under experienced members and repeated partners who have work together in other SCN constituted in the past. Another important point is the concentration on the SCN that are built. It is a case of a giant SCN restricted in space and on the same members. About 100% of companies belong to the SCN generated. To have an idea of complexity of SCNs generated, the average SCN size reaches 78 companies which is almost 20 times the size of initially SCNs established for simulation (See Fig. 2).

4.2 Individualistic Versus Collaborative Approach

The second simulation was the comparison of individualist and the collaborative approaches. As we can notice from simulated results, the links counts about 392. The

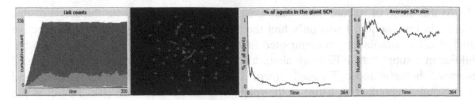

Fig. 2. Increase of experienced members in deterrence of new members.

major parts of them are connections between new members and experienced members followed by connections only within new members. So it seems there is a tendency to have dispersive SCNs, where new members prefer to adopt an individualistic strategy after gaining experience from experienced members. The percentage of agents in a giant SCN starts with 100% agents and breaks down to 90%. The average SCN size is highly volatility reaching 156 agents, the double of the last simulation. However, it ends with less than 40 agents in a SCN. This happens because at the beginning, companies started to be collaborative and building huge SCNs, when the links between experienced members were the majority. Then, the number of companies drops because of the individualistic strategy among inexperienced members (See Fig. 3).

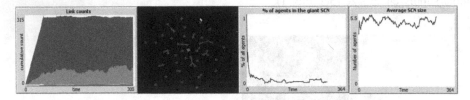

Fig. 3. Individualist vs. collaborative approach comparison

4.3   Action of Risk Avoidant Companies

The third simulation done under the scope of this work was to verify the risk profile impact on the constitution of SCN. According to the output results, the greater is the risk aversion of agents, the higher is the number of links between new members in SCNs. It was established 315 links among companies. The major of SCNs built are dispersed or fragmented in the market with few members on average. The simulation reports 5.5 companies on average, which is one more company from the start point of the simulation. It is also present a deeply decline on the percentage of agents in a giant SCN during the simulation (See Fig. 4).

4.4   Predisposition for Problem Solving

Finally, the last simulation was concerned with the understanding of the impact of predisposition of solving problems in a SCN about their needs. As we can see from reported results, the SCNs are constituted fundamentally with connections between experienced members and new members. The second major group of links is the ones

Fig. 4. Agents' risk profile impact

among new members without experience at all in a SCN followed by the links established among experienced members. In total, we have 391 links during this simulation.

At the beginning of the simulation, the percentage of agents being part of a giant SCN was 100%. Then, we can notice a significantly decline on the percentage of agents that constitutes a giant SCN. An average SCN size reaches a total of 100 companies that during the simulation has a vertiginous break, situating its value around 20 companies (See Fig. 5).

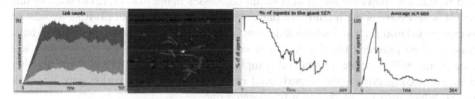

Fig. 5. Problem solver impact

5 Results Discussion

When we make a deep analysis about the results, we can detect interesting results. First of all, we have more connections on SCN when the majority of the partners have experience from past SCN's. Experienced companies prefer to establish links with other experienced partners or repeated on a new SCN. However, these connections don't give the companies the predisposition to expand their position in the market. They stay together, concentrated in their own market. This result is also evident when we take a look on risk analysis. Companies who are risk avoiders felt less available in constituting a SCN. For this reason, most of links are established among new members who generate small SCNs, spread all over the market. This wants to demonstrate that experienced members are more reluctant to enter in a risky SCN, then leaving this space for new members who had form some networks with the experienced companies, during the simulation. These players excluded from the principal centre of the market, try to explore some opportunities in filling existent gaps in the market. For this reason, they are completely dispersed on the market.

Another important achievement is to verify that a giant SCN in the market with 100% of their member included, doesn't mean it is constituted by a large number of players. The largest SCN was found when it was simulated the interaction between individualistic members and collaborative. This result reveals some interesting signs about the efficiency and effectiveness work. It suggests that a giant component could be losing performance over the time. But, to proof this it is necessary to perform other simulations, unfortunately they are not contemplated on the scope of this work.

Finally, the case of the problem solver predisposition members in order to satisfy the SCN needs. It is evident that this feature catches a lot of members building another huge SCN at the beginning of simulation. After reaching the global needs of a SCN, there is a significant decline in the percentage of agents compounding the giant SCN. It means that after attending SCN needs, most of the participants start to leave giant SCN and explore gaps in the market incorporated in small SCNs.

6   Conclusions

This article had the objective to discuss the constitution or assembling of Supply Chain Networks. After several and distinct simulations we achieve some interesting results: (1) Supply Chain Networks were built fundamentally based on experienced members and repeated partners for the most relevant businesses in the market; (2) to achieve this result is necessary some quantity of players but not the largest one; (3) Risk avoidance is critical to build high and sustainable supply chain networks. Companies need to have trust on their partners; (4) the fact of having a lot of players in the market does not means they will generate a giant and complex SCN. Most of the players come together after some connections with experienced members and explore market gaps opportunities, which turn the market in a fragmented one.

Following this reasoning, SCNs can be very advantageous for the companies which integrate them, but can also have some disadvantages. The effect on the market is also discussed on this work. Considering this, we can affirm that relevant businesses attract more often, the experienced and repeated partners for SCNs. New members without experience get the experience needed in some giant SCNs and then start to explore some gaps dispersed in the market, competing against other players.

References

1. Harland, C.M.: Supply chain management: relationships, chains and networks. Br. J. Manag. 7(s1), S63–S80 (1996)
2. Guimerà, R., Uzzi, B., Spiro, J., Amaral, L.A.: Team assembly mechanisms determine collaboration network structure and team performance. Science 308(5722), 697–702 (2005). https://doi.org/10.1126/science.1106340
3. Vitasek, K.: Supply Chain and Logistics: Terms and Glossary. Supply Chain Visions, Bellevue (2006)
4. Webster, S.: Principles and Tools for Supply Chain Management. McGraw-Hill Irwin, Boston (2008)
5. Slack, N., Chambers, S., Johnston, R.: Operations and Process Management: Principles and Practice for Strategic Impact. Prentice Hall/Financial Times, Upper Saddle River (2009). ISBN 9780273718512

6. Chopra, S., Meindl, P.: Supply Chain Management. Pearson International Edition, Thousand Oaks (2007)
7. Klibi, W., Martel, A.: Scenario-based supply chain network risk modeling. Eur. J. Oper. Res. **223**(3), 644–658 (2012). https://doi.org/10.1016/j.ejor.2012.06.027
8. Watson, M., Lewis, S., Cacioppi, P., Jayaraman, J.: Supply Chain Network Design: Applying Optimization & Analytics to Global Supply Chain, p. 1. Pearson Education, Inc., Thousand Oaks (2013). ISBN 978-0-13-301737-3
9. Wang, F., Lai, X., Shi, N.: A multi-objective optimization for green supply chain network design. Decis. Support Syst. **51**, 262–269 (2011)
10. Fattahi, M., Govindan, K., Keyvanshokooh, E.: Responsive and resilient supply chain network design under operational and disruption risks with delivery lead-time sensitive customers. Transp. R. Part E: Logistics Transp. Rev. **101**, 176–200 (2017)
11. Trkman, P., McCormack, K.: Supply chain risk in turbulent environments: a conceptual model for managing supply chain network risk. Int. J. Prod. Econ. **119**(2), 247–258 (2009). https://doi.org/10.1016/j.ijpe.2009.03.002
12. Pishvaee, M., Razmi, J.: Environmental supply chain network design using multi-objective fuzzy mathematical programming. Appl. Math. Model. **36**(8), 3433–3446 (2012). https://doi.org/10.1016/j.apm.2011.10.00
13. Guide Jr., V., Van Wassenhove, L.: The reverse supply chain. Harvard Business Review (2002)
14. Pishvaee, M.S., Torabi, S.A.: A possibilistic programming approach for closed-loop supply chain network design under uncertainty. Fuzzy Sets Syst. Theme: Games Optim. Discrete Struct. **161**(20), 2668–2683 (2010). https://doi.org/10.1016/j.fss.2010.04.010
15. Lonsdale, C.: Effectively managing vertical supply relationships: a risk management model for outsourcing. Supply Chain Manag.: Int. J. **4**(4), 176–183 (1999)
16. Wilensky, U.: NetLogo. Center for Connected Learning and Computer-Based Modeling, Northwestern University, Evanston, IL (1999). http://ccl.northwestern.edu/netlogo/
17. Bakshy, E., Wilensky, U.: NetLogo Team Assembly Model. Center for Connected Learning and Computer-Based Modeling, Northwestern University, Evanston, IL (2007). http://ccl.northwestern.edu/netlogo/models/TeamAssembly

Using Agent Base Simulation to Model Operations in Semi-automated Warehouse

Pawel Pawlewski[1]([⊠]) and Tomasz Kunc[2]

[1] Poznan University of Technology, ul. Strzelecka 11, 60-965 Poznań, Poland
pawel.pawlewski@put.poznan.pl
[2] ZREMBUD, ul. Mała Łąka 10, 43-400 Cieszyn, Poland
tomasz@zrembud.com.pl

Abstract. The paper presents the results of research carried out in recent years in the area of warehousing. The main goal of the article is to show the project of simulation modeling semi-automated warehouse using multi-agent technologies. The most important points of the article are: the presentation of the new kind of automated drawer racks, originality of this project and basis for defining the methodology of modeling this kind of warehouse using ABS – agent based simulation. Extension of the script language for agent's behavior describing is proposed.

Keywords: Agents · Warehouse systems · Agent based simulation · Modeling

1 Introduction

The paper presents results of our researches performed in area of warehousing. By this term we understand a facility whose main function is buffering and storage of SKUs or items. If storage hardly plays a role - transshipment, cross-dock, or platform center often are used [1]. A distribution warehouse is defined as a facility that store products from multiple suppliers which ultimately are to be delivered to a number of customers [2]. We treat the warehouse as an object it consists of a number of parallel aisles with products being stored vertically alongside. During our researches we developed new kind of racks. It is semi-automated racks where some sections of racks are moved by carriages. To model it we developed the modeling approach used agent base thinking. The goal of this paper is to present the project of simulation modeling semi-automated warehouse using multi-agent technologies.

The highlights of the paper are:

– easiest of modeling logistics using agent based approach,
– methodology of modeling operations at warehouse using ABS (Agent Based Simulation),
– presentation of new kind of semi-automated racks.

The main contribution is indication of the possibility of implementing agent technologies for modeling drawer shelves - development of the basis for the methodology of rapid design of warehouses.

F. De la Prieta et al. (Eds.): PAAMS 2019 Workshops, CCIS 1047, pp. 50–61, 2019.
https://doi.org/10.1007/978-3-030-24299-2_5

The paper is organized as follow: Sect. 2 about literature background is divided in two part: warehouse equipment and agent based simulation. Section 3 defines the problem – how to build the simulation model to show the benefits of implementation of drawer racks in comparison with other technologies. Proposed solution based on cyclic and agents approach is presented in Sect. 4. Section 5 provides conclusions and plans for further research.

2 Literature Background

2.1 Warehouse Equipment

As mentioned earlier we treat the warehouse as an object it consists of a number of parallel aisles with products being stored vertically alongside. The term warehousing (and all that goes along with it) is treated as part of logistics management. Logistics includes procurement, inventory management, and distribution. Logistics with product development, marketing, sales, and other product-related disciplines form supply chain. Warehouse plays a vital role in the success or failure of the company [3].

In [4] warehouse design problem is defined as five groups of decisions: determination of the general structure of the warehouse (conceptual design); its sizing; layout calculation; warehousing equipment selection; and selection of its operational strategy. [4] and [5] add that a warehouse project must also include definitions of policies about order fulfillment/picking, stocking, and stock rotation. The best storage method, the most appropriate selection of material handling equipment and warehouse layout are the goals of the warehouse design [6]. In other words warehouse layout plan, material handling plan and warehouse operations are three factors that affect the warehouse layout design, but literature includes studies which grouping that factors differently [3, 4, 7, 8].

Storage area plan, aisle plan, shelf types and sizes, dock plan form warehouse layout plan. Warehouse material handling plan contains material handling equipment plan and personnel plan. Placement/picking policies and assignment policies are the parts of warehouse operations plan. In [9] are defined 3 dimensions of warehouse design: selection of material handling equipment, movement of material handling equipment in the corridor, input/output quantities.

We think that two from three factors in some situations are dependent on each other. Material handling equipment (warehouse equipment) has an influence on general structure of the warehouse – on warehouse layout plan.

Now on the market are available following types (technologies) of equipment used for material handling in warehouse.

RR-Row racks - goods are laid in rows on several or several levels of storage, parallel to the working corridor. The device or operators operating the rack have access to units that are located parallel to the transport channel. In row racks it is possible to handle carriers located directly at the working corridor. Dedicated to the centers where the so-called general cargo or completing shipments. An important disadvantage of the solution is the small surface ratio that the shelves occupy in relation to the one that is needed for efficient stacking of goods using special devices.

DDS-Double deep shelves - the most common storage system for fully automated systems. Carriers stored in the same way as in row racks with the difference that in two rows. This means access from the working corridor to two carriers from the point of view of the shelving depth. Support for media located in a deeper location is possible after changing the location of the media from a shallow location and unveiling it. The system has fixed work corridors for stackers. Have similar advantages as row racks. However, they significantly increase the ratio of the space occupied by the shelves to the working corridors. The disadvantage is the extended stock uptake and picking up of goods from the rack.

Block - Laying in a block system on shelves. Multideep rack, drive in (drive-in), Shuttle system - such systems are characterized by the possibility of multiplying the depth of storage, this means storing more than 2 units in the Z-axis (depth). The method of operation depends on the type of shelving system. In the case of Drive In racks, the order of placing is as follows: the operator picks up the goods and enters the end of the "zero" rack. It leaves the load, then takes another unit, it enters the end of the block, but sets it at a higher level. The situation is repeated at subsequent levels. The stocking takes place from the end to the beginning of the rack.

The system of shelves supported by the Shuttle trolley consists in using a special trolley moving in the Z axis of the rack on special rails. The trolley supports a single channel (depth), in case it is to be changed, the Shuttle is transported using a trolley or automated systems. Channel support looks as follows. The shuttle is at the beginning of the rack. Operator places a palett on it. The trolley transports the carrier to the depth indicated by the system and deposits the carrier. Stacking order from the end to the beginning - without having to keep the order of levels. These systems have the best ratio of space for storage of goods in relation to working corridors. Regardless of the solutions of the installation method, whether by means of automatic stackers, roller guides or forklifts, they do not work well in warehouses where there is a large quantity of goods where a fifo system is required.

ROT - Rotational (flow) racks. Goods stacked on a rack one by one thanks to the use of roller conveyors. In addition, goods due to the fact that the rack is inclined under the account of several% are automatically moved to the beginning of the rack. Stocking from beginning to end without having to keep the order of levels. To gain access to the palett, the rows are extended to reveal the chosen sector. The process is slow and limits access to other pallet units.

MOB-Storage racks (mobile). A system similar to row storage with the basic difference that there are no fixed work corridors and shelves are placed on special platforms. The shelves divide into a working corridor by means of which goods are manipulated on the shelves.

MEZ-Mezzanine - this solution divides the storage space into several levels. They are mainly used for storing general cargo, where additional work is usually required when handling goods.

2.2   Agent Based Simulation

In [10] was presented the program of the library of agents called LogABS designed and implemented in FlexSim DES. In this work was described arguments to use the method based on mixing DES (Discrete-Event Simulation) and ABS (Agent Based Simulation).

DES has been the main way for the process simulation of manufacturing and logistics for about four decades. This is adequate for problems that consist of queuing simulations and a variability is represented through stochastic distributions [11]. This approach is applicable in simulating the manufacturing and supply chain processes. DES models are characterized by [12] a process oriented approach (the focus is on modeling the system in detail, not the entities). They are based on a top-down modeling approach and have one thread of control (centralized). They contain passive entities (i.e. something is done to the entities while they move through the system) and intelligence (e.g. decision making) is modeled as part of the system. In DES, queues are the crucial element; a flow of entities through a system is defined; macro behavior is modeled and input distributions are often based on collected/measured (objective) data.

ABS is a simulation technique that models the overall behavior of a system through the use of autonomous system components (also referred to as agents) that communicate with each other [13]. The behavior incorporated into an agent determines its role in the environment, its interaction with other agents, its response to messages from other agents, and indeed whether its own behavior is adaptable [14]. Agent based modeling is a relatively new method compared to system dynamics and discrete event modeling. Agent based modeling offers a modeler another way to look at the system. You may not know how the system behaves or be able to identify its key variables and dependencies, or recognize the process flow, but you can have an insight into how the system objects behave. It is possible to start building the model by identifying the objects (agents) and defining their behaviors. Next, it is possible to connect the created agents and allow them to interact or put them in an environment which has its own dynamics. The system's global behavior emerges from many concurrent individual behaviors [15].

There is no standard language for agent based modeling, and the structure of an agent based model comes from graphical editors or scripts. There are many ways to specify an agent's behavior. Frequently, an agent has a notion of state and its actions and reactions depend on the state; then the behavior is best defined with statecharts. Sometimes the behavior is defined in rules executed by means of special events [15].

Academics still debate which properties an object should have to be an "agent": proactive and reactive qualities, spatial awareness, an ability to learn, social ability, "intellect", etc. In applied agent based modeling, however, you will find all kinds of agents: some communicate while others live in total isolation, some live in a space while others live without a space, and some learn and adapt while others never change their behavior patterns. According to [16], agent characteristic can be defined as:

1. identifiable, a discrete individual with set of characteristics and rules governing its behaviors and decision-making capabilities,
2. autonomous and self-directed,
3. situated, living in an environment where it interacts with other agents – has protocols for interaction with other agents,
4. goal directed – having goals to achieve,
5. flexible – having the ability to learn and adapt its behaviors based on experiences.

3   Problem Definition

The Zrembud Cieszyn (http://www.zrembud.com.pl/regaly.html) company has developed an innovative storage method that uses a properly modified shelving system based on single or double sections of row systems reversed by 90°, set perpendicular to the working corridor.

Fig. 1. Visualization of new type of automatic storage rack (*Source*: Zrembud Cieszyn, Poland)

The whole system creates a block where the depth of the rack and the number of storage levels is adapted to the requirements of users. The shelving sections are placed on a suitably designed platform that allows automatic system movement Fig. 1. The **DR - drawer racks** system will be widely used in logistic centers and other areas designated for storing goods. This type of solution will allow independent operation of each platform and effective management of their traffic.

The new type of automatic storage rack developed has the ability to easily be temporarily adapted to the variable demand for storage space by expanding or reducing it to further drawers without the need to perform work in the floors or foundations of storage halls. The concept of sliding drawers was used, on which shelves for storage of goods on pallets or on shelves are placed. The drawer is placed on the platform. The transfer and retraction of the platform is made possible by a transfer carriage moving perpendicular to the direction of movement of the transport platform. The carriage's task is to enable the movement of the unit indicated by the operator.

Communication between the forklift operator, the rack control system and the WMS (Warehouse Management System) system allows the drawer to be pulled out shortly before reaching the positions via the forklift, which limits the time for loading or unloading. Installing or changing the arrangement of shelves does not require the necessity to build infrastructure in the warehouse floor.

The designed solution optimizes the storage space by reducing the number of transport corridors. As a result, there is an increase in the storage capacity of goods at the same storage area. Customers are able to reduce their storage space, which directly translates into a reduction in the cost of investment in the construction of logistic centers as well as more efficient use of internal transport (Table 1).

Table 1. Comparison of technologies used for material handling in warehouse (assessment range from 1 to 5) (*Source*: own study)

Criterion	RR	DDS	Block	ROT	MOB	MEZ	DR
The use of space	2	4	5	5	4	5	4
Operations according to FIFO, FEFO or LIFO	5	4	2	2	3	5	5
Access to each carrier	5	4	1	1	3	5	5
Variety of assortments	5	4	3	1	3	5	5
Innovation	1	3	3	3	3	2	5
Automation of processes	4	5	3	1	1	1	5
Impact on the structure of the object - including damage to the floor by anchoring the shelves	2	2	3	3	3	1	5
Storage according to ABC	5	4	1	1	3	5	5
Speed of manipulation	4	4	4	3	3	2	5
The sum of points	**33**	**34**	**25**	**20**	**26**	**31**	**44**

The automatic drawer rack system offers a number of advantages over competing solutions present on the market:

- Radical improvement in the ratio of the number of storage places to the area – Fig. 2,
- Better use of warehouse space,
- Better use of internal transport,
- Better organization of work in the warehouse,
- Less consumption of internal transport by reducing storage space, Less electricity consumption in forklift trucks - by eliminating unnecessary movements on handling.

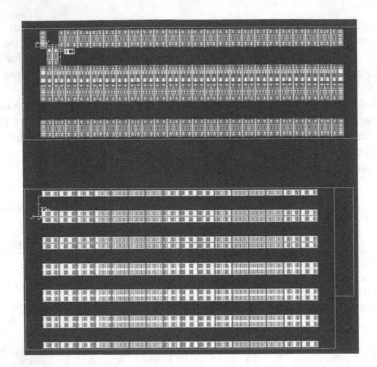

Fig. 2. View of layouts: upper – drawer racks, bottom - row racks (*Source*: own study)

The customer is interested in researching, analyzing the designed racking system. First of all, logistic parameters of the rack will be taken into account - speed, acceleration and deceleration of shelves' extension. To this end, a simulation model will be built.

The aim of the research will be to find answers to questions about coordinating the work of retractable shelves in time and space: will the movable frame be ejected before picking up or loading the pallet?, how much earlier does the frame have to get a signal?, what is the acceleration and deceleration of the frame movement and their impact on efficiency (throughput) of the rack?

The simulation model of the automatic drawer shelf will be able to define various work scenarios (what-if analysis?), Which in turn will allow you to choose the appropriate rack parameters from the customer's point of view. The built-in simulation model - logistic of the rack will allow local and system analysis, i.e. the work of many automatic shelves connected in the system. In the logistics (systemic) and economic area, it is essential to identify key logistics parameters and their connections in the drawer shelving system.

From the customer's point of view (user of new rack system), it is important to answer the question of how many shelves and how they are set to provide the customer with an optimal flow of material in the warehouse from his point of view. Simulation studies will concern the location of a drawer shelf as part of a shelving system and examine the behavior of a system built from several, several dozen or so dozens of such shelves. The key will be to find the answer to the question: what are and are the risks associated with combining racks in the system, the bandwidth of such a system, rules of behavior, control rules.

4 Designed Solution

To form the basis to solve defined in previous section problem we used our earlier experiences [10, 17, 18]. In [17] was defined the script language for agent's behavior describing. To build the logic of designed simulation model we concentrate on:

- levels of control and analysis,
- using cyclic and agents approach.

We identify work cycles on following levels:

- level of automation (PLC - programmable logic controller)
- level of rack's transfer carrier and forklift,
- level of control/management – MFC/WMS (MFC – Material Flow Control system, WMS – Warehouse Management System).

Agent approach consists in describing and implementing the logic of system operation in a distributed and autonomous way (as in reality). Central control and management (equivalent of MFC/WMS) is treated as operation of the agent as well.

To build the simulation logistics model that will have possibilities to answer defined in Sect. 3 questions – it is not necessary to focus on level of automation. So we focus on level of rack's transfer carriers and forklifts.

We define the rules for rack's carriers, forklifts and for level of control/management.

4.1 Level of Rack's Transfer Carrier

We use following structure of addresses in designed warehouse: 1A_18_b_2.

- 1 – number of corridor
- A - A or B – side of corridor
- _18 – number of rack in row
- _b – level - shelf (5 levels/shelfs are: a, b, c, d, e)
- _2 – position on the level/shelf

These addresses are used by Warehouse Management System to form transport orders for forklifts and to control transfer carriers by Material Flow Control System.

Two racks form the section that can be moved by transfer carrier – Fig. 3. The rules of transfer carrier are defined as:

- Start position racks 2&3 – Sect. 2,
- R motion from Sect. 2 till the Sect. 9
- B motion from position 1 (on the level/shelf) till the position 5.

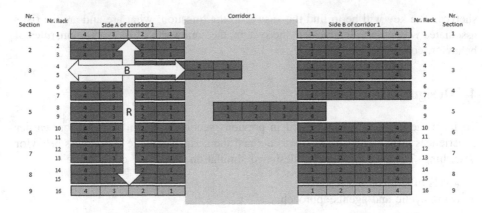

Fig. 3. View of layout for transfer carrier rules (*Source*: Zrembud Cieszyn, Poland).

Table 2 contains the list of tasks of transfer carrier cycle work. The task is formed by row, where "Address" defines position (point on floor) or section, "Task" defines operation according to description in [17] and "Parameter" – time or number.

Table 2. List of tasks of transfer carrier cycle work. (*Source*: own study)

Address	Task	Parameter	Description
	ReadyForTask		Start of cycle – waiting for request from WMS
GG_001	Travel		Moving under the section
/S1A_5	PickUp		Pick Up the section
GG_002	TravelLoaded		Ejection of the section
	ReadyForTask		Waiting for request from MFC
GG_001	TravelLoaded		Moving back of the section
/S1A_5	Lowercontain		Lowering of the section
	Call	1	Return to the beginning of the cycle – to the first row of this table

4.2   Level of Forklift

Foklift (one or more) works in two cycles:

- Receiving – from receive area where materials are unloaded from trucks, to addressed rack,
- Production – from addressed rack to production area

Transport orders with addresses are prepared by WMS. Forklift drives up to the extended shelf always at the row from which the shelf has moved out - gets from the first position, i.e. the nearest row. Tables 3 and 4 contain lists of tasks for "Receiving" cycle and for "Production" cycle.

Table 3. List of tasks of forklift – Receiving Cycle (*Source*: own study)

Address	Task	Parameter	Description
	ReadyForTask		Start of cycle – waiting for request from WMS
GG_015	Travel		Moving to Receiving area
P_13	Load	1	Loading 1 pallet
GG_023	TravelLoaded		Moving to the entry of corridor
N_07	TravelLoaded		Entry ahead to the corridor and moving to the rack
P_07	Unload	1	Unloading 1 pallet to the rack
GG_023	Travel	−1	Coming back to the entry to corridor
	Call	1	Return to the beginning of the cycle – to the first row of this table

Table 4. List of tasks of forklift – Production Cycle (*Source*: own study)

Address	Task	Parameter	Description
	ReadyForTask		Start of cycle – waiting for request from WMS
GG_023	Travel		Moving to the entry of corridor
N_02	Travel		Entry ahead to the corridor and moving to the rack
P_02	Load	1	Loading 1 pallet
GG_023	TravelLoaded	−1	Coming back to the entry to corridor
GG_017	TravelLoaded		Moving to the Production area
	Unload	1	Unloading 1 pallet
	Call	1	Return to the beginning of the cycle – to the first row of this table

4.3 Level of Control/Management

The logic of communication between agents representing transfer carriers, forklifts and WMS/MFC control/management is presented on Fig. 4.

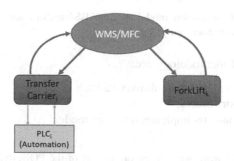

Fig. 4. The logic of communication between agents representing transfer carriers, forklifts and control/management. (*Source*: own study)

These agents work on cycles too. On the level of control/management (WMS/MFC) the cycle is defined generally in for steps:

1. Start of cycle,
2. Check the status of warehouse and take decision,
3. Send the transport order to Transfer Carrier or Forklift
4. Go to the 1 – Start of cycle

On the level of Transfer Carriers/Forklift cycles are performed according to list of tasks showed in Tables 2, 3 and 4.

5   Conclusions and Future Research

In [17] was defined the script language to describe agent's behaviors. This language was implemented in FlexSim Simulation Software. In [18] was presented the methodology for layout and intralogistics redesign using simulation. This methodology is dedicated for assembling system and available as LogABS Simulation Program. Now we develop LogABS for this kind of warehouse that uses designed drawer racks. The first step was to extend the script language defined in [17] by two commands: PickUp and Lower. Figure 5 shows the corridor with drawer racks, transfer carriers and forklift as part of simulation model built in LogABS/FlexSim 3D environment.

Fig. 5. The view 3D of simulation model in LogABS/FlexSim with one corridor, transfer carriers and forklift (*Source*: own study)

Next steps to build methodology are:

– Preparing allocation of items on drawer racks,
– Preparing of transport orders,
– Defining measures and its implementation in model.

Acknowledgements. The work was carried out as part of the POIR.01.01.01-00-0373/17 project, "Development of an automatic drawer shelf using modified 90° reverse row shelving systems dedicated to internal warehouse logistics", financed by NCBiR.

References

1. De Koster, R., Le-Duc, T., Roodbergen, K.: Design and control of warehouse order picking: a literature review. Eur. J. Oper. Res. **182**(2), 481–501 (2007)
2. van den Berg, J.P., Zijm, W.H.M.: Models for warehouse management: classification and examples. Int. J. Prod. Econ. **59**, 519–528 (1999)
3. Baker, P., Canessa, M.: Warehouse design: structured approach. Eur. J. Oper. Res. **193**, 425–436 (2009)
4. Gu, J., Goetschalckx, M., McGinnis, L.F.: Research on warehouse design and performance evaluation: a comprehensive review. Eur. J. Oper. Res. **203**(3), 539–549 (2010)
5. Chan, F.T.S., Chan, H.K.: Improving the productivity of order picking of a manual-pick and multi-level rack distribution warehouse through the implementation of class-based storage. Expert Syst. Appl. **38**(3), 2686–2700 (2001)
6. Ashayeri, Y., Gelders, L.F.: Warehouse design optimization. Eur. J. Oper. Res. **21**, 285–294 (1985)
7. Gu, J., Goetschalckx, M., McGinnis, L.F.: Research on warehouse operation: a comprehensive review. Eur. J. Oper. Res. **117**, 1–21 (2007)
8. Rouwenhorst, B., Reuter, B., Stockrahm, V., Van Houtum, G.J., Mantel, R.J., Zijm, W.H. M.: Warehouse design and control_framework and literature review. Eur. J. Oper. Res. **122**, 515–533 (2000)
9. Park, Y.H., Webster, D.B.: Modelling of three-dimensional warehouse systems. Int. J. Prod. Res. **27**, 985–1003 (1989)
10. Pawlewski, P.: DES/ABS approach to simulate warehouse operations. In: Bajo, J., et al. (eds.) PAAMS 2015. CCIS, vol. 524, pp. 115–125. Springer, Cham (2015). https://doi.org/10.1007/978-3-319-19033-4_10
11. Siebers, P.O., Macal, C.M., Garnett, J., Buxton, D., Pidd, M.: Discrete-event simulation is dead, long live agent-based simulation! J. Simul. **4**(3), 204–210 (2010)
12. Korytkowski, P., Wisniewski, T., Rymaszewski, S.: An evolutionary simulation-based optimization approach for dispatching scheduling. Simul. Model. Pract. Theory **35**, 69–85 (2013)
13. North, M.J., Macal, C.M.: Managing Business Complexity: Discovering Strategic Solutions with Agent-Based Modeling and Simulation. Oxford University Press, New York (2007)
14. Mustafee, N., Bischoff, E.E.: A multi-methodology agent-based approach for container loading. In: Jain, S., Creasey, R.R., Himmelspach, J., White, K.P., Fu, M. (eds.) Proceedings of the 2011 Winter Simulation Conference (2011)
15. Weimer, Ch.W., Miller, J.O., Hill, R.R.: Introduction to agent based modeling. In: Roeder, T.M.K., Frazier, P.I., Szechtman, R., Zhou, E., Huschka, T., Chick, S.E. (eds.) Proceedings of the 2016 Winter Simulation Conference (2016)
16. Macal, Ch.M., North, M.J.: Agent-based modeling and simulation: desktop ABMS. In: Henderson, S.G., Biller, B., Hsieh, M.H., Shortle, J., Tew, D.J., Barton, R.R. (eds.) Proceedings of the 2007 Winter Simulation Conference (WSC) (2007)
17. Pawlewski, P.: Script language to describe agent's behaviors. In: Bajo, J., et al. (eds.) PAAMS 2018. CCIS, vol. 887, pp. 137–148. Springer, Cham (2018). https://doi.org/10.1007/978-3-319-94779-2_13
18. Pawlewski, P.: Methodology for layout and intralogistics redesign using simulation. In: Rabe, M., Juan, A.A., Mustafee, N., Skoogh, A., Jain, S., Johansson, B. (eds.) Proceedings of the 2018 Winter Simulation Conference (2018)

Second International Workshop on Blockchain Technology for Multi-agent Systems (BTC4MAS)

Second International Workshop on Blockchain Technology for Multi-agent Systems (BTC4MAS)

Multi-agent systems (MAS) are composed of loosely coupled entities (agents) interconnected and organized in a network. Every agent has the ability to solve problems and attain its goals by interacting with each other through collaboration, negotiation, and competition patterns. MAS are increasingly dealing with sensitive data. Therefore, enforcing the notion of reputation, ensuring trust and reliability, is essential for modern MAS. Blockchain (BCT) is a P2P distributed ledger technology providing shared, immutable, transparent, and updatable (append-only) registers of given values characterizing a given network (e.g., all the actions intercurred among the participants and information about the participants themselves). However, employing the BCT "as-is" and by itself in dynamic and quickly evolving scenarios can represent an unlucky choice. The reasons span from fundamental properties of BCT to application/domain-specific constraints. Reaching consensus in distributed multi-stakeholder networks with possible unaligned interests can be considerably complex or unsustainable.

Therefore, if properly managed, combining BCT and MAS can represent a win–win solution:

1. The adoption and adaption of BCT can help to overcome trust and reliability limitations broadly known in the MAS literature, enabling secure, autonomous, flexible, and even profitable solutions.
2. MAS can contribute with its features to address limitations of BCT.

Organization

Organizing Committee

Davide Calvaresi	HES-SO Valais-Wallis, Switzerland
Michael Schumacher	HES-SO Valais-Wallis, Switzerland
Andrea Omicini	University of Bologna, Italy
Alevtina Dubovitskaya	HSLU and Swisscom, Switzerland
Sooyong Park	Sogang University, South Korea

Publicity Chairs

Amro Najjar	UMEA University, Sweden
Timotheus Kampik	UMEA University, Signavio GmbH, Sweden

Program Committee

Alexander Norta	Tallinn University of Technology, Estonia
Andrea Omicini	Alma Mater Studiorum-Università di Bologna, Italy
René Schumann	University of Applied Sciences and Arts Western Switzerland, Switzerland
Jean-Paul Calbimonte	University of Applied Sciences and Arts Western Switzerland, Switzerland
Stéphane Galland	Université de Technologie de Belfort-Montbéliard, France
Luciano Garcia Banuelos	University of Tartu, Estonia
Ingo Weber	CSIRO, Australia
Claudiuo Di Ciccio	Vienna University of Economics and Business, Austria
Ermo Täks	Tallinn University of Technology, Estonia
Fusheng Wang	Stony Brook University, USA
Amro Najjar (Publicity Chair)	UMEA University, Sweden
Paolo Sernani	Università Politecnica delle Marche, Italy
Timotheus Kampik (Publicity Chair)	Umea University, Sweden
Yazan Mualla	UTBM, France
Önder Gürcan	CEA, France
Giuseppe Albanese	University of Applied Sciences and Arts Western Switzerland, Switzerland
Petr Novotny	IBM, USA
Giovanni Ciatto	University of Bologna, Italy

A Startup Assessment Approach Based on Multi-Agent and Blockchain Technologies

Davide Calvaresi[1]([⊠]) [iD], Ekaterina Voronova[2], Jean-Paul Calbimonte[1], Valerio Mattioli[1], and Michael Schumacher[1]

[1] University of Applied Sciences and Arts Western Switzerland, Sierre, Switzerland
davide.calvaresi@hevs.ch
[2] Innovare Digital s.a.r.l., Lausanne, Switzerland
k.voronova@innmind.com

Abstract. The dynamic nature of startups is linked to both high risks in investments as well as potentially important financial benefits. A key aspect to manage interactions among investors, experts, and startups, is the establishment of trust guarantees. This paper presents the formalization and implementation of a system enforcing trust in the startup assessment domain. To do so, an existing architecture has been extended, incorporating a multi-agent community and related interactions via private blockchain technology. The developed system enables a trust-based community, immutably storing, tracking, and monitoring the agents' interactions and reputations.

Keywords: Multi-Agent Systems · Blockchain · Startup assessment

1 Introduction

Startups have become a driving force fostering innovation in several fields. An intense competition pushes entrepreneurs to strive in creating new opportunities and solutions for existing problems, employing new or combining existing technologies. Startups are demanded to provide disruptive technological solutions able to challenge big corporations, which are less flexible and fast-reacting due to their size and complex decision-making processes. Both novelty and potential flexibility to quickly adapt to new market conditions are favorable for startups to *(i)* create additional value for possible consumers, and to *(ii)* increase financial benefits for investors and technological contributions for all players in the market. In fact, this value has shown continuous growth in the latest years. Between (2015–2017) the global startup economy generated a worth of about 2.3 trillion USD (value growing steadily), according to the Global Startup Ecosystem Report [17]. However, although the startup ecosystem attracts massive investment (i.e., more than 207 billion USD of funds have been raised in 2018 [18]),

F. De la Prieta et al. (Eds.): PAAMS 2019 Workshops, CCIS 1047, pp. 67–79, 2019.
https://doi.org/10.1007/978-3-030-24299-2_6

it cannot be neglected that startups are highly vulnerable to numerous external and internal factors. Not all startups succeed: according to [16], around three quarters of venture-backed US projects do not return investors' capital. The most common reasons why projects fail are: *(i)* no market need, *(ii)* lack of funds, *(iii)* improper balance of the team's competences, and *(iv)* unsustainable competition [23]. Such concerns make investing in startups potentially highly profitable and risky at the same time. Besides startups and investors, other players participate in the process of creating innovation, who, at the same time, can benefit and are vulnerable to the high-rate of startup failures. For example, we can mention early adopters, contributors, and *participants* of the startup ecosystem. Such participants contribute to the ecosystem by providing specific services to the startups, such as mentoring, testing new products, and facilitating their communication with investors. Tight collaboration with the startups can increase the potential of success. Hence, conducting an in-depth analysis of the project they consider investing in, investors and other players drastically reduce the risks of failure.

In this domain, which requires dealing with sensitive and classified data (e.g., intellectual property and business plans), the employment of intelligent systems is increasing at a fast pace, and privacy, security, and integrity are becoming outstanding concerns. One possible way to address these challenges is by relying on Multi-Agent Systems (MAS), which have been successfully employed even in data-sensitive domains (e.g., e-health [10], telerehabilitation [6], manufacturing [12], etc.). In particular, the establishment of trust mechanisms and guarantees, constitutes a fundamental step towards the deployment of agent-based systems that can help managing interactions among investors, experts and startups. In this respect, the MAS community has explored the usage of blockchain technology (BCT) [4,21,22], in order to manage agent reputation, while enhancing transparency and trust (even in the case of unknown intentions/nature of the agents), removing the need for conventional *trusted third parties* [5].

In the context of startups assessment and incubation, this paper presents a system enabling dynamics among startups, expert evaluators, and investors based on the computation of their reputation relying on Multi-Agent Systems (MAS) and blockchain technology (BCT). In particular, a Jade-based (MAS) and Hyperledger-based (BCT) system has been implemented, including: two-folded actors and services evaluation, a relational-like world-state DB, policies and mechanisms for disagreement resolution, smart contracts computing, and monitoring agent reputation. Finally, the system has been tested with alpha and beta testers.

The paper is organized as follows: Sect. 2 describes the state-of-the-art in business assessment, trust and MAS technologies, Sect. 3 describes a motivating case study, Sect. 4 provides details about the system design, which is discussed in Sect. 5 before the conclusions.

2 State of the Art

Nowadays, communities play a major role in the success of business projects. Many startups defined as unicorns[1] owe a considerable part of their success to the *relationships* built thanks to their communities. However, communities can provide more than just connecting the players. For example, sharing visions, estimating certain aspects crucial for the evolution of a startup, supporting other players in the decision-making process, and building a solid understanding about product markets. By creating a trustworthy common ground, it is possible to distinguish the most promising and robust ideas, projects, and companies in a faster and more precise manner.

InnMind [14] is an example of a platform establishing a common ground for startups, investors, service providers, and all the relevant professionals. It comprises complex B2B2C solutions that combine *(i)* online database (marketplace) of innovative startups, *(ii)* online hub of investment organizations (VCs, angels, etc), *(iii)* industrial players and service providers, and *(iv)* educational sources with comprehensive information for innovative business owners. InnMind connects providers and suppliers of innovative technologies and startups, providing an efficient multi-functional instrument to help them to be more productive and successful. Platforms such as InnMind, address numerous challenges, e.g. access to promising projects, listings of experienced professionals, potential partners and investors from all around the world. However, currently, there is still the need for providing a profound assessment of given projects in a transparent and comprehensive form. Moreover, it is currently not possible to provide manual communication or deliver in-depth analysis and assessment of a company's current position and future potential.

Although there are many platforms operating as a listing service for the registered projects [13], only a few of them consider the reputation as an important discriminant factor. Some platforms provide assessment conducted by their own team of experts, keeping the ranking private or disclosing only partially the assessment process/methodology [2]. The most popular providing such services are listed below: *StartupRANKING* [19] provides a two-factor ranking system. The first factor is closely linked with search engine optimization (SEO) of the project website (e.g., the number of backlinks to the webpage, traffic on the webpage, and content). The second factor is calculated based on users' engagement on Facebook and Twitter. It is also planned to add analysis of audience engagement in such social media channels as LinkedIn, Pinterest, Youtube, and others. *Crucnchbase* [9] introduced Crunchbase Rank (CB Rank) and Trend Scores. According to [20], CB Rank combines factors such as the number of connections a profile has, the level of community engagement, funding events, news articles, and acquisitions, etc. While CB Rank is linked to the activities of the

---

[1] "unicorns": startups companies which have market value of 1 billion dollars (or more). This term is widely used in venture investment industry. Highly successful startups. It commonly refers to businesses having valuation higher than a certain amount (e.g., 1 BLN dollars).

entity, Trend Score considers changes in the Rank. CB Rank is reflected on the companies' profiles, and Trend Score can be used for building a search filter for users who have paid subscription. *CB Insights* [8] uses a system called Mosaic to assess the startups. There are three key elements at the basis of each score proposed by the platform: market (e.g., competition and saturation on the market), money (financial situation of the company) and momentum (marketing, social sentiment, customers and partnerships).

Moreover, many ratings operate with Initial Coin Offering (ICO) or Security Token Offering (STO) projects. For example, *ICO Bench* delegate the ranking score to community, evaluating the companies based on three factors: team, vision, and product (marks then averaged by the platform). The lack of transparency in the criteria, mechanisms, and score assignment generate considerable skepticism and mistrust, especially in platforms allowing the users to rank each other.

Aiming at fostering transparency and reliability in ranking platform and firms, several paradigms and approaches from the Artificial Intelligence (AI) field can be employed. For example, MAS are characterized by models and dynamics, emulating human behaviors. Ensuring accountable and trusted interactions between agents is essential, and although not straightforward, many remarkable efforts have been invested in the cause [11,15,24]. Yet, constantly evolving scenarios and technologies demand new, viable, and sustainable solutions. As reported in [4] binding MAS and BCT is a promising approach and represents a new frontier in the AI field. Studies such as [5] and [7] provided early proof of concept and architectures addressing trust and security requirements by combining MAS and BCT.

3   Case Study

In the scenario of startup assessment, we aim at implementing a two-folded evaluation to foster the computation of reputation of the actors operating in the InnMind Platform in a system combining MAS and BCT. Following the agent-based approach, let us define the set of high-level behaviors (autonomous or user-dependent):

B0: *actor profiling:* filling the user profile with personal/professional information according to his/her role.

B1: *startup self-assessment:* evaluation of the startup features;

B2: *request of assessment:* demand for an evaluation of the startup features;

B3: *request visualization:* demand for a visualization of profile and expert(s) assessment(s) (data on/off-chain under evaluation);

B4: *expert assessment:* assessment of an expert's skills and past startups assessments (executed on a voluntary basis);

B5: *assessment response:* if the request is accepted, B11 follows. If the request for B11 is rejected, a motivation has to be provided;

B6: *suggestion:* recommending a project as promising investment;

B7: *success rate:* assessment of the percentage of successful deals of an investor;

B8: *demand for an expert assessment:* request a startup to get some features assessed by one or more experts with particular expertise and competence;

B9: *demand for assessing a startup:* request an expert to assess a startup or to evaluate an assessment produced by another expert about a given startup;

B10: *assessment negotiation:* negotiation of cost/delivery time of a given evaluation. It can be delegated to the agent representing the user, which according to a customizable cost function, can negotiate autonomously;

B11: *startup evaluation:* evaluation of the startup and its products/services. Such a value impacts on the computation of the agent reputation;

B12: *assessment proposal:* proposal to perform B11 for a given cost and deadline;

Table 1 provides the association agent - behaviors. The diagonal elements (cells in blue) indicate the behaviors involving a single agent. The others, reading the table rows to columns indicate the initiator and the recipient of a given behavior. It is worth to recall that the primary objective of creating such a system for startup assessment is to ensure transparency and achieve trust in the community. According to the evidence provided in Sect. 2, the current practices of fundraising, expanding to new markets, and finding new partners/projects are eager of resources and time. A trustworthy assessment system can play a crucial role during preliminary screenings, semi-automating the process of pre-selecting promising projects/partners in the early stage.

Table 1. High-level agent behaviors; STUP: startup, EXP: expert, and INV: investor.

	STUP	EXP	INV
STUP	B0, B1	B2, B5, B10, B11	B3, B11
EXP	B5, B10, B11, B12	B0, B4*	B6, B11
INV	B8, B11	B9, B10, B11	B0, B7

* indicates behaviors among actors of the same category.

4   System Design and Implementation

Regardless of the scale, startup assessment systems are classified as private distributed systems composed of both collaborative and/or competitive actors (i.e., agents). Such entities aim at *(i)* maximizing their interests (e.g., earning money for a given evaluation, credits, expertise, knowledge, and reputation) and *(ii)* having freedom of joining, serving, and leaving the platform at any time. However, besides the high-level behaviors presented in Table 1, the agents can show/evolve malicious behaviors such as *(iii)* organize coalitions and *(iv)* foster selfish interests manipulating and exploiting other actors or some dynamics in the platform. To reduce such risks and to enable the agents' autonomous interactions on behalf of the human actors, it is necessary to understand and monitor agent reliability. The high-level behaviors introduced in Sect. 3 have been modeled as simple and composite behaviors. Moreover, a set of low-level behaviors such as send/receive messages, search agents in the platform, registration, and identification, has been developed extending the architecture in [7].

Acknowledging the risk of not having *fully* trustworthy agents, there is the need for computing the reputation with uniform and unbiased techniques. In the underlying architecture (see Fig. 1) the reputation management is handled by smart contracts, thus enforcing the main BCT properties (e.g., data transparency, immutability, integrity). Moreover, a given reputation threshold can be set to discriminate whether to suspend or expel an agent from the community. The agents operating in the system respect the loosely coupled, interconnected, and organized networks of the human actors of the InnMind Platform [14]. The mapping actors - agents have been realized at the JADE level (the underlying agent framework [1]). Considering the InnMind community as "restricted", we have employed the *Certification Authority* of Fabric Hyperledger (v1.2) [3].

4.1 System Architecture, Agent Identity, and Certificates Management

The underlying architecture supports the implementation of two cases of agents.

- CA-A: it handles registration, interacts with the certification authority component of Hyperledger, and can define rules and conditions for enrollment.
- BC-A: regular agent operating in the community. All its interactions/ behaviors are stored on the blockchain;

The *administrator* of the InnMind platform is an instance of CA-A. The actors *startup, expert, investor, business angel, freelancer, consultant, mentor*, and *advisor* are instances of BC-A. To operate in the community (and on the ledger(s)), the BC-A(s) have to be registered by CA-A (obtaining credentials and certificates of the corresponding public keys) and to operate according to rules and policies of the platform (see Sect. 4.2).

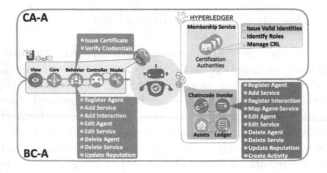

Fig. 1. Conceptual design of the system components.

In the current implementation, the blockchain network is composed of one ledger with three peers running on different machines. This configuration is contrasting with the policy of the underlying architecture assigning a peer to every $(BC - A_i)$. Such a strategical choice is due to legal and privacy obligations over the shared data. The World State database (maintaining the current state of the ledger state) used in the presented systems is shown in Fig. 2 (where it is also possible to notice the handcrafted relational properties).

The structure of the world-state (Level-DB) respects the composite keys-indexes mechanism offered by the underlying architecture. However, it has been introduced the concept of *composite service* which allows a hierarchical aggregation of services. Such a choice has been demanded by the dynamical nature of some services. For example, a startup can operate in diverse domains, therefore the fields composing the self-assessment can be different and must be configurable dynamically. By doing so, it is possible to track the reputation of a given agent (startup or expert) down to the single instance and then aggregating it up to the composite service.

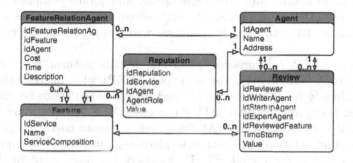

Fig. 2. Basic structure of the InnMind WSDB

Concerning Fig. 2, *Agent* contains the details of the agent. *FeatureRelation-Agent* relates the services to the agent. *Review* defines the registration of the feature evaluation, tracking service, actors, and *WriterAgent* (e.g., STUP or EXP) for implementing the two-folded reputation evaluation mechanism. Moreover, there is the *timestamp* field which serves to purpose of tracking the evolution over the time of the reputation values (see Fig. 3). *Reputation* relates a given agent, service, and reputation. Finally, *Feature* details the service and its possible composition.

The correctness of structures and functionalities have been tested following the Test Driven Development (TDD) approach. By doing so, it has been possible to avoid setting up the network (e.g., download and install the docker images of Hyperledger) when not strictly required. Moreover, the TDD approach allows to verify if the latest functionalities have compromised the existing and stable functionalities. Finally, the TDD has been employed to execute a predetermined set of scenarios.

Chaincode invoke successful. result: status:200 payload:[[{"Int

Fig. 3. getHistory function for tracking the reputation evolution

4.2 System Dynamics

Being a permissioned community, the first step is to register and get the certificates enabling interactions with other actors/agent via the underlying blockchain. To do so, the current implementation demands proof of identity of the registering actor and code (in the future proof of payment). Focusing on the two main actors, after the registration, and profile completion (B0), a given startup (STUP) must provide the *self-assessment* (B1)[2]. Hence, if a STUP has not completed B0 and B1, it is not allowed to operate in the community (Fig. 4(b)).

Viceversa, STUP can proceed according to the natural flow of actions demanding to be assessed (B2) by an expert (EXP) who, on the other hand, must have already filled his/her profile and expertise (B12)[3] to be visible and eligible (Fig. 4(a)). In particular, STUP can read the ledger screening the EXP possibly eligible to perform B11. At this point, a human-based or agent-based (autonomous) negotiation (B10) can take place (e.g., based on cost and delivery time). When B11 is completed, STUP can check the assessment received and

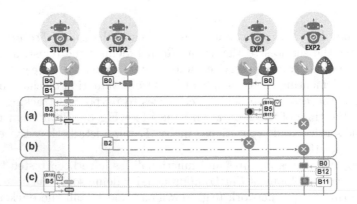

Fig. 4. Agents interactions

---

[2] The features implemented in the ledger are listed in Appendix A.

[3] The features implemented in ledger are listed in Appendix B.

release a mark based on its quality. In case no EXP is available to evaluate a STUP, B11 need by a given STUP remains pending. If an EXP registers and becomes eligible to perform it, he/she will send an assessment proposal (B12), possibly triggering acceptance, rejection, or a negotiation (Fig. 4(c)).

4.3 Actors Reputation: Misalignment and Conflict Resolution

The agent reputation is computed averaging and weighing the marks received on previous and current behaviors (e.g., self-assessment and service evaluation). To maintain a high level of trust and quality services in the platform, the system administrator can regularly trigger smart contracts monitoring the evolution of the reputation of the various actors (in terms of both single behaviors and trends). By doing so, it is possible to monitor if given behaviors can lead to malicious trends, systematic errors, or just to a single (involuntary fault).

However, the assessments can be subject to personal biases and therefore showing relatively diverging marks. If the marks given by two actors about the evaluation of a given content differ more than a customizable threshold, the actors are required to revise their judgment. In turn, if either one accepts to revise his/her mark and the difference goes below the threshold, the new reputation is computed, and the ledger is updated. Viceversa, if the difference persists, the system or the administrator identifies a third actor (e.g., an expert) to provide a third evaluation and review the two disagreeing assessments.

Another risk concerning the reputation and existing solutions is that once deleted a profile and abandoned the platform, in many cases, it is possible to come back with new registration and a *clean* profile. To study the robustness of the developed systems with respect to such a possibility, we tested the following scenario: An expert newly registered in the platform is given a fair reputation of 6 out of 10. Performing "arguable" behaviors, his reputation assumes an almost monotonic negative trend. Reaching the minimum value of 4, the expert decides to leave the platform and delete his account. After a given period the expert registers himself again in the platform. In turn, we tested two different approaches:

(i) we handcrafted the possibility of bypassing the certification authority mechanisms (e.g., providing fake Id and codes). In such a case, the expert gains again the initial reputation value of 6. This time, we performed positive behaviors gaining quickly reliability (Fig. 5 - red line).

(ii) we registered using the actual id and a new code (received after the simulation of a new payment). Even if its profile has been previously deleted (from the WD-Database), exploring the ledger his history and reputation have been restored. Performing the same positive behaviors of the scenario *(i)*, however, generate a different outcome (Fig. 5 - blue line).

The development of smart contracts to compute and monitor the reputation trends is still in its early stage. In the upcoming implementation, factors such as *(i)* how long a given value is kept), *(ii)* the number evaluated behaviors, and *(iii)* the derivative of the reputation curve will play a crucial role.

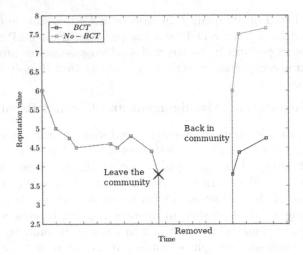

Fig. 5. Possible evolution of agent reputation. (Color figure online)

5   Discussion

Independently from the application domain, unveiled or merging new technologies can generate a valuable breakthrough, as well as rising even more questions and challenges. Currently, the InnMind platform operates connecting startups, experts, and investors. The developed system enriches the value of the platform by adding a reliable social assessment (reputation/trust assessment) based on MAS and BCT. Such technologies and transparent mechanisms promote more trustworthy interactions and investments among the actors. The system is still in its early stage, and dynamics such as conflict resolution and arbitrage still need a fine-tuning. In a later stage, a considerable number of dynamics will be directly delegated to automated behaviors and predefined smart contracts. Further, InnMind plans to integrate machine learning and AI algorithms within the MAS aiming at delivering predictions based on the collected historical data (e.g., company's development and founders' reputation).

However, several concerns from the real world still need to be assessed. For example, a legal basis for the data on/off-chain need to be developed, as well as policies for cross-border distributed peers. Currently, no comprehensive legal base explains and regulates integration of the blockchain into the business sector. There is a need for clear laws connected to the privacy, and personal data use, that will help further to develop "healthy" markets. Moreover, a low level of trust in the virtual world could be considered relevant for undertaking legal actions in the real world. From the technological point of view, besides their tamper-proof mechanism once already in the system, verifying the correctness of the smart contracts remains an open challenge, as well as how to verify the identity and intentions of who is in charge of updating or developing new ones.

6   Conclusions

This paper presented the formalization and implementation of a system enforcing trust in the startup assessment domain. To do so, it has been extended an existing architecture presented in [7] by implementing a multi-agent community and related interactions via private blockchain technology. The developed system enables a trust-based community, immutably storing, tracking, and monitoring the agents' interactions and reputations.

The observations show promising directions to undertake. Although the benefits of combining MAS and BCT are justified by several studies and the acceptance of the developed prototype satisfied the InnMind managers, the employed technologies are not fully framed by standards nor been widely adopted yet.

The planned future works are: *(i)* extending B10 (given the shared benefits, we aim at involving startups in sharing the assessment costs in the negotiation, adapting the behavior accordingly.), *(ii)* implementing smart contracts to infer possible future behaviors reasoning on historical data (e.g., reputation), *(iii)* implement autonomous behaviors and smart contracts to timely spot malicious behaviors, and *(iv)* implement behaviors regulating lack of commitment (both startups and experts side).

A   Startup Self-evaluation Features

- **Product:** technology/product, value proposition, scalability, and IP rights;
- **Customer:** customer development, targeted market, and regional coverage;
- **Market competition:** competition, current partnerships, need in the market, marketing, and PR Strategy
- **Finance:** business model/tokenomics, current financial situation, pace of ROI, and exit Strategy.
- **Team and administrative:** components, team experience, company registration, and legal aspects;

B   Startup Assessment Features for Expert Evaluation

- **Team:** experience, roles covered, traditional Media, and social media proof (in regards to the team and their connection to the project), blockchain knowledge and experience, and advisory board;
- **Product/Service development:** stage of development, proof of stage of development, speed of development, roadmap, correlation between, plans and capacities, innovativeness of the product/service, sufficiency of resources/assets for creation of the product, specialised conferences participation, and comments;
- **Technology chosen:** technology fits the goals of the product/service, technology helps to create the value added in the best way, the level of internal risk wrt. the use of the technology, coding activity, blockchain added value, and comments;

- **Added value and problem solved:** product/market fit, relevance added value, solved problem, difficulty in creating value, and comments;
- **Market research:** differentiation, Economies of scale, competition analysis and understanding, real competition, and comments
- **Customer development:** target audience (analysis), market size, market fit, market share potential, and comments;
- **Marketing strategy:** marketing documentation, channels of distribution, clear positioning, partners, media coverage, online marketing activities, offline marketing activities, power of buyer, and comments;
- **Business model and tokenomics:** financial planning, business model validity, tokenomics margin, power of buyer and supplier, access to finance, and comment;
- **Risks:** political, economic, social, technological, environmental, legal, and internal;

References

1. Bellifemine, F.L., Caire, G., Greenwood, D.: Developing Multi-agent Systems with JADE, vol. 7. Wiley, Hoboken (2007)
2. BV4: Certified expert evaluation (2018). https://www.bv4.ch/startup-rating. Accessed 24 Mar 2019
3. Cachin, C.: Architecture of the hyperledger blockchain fabric (2016)
4. Calvaresi, D., Dubovitskaya, A., Calbimonte, J.P., Taveter, K., Schumacher, M.: Multi-agent systems and blockchain: results from a systematic literature review. In: Demazeau, Y., An, B., Bajo, J., Fernández-Caballero, A. (eds.) PAAMS 2018. LNCS (LNAI), vol. 10978, pp. 110–126. Springer, Cham (2018). https://doi.org/10.1007/978-3-319-94580-4_9
5. Calvaresi, D., Dubovitskaya, A., Retaggi, D., Dragoni, A.F., Schumacher, M.: Trusted registration, negotiation, and service evaluation in multi-agent systems throughout the blockchain technology. In: 2018 IEEE/WIC/ACM International Conference on Web Intelligence (WI), pp. 56–63. IEEE (2018)
6. Calvaresi, D., Marinoni, M., Dragoni, A.F., Hilfiker, R., Schumacher, M.: Real-time multi-agent systems for telerehabilitation scenarios. Artif. Intell. Med. (2019)
7. Calvaresi, D., Mattioli, V., Dubovitskaya, A., Dragoni, A.F., Schumacher, M.: Reputation management in multi-agent systems using permissioned blockchain technology. In: 2018 IEEE/WIC/ACM International Conference on Web Intelligence (WI), pp. 719–725. IEEE (2018)
8. Cbinsights: Understanding the health of tech startups (2018). https://www.cbinsights.com/company-mosaic. Accessed 24 Mar 2019
9. Crunchbase: Crunchbase web startup ranking platform (2018). https://about.crunchbase.com/blog/influential-companies/. Accessed 24 Mar 2019
10. Dubovitskaya, A., Urovi, V., Barba, I., Aberer, K., Schumacher, M.I.: A multiagent system for dynamic data aggregation in medical research. BioMed. Res. Int. (2016)
11. Hedin, Y., Moradian, E.: Security in multi-agent systems. Procedia Comput. Sci. **60**, 1604–1612 (2015). https://doi.org/10.1016/j.procs.2015.08.270. http://www.sciencedirect.com/science/article/pii/S1877050915023972. Knowledge-Based and Intelligent Information and Engineering Systems 19th Annual Conference, KES-2015, Singapore, September 2015 Proceedings

12. Hsieh, F.S.: Modeling and control of holonic manufacturing systems based on extended contract net protocol. In: Proceedings of the 2002 American Control Conference, vol. 6, pp. 5037–5042 (2002)
13. InnMind: 62 top listings to promote your startup (2018). https://innmind.com/articles/1816. Accessed 24 Mar 2019
14. InnMind: Global sturtup community for supporting innovation (2018). https://innmind.com/. Accessed 24 Mar 2019
15. Ramchurn, S.D., Huynh, D., Jennings, N.R.: Trust in multi-agent systems. Knowl. Eng. Rev. 19(1), 1–25 (2004). https://doi.org/10.1017/S0269888904000116
16. Harvard Business School: The venture capital secret (2018). https://www.hbs.edu/news/Pages/item.aspx?num=487. Accessed 24 Mar 2019
17. Startupgenome: Global startup ecosystem report 2018: Succeeding in the new era of technology (2018). https://startupgenome.com/all-report-thank-you/?file=2018. Accessed 24 Mar 2019
18. Startupgenome: PWC G4 2018 evaluation (2018). https://www.pwc.com/us/en/industries/technology/moneytree.html. Accessed 24 Mar 2019
19. StartupRANKING: SR web startup ranking platform (2018). https://www.startupranking.com/how-it-works. Accessed 24 Mar 2019
20. Stephan, D.: Crunchbase rank and trend score (2018). https://about.crunchbase.com/blog/crunchbase-rank-trend-score. Accessed 24 Mar 2019
21. Swan, M.: Blockchain: Blueprint for a new economy (2015)
22. Tapscott, D., Tapscott, A.: Blockchain Revolution: How the Technology Behind Bitcoin is Changing Money, Business, and the World. Penguin, Westminster (2016)
23. TILab: cbinsights research (2018). https://www.cbinsights.com/research/startup-failure-reasons-top/. Accessed 24 Mar 2019
24. Yu, B., Singh, M.P.: An evidential model of distributed reputation management. In: Proceedings of the First International Joint Conference on Autonomous Agents and Multiagent Systems: Part 1, pp. 294–301. ACM (2002)

Comparative Analysis of Blockchain Technologies Under a Coordination Perspective

Giovanni Ciatto[1]($\boxtimes$) (iD), Michael Bosello[1] (iD), Stefano Mariani[2] (iD),
and Andrea Omicini[1] (iD)

[1] Università di Bologna, Cesena, Italy
{giovanni.ciatto,andrea.omicini}@unibo.it,
michael.bosello@studio.unibo.it
[2] Università di Modena e Reggio Emilia, Reggio Emilia, Italy
stefano.mariani@unimore.it

Abstract. Many research works apply blockchain technologies to several different application domains ranging from supply chain and logistics to healthcare and real-estate. There, nevertheless, the blockchain performs the same two core tasks: identity management and asset tracking. In this paper we analyse how the blockchain can be exploited beyond these traditional tasks, towards coordination of distributed processes. To this end, we design and develop proof-of-concept implementations of the LINDA model on top of different blockchains, and compare their strengths and shortcomings.

Keywords: Blockchain-based coordination · Smart contracts ·
LINDA on Ethereum · LINDA on Fabric · LINDA on Corda

1 Introduction

The *blockchain* concept and technology is rapidly shaking up many different areas in both academic research and industrial practice. Its ability to *secure* both data and computation in a distributed setting *with no need* to rely on reciprocal trust or a centralised authority is an appealing way to re-think current applications and functionalities requiring a middle-man, as well as to promote brand-new business opportunities—such as, cryptocurrencies.

Besides cryptocurrencies, it is more and more clear that the blockchain naturally fits many heterogeneous application domains, such as supply chain for tracking goods [12], healthcare for auditing EMR exchange [2], real estate market to track ownership [4], etc. Despite diversity of applications, the blockchain actually performs mostly the *same* task everywhere, hence is used for the same core functionality across domains: *identity management* and *asset tracking*. In cryptocurrency applications, for instance, the asset is money, whereas in supply chain it is goods, and in healthcare could be the EMR of patients: regardless,

F. De la Prieta et al. (Eds.): PAAMS 2019 Workshops, CCIS 1047, pp. 80–91, 2019.
https://doi.org/10.1007/978-3-030-24299-2_7

the blockchain provides a way to track ownership of the asset while protecting integrity of owners identity.

Along this line, we investigate whether the blockchain can be used for other tasks, stretching its reach *beyond* identity management and asset tracking. In particular, we look at the growing interest of the *multi-agent systems* (MAS) community towards the blockchain as a promising solution to long-stading open challenges, such as reputation management, data consistency, accountability of interactions [3].

On interaction, in fact, the contribution of this paper is focussed, aimed at answering the question *"can the blockchain work as a coordination medium?"*. Indeed, we are interested in investigating whether the appealing features of most blockchain technologies – such as global *ordering* of distributed events, data *consistency* despite replication, and *accountability* of interactions – could be efficiently and effectively exploited to realise the *coordination models* governing interactions in MAS towards satisfaction of desired system properties [3].

Accordingly, the contribution of this paper is as follows:

- *proof-of-concept* implementations of the LINDA coordination model [8] on top of selected blockchain technologies—namely, Ethereum [16], Hyperledger Fabric [1], and R3 Corda [11]
- a *comparative analysis* of the implementations under a coordination perspective—namely, in terms of the properties, assumptions, and design choices behind a coordination model like LINDA
- a *discussion* of the strengths and limitations of each blockchain technology analysed so as to reveal their actual potential as the backbone of novel coordination technologies

The paper is hence structured as follows: Sect. 2 overviews the main features of a coordination model in terms of requirements, design choices, and provided properties, taking the archetypal LINDA as a reference; Sect. 3 first describes the blockchain technologies considered in this study, then our implementation of LINDA on top of them; Sect. 4 focuses on the strength and shortcomings of each implementation in an attempt to clarify to what extent the blockchain can support coordination mechanisms and policies; Sect. 5 concludes the paper.

2   The Coordination Perspective

Coordination is the practice of governing the *interaction space* [5], that is, defining the dependencies amongst activities and how to handle them so as to avoid unwanted interference or undesirable side-effects, while achieving target properties at the level of the global, coordinated system.

Many coordination models, languages, and technologies have been proposed for about thirty years now, especially in the MAS community—see [7,14,15] for a survey. Among those, *tuple-based* coordination has been extensively studied mainly for its greater expressiveness and openness w.r.t. approaches based on message-passing. LINDA [8], in particular, is widely considered as the archetypal tuple-based coordination model, and as such has been comprehensively and deeply studied and extended throughout the years along many dimensions: formal expressiveness, suitability to diverse application domains, strengths and weaknesses, implementation choices, etc.

For the purpose of this paper, it is useful to highlight the requirements LINDA implementations must abide to, the design choices they possibly have the freedom to make, and the properties granted to the coordinated system, so as to better ground the discussion presented in Sect. 4 and let us focus on the most impactful characteristics of the implementations described in Sect. 3.

LINDA has three distinctive properties that define the model, and translate to requirements for implementors:

generative communication — hence the fact that information produced by interacting parties has its own lifecycle *independent* of that of its producer; in other words, information has to be stored on a dedicated repository (the *tuple space*) whose lifetime can extend beyond that of interacting agents

associative access — as the capability to locate and handle information based on *content*, not on name or address; this implies that a language for (possibly, partially) describing the content of information items is needed (a *template*), and that search and retrieval should be based on such a language

suspensive semantics — that is, the fact that operations accessing information not yet available should not fail, but *block and wait* until information becomes available; this is what ultimately enables coordination through *synchronisation* of activities

The above requirements may actually be satisfied in different ways, hence a few design choices are available to LINDA-based coordination technologies, for instance regarding the tuple and template languages – that is, the languages to describe either actually or potentially existing information items, respectively –, the matching mechanisms enabling associative access, as well as the *primitives* available to coordinated entities—usually, three: OUT to produce information, RD to read it, IN to consume (read and delete) it.

Based on whether these design choices fully respect the requirements above, the LINDA implementation at hand may fully support or not the peculiar benefits of LINDA-based coordination: *synchronisation* based on information availability and *decoupling* in reference, space, and time. The former means that no special constructs are devoted to check conditions and decide to synchronise on specific events, hence no dedicated actions have to be performed by interacting agents: LINDA primitives embed synchronisation through suspensive semantics. The latter means that in order to coordinate, processes need not to know each other identifiers or addresses, nor do they need to co-exist in time or space, because coordination happens through availability on information, and such information has its own lifetime and addressable content.

In Sect. 4 we discuss how the blockchain relates to these requirements and design choices, hence whether a coordination model like LINDA can be faithfully modelled and implemented on top of currently available blockchain technologies.

3   Comparison of LINDA on Selected BCT

Regardless of specific implementations, blockchain technologies (BCT) consist of a peer-to-peer network of nodes enacting a *consensus protocol* that lets them globally behave as a single *state machine*, aimed at consistently managing the data jointly manipulated by a number of clients—which may be either human or software agents. Handling of clients read/write requests, as well as their *chronological ordering*, is responsibility of special nodes of the blockchain, which commit the results to blocks of data linked by hash chains, following the principles described in [10]. This process creates a hard-to-tamper sequence of blocks – indeed, the *block*-chain – tracking the whole history of system evolution. Indeed, the interest around the blockchain lies essentially in that capability of maintaining a consistent *shared state* between mutually- untrusted parties.

When the state machine is an interpreter executing some custom program defined by external agents – that is, what is commonly meant by *smart contract* (SC) nowadays [9] –, we call that BCT "SC-enabled". There, distributed consensus is exploited to ensure that all SC are consistently executed in the exact same way on all replicated nodes. The many SC-enabled BCT currently available implement the concept of SC in several diverse ways. For instance, some are very strict in the way new agents are admitted to be part of the system, thus allowing for finer access control mechanisms—which are desirable in many real-world contexts: they are therefore called "*permissioned*". Others let agents create their own identities, usually by means of public keys, thus virtually letting anyone join the system: they are therefore called "*permissionless*". In permissionless blockchains, each SC may virtually interact with any off-chain agent – and vice versa –, therefore SC policies and constraints based on identity must be programmed ex-novo every time by developers. Conversely, in *permissioned* blockchains access control policies can be set up and managed by exploiting dedicated services and API.

Every SC-enabled blockchain implementation supports the creation of some non-forgeable token which may be used for value exchange, but some of them *require* a native currency to make their approach to distributed consensus secure. This is the case, for instance, of Ethereum [16], but not of Fabric [1] and Corda [11].

From a computational perspective, SC-enabled BCT also differ in *(i)* how they represent the shared replicated state, there including what sorts of information SC can store and handle; *(ii)* the admitted operations on such state, there including rules concerning how SC can be instantiated, destroyed, or updated; *(iii)* what sorts of computation SC are able to perform, and on which data; *(iv)* how data is expected to flow from agents to SC – or among them – and vice versa. Finally, BCT can also be classified w.r.t. how they handle the problem of termination. Off-chain agents can deploy custom programs (the SC) to the blockchain, which may be non-terminating in the general case. Hence they may prevent the BCT from working correctly, since non-terminating computations may make nodes starve. To avoid this, BCT must implement some sort of countermeasure to forbid, prevent, or discourage long or non-terminating computations from being executed.

The following subsections describe three specific BCT w.r.t. all these aspects.

3.1 Ethereum

Ethereum [16] is a permission*less* BCT with a native currency, the Ether (ETH), employed in a Proof-of-Work based approach to consensus, which is enacted by "miners", i.e., the special nodes in charge of producing blocks.

Ethereum shared state consists of a number of *accounts*, each one associating information to either off-chain agents or SC. Such information include a *balance*, in terms of ETH – which implies that both agents and SC can own money –, and, in case of SC, a *storage* area for anything that can be represented as byte strings. SC encapsulate custom and stateful *behaviours*, whose state consists of the aforementioned storage, whereas behaviour is expressed in terms of an ad-hoc bytecode. State may change as a consequence of *transactions* (TX) being published by off-chain agents. In particular, the admissible operations that transaction may convey are: *(i)* deployment TX to create new SC, *(ii)* money transfer TX to exchange money, *(iii)* invocation TX to send a message to a SC, triggering one of its behaviour—whose effects may depend on both the message content and the current SC state. Once triggered, SC can interact with each other through *synchronous* function call, and with off-chain agents through a publish subscribe mechanism where the blockchain itself is used as a blackboard where events of interest are published by SC and read by off-chain agents.

Ethereum discourages long/non-terminating computations in SC through the notion of *gas*, that is, a sort of fuel which must be included into TX by the agents publishing them. Gas is literally bought by agents by consuming their ETH, and TX processing always consumes some gas, depending on which and how many bytecode instructions are actually executed. If the provided gas for a TX is not enough for it to complete, then its effects on the system state are completely reverted, except for gas consumption. Since the total amount of ETH is finite, there cannot be infinite computations, whereas long ones are still possible but made extremely costly—hence, discouraged.

As pointed out in [6], and briefly summarised in Subsect. 3.4, this trait of Ethereum has consequences on how Ethereum-based coordination works.

3.2 Hyperledger Fabric

Fabric [1] is a permission*ed* BCT with no native currency, made of several peers (or nodes), possibly playing different roles, and the offchain agents interacting with and through them. There must be one or more *ordering* nodes (or *orderers*) composing the *Ordering Service* in charge of a consensus protocol of choice, aimed at ordering the many transactions possibly issued by off-chain agents.

Fabric-based systems are conceived for being simultaneously adopted by several organisations—possibly and likely having competing interests. To this end, *several* block-chain data structures may be in principle created and stored by non-ordering peers, in the form of *channels* that share the view on the order of events given by the Ordering Service. A many-to-many relation binds channels and organisations. A *Membership Service* is in charge of assigning peers to roles, verify their membership to a particular organisation, and define organisations' rights and roles w.r.t. channels. The set of organisations joining a channel, as well as the set of peers composing an organisation, are dynamic configurations of the Fabric system, which may vary over time.

For a given channel, one or more *chaincodes* (i.e., smart contracts) may be dynamically installed, executed, or queried similarly to what happens in Ethereum. This is where custom business logic of organisations is injected. Chaincodes in Fabric may be written in one or more mainstream programming languages – e.g., Go, JavaScript, or Java –, and rely on the Shim API[1]. Similarly to what happens for Ethereum SC, the internal state of Fabric chaincode is composed of key-value pairs containing arbitrary data. Such a state may evolve as a consequence of the chaincode being executed, as triggered by off-chain agents through requests (i.e., messages). Again similarly to Ethereum, chaincodes may interact with each other through synchronous method calls, and with off-chain entities through a channel-wise event bus.

For each channel, one or more *endorsing* peers (or *endorsers*) must be defined – usually, at least one for each organisation – to execute chaincodes. More precisely, when a chaincode invocation TX is published, the corresponding code is *simulated* by as many endorsing peers as requested by that chaincode *endorsement policy*—that is, essentially, a boolean formula stating *which* endorsers must approve the transaction. Only if the endorsement policy is satisfied – i.e. a sufficient amount of endorsements has been gathered – the transaction can be ordered by the Ordering Service and then, finally, registered on the channel. This last step is where the side effects possibly produced by the invocation TX are reified.

This is Fabric peculiar *execute-order-validate* architecture, better described in [1], whose ultimate purpose is to prevent non-terminating chaincodes from starving the system.

3.3   Corda

Corda [11] is another permission*ed* BCT with no native currency, designed specifically for financial applications. A Corda system is made of several nodes, each identified by the system *doorman* service – i.e., a certification authority –, which is the only entity capable of issuing *certificates* to cryptographically bind real world organisations to some public key.

Corda is designed considering *privacy* as its very first concern, thus there is no such a thing like a global, shared state, by default: information, there including the asset tracked by the system and the transactions issued by nodes, is shared among nodes only if and when it is strictly necessary. Therefore, each node only

---

[1] https://hyperledger-fabric.readthedocs.io/en/latest/chaincode4ade.html.

perceives a portion of (or a point of view on) the system state, called *Vault*. What makes this possible is the idea of *Unspent Transaction Output* (UTXO)—which is strongly inspired to how BitCoin works. The *State* is the most simple chunk of information that can be represented, whose structure is application specific and must be defined by developers. Variations may be applied to each State by nodes, through transactions, each encoding consumption of the output of zero or more pre-existing transactions, and producing some new output states to be eventually consumed—thus the name UTXO. This mechanism iteratively builds a directed acyclic graph (DAG) of transactions, whose unconsumed fringe represent the current state, and whose portion of interest for a given node represents its Vault.

In Corda SC are simply called *Contracts* and they are not dynamically deployed by users but by system administrators at deployment time. Conversely, they are meant to state transactions validity w.r.t. their senders and their intended receivers, other than, of course, their input and output states. Even though such design choices may appear constraining, they are actually quite flexible since States may represent virtually any data structure, and TX any sort of operations upon them, whereas Contracts simply define the contexts where such operations are admissible.

Transactions ordering and certification is the sole responsibility of *Notary Services*, very similar to Ordering Service in Fabric: a number of nodes enacting some consensus protocol. The main difference is that Corda allows multiple Notary Services within the same system, each possibly employing different consensus protocols. When a node issues a TX, all the involved nodes must receive a copy of the TX data to be signed. Then, the TX must be notarised by one or more Notary Services, and finally it must be sent back to the involved nodes to let themto update their Vaults.

Any control-flow related aspect involving the coordination of one or more nodes can be performed in Corda through *Flows*. A library of basic Flows to be composed is made available to the developers of Corda-based applications. Flows are the place where articulated business logic is put, given the constraints affecting Contracts. For instance, as it is further discussed in Subsect. 3.4, we exploit Flows to mimic LINDA' suspensive semantics.

3.4 LINDA on Ethereum, Hyperledger Fabric, R3 Corda

In the following subsections, we describe three proof-of-concept implementations of blockchain-based coordination, namely: implementing LINDA on Ethereum (in two different ways), implementing LINDA on Fabric, and finally on Corda. The purpose is that to investigate feasibility of blockchain-based coordination, suitability of the different BCT, and impact of BCT features on coordination-related properties.

LINDA on Ethereum. Designing and implementing LINDA over the Ethereum platform has been the purpose of [6]. There, a LINDA implementation is proposed where:

- tuple spaces are mapped to smart contracts
- tuples and templates are represented as raw strings
- template matching coincides with string inclusion
- primitive *invocations* are performed through SC methods calls
- primitive *completions* are performed through Ethereum's publish-subscribe mechanisms or method calls as well—depending on which of the two proposed implementations is considered

The peculiarities of the Ethereum-based implementation are mainly dictated by *(i)* the openness deriving from Ethereum being a permission*less* BCT, *(ii)* the presence of a native cryptocurrency, and, in particular, *(iii)* the requirement forcing smart contracts callers to pay some fee – in terms of gas – in order for the called smart contract execution to have an effect. More precisely, [6] discusses how the inherent bound between the native currency and SC computation forces designers to take the economical dimension of coordination into account: an aspect which is instead missing in the upcoming implementations on Fabric and Corda.

LINDA **on Fabric.** The implementation of LINDA on Fabric recalls the one on top of Ethereum presented in [6]. Client applications that reside off-chain are the *coordinated entities* whereas the chaincode represents the *coordination media* and provides a LINDA-like interface which exposes the *communication primitives*. A chaincode can be instantiated multiple times even in the same channel: as a result, every chaincode instance is a separated tuple space. Since in a chaincode the execution flow cannot be suspended to wait for a specific value in the ledger, *invocation* and *completion* of the primitives are divided into two phases in order to emulate LINDA *suspensive semantics.*

At first, the client selects a tuple space (i.e. the chaincode instance name) and invokes an operation on it with the regular proposal-transact protocol supported by Fabric. In the proposal, the client specifies a LINDA operation and its argument, i.e., the tuple or the tuple template. For simplicity, in this proof-of-concept, the tuple and tuple template languages are the same, hence the matching mechanism is pure equality, but Fabric provides facilities for rich queries, so, more expressive matching mechanisms can be easily built. The transaction procedure returns a promise that will be completed when the transaction has been immutably appended to the ledger, decreeing that primitive invocation has been registered. Instead, completion is notified with the *event* mechanism, so, another promise is attached to the previous one waiting for the completion event that will be eventually produced by another transaction. We anticipate that the client may decide to either add a callback to the promise or wait for its completion, being thus free to choose the preferred invocation semantics—respectively, *async*hronous or *synch*ronous.

The Chaincode maintains tuples and pending requests in the key-value store, in particular, the key is the tuple and the value is related information: available quantity and the associated queue of pending requests. The transaction id (TxId) is used as unique identifier of the request. When a matching tuple is not present, the TxId and the operation type are bundled and added to the queue.

In Fabric, only *one event per transaction* can be set. This limitation requires the out primitive to potentially resume multiple clients with a single event, thus, to work properly, the event has a common name known by the clients (TUPLEEVENT). The payload of the event contains the list of TxId of the processes to resume and the corresponding retrieved tuples. Every time a TUPLEEVENT is logged in a block, *all* the waiting clients are woken up by the Event Hub: they inspect the queue searching for their TxId, and if it is found, the promise (thus the primitive as well) is completed with the corresponding tuple—otherwise, the process goes back to waiting.

As far as the body of the chaincode is concerned, three coordination primitives are provided: OUT, IN, and RD. When an agent invokes the OUT operation, the chaincode immediately creates a TUPLEEVENT and adds to it the current TxId. Then, it increases the quantity of the tuple and pops an element from the pending requests queue if any. Its TxId is appended to the event payload and, if the waiting request is a IN, the quantity of the tuple is decreased. The chaincode continues until the tuple quantity reaches zero or the queue is empty. In the IN and RD operations, the chaincode produces a TUPLEEVENT with the current TxId if a matching tuple is found, otherwise it adds the request to the queue. The only difference is that IN decreases the tuple quantity in the matching case.

LINDA **on Corda.** In Corda, tuples are represented by a State, namely TUPLESTATE, which contains the tuple itself, the parties involved in the tuple space and other information about the tuple, such as who produced it. Consequently, the Vault becomes the tuple space. A contract imposes the rules for the tuple space evolution over time. We impose that, in order to produce a tuple, a TUPLESTATE must be created and no TUPLESTATE must be consumed. In addition, the transaction must be signed by the producer. For the tuple consumption case, one TUPLESTATE must be consumed and no TUPLESTATE must be produced. The required signers are the producer and the consumer.

The client who invokes the RPC is the *coordinated entity*. The coordination primitives are not explicitly represented but *emerge* from the cooperation of client and Flows, as follows. We implement two Flows: PUTFLOW and TAKEFLOW. PUTFLOW takes a tuple and creates a transaction with the new TUPLESTATE, then, it signs and finalises the transaction. TAKEFLOW accepts a tuple template and searches in the Vault a matching tuple that is unconsumed. If a valid tuple is found, the Flow builds a transaction that spends the TUPLESTATE and signs it. Afterwards, TAKEFLOW requires the signature of the producer and finalises the transaction. If everything goes well, the tuple is returned. If a tuple is not found, the Flow fails.

The client uses the two procedures above to mimic the *coordination primitives*. For the OUT operation, the invocation of PUTFLOW is sufficient. For RD instead, the client searches for a matching unconsumed tuple in the Vault and subscribes to future updates of the TUPLESTATE type. After that, the method waits on an *event semaphore*. If a matching unconsumed tuple is found in the Vault, or when it comes from an update notification, the semaphore is released and the update subscription is revoked. Finally, the method returns the retrieved tuple. The IN operation behaves like RD, except that it needs to use TAKEFLOW to acquire the tuple. So, when the semaphore is released, TAKEFLOW is invoked. If the acquisition fails, the client goes back to waiting on the semaphore and retries when the notification of a new adequate tuple comes. The procedure is repeated until a successful invocation occurs.

Let us recall that communications in Corda are *point-to-point*, and that a Flow is suspended until *all* the involved parties respond to the transaction—so as to guarantee message delivery. In order to spread the tuples, then, *all* the nodes participating in the tuple space are indicated in the parties field. As imposed by Flows operation, all the nodes must be available to complete any of the aforementioned operations and, as a result, there cannot be *time* or *reference uncoupling* between those nodes—two of the peculiar LINDA properties. To achieve that, one has to design alternatives to Flow procedures for spreading the transactions containing tuples and their consumption, being careful to eventually deliver the messages also to the nodes temporarily unavailable. We discuss similar limitations and opportunities in the upcoming section.

4   Discussion

By comparing the different implementations proposed in Sect. 3 against the requirements and design choices described in Sect. 2, a few interesting considerations regarding strengths and limitations of the considered BCT in supporting coordination emerge.

Economy of Coordination. By comparing LINDA on Fabric and Corda to LINDA on Ethereum, we observe that the "economy of coordination" dimension is typical of BCT coming with some notion of native currency [6]. Although the need to bound coordination primitives execution to currency consumption may appear limiting and undesirable, in [6] a few economic models are discussed which actually resemble real-world scenarios, hence can be proficiently used to either incentivise or discourage selected coordination patterns.

Observability. Permission*ed* BCT allow for a finer control on *visibility* of tuple spaces and of tuples within tuple spaces. In fact, through the notions of *Channel* or *Vault*, for instance, tuple spaces and therein tuples can be partitioned and made available to different, possibly dynamically established sub-sets of nodes. This may greatly help in all those scenarios requiring privacy or confidentiality.

Efficiency. By employing Fabric endorsement policies or Corda programmable contracts it is also possible to chose which and how many nodes are in charge of actually operating tuple spaces—namely, performing the computations associated to system functionalities. Furthermore, by separating nodes responsible for consensus and those responsible for business logic execution, permission*ed* BCT make it possible to leverage replication in a controlled way, avoiding to always include *all* validating nodes.

Both opportunities may greatly enhance efficiency and scalability of blockchain-based coordination.

Correctness. Nevertheless, regardless of the many desirable properties mentioned above, implementation of LINDA is not always fully faithful w.r.t. the discussion of Sect. 2. In Corda, for instance, registered transactions are not publicly available by default, but only visible to the nodes they *explicitly* involve. This is very constraining when it comes to LINDA tuple spaces, as it implies that whenever an agent performs an OUT operation it must explicitly list the peers potentially interested to later read or consume it, otherwise they cannot even be aware of its existence. Put in other terms, reference uncoupling is lost.

Concurrency. Both Fabric and Corda architectures, neatly separating participant nodes in orderers and endorsers, could actually positively impact the level of concurrency achievable in a LINDA-coordinated systems, as it allows to perform in parallel computations related to coordination taking place in different channels or involving different Vaults. This could greatly help in dealing with a notable shortcoming of blockchain-based coordination, that is, serialisation of interactions which instead, as for LINDA, could be processed in parallel—e.g. read operations.

5   Conclusion and Further Work

In this paper, we implement the archetypal LINDA coordination model on top of three different blockchain technologies – namely, Ethereum, Hyperledger Fabric, and R3 Corda – so as to assess the potential of *blockchain-based coordination*. To the best of our knowledge, this is unprecedented in literature investigating integration opportunities between blockchain and multi-agent systems. Our preliminary results show that blockchain is a promising technology to work as the backbone of coordination approaches, but that along with the many opportunities it brings, a few open issues are still to be fully assessed and dealt with. Since we believe that research in this topic is worth the effort, our future works will insist on unravelling the potential of blockchain-based coordination.

References

1. Androulaki, E., et al.: Hyperledger fabric: a distributed operating system for permissioned blockchains. In: 13th EuroSys Conference (EuroSys 2018). ACM, New York (2018). https://doi.org/10.1145/3190508.3190538
2. Azaria, A., Ekblaw, A., Vieira, T., Lippman, A.: MedRec: using blockchain for medical data access and permission management. In: 2nd International Conference on Open and Big Data (OBD 2016), pp. 25–30, August 2016. https://doi.org/10.1109/OBD.2016.11

3. Calvaresi, D., Dubovitskaya, A., Calbimonte, J.P., Taveter, K., Schumacher, M.: Multi-agent systems and blockchain: results from a systematic literature review. In: Demazeau, Y., An, B., Bajo, J., Fernández-Caballero, A. (eds.) PAAMS 2018. LNCS (LNAI), vol. 10978, pp. 110–126. Springer, Cham (2018). https://doi.org/10.1007/978-3-319-94580-4_9

4. Chavez-Dreyfuss, G.: Sweden tests blockchain technology for land registry. Reuters, June **16** (2016)

5. Ciancarini, P.: Coordination models and languages as software integrators. ACM Comput. Surv. **28**(2), 300–302 (1996). https://doi.org/10.1145/234528.234732

6. Ciatto, G., Mariani, S., Omicini, A.: Blockchain for trustworthy coordination: a first study with Linda and Ethereum. In: 2018 IEEE/WIC/ACM International Conference on Web Intelligence (WI), pp. 696–703, December 2018. https://doi.org/10.1109/WI.2018.000-9

7. Ciatto, G., Mariani, S., Louvel, M., Omicini, A., Zambonelli, F.: Twenty years of coordination technologies: state-of-the-art and perspectives. In: Di Marzo Serugendo, G., Loreti, M. (eds.) COORDINATION 2018. LNCS, vol. 10852, pp. 51–80. Springer, Cham (2018). https://doi.org/10.1007/978-3-319-92408-3_3

8. Gelernter, D.: Generative communication in Linda. ACM Trans. Program. Lang. Syst. **7**(1), 80–112 (1985). https://doi.org/10.1145/2363.2433

9. Governatori, G., Idelberger, F., Milosevic, Z., Riveret, R., Sartor, G., Xu, X.: On legal contracts, imperative and declarative smartcontracts, and blockchain systems. Artif. Intell. Law **26**(4), 377–409 (2018). https://doi.org/10.1007/s10506-018-9223-3

10. Haber, S., Stornetta, W.S.: How to time-stamp a digital document. J. Cryptol. **3**(2), 99–111 (1991). https://doi.org/10.1007/BF00196791

11. Hearn, M.: Corda: a distributed ledger (2016). https://docs.corda.net/releases/release-V3.1/_static/corda-technical-whitepaper.pdf

12. Kim, H.M., Laskowski, M.: Toward an ontology-driven blockchain design for supply-chain provenance. Intell. Syst. Acc. Finan. Manag. **25**(1), 18–27 (2018)

13. Omicini, A., Zambonelli, F., Klusch, M., Tolksdorf, R. (eds.): Coordination of Internet Agents: Models, Technologies, and Applications. Springer, Heidelberg (2001). https://doi.org/10.1007/978-3-662-04401-8

14. Papadopoulos, G.A.: Models and technologies for the coordination of Internet agents: a survey. In: Omicini et al. [13], chap. 2, pp. 25–56. https://doi.org/10.1007/978-3-662-04401-8_2

15. Rossi, D., Cabri, G., Denti, E.: Tuple-based technologies for coordination. In: Omicini et al. [13], chap. 4, pp. 83–109. https://doi.org/10.1007/978-3-662-04401-8_4

16. Wood, G.: Ethereum: a secure decentralised generalised transaction ledger (2014). http://ethereum.github.io/yellowpaper/paper.pdf

Multi-Agent Modelling of Fairness for Users and Miners in Blockchains

Önder Gürcan$^{(\boxtimes)}$ (iD)

CEA, LIST, Point Courrier 174, 91191 Gif-sur-Yvette, France
`onder.gurcan@cea.fr`

Abstract. Due to the open and dynamic nature of blockchain systems, the participants (users and miners) have to take into accounts uncertain constraints (e.g., the transaction confirmation times, the delays in the network, and the topology of the network) during their decision-making processes for carefully balancing their objectives. One of these objectives is to operate in a *fair* environment. This is important since participants may decide to leave the system if they cannot satisfy this objective, which may imply reduced security and sustainability of the system. Yet, existing approaches to modelling fairness are based on formalisms that do not capture the open and complex nature of the blockchain systems. In this paper, we discuss the current status of modelling of fairness based on a high-level description of blockchains and we exploit multi-agent modelling of fairness for users and miners.

Keywords: Fairness · Decision making · Uncertainty

1 Introduction

The success of Bitcoin [11] largely relies on the perception of a trustworthy underlying peer-to-peer protocol: blockchain. This perception gave rise to many other successful blockchains also [2,3,7,19]. However, in order to have a sustainable success, blockchains should provide *fair* mechanisms in order to avoid participants to leave the system. Without such fairness, participant might be disincentivized to use blockchains, reducing the security of them. However, such systems are open and complex systems and thus providing fairness is not trivial.

The studies focusing on *fairness* in the literature [4–6,12,16] try to formalize the system model in a simplified manner and thus the open and complex nature of blockchains are not captured. In this paper, however, we claim that the use of multi-agent systems (MAS) will make it possible to harness the complexity of fairness problem by delegating software agents to represent participants. Because in MAS the system is composed of agents where each agent behaves according to its local perceptions and local knowledge, has the ability to model uncertainty, and *chooses* to perform the actions based on decision making process. In addition, MAS modelling allows us to use agent-based modelling and simulation (ABMS) as an adjunct to theoretical research since ABMS is a powerful tool for

© Springer Nature Switzerland AG 2019
F. De la Prieta et al. (Eds.): PAAMS 2019 Workshops, CCIS 1047, pp. 92–99, 2019.
https://doi.org/10.1007/978-3-030-24299-2_8

determining the dynamics of open and complex systems and, consequently, for quantitatively testing theoretical predictions where mathematical modelling is not sufficient.

This paper is organized as follows. The next section describes blockchains in general. In Sect. 3, the fairness in blockchains problem is explained. Section 4 states how multi-agent modelling can be used for tackling the fairness problem. A comprehensive discussion is made in Sect. 5 and finally, Sect. 6 concludes the paper and gives future prospects.

2   Blockchain Systems

The blockchain protocol, introduced by Satoshi Nakamoto [11], is the core of the decentralized crypto-currency systems. Participants following this protocol can create together a distributed economical, social and technical system where anyone can join (or leave) and perform transactions in-between without neither needing to trust each other nor having a trusted third party. It is a very attractive technology since it maintains a *public*, *immutable* and *ordered* log of transactions which guarantees an *auditable* ledger accessible by anyone.

Technically speaking, a blockchain system is an open and distributed electronic payment system composed of participants called *users* and *block creators* (Fig. 1). All participants of a blockchain system store unconfirmed transactions in their memory pools and confirmed transactions in their blockchains.

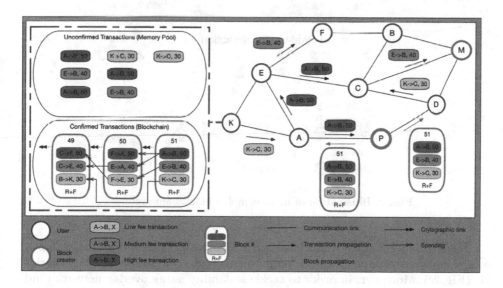

Fig. 1. Illustration of a blockchain system.

Users create transactions with a fee and then broadcast them across the blockchain network for being confirmed. During the diffuse of transactions, every node validates them before diffusing to their neighbours. Note that, due to the characteristics of the network, every node will receive in different orders and also some transactions might be lost during communication. In this sense, ordering them totally for appending to the blockchain in an immutable manner is the responsibility of *block creators*. After receiving a certain number of transactions, block creators try to confirm them as a block by using a consensus algorithm like Proof-of-Work (PoW), Proof-of-Stake (PoS), Delegated Proof-of-Stake (DPoS), Practical Byzantine Fault-Tolerance (PBFT) and so on (see [18] for a review). Based on the algorithm used and the blockchain technology, block creators are name as miners [11], validators [19], bakers [7], committee members [2,3] etc. respectively.

The created block contains the transactions chosen by the creator of the block, the unique hash value of the block, the unique hash value of its previous block and a block reward, which is composed of a static block reward plus the total fees of transactions, expressed as a transaction to its creator. Note that, similar to the diffuse of transactions, every node validates the diffused blocks before diffusing to their neighbours.

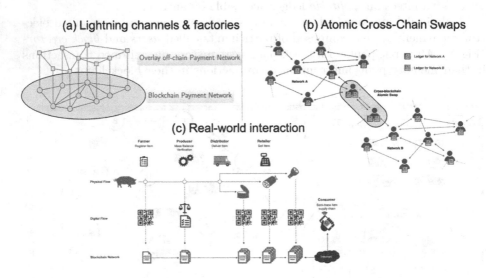

Fig. 2. Illustration of more complex blockchain systems.

Besides, blockchain systems have real-world interactions in case, for example, a user orders a product from an online marketplace, or supply-chain scenarios [1] (Fig. 2c). Moreover, in order to tackle scalability issues overlay network (2nd layer) protocols called lightning networks[1] and lightning factories (networks of these channels) [14] are being used (Fig. 2a). Furthermore, there are also mechanisms that allow making atomic cross-chain swaps [10], i.e. payments issued

---

[1] Lightning Network, https://lightning.network, last access on 24 March 2019.

using several different blockchains (Fig. 2b). In short, blockchain systems are in fact groups of multiple blockchains including also the real-world.

3 Fairness in Blockchains

Regardless of being a user or a miner, every participant keeps a replication of the whole blockchain. Thus, the more participants a blockchain system has, the more replications it has, and the more the blockchain is replicated, the more secure and sustainable the blockchain system is. Moreover, the more participants there are, the more validators the system will have during the diffuse of data. However, such participation is not trivial and is driven by the *incentives* that the system provides to its participants. As a result, blockchain systems should provide a *fair* environment in which both users and miners consider worthwhile to join and stay over time in the system [8].

Users are willing to issue transactions in-between without neither needing to *trust each other* nor having a *trusted third party*. Consequently, they expect the system to provide a *trusted* transactional service at a reasonable cost, speed and acceptable quality. Hence, a trend on a growing number of unconfirmed transactions may create a service degradation, and may result decreased participation of users [8]. If no user stays in the system, miners will have no transactions to confirm[2] and thus the system will be confined to end[3].

Block creators, on the other hand, are willing to make profit from (or at least compensate) their service of confirming transactions as blocks. Consequently, block creators are incentivized by a reward for each successful block creation. However, the expected time and variance of receiving payouts can be quite large for them. Such a situation disincentivizes the block creators with relatively lower capital. Hence, such block creators either leave the system or combine their resources with the others (creating mining pools, delegating stakes etc.). Such collaborations may lead to the centralization of the block creation power in the network, which may make the entire network to be controlled by a small number of collaborations. Such a situation will decrease the *trust*, and may result, decreased user participation that reduces the *trust* even more.

4 Multi-Agent Modelling of Fairness in Blockchains

In this section, we will discuss how multi-agent modelling can be used for tackling the fairness problem of blockchain systems.

---

[2] Technically the miners can create empty blocks and get block rewards. But this is not the purpose of blockchain systems.

[3] Although it is open system and we can expect that participants may come back in the future, once they lose their trust it is harder to expect them to come back.

4.1   A Rational Multi-Agent Model for Fairness

In [8,9], it has been shown that, a blockchain system can be modelled as a multi-agent system where the system is composed of agents where each agent behaves according to its local perceptions and local knowledge (*belief*), models uncertainty via expected values of variables or *actions*, and always *chooses* to perform the actions with the optimal *expected* outcome (among all feasible actions) for maximizing its utility [15].

The multi-agent approach proposed in [8,9] models a blockchain system as follows. *User agents* have the *action* of issuing transactions where they need to *choose* a fee. After issuing a transaction, a user agent *expect* it to be confirmed. Besides, each user agent has the action of validating the diffused data. Finally, a user agent may *think* that the system is fair or unfair and behave according to this belief. *Block creator* agents have the *action* creating blocks. Their block creation power depends on the investment *choice* they made. Block creator agents are free to *choose* to select the unconfirmed transactions they want into their blocks. In return, due to the creation of blocks, they *expect* rewards from the system.

Both user and block creator agents in the blockchain system are modelled as rational agents where each rational agent n has a set of actions A_n and a utility function $\mathcal{U}_n$. Using A_n and $\mathcal{U}_n$, n uses a decision process where it identifies the possible sequences of actions to execute. These sequences as rational behaviours of n and denoted as β. The objective of n is to choose the behaviours that selfishly keep $\mathcal{U}_n$ as high as possible. When an agent needs to choose a behaviour for execution, it needs to calculate its expected value. The expected value $\mathcal{E}(\beta_i)$ depends on the probabilities of the possible outcomes of the execution of β_i. Fairness can then be modelled as the situation in which the total satisfaction of a rational agent's expectations $\mathcal{U}_n$ is above a certain degree. If, at any time, an agent finds the system unfair (i.e. if its overall expected utility in a sufficiently long time window is below the certain degree), it may either try to improve its abilities (e.g., choosing more investment for miners) or may decide to leave.

Based on this multi-agent based fairness model, probabilistic strategies then designed for users and miners [8,9], and their mathematical analyses are made. However, agent-based simulations are needed for more realistic results. Mathematical analyses are not able to express openness and to capture complex dynamics.

4.2   Exploiting Multi-Agent Modelling for Fairness

In fact, the aforementioned fairness model focuses only on rational agents and does not capture all the properties needed for tackling with the complexity of the fairness problem. For a better multi-agent model, we claim that the following question should be asked:

Who can take the decisions about fairness and/or affect the fairness?

We answer this in three-levels: system-, block creator- and user-level. While the system-level preferences are the same for the whole network, block creator and user agents may have individual preferences for fairness and have different expectations. Overall, fairness improvements should drive the system towards a more fair state.

System-Level. The blockchain system has properties like security, liveness, scalability, trust and fairness; characteristics like delay, reliability and topology; and rules like validation and rewarding. The system can improve fairness by using the information visible to everyone and thus validatable by everybody (as less uncertain as possible), i.e., the information on the blockchain. It can introduce mechanisms to prevent/reduce the attacks using such reliable information. For example, the system can provide a more fair (proportional nearly to the effort spent) reward distribution for the successful block creators to avoid unfair distribution of rewards, by, e.g., not allowing the same agent(s) to win successively. In PoW for example, the creator of block (n) is obviously has more chance for mining the block (n + 1) and also some agents can make selfish mining (block creation) attacks. The system can also improve fairness by allowing cancellation of transactions for users under certain conditions as proposed in [9].

Block Creator-Level. Block creator agents are naturally *competitive*. They can decide with local information to improve their situations. For instance, they can modify their neighbourhood if they think that their data are diffused slowly. They behave selfishly in order to increase their revenue.

User-Level. Users agents are, on the other hand, can be *cooperative*. They can detect unfair situations with local, incomplete and uncertain information [17], e.g., unconfirmed transactions by using time-stamped memory pooling. User agents can force block creator agents to be cooperative when needed, since each user agent has the power of validating and diffusing data. For example, if a transaction is unconfirmed since for a long time, the user agents may begin to invalidate the blocks that do not contain this transaction. User agents can detect locally misbehaviors of the others, such as diffusion of invalid transactions and/or blocks, and detection of fraud (misbehaving block creators and/or users).

5 Related Work

To model and analyse unfairness situations in Bitcoin-like blockchains [11], several *formal studies* have been conducted so far [4–6,12,16]. Garay et al. [6] showed that, assuming that all miners follow the protocol, the number of blocks created by miners is proportional to their fraction of computation powers. Eyal et al. [5] were the first to formally show that Bitcoin protocol is not incentive compatible by presenting a deviant mining strategy called *selfish mining*. Their main result states that a miner whose hash rate is 33% of network can generate 38.4% of the blocks by employing this strategy. This consequently shows that Bitcoin protocol is not *fair*, i.e., fraction of blocks contributed by a miner to the blockchain can deviate significantly from his hash rate fraction. Work of Sapir-shtein et al. [16] further analyse and optimize this strategy. Carlsten et al. [4] shows that selfish mining becomes even more profitable in a setting where there is no fixed block reward, i.e. miners earn their revenue solely through transaction fees. In addition to that, they show it is likely for Bitcoin to become unstable due to miners bribing each other to fork the chain. To tackle such problems, a solution proposed by Fruitchain [13] is to incentivize solo mining by using a novel rewarding scheme.

However, in all these studies, in order to formalize the system model, the system is simplified (e.g., [6] defines rounds) and thus the open and complex nature of blockchains are not captured. In this paper, however, we show that using a multi-agent system approach allow effectively capturing necessary details for the fairness problem.

6   Conclusion and Prospects

In this paper, we made a high-level (technology and algorithm independent) description blockchain systems where there are users, block creators and the system itself. All these actors affect and are affected by *fairness*, and unfairness situations may derive all or some of them to a less secure and stable state. To capture the necessary details of fairness effectively, we proposed a multi-agent modelling approach. We proposed agent-based fairness improvements which are supposed to be better aligned with user and block creator expectations and the system's properties.

In a nutshell, we claim that blockchain systems are complex systems with intricate open and dynamic network structures exchanging information. There-fore, while a better fairness will increase the number of participants in the system and increase the scale, it is not known yet if the fairness will increase sub-linearly, linearly or super-linearly with the scale. The result can be an equilibrium state where fairness and participation are balanced or a chaotic situation where fairness and participation are fluctuating continuously. Consequently, a quantitative framework for fairness in blockchains which will allow the analysis of fairness with respect to scale should be developed for quantitatively testing theoretical predictions where mathematical modelling is not sufficient. To this end, agent-based modelling and simulation should be used for building simulations dedicated to blockchain systems.

References

1. Alzahrani, N., Bulusu, N.: Block-supply chain: a new anti-counterfeiting supply chain using NFC and blockchain. In: Proceedings of the 1st Workshop on Cryptocurrencies and Blockchains for Distributed Systems, CryBlock 2018, pp. 30–35. ACM, New York (2018). https://doi.org/10.1145/3211933.3211939
2. Androulaki, E., et al.: Hyperledger fabric: a distributed operating system for permissioned blockchains. In: EuroSys 2018, Porto, Portugal, April 2018

3. Buchman, E., Kwon, J., Milosevic, Z.: The latest gossip on BFT consensus. arXiv preprint arXiv:1807.04938 (2018)
4. Carlsten, M., Kalodner, H., Weinberg, S.M., Narayanan, A.: On the instability of bitcoin without the block reward. In: Proceedings of the 2016 ACM SIGSAC Conference on Computer and Communications Security, pp. 154–167. ACM (2016)
5. Eyal, I., Sirer, E.G.: Majority is not enough: bitcoin mining is vulnerable. In: Christin, N., Safavi-Naini, R. (eds.) FC 2014. LNCS, vol. 8437, pp. 436–454. Springer, Heidelberg (2014). https://doi.org/10.1007/978-3-662-45472-5_28
6. Garay, J., Kiayias, A., Leonardos, N.: The bitcoin backbone protocol: analysis and applications. In: Oswald, E., Fischlin, M. (eds.) EUROCRYPT 2015. LNCS, vol. 9057, pp. 281–310. Springer, Heidelberg (2015). https://doi.org/10.1007/978-3-662-46803-6_10
7. Goodman, L.M.: A self-amending crypto-ledger. Tezos white paper (2014)
8. Gürcan, Ö., Del Pozzo, A., Tucci-Piergiovanni, S.: On the bitcoin limitations to deliver fairness to users. In: Panetto, H., et al. (eds.) OTM 2017. LNCS, vol. 10573, pp. 589–606. Springer, Cham (2017). https://doi.org/10.1007/978-3-319-69462-7_37
9. Gürcan, Ö., Ranchal Pedrosa, A., Tucci-Piergiovanni, S.: On cancellation of transactions in bitcoin-like blockchains. In: Panetto, H., Debruyne, C., Proper, H.A., Ardagna, C.A., Roman, D., Meersman, R. (eds.) OTM 2018. LNCS, vol. 11229, pp. 516–533. Springer, Cham (2018). https://doi.org/10.1007/978-3-030-02610-3_29
10. Herlihy, M.: Atomic cross-chain swaps. In: Proceedings of the 2018 ACM PODC 2018, pp. 245–254. ACM, New York (2018)
11. Nakamoto, S.: Bitcoin: a peer-to-peer electronic cash system (2008). https://bitcoin.org/bitcoin.pdf
12. Pass, R., Seeman, L., Shelat, A.: Analysis of the blockchain protocol in asynchronous networks. IACR Cryptology ePrint Archive 2016, 454 (2016)
13. Pass, R., Shi, E.: Fruitchains: a fair blockchain. Cryptology ePrint Archive, Report 2016/916 (2016). http://eprint.iacr.org/2016/916.pdf
14. Pedrosa, A.R., Potop-Butucaru, M., Tucci-Piergiovanni, S.: Scalable lightning factories for bitcoin. In: SAC DADS (2019, to appear)
15. Russell, S.J., Norvig, P.: Artificial Intelligence - A Modern Approach, 3rd edn. Pearson Education, London (2010)
16. Sapirshtein, A., Sompolinsky, Y., Zohar, A.: Optimal selfish mining strategies in bitcoin. In: Grossklags, J., Preneel, B. (eds.) FC 2016. LNCS, vol. 9603, pp. 515–532. Springer, Heidelberg (2017). https://doi.org/10.1007/978-3-662-54970-4_30
17. Serugendo, G.D.M., Gleizes, M.P., Karageorgos, A. (eds.): Self-organising Software - From Natural to Artificial Adaptation. NCS. Springer, Heidelberg (2011). https://doi.org/10.1007/978-3-642-17348-6
18. Wang, W., et al.: A survey on consensus mechanisms and mining strategy management in blockchain networks. IEEE Access 7, 22328–22370 (2019). https://doi.org/10.1109/ACCESS.2019.2896108
19. Wood, G.: Ethereum: a secure decentralised generalised transaction ledger (2014). http://bitcoinaffiliatelist.com/wp-content/uploads/ethereum.pdf

Integrating Multi-agent Simulations into Enterprise Application Landscapes

Timotheus Kampik[1,2]([⊠]) and Amro Najjar[1,3]

[1] Department of Computing Science, Umeå University, 90187 Umeå, Sweden
{tkampik,najjar}@cs.umu.se
[2] Signavio GmbH, 10787 Berlin, Germany
[3] AI-Robolab/ICR, Computer Science and Communications,
University of Luxembourg, 4365 Esch-sur-Alzette, Luxembourg

Abstract. To cope with increasingly complex business, political, and economic environments, agent-based simulations (ABS) have been proposed for modeling complex systems such as human societies, transport systems, and markets. ABS enable experts to assess the influence of exogenous parameters (*e.g.*, climate changes or stock market prices), as well as the impact of policies and their long-term consequences. Despite some successes, the use of ABS is hindered by a set of interrelated factors. First, ABS are mainly created and used by researchers and experts in academia and specialized consulting firms. Second, the results of ABS are typically not automatically integrated into the corresponding business process. Instead, the integration is undertaken by human users who are responsible for adjusting the implemented policy to take into account the results of the ABS. These limitations are exacerbated when the results of the ABS affect multi-party agreements (*e.g.*, contracts) since this requires all involved actors to agree on the validity of the simulation, on how and when to take its results into account, and on how to split the losses/gains caused by these changes. To address these challenges, this paper explores the integration of ABS into enterprise application landscapes. In particular, we present an architecture that integrates ABS into cross-organizational enterprise resource planning (ERP) processes. As part of this, we propose a multi-agent systems simulator for the Hyperledger blockchain and describe an example supply chain management scenario type to illustrate the approach.

Keywords: Agent-Based Simulation · Business rules ·
Decision support systems · Business process management

1   Introduction

In recent years, agent-based simulations (ABS) have proven their merits in providing assistance to decision makers. Notable ABS have been proposed to address societal challenges such as the sustainable development of rural areas [4], modeling population displacement and its consequences [31], and crisis and disaster

© Springer Nature Switzerland AG 2019
F. De la Prieta et al. (Eds.): PAAMS 2019 Workshops, CCIS 1047, pp. 100–111, 2019.
https://doi.org/10.1007/978-3-030-24299-2_9

management [3,23]. Moreover, ABS can be applied in user-centric scenarios, for instance, to understand driver behaviors in urban environments [5], or to represent user satisfaction of cloud computing services [20]. In most of these applications, ABS are used to enable experts to assess the influence of exogenous variables (*e.g.*, global warming), and the impact of potential policies and their consequences (*e.g.*, the consequences of increasing government spending in rural regions).

On the technical side, multiple ABS tools and development environments have been proposed [1]. For example, MASON [18], RePast Simphony [22], and Netlogo [30] are frequently used general-purpose and social simulation environments that help users build complex ABS and provide ready-to-use plugins and support functionalities, such as data visualization and analysis tools.

Despite these technical advances, and although ABS have been employed to address practical problems, ABS are still mainly used by experts in research institutes and consulting firms. Consequently, the results of the simulations cannot easily be translated into policies, as this requires intensive coordination among the different actors involved (experts, executive directors, clerks, *et cetera*). This situation is aggravated in cross-organizational contexts as the recommendations learned from the ABS will likely lead to changes/updates of existing agreements that bind the involved parties. In such cases, implementing these recommendations will typically lead to a time and resource-consuming process to reach a new consensus among the involved stakeholders. Figure 1 illustrates the *status quo* approach to integrating ABS into enterprise application landscapes. As can be seen from the figure, organization A develops the ABS based on expert knowledge and historical data. The results of the simulation are then used to provide decision support for decision makers. In case the decision is used in-house in the same organization (A), the results of the simulation can be integrated into the local enterprise application landscape, for example by configuring corresponding business rules. However, integrating the results of the simulation into the decision-making process of multiple organizations–*i.e.*, to facilitate cross-organizational agreements–is difficult since the results may lead to updates to be applied to binding contracts.

To overcome these difficulties, in this paper we explore integrating of ABS into cross-organizational enterprise application landscapes. In particular, we investigate the use of blockchain technology (BCT) to facilitate the consensus-reaching process for updating the business rules to take the results of the ABS into account. The contributions of this paper are as follows:

1. Propose an integrated ABS allowing to facilitate cross-organizational automation, in particular in supply chain scenarios.
2. Present an architecture, generic simulation component, and running example for the proposed approach.
3. Provide an overview of the advantages and disadvantages of decentralized environments for the use case type in focus.
4. Outline technical challenges and societal risks that are associated with deploying MAS simulations as smart contracts in public blockchain environments.

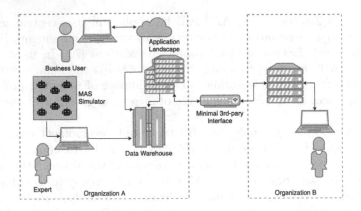

Fig. 1. Stand-alone MAS simulation, minimal organizational interface

The rest of this paper is organized as follows. In Sect. 2, we provide an overview of existing related research on MAS simulations for business scenarios and decentralized business rule execution. We then introduce the concept of MAS simulations as decentralized business rules in Sect. 3. We specify the architecture of a generic MAS simulation component for blockchain environments, as well as a set of feasible technologies, and describe a simple supply chain management example in Sect. 4. In Sect. 5, we give an overview of the advantages and disadvantages of decentralized ("blockchain-based") environments for our use case type, highlight key challenges and opportunities the proposed approach implies for *public blockchain* environments, discuss the limitations of the presented research, and outline relevant future research.

2   Background

2.1   Multi-agent Simulations for Decision Support

ABS have been used to simulate a variety of social phenomena and business environments, with the objective of providing decision support for decision makers in various domains. The use of agent technology for simulating social phenomena on a computer, a sub-domain known as Agent-Based Social Simulation (ABSS) [8], has been applied to different use cases. Examples include evaluating the effects of marketing strategies [28] and assessing the impact of rumors on social networks [29]. In a business context, ABS have been applied in manufacturing systems and supply chain management [16], and to assist Software-as-a-Service (SaaS) providers strike a balance between business gains and end-user satisfaction [21].

2.2   Decentralized Process and Business Rule Execution

With the advent of *blockchain* technology as a potential solution allowing for cross-organizational record-keeping without the requirement of a trusted central authority, the decentralized execution of business processes and business rules has gained increased attention in academia [19] and industry [10]. In particular, engines that compile business process (BPMN [24]) and business decision diagrams (DMN [25]) and execute the resulting program code have been proposed and implemented as prototypes for private blockchain solutions, *i.e.* for *Ethereum* [11,17]. While these works aim to facilitate cross-organizational process-execution, *this* paper explores the integration of agent-based simulations into the emerging ecosystem of cross-organizational enterprise software. With this integration, information obtained from the simulation can be automatically employed to update cross-organizational business rules, which allows organizations to accommodate the rapid pace of today's business environment.

In contrast to our previous work [12], whose main aim is to introduce a MAS simulation architecture to support policy-makers when determining whether to tolerate bypassing a decentralized business process, this article explores the benefits of integrating ABS with enterprise-ready BCT. The next section discusses the merits of the solution proposed in this paper.

3   MAS Simulations as (Decentralized) Business Rules

To overcome the shortcomings discussed in Sect. 1 and illustrated by Fig. 1, this section proposes to integrate ABS simulations into cross-organizational enterprise application landscapes. The proposed solution is illustrated in Fig. 2. Similar to Fig. 1, organization A runs an ABS engine integrated with its application landscape. Yet, unlike in Fig. 1, where a minimal third-party interface for cross-organizational communication is used, in the proposed solution we rely on a decentralized and autonomous interface that hosts the simulation. Input parameters and output are stored transparently for all participating organizations in the trusted and decentralized autonomous interface (*e.g.*, on a distributed ledger). This facilitates the consensus-reaching process and makes it possible for other partners such as organization B to keep track of the simulation runs. Consequently, with this decentralized consensus making process, the empowered business user in Fig. 2 is able to integrate changes, updates, and lesson-learned from each simulation and feed them into the decision-making process of organization A even if this would entail changes in commitment and binding agreements with B. Because of the decentralized autonomous interface, the proposed updates require little or no human intervention for a new agreement to be reached and implemented. Depending on the nature of the changes, either the simulation parameters or the simulation code itself can be updated. The update can be approved by the other organization in a semi-automated or fully automated manner. Such an approach can facilitate the time it takes to accommodate changes in an organization's business environment, and help avoid disagreements among stakeholders since *(i)* the fact that the simulation is recorded on the ledger ensures its validity, *(ii)* business rules of how and when to undertake the updates, and on how to split the losses/gains caused by these changes are also predefined and stored on the ledger.

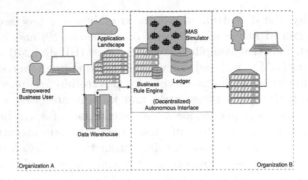

Fig. 2. Integrated MAS simulator at organizational interface

4 Hyperledger-Based Decentralized ABS: An Implementation Proposal

4.1 Architecture

To implement the approach as suggested above, we propose an architecture with the following three core components:

Decentralized business rule execution (DBREX) environment. This environment allows for *(i)* data exchange, *(ii)* ABS and business rule execution, *(iii)* consensus-finding, and *(iv)* record-keeping, all in a decentralized fashion. Exactly one DBREX environment exists, independent of the number of organizations that participate in the scenario. As a distributed system, the DBREX environment crosses organizational boundaries: all participating organizations should maintain a DBREX environment node.

DBREX user interface (UI) application. The DBREX user interface (UI) application (DBREX UI) allows a participating organization to interact with the DBREX to specify its business offers and needs (and the corresponding requirements). Each organization has its own DBREX UI. However, it makes sense to have identical or nearly-identical DBREX UIs for each participant *type* in a given scenario. For example, all organizations that are in a *supplier* role can use the same DBREX UI (with minor configuration changes or custom adjustments), whereas all organizations in a *purchaser* role can use another specific DBREX UI.

Internal ERP system entry point. The internal ERP system entry point is a custom data interface that connects an organization's IT system landscape via the DBREX UI to the DBREX environment. Given the heterogeneous nature of ERP system landscapes, each organization is likely to have its own custom-implemented entry point.

Figure 3 provides a high-level graphical overview of the proposed architecture in a simplified two-organization scenario.

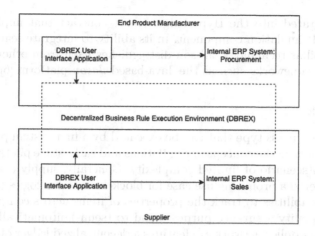

Fig. 3. Architecture proposal: graphical representation

4.2 Technologies

We suggest the following set of technologies to implement a first prototype of the proposed architecture:

Application execution runtime: Node.js. *Node.js*[1] is a JavaScript execution environment that allows running JavaScript programs outside of the browser (*e.g.*, on a server). Because there are both JavaScript-based ABS tools and smart contract execution environments (see below) and because of its rich ecosystem of plug-and-play dependencies, Node.js is a feasible choice for powering the decentralized business rule execution environment, as well as the front end and back end of the centralized applications that interface with it.

Decentralized execution environment: Hyperledger Fabric. *Hyperledger Fabric* (short: Hyperledger) is a *partial trust* smart contract engine [2]. In contrast to *public blockchain* ecosystems, Hyperledger is a private, *partial trust* blockchain solution; *i.e*, participants have to be authorized as eligible users. This has the advantage that a cryptocurrency-based incentive scheme (*mining* feature) is not required, which improves performance and prevents volatility. Hyperledger smart contracts can be specified in a range of mainstream programming languages such as Go and JavaScript. In contrast to *public* blockchain solutions like *Ethereum* [32], the *partial trust* approach of Hyperledger allows for faster and cheaper transactions [26,27].

Multi-agent simulation library: JS-son. *JS-son* is a JavaScript library for running belief-desire-intention (BDI) agents [13][2]. Because JS-son can be installed as a light-weight *Node Package Manager*[3] dependency, it can be

---

[1] https://nodejs.org/.

[2] Note that JS-son does not *require* a BDI approach; instead, beliefs can activate plans right away.

[3] https://www.npmjs.com/.

easily integrated into the Hyperledger smart contract that implements the agent-based simulation component. In its ability to integrate seamlessly with the Hyperpillar technology, JS-son distinguishes itself from other agent programming frameworks such as the Java-based *Jason* platform [6][4].

4.3   Example

As an example process type that can be executed by a first system prototype, as well as for evaluating the concept in simulations and early-stage pilots, we suggest a supply chain scenario of limited complexity. Generally, supply chain management is considered a promising use case for blockchain technologies (*c.f.* [14]). In particular, the abilities to track the properties of items across complex delivery networks for quality assurance purposes and to (semi-)automatically adjust an organization's supplier network are features a decentralized ledger offers as value propositions in supply chain management scenarios.

To illustrate the proposed approach, we introduce a simplified generic supply chain management business process for issuing invitations to tender (to supply certain goods). To improve intelligibility, we describe a scenario with one *purchaser* that requests an offer to supply parts and one *supplier* that agrees to deliver the requested product(s) and focus on the *happy path*; *i.e.*, we ignore possible exceptions (and also low-level details).

The process covers two levels: the initial agreement (human-in-the-loop) level and the automated run-time level.

The top-level process describes the supplier management process, abstracting from the details of the delivery cycles. The process flow can be described as follows (Fig. 5):

1. The process starts with the *purchaser* issuing an invitation to tender with specific conditions.
2. For the process to continue, a *supplier* needs to accept the invitation.
3. As soon as a supplier has accepted the invitation, the agreement is persisted to the ledger of the DBREX environment as a *smart contract*, and the planning and delivery cycle (subprocess) starts. As part of the smart contract, an ABS is specified that informs the dynamic adjustment of the product quantity over the different delivery cycles[5].
4. When the contract expires, the DBREX environment automatically terminates the supplier relationship.

The process flow of a delivery cycle can be described as follows (Fig. 4):

1. A delivery cycle starts with the purchaser proposing the current simulation parameters. For example, key indicators that describe the purchaser's business environment might have been specified as variables in the smart contract's ABS specification.

---

[4] For a comprehensive overview of agent platforms, see Kravari and Bassiliades [15].
[5] Potentially, product *quality* could be dynamically adjusted as well.

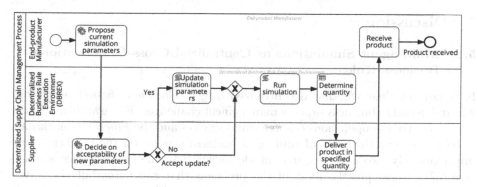

Fig. 4. Example: planning and delivery cycle

2. Then, the supplier decides on the acceptability of the parameters. As an alternative to this step, upper and lower bounds, within which the product quantity needs to be, could be specified in advance.
3. If the purchaser has approved the parameter update, the DBREX environment updates simulation parameters; otherwise, the previously (or: initially) specified parameters are kept.
4. Subsequently, the DBREX environment executes the simulation.
5. Based on the simulation result, the DBREX environment adjusts the product quantity that has to be delivered this cycle.
6. Then, the supplier delivers the product in the specified quantity.
7. Once the purchaser receives the project, they register this in the decentralized ledger of the DBREX environment.

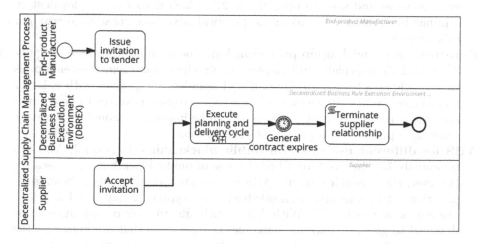

Fig. 5. Example: supply chain management process

5   Discussion

5.1   Multi-agent Simulations as Centralized Cross-Organizational Business Rules

It is not yet clear whether decentralized ledger (*blockchain-based*) technology will indeed solve business process management challenges. For example, a recent comparison of the operations costs of cloud services and the *Ethereum* blockchain determined that the costs of running a business process on the blockchain are approximately two orders of magnitude higher than the cloud service alternative [27][6]. Consequently, most of the problems that can potentially be solved by a decentralized ledger might instead be addressed by managing trust purely on a socio-organizational level (*i.e.*, by a trusted third party) or through alternative decentralized consensus techniques that do not rely on *blockchain*-like technologies. Hence, it is important to highlight that the proposed approach is blockchain-agnostic; *i.e.*, alternatively, a trusted third-party can take the role of the decentralized business rule execution environment.

5.2   Multi-agent Simulations on Public Blockchains

In this paper, we propose deploying using a private/partial trust blockchain as the decentralized execution environment. Yet, it is worth discussing the feasibility and potential risks of deploying technologies that follow the proposed approach to *public* blockchains, like *Ethereum*. Below, we briefly elaborate on the implications of deploying three variants of the proposed solution type in a public blockchain context:

Enterprise ABS on public blockchains. Public blockchains like Ethereum are expensive and slow to operate [26,27], which makes the deployment to a public blockchain infeasible, if no practical advantages that counterweight this issue exist.

Enterprise ABS with open participation. One possible advantage of a public blockchain–especially in complex supply chain management scenarios–is that it allows ad-hoc participation and seamless integration with a larger financial ecosystem. If the public blockchain ecosystem evolves to be cheaper and faster in the future, this advantage can be important enough to motivate selecting a public over a private blockchain solution.

ABS for different use cases on public blockchains. In general, ABS can potentially be employed for a broad range of public blockchain use cases [7]. However, the possibility to run ABS in a cryptocurrency context bears societal risks. It is generally acknowledged that cryptocurrency fraud is a serious economic problem [9]. With ABS, which–due to their complexity–can be designed to generate extreme outcomes in edge cases that are known to the simulation designer and unknown to other users, cryptocurrency fraudsters have an additional tool at their disposal.

---

[6] Other concerns are performance [26] and security issues.

5.3   Limitations and Future Research

In this paper, we have presented an architecture and toolchain for integrating ABS into enterprise application landscapes. The presented work is purely conceptual and lacks an implementation and evaluation. In addition, the relevance of a decentralized, *blockchain*-based solution can generally be questioned, as no strong evidence of business benefits such solutions may provide seems to exist, yet. The latter issue is, however, not central to the contribution of this paper: as explained above, the proposed architecture can also implemented as a solution that can be deployed in a centralized environment, *i.e.* as an interface operated by a trusted third party.

To further advance the approach we propose in this paper, we suggest the following research:

- Implement the proposed architecture as a generic Node.js library for Hyperledger environments and provide a simple running example scenario.
- Evaluate the architecture and its implementation by running simulations that compare business performance (time, costs) in a traditional environment with the performance that can be achieved by employing the proposed architecture, *ceteris paribus*.
- Evaluate the approach in a first pilot project of limited complexity.
- Provide an in-depth perspective of the alternative *centralized* architecture for integrating ABS into enterprise application landscapes.

Acknowledgements. This work was partially supported by the Wallenberg AI, Autonomous Systems and Software Program (WASP) funded by the Knut and Alice Wallenberg Foundation and partially funded by the German Federal Ministry of Education and Research (BMBF) within the Framework Concept "Industrie 4.0 – Kollaborationen in dynamischen Wertschopfungsnetzwerken (InKoWe)"/managed by the Project Management Agency Forschungszentrum Karlsruhe (PTKA).

References

1. Abar, S., Theodoropoulos, G.K., Lemarinier, P., O'Hare, G.M.: Agent based modelling and simulation tools: a review of the state-of-art software. Comput. Sci. Rev. **24**, 13–33 (2017)
2. Androulaki, E., et al.: Hyperledger fabric: a distributed operating system for permissioned blockchains. In: Proceedings of the Thirteenth EuroSys Conference, p. 30. ACM (2018)
3. Bañgate, J., Dugdale, J., Beck, E., Adam, C.: A multi-agent system approach in evaluating human spatio-temporal vulnerability to seismic risk using social attachment. WIT Trans. Eng. Sci. **121**, 47–58 (2018)
4. Berger, T., Schreinemachers, P., Woelcke, J.: Multi-agent simulation for the targeting of development policies in less-favored areas. Agric. Syst. **88**(1), 28–43 (2006)
5. Bessghaier, N., Zargayouna, M., Balbo, F.: Management of urban parking: an agent-based approach. In: Ramsay, A., Agre, G. (eds.) AIMSA 2012. LNCS (LNAI), vol. 7557, pp. 276–285. Springer, Heidelberg (2012). https://doi.org/10.1007/978-3-642-33185-5_31

6. Bordini, R.H., Hübner, J.F., Wooldridge, M.: Programming Multi-Agent Systems in AgentSpeak Using Jason. Wiley Series in Agent Technology. Wiley, Hoboken (2007)

7. Calvaresi, D., Dubovitskaya, A., Calbimonte, J.P., Taveter, K., Schumacher, M.: Multi-agent systems and blockchain: results from a systematic literature review. In: Demazeau, Y., An, B., Bajo, J., Fernández-Caballero, A. (eds.) PAAMS 2018. LNCS (LNAI), vol. 10978, pp. 110–126. Springer, Cham (2018). https://doi.org/10.1007/978-3-319-94580-4_9

8. Davidsson, P.: Agent based social simulation: a computer science view. J. Artif. Soc. Soc. Simul. **5**(1), 1–7 (2002)

9. Drozd, O., Lazur, Y., Serbin, R.: Theoretical and legal perspective on certain types of legal liability in cryptocurrency relations. Baltic J. Econ. Stud. **3**(5), 221–228 (2018)

10. Gregor, K.: IBM wants to make 2017 the year of blockchain enterprise deployment (2017). https://www.ibm.com/blockchain/in-en/assets/IDC_Report_IBM_wants_to_make_2017_the_year_of_BlockChain_Enterprise_Deployment.pdf (2017)

11. Haarmann, S., Batoulis, K., Nikaj, A., Weske, M.: DMN decision execution on the ethereum blockchain. In: Krogstie, J., Reijers, H.A. (eds.) CAiSE 2018. LNCS, vol. 10816, pp. 327–341. Springer, Cham (2018). https://doi.org/10.1007/978-3-319-91563-0_20

12. Kampik, T., Najjar, A., Calvaresi, D.: MAS-aided approval for bypassing decentralized processes: an architecture. In: 2018 IEEE/WIC/ACM International Conference on Web Intelligence (WI), pp. 713–718. IEEE (2018)

13. Kampik, T., Nieves, J.C.: JS-son - a minimalistic JavaScript BDI agent library. In: 7th International Workshop on Engineering Multi-Agent Systems (EMAS 2019), Montreal, Canada, 13–14 May 2019 (2019)

14. Korpela, K., Hallikas, J., Dahlberg, T.: Digital supply chain transformation toward blockchain integration. In: Proceedings of the 50th Hawaii International Conference on System Sciences (2017)

15. Kravari, K., Bassiliades, N.: A survey of agent platforms. J. Artif. Soc. Soc. Simul. **18**(1), 11 (2015)

16. Lee, J.H., Kim, C.O.: Multi-agent systems applications in manufacturing systems and supply chain management: a review paper. Int. J. Prod. Res. **46**(1), 233–265 (2008)

17. López-Pintado, O., García-Bañuelos, L., Dumas, M., Weber, I.: Caterpillar: a blockchain-based business process management system. In: Proceedings of the BPM Demo Track and BPM Dissertation Award Co-Located with 15th International Conference on Business Process Modeling (BPM 2017), Barcelona, Spain (2017)

18. Luke, S., Cioffi-Revilla, C., Panait, L., Sullivan, K., Balan, G.: MASON: a multi-agent simulation environment. Simulation **81**(7), 517–527 (2005)

19. Mendling, J., et al.: Blockchains for business process management-challenges and opportunities. ACM Trans. Manag. Inf. Syst. (TMIS) **9**(1), 4 (2018)

20. Najjar, A.: Multi-agent negotiation for QoE-aware cloud elasticity management. Ph.D. thesis, École nationale supérieure des mines de Saint-Étienne (2015)

21. Najjar, A., Mualla, Y., Boissier, O., Picard, G.: AQUAMan: QoE-driven cost-aware mechanism for SaaS acceptability rate adaptation. In: Proceedings of the International Conference on Web Intelligence, pp. 331–339. ACM (2017)

22. North, M.J., et al.: Complex adaptive systems modeling with repast simphony. Complex Adapt. Syst. Model. **1**(1), 3 (2013)

23. Ogie, R., Adam, C., Perez, P.: A review of structural approach to flood management in coastal megacities of developing nations: current research and future directions. J. Environ. Plann. Manag. 1–21 (2019)
24. OMG: business process model and notation (BPMN), version 2.0, January 2011
25. OMG: decision model and notation (DMN), version 1.1, June 2016
26. Pongnumkul, S., Siripanpornchana, C., Thajchayapong, S.: Performance analysis of private blockchain platforms in varying workloads. In: 26th International Conference on Computer Communication and Networks (ICCCN), pp. 1–6. IEEE (2017)
27. Rimba, P., Tran, A.B., Weber, I., Staples, M., Ponomarev, A., Xu, X.: Comparing blockchain and cloud services for business process execution. In: 2017 IEEE International Conference on Software Architecture (ICSA), pp. 257–260. IEEE (2017)
28. Serrano, E., Iglesias, C.A.: Validating viral marketing strategies in Twitter via agent-based social simulation. Expert Syst. Appl. **50**, 140–150 (2016)
29. Serrano, E., Iglesias, C.A., Garijo, M.: A survey of Twitter rumor spreading simulations. In: Núñez, M., Nguyen, N.T., Camacho, D., Trawiński, B. (eds.) ICCCI 2015. LNCS (LNAI), vol. 9329, pp. 113–122. Springer, Cham (2015). https://doi.org/10.1007/978-3-319-24069-5_11
30. Sklar, E.: NetLogo, a multi-agent simulation environment (2007)
31. Sokolowski, J.A., Banks, C.M., Hayes, R.L.: Modeling population displacement in the Syrian city of Aleppo. In: Proceedings of the Winter Simulation Conference 2014, pp. 252–263. IEEE (2014)
32. Wood, G.: Ethereum: A secure decentralised generalised transaction ledger. Ethereum project yellow paper, vol. 151, pp. 1–32 (2014)

Contesting the Truth - Intentional Forking in BFT-PoS Blockchains

Wolf Posdorfer$^{(\boxtimes)}$ and Julian Kalinowski

Department of Informatics, University of Hamburg,
Vogt-Kölln-Straße 30, 22527 Hamburg, Germany
{posdorfer,kalinowski}@informatik.uni-hamburg.de

Abstract. Byzantine-Fault-Tolerant Proof-of-Stake Blockchains usually make strong guarantees regarding transaction and block finality,
which makes them suitable technologies for consortium usage, where
fluctuations in state are disturbing to business processes. Proof of Work
Consensus however can not make finality guarantees as it employs the
longest-chain-rule, where the longest chain dictates the current state,
which can always be replaced by another longer chain.

In this paper we propose a dispute mechanism for BFT-PoS
Blockchains, where intentional forking is used to replace non-optimal
transactions for business cases, where the blockchain is used to store
only optimal solutions. Based on the longest-chain-rule of PoW algorithms validator nodes agree upon a more optimized chain via their
regular consensus to make adjustments to the previously agreed upon
state.

Keywords: Blockchain · Mempool · Byzantine fault tolerance ·
Proof of Stake · Fork

1 Introduction

With the introduction of Bitcoin [14] the underlying blockchain technology itself
has gained a lot of traction in various domains other than cryptocurrencies. The
key features blockchain technology offers are its decentralization, transparency,
integrity and immutability.

While the Proof-of-Work (PoW) or Nakamoto-consensus is geared towards
full decentralization in trustless environments it is not suited for the usage in
federations or consortiums where participants are known and more trustworthy.
The required hashing power and waste of energy makes PoW unattractive for
high frequency business processes like stock or energy trades. Proof-of-Stake
algorithms however offer less wasteful consensus algorithms more suited for this
purpose.

Due to competing blocks for the same height (forks) and the longest chain
rule in Bitcoin transaction- or block finality can only be assured after a certain
amount of succeeding blocks have extended the chain thus also extending the

© Springer Nature Switzerland AG 2019
F. De la Prieta et al. (Eds.): PAAMS 2019 Workshops, CCIS 1047, pp. 112–120, 2019.
https://doi.org/10.1007/978-3-030-24299-2_10

time for business processes. Byzantine Fault Tolerant based PoS (BFT-PoS) algorithms do not employ the longest chain rule as they usually don't have a fork process and thus do not require any succeeding blocks to make strong guarantees on block finality. Thus BFT-PoS Blockchains are more suited for business processes that require immediate transaction finality and a single state over a set of known and trustworthy nodes.

In previous work [18] we have devised a Mempool model for a BFT-PoS blockchain that allows for cooperative scheduling amongst Virtual Power Plants. Based on a cost-function transactions can be graded on their optimality for the given scheduling period, which enables nodes to select the most optimized transactions to be included into a block and discarding the rest. This greatly minimizes clutter in the blockchain and saves storage. However due to external factors such as network partitioning or packet loss it is possible that a sub-optimal transaction was deemed as the most optimized and included into the block granting it finality.

In this paper we propose the addition of an intentional consensus based forking process into BFT-PoS Blockchains. In order to contest the finality of sub-optimal transactions a dispute mechanism is necessary to replace transactions with more optimized ones. By introducing an intentional forking process into a BFT-PoS consensus we can achieve a chain that only consist of most optimized transactions but also delaying the block finality to a certain extend.

2   Related Work

Blockchains grant strong immutability guarantees to their underlying data structure by using standardized hash functions. By additionally including the hash of previous blocks into the current hash, the necessary computational effort to change data and brute-force hash collisions increases the further the data is away from the latest block.

Instead of utilizing standard hash functions, e.g. SHA-1, Chameleon Signatures [10] can be used as an alternative. These special hash functions contain trapdoors, which, given proper knowledge of the trapdoor, decrease the difficulty of finding collisions. This essentially allows previous blocks to be rewritten with different data but resulting in the same hash. This eliminates the need for an additional consensus over this de facto new block as it does not break any of the succeeding blocks integrity, as shown by [2]. A drawback in this method is the necessity to know the trapdoor-key, either in a central institution or on every node, which can lead to security risks. Instead of directly rewriting existing data, we chose our approach of a consensus based replace mechanism, because it favors decentralization and does not require parties with special entitlements. Also, disputed blocks can still be stored if nodes choose to do so, which might also be necessary for legal or regulative purposes.

3   Blockchain

Blockchains are decentralized data structures, whose internal consistency are guaranteed and maintained by a consensus algorithm over a distributed state. Every node holds a full and synchronized replication of the state [1].

To apply changes to the state of the blockchain a transaction has to be submitted. A fixed number of transactions are joined to form a block. Every block also contains a hash of its predecessor block, thus forming a chain of blocks.

The predecessors block hash is constructed by hashing a timestamp, a nonce, the transactions merkle-tree hash and the respective predecessors hash. Figure 1 depicts an exemplary blockchain datastructure showing three blocks and their linking via the predecessors hash (Prev_Hash).

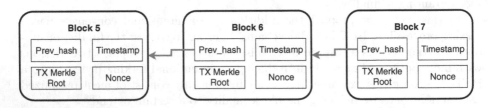

Fig. 1. Simplified blockchain data structure [16]

Transactions are created by network participants and propagated to other nodes through a peer-to-peer network. Depending on the blockchain technology used transactions can contain currency or trade information, function calls or other application specific data.

3.1   Consensus

The key properties of every blockchain are guaranteed transaction and block-validity, which is ensured through a consensus algorithm. Every participating node will eventually reach the same valid shared state.

Bitcoin, Ethereum and similiar public ledger technologies use a consensus algorithm that is referred to as *Proof-of-Work* (PoW) [5,14,19]. By solving a cryptographic challenge trust is ensured throughout the participants. Usually PoW algorithms require that the *Miners* (nodes interested in solving the challenge) find a specific *Nonce*. The resulting requirements for the nonce are defined by what is called the "difficulty". The difficulty specifies how many zeros the resulting hash of nonce and merkle-tree hash requires. Finding a suitable nonce that meets the difficulty is a brute-force task, that is computationally hard to perform, but trivial to verify.

By automatically adjusting the difficulty (increasing or decreasing the required amount of leading zeros) at certain fixed intervals it is ensured that very rarely two different blocks for the same height are distributed amongst the participants. When two blocks compete for the same height, this state is called a *fork*. To resolve this unintentional fork the "winning" block of the two is decided upon by whoever has more succeeding blocks. This is referred to as the *longest chain rule*. Once a block has more successors than its competing block, all nodes will synchronize their state to the longest chain and discard the other. By discarding the shorter chain all transactions within it will be also discarded.

In contrast to PoW the *Proof-of-Stake* (PoS) algorithms try to mitigate the waste of resources of brute-forcing nonces [7–9]. By staking their own coins (or stake) they decrease the difficulty for themselves to create a block. The more coins a miner stakes the easier it becomes. There are some other requirements that coins must uphold to, like coin-age, depending on the blockchain technology in use [3,9]. This is most often used to mitigate the results of coin hoarders owning large amounts of stake, which could potentially impact the system.

3.2 BFT-Based PoS Consensus

The Byzantine Fault Tolerant (BFT) based PoS algorithms address different requirements than the consensus algorithms used in public chains. The BFT-PoS family of algorithms try to solve the byzantine generals problem in a set of mostly known participants. Most BFT-PoS algorithms are loosely based on the PBFT-algorithm [6] and other 2-Phase-Commit-algorithms [12]. Tendermint [11], Ripple [17] and Stellar [13] are some of the BFT-PoS algorithms currently in wider use.

In BFT-based PoS algorithms nodes can have different roles. Validator nodes are directly responsible for consensus. They are a set of nodes that vote on proposed blocks by signing their hashes. All of the validators take turns proposing a new block - they become the *proposer*. By only allowing one proposer per round and per height it is ensured that only one block exists for any height. This prevents the blockchain from unintentionally forking due to two competing blocks, which also means that every block is final as there can be no competing longer chain.

4 Mempool Model

In PoW- and PoS-Blockchains miners select transactions from Mempool to be included in the next potentially mined block. Since there are no fixed selection criteria, miners prefer transactions which give them high rewards in the form of a transaction fee [15]. This introduces a highly competitive transaction selection process, as transactions with higher fees are generally favored. In contrast, BFT-PoS-Blockchains (e.g. Tendermint) usually employ a first-in-first-out rule when picking transactions from the Mempool. In both cases, transaction selection does not follow any business criteria.

Another approach would be to use the blockchain-layer protocol to support the business case it is used for. In order to enable cooperative scheduling in

Virtual Power Plants (VPPs), the Mempool transaction selection process of a BFT-PoS-Blockchain was adapted in [18]. In this scenario, each peer may propose a solution for a given timeslot, given by a scheduling vector put into a blockchain transaction. A scheduling vector essentially represents the distribution of energy supply among the energy sources. This problem can only be solved numerically and thus, there may be many valid and good solutions. However, the blockchain should agree upon a solution after a given time to move forward. The aim was to only persist a single optimal transaction (scheduling vector) in order to minimize clutter. By caching transactions in the Mempool and selecting only the optimal transaction we ensured that only a single transaction was persisted in a block for any given scheduling slot. Also every transaction is atomic, meaning it does not have any dependencies on other transactions, as every scheduling vector is also atomic in its nature.

5   Filing Disputes

One of the main problems of this approach can be the nature of message propagation in peer-to-peer networks. Due to packet loss, network segregation or even malicious intent, it is possible that certain transactions do not get broadcasted to all validator nodes. For the example, let T_a be a transaction which provides a valid, possible good solution and T_x a transaction containing a proposal that is optimal for the business case. In the case T_x, has not reached the current proposer, but T_a has and is the best available option, the proposer will obviously include T_a in the next block B_a. This will lead to one of two different outcomes, depending on which nodes have T_x in their Mempool.

> $>2/3$ received T_x, the proposal will not reach consensus. A new proposer will propose another block.
> $\leq 1/3$ received T_x, the proposal will reach consensus. Allowing for the less optimized transaction T_a to be persisted.

One possible solution would be to create a special dispute consensus message that instantly stops the current voting round, if it contains a revised, better transaction. This would prevent the creation of unnecessary blocks. However the same problems that already applied to transaction propagation applies to this special dispute message. Nodes might not receive the message or receive it after the consensus for a block has already been completed.

A better approach is to deploy a dispute protocol implementing a *rollback and replace* scenario. Our approach resembles the longest-chain mechanism in Bitcoin [14] and other "cryptocurrencies", where a block on an alternate side-chain can be replaced by a different block on a longer side-chain. An exemplary instance of this block replacing protocol can be seen in Fig. 2.

Whenever a sub-optimal transaction was included in a block a dispute message can be broadcasted to the network. The protocol is initiated by at least one of the nodes that knows about the better transaction T_x for the block B_a simply by broadcasting a special message indicating that this is a dispute.

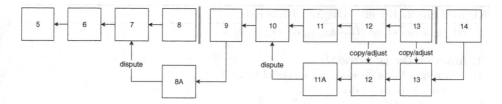

Fig. 2. Exemplary replacement of disputed Blocks

Once a proposer receives the dispute message, a new block B_x containing T_x is created, replacing the currently existing block B_a. A proposal round is initiated to replace the previous block B_a instead of creating a new block. The proposer will have to include the same transactions that were previously included and only replace T_a for the optimal transaction T_x (see algorithm 1). All other block data, like height and metadata, are left unmodified.

This is a rather trivial protocol when the disputed block is the most current block. When the dispute was found in an earlier block, all following blocks will have to be adjusted, as their hashes will not match anymore. The necessary steps for receiving a dispute can be seen in algorithm 2.

Algorithm 1. Create Dispute Proposal
```
 1: BC ← Blockchain[Block₀, ..., Blockₙ]
 2:
 3: function CREATE_DISPUTE(blockheight, txOrig, txOpt)
 4:     M ← [ ]
 5:     for i ← blockheight, sizeof(BC) do
 6:         B ← BC[i]
 7:         if B ∋ txOrig then
 8:             B[txOrig] ← txOpt
 9:         end if
10:         Bₕₐₛₕ ← hash(B, B − 1ₕₐₛₕ)
11:         M[] ← B
12:     end for
13:     broadcast M for consensus
14: end function
```

---

6 Evaluation and Future Work

The proposed approach allows for a blockchain containing only optimal transactions, depending on business scenario, in the long run. The proposed dispute mechanism aides in keeping the storage requirements low by in-situ replacing less optimized transactions, while appending them instead would needlessly clutter

---

Algorithm 2. Receive Dispute Proposal

1: $BC \leftarrow Blockchain[Block_0, ..., Block_n]$
2:
3: **function** ON_DISPUTE(M)
4:     $archiveNode \leftarrow$ node preserves old state?
5:     **for** $i \leftarrow 0, M[n]$ **do**
6:         $B \leftarrow M[i]$
7:         **if** $archiveNode$ **then**
8:             $OB \leftarrow BC[B_{height}]$ ▷ retrieve previous original block
9:             $Archive[OB_{height}, OB_{hash}] \leftarrow OB$
10:         **end if**
11:         $BC[B_{height}] \leftarrow B$
12:     **end for**
13: **end function**

---

the blockchain. Using less storage as a side effect allows for a faster synchronization of new blockchain nodes, which enable new parties to participate sooner.

For a preliminary evaluation the proposed dispute mechanism was implemented in the *cadeia*[1] blockchain framework. The cadeia-blockchain is a full-fledged standalone blockchain framework. It is further a multi agent framework allowing for simple replacement of core components that make up a blockchain. Based on the Jadex [4] framework every core component, e.g. Consensus-Agent, can be replaced by a different agent adhering to the same interface description, thus allowing for rapid prototyping of different consensus, peer-to-peer or database technologies. By connecting different agents to the cadeia chain a variety of use cases can be implemented.

By utilizing a multi agent platform like Jadex it is further possible to separate a single blockchain node onto multiple different devices, allowing for the application logic, consensus- and P2P-components to be run on low-end hardware while the data storage resides on cloud or edge storage devices, which can lead to new uses cases in IoT, fog- or edge-computing scenarios.

The proposed approach is not applicable to all types of transactions as it requires that all transactions are of atomic nature. If transactions are dependent on one another (e.g. in Bitcoin), further adjustments need to be made to the blocks. In future work we aim to further enhance the intentional forking mechanism to allow for squashing or cherry-picking of transactions to only hold current and viable transactions. It will also require the detection and resolution of interdependencies of the transactions. This will in turn lead to a blockchain that is capable of reducing its size while running, to allow for faster on-boarding and synchronization of new participants in consortium blockchains.

---

[1] cadeia project site - https://git.informatik.uni-hamburg.de/cadeia/cadeia.

7   Conclusion

In this paper we presented a transaction dispute mechanism for Byzantine-Fault-Tolerant Proof-of-Stake Blockchain consensus. BFT-PoS has strong guarantees on transaction and block-finality, which means that there is only one chain at any given time. We chose to borrow the longest chain rule of Proof-of-Work consensus' to make corrections to previous blocks.

The presented algorithm intentionally creates forks at the contested height, by replacing a non-optimal transaction in a given block and adjusting the hashes and metadata of any succeeding block. By resubmitting the resulting new fork into the consensus mechanism it is guaranteed that all participating validators are agreeing to the adjustment.

References

1. Antonopoulos, A.M.: Mastering Bitcoin: Unlocking Digital Cryptocurrencies. O'Reilly Media Inc., Sebastopol (2014)
2. Ateniese, G., Magri, B., Venturi, D., Andrade, E.: Redactable blockchain-or-rewriting history in bitcoin and friends. In: 2017 IEEE European Symposium on Security and Privacy (EuroS&P), pp. 111–126. IEEE (2017)
3. Bentov, I., Lee, C., Mizrahi, A., Rosenfeld, M.: Proof of activity: extending bitcoin's proof of work via proof of stake. IACR Cryptology ePrint Archive 2014/452 (2014)
4. Braubach, L., Pokahr, A.: Developing distributed systems with active components and jadex. In: Scalable Computing: Practice and Experience, pp. 100–120 (2012)
5. Buterin, V., et al.: A next-generation smart contract and decentralized application platform. White paper (2014)
6. Castro, M., Liskov, B., et al.: Practical Byzantine fault tolerance. In: OSDI, vol. 99, pp. 173–186 (1999)
7. David, B.M., Gazi, P., Kiayias, A., Russell, A.: Ouroboros praos: an adaptively-secure, semi-synchronous proof-of-stake protocol. IACR Cryptology ePrint Archive 2017/573 (2017)
8. Jain, A., Arora, S., Shukla, Y., Patil, T., Sawant-Patil, S.: Proof of stake with casper the friendly finality gadget protocol for fair validation consensus in ethereum. Int. J. Sci. Res. Comput. Sci. Eng. Inf. Technol. 3(3), 291–298 (2018)
9. King, S., Nadal, S.: PPCoin: peer-to-peer crypto-currency with proof-of-stake, 19 August 2012. Self-published paper
10. Krawczyk, H., Rabin, T.: Chameleon signatures. In: NDSS (2000)
11. Kwon, J.: Tendermint: consensus without mining. Draft v. 0.6, fall (2014)
12. Lampson, B., Sturgis, H.E.: Crash recovery in a distributed data storage system, January 1979. https://www.microsoft.com/en-us/research/publication/crash-recovery-in-a-distributed-data-storage-system/
13. Mazieres, D.: The stellar consensus protocol: a federated model for internet-level consensus. Stellar Development Foundation (2015)
14. Nakamoto, S.: Bitcoin: a peer-to-peer electronic cash system (2008)
15. Pontiveros, B.B.F., Norvill, R., State, R.: Monitoring the transaction selection policy of bitcoin mining pools. In: 2018 IEEE/IFIP Network Operations and Management Symposium, NOMS 2018. IEEE (2018)

16. Posdorfer, W., Kalinowski, J., Bornholdt, H., Lamersdorf, W.: Decentralized billing and subcontracting of application services for cloud environment providers. In: Proceedings of the ESOCC 2018 Workshops, pp. 79–89. Springer, Heidelberg (2018)
17. Schwartz, D., Youngs, N., Britto, A., et al.: The ripple protocol consensus algorithm. Ripple Labs Inc., White Paper, 5 (2014)
18. Stübs, M., Posdorfer, W., Kalinowski, J.: Business-driven blockchain-mempool model for cooperative optimization in smart grids. In: International Conference on Smart Trends for Information Technology and Computer Communications. Springer, Heidelberg (2019)
19. Wood, G.: Ethereum: a secure decentralised generalised transaction ledger. Ethereum Project Yellow Paper, 151, pp. 1–39 (2018)

Cross Chain Bribery Contracts: Majority vs Mighty Minority

Quang Tran, Lin Chen, Lei Xu, Yang Lu(✉), and Weidong Shi(✉)

Computer Science Department, University of Houston, Houston, TX 77054, USA
qtran@uh.edu, chenlin198662@gmail.com, xuleimath@gmail.com,
shisunny.yang@gmail.com, wshi3@uh.edu

Abstract. Bribery is a perilous issue in the real world, especially in an economical aspect. This fraudulence is unavoidable, and more importantly, it is more difficult to trace in case smart contracts are utilized for bribing on a distributed public blockchain. In our paper, we propose a new threat to the security of a blockchain system, cross-chain bribery using smart contracts. An arbitrary wealthy briber can utilize cross-chain smart contracts to manipulate a consensus mechanism on a victim's blockchain or to disgrace a victim's blockchain. To better understand this threat, our paper proposes a framework to analyze bribery using cross-chain smart contracts. We analyze the amount of incentive to bribe rational miners in a victim's blockchain and also a full cost of conducting a cross-chain bribery attack. The result is that such attacks can be carried out with a reasonable amount of money or cryptocurrencies.

Keywords: Blockchain · Smart contract ·
Cross-chain bribery contract · Security threat · Selfish mining ·
Rational miner

1 Introduction

Blockchain [8,16,19] provides a decentralized method for records keeping and information/transactions validation. Various applications are developed on top of the blockchain platform. One of these applications is a smart contract, which brings many advantages, e.g., saving time, reducing conflicts, and saving money. Several popular blockchain platforms support smart contracts such as Ethereum, EOS, Hyperledger Fabric, and Stellar, which can be feasible for solving a range of business challenges [2]. Even though smarts contracts provide a fundamental feature to extend usages of the blockchain, people tend to consider an actual usage of them while underestimating adverse effects they can cause. Smart contracts can be utilized in a destructive manner, i.e., bribery to undermine existing consensus mechanisms to gain financial benefits [3,5,18].

As one of the most popular blockchain construction method, the proof-of-work (PoW) based mining process requires a vast computational power to solve

© Springer Nature Switzerland AG 2019
F. De la Prieta et al. (Eds.): PAAMS 2019 Workshops, CCIS 1047, pp. 121–133, 2019.
https://doi.org/10.1007/978-3-030-24299-2_11

mathematical puzzles to produce a valid block. It is tough, if not impossible, for individual miners to compete with professional mining farm corporations. Therefore, individual miners usually join a mining pool to maximize their profits. In other words, we can claim that the miners in public blockchain are not united, and consolidated. They are forming up as a group based on the fundamental factor-maximizing efficiency and incentives. Thus, they can quickly change their mind and easily be manipulated, targeted in a bribery contract attack.

Unlike prior efforts primarily focusing on analyzing selfish mining behaviors using incentives restricted within a specific blockchain system to maximize a briber's beneficial rewards, we aim at outlining the possibility of security and stability of public blockchains and cryptocurrency systems as an economy driven game. We propose a cross-chain bribery attack scheme in which a briber targets at a distributed public blockchain to undermine consensus mechanism on a victim chain through a short-term bribing and manipulating bribed miners. The example scenario in our paper uses the Ethereum blockchain platform as a model to analyze how such an attack can be carried out. The cross-chain attack can be applied to any public blockchain since there always exists selfish behaviors within a public blockchain.

Our contributions in this paper include:

- Providing a holistic view of selfish behaviors on blockchain by showing the feasibility of external influences in the form of cross chain bribery smart contracts.
- Investigating the effect of cross chain external incentives to consensus mechanism of victim blockchain.
- Analyzing possible scenarios and consequences using selfish miners and validators in Ethereum blockchain as an example.
- Providing a possibility of strategy by rational players who maximize profit in a multi-chain and multi-currency setting.
- Suggesting the necessity of additional research on selfish behaviors of rational miners in mining pools.

The rest of the paper is organized as follows. In Sect. 2, we discuss selfish behaviors in blockchain and related works. Then we introduce cross chain incentives in the form of bribery smart contracts and analyze their influences on selfish behaviors on the victim chain. After the analysis, we discuss future research direction and open problems. In the end, we conclude the paper.

2   Selfish Mining Strategy and Related Works

In a blockchain system built on proof-of-work (PoW) and longest chain principle, a regular user works on the latest block on the longest branch to produce a new block. After the user successfully makes a valid block, he/she broadcasts the new block to the whole network immediately to claim the reward. However, selfish miners who want to maximize their benefits can adopt a different strategy to

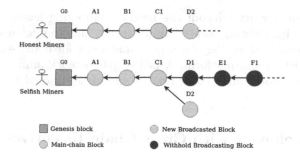

Fig. 1. Selfish miners withhold broadcasting new blocks.

get more rewards. One possible strategy is to hold produced blocks and submits them together to the system (Fig. 1).

The idea of selfish mining gains more attention since it was first proposed in 2014 [11]. The paper pointed out that a simple majority is not enough to protect the security of Bitcoin in a case of the existence of selfish miner. Specifically, they propose an attack that selfish miners can push their revenue up while gaining more rational miners to join the selfish mining pool until it becomes a majority. Following this inspiration, other models are proposed to stir up the attention of researchers and developers in understanding such a potential threat of selfish mining in a public blockchain platform [3,18]. Jian Niu and Chen Feng analyzed selfish mining in the Ethereum platform using a 2-dimensional Markov model to determine a threshold that makes such fraud strategy profitable, which is lower than the one in Bitcoin. However, in reality, the chance of selfish mining occurrence can be meager, or it might not happen. Two essential conditions need to be met which are computational power, and hashing power. Selfish miners must have a strong computational power and control enough hashing power so that they can generate blocks quicker than honest and majority miners. It becomes a game of cat and mouse.

Besides controlling computation to perform selfish mining, a new methodology, known as a bribery contract, is also considered which can achieve similar effects [14,15]. A smart contract is an application written in a programming language by developers running on top of a supported blockchain platform. A smart contract contains a set of rules proposed by a creator to those who interact and accept these rules. When these pre-defined conditions are met, a contract agreement is automatically enforced, and a transaction is also automatically generated to a network to verify before inserting it into a blockchain. A smart contract feature can cause an impact on the current incentive and fairness mechanisms in a blockchain consensus protocol. Selfish miners make use of electronic contracts to create a bribery attack on a targeted blockchain platform by giving bribees incentive rewards for doing fraudulence. One of an example is that briber creates a bribery contract to give an amount of coin token as a reward for those miners who withhold announcing new successful mining block until briber successfully mines and announces this block to a network. This attack can be achieved easily by any wealthy adversary without the need of competing hashing and computational power with existing miners. Importantly, this fraudulence favors both the briber and bribee since they both get some profit for doing so, especially in the case of the Ethereum platform. A briber gets a block mining reward while a bribee also gets both uncle block reward and an additional bribery contract reward.

3   Selfish Behavior with Cross-Chain Incentives

3.1   Bribery Contracts - The New Threat to Consensus

Blockchain has been used to build various applications across many business platforms [20,21], and the smart contract is a fundamental feature to extend blockchain's impacts [7,13,22]. Most existing works consider an actual usage of smart contracts, but tend not to pay attention to the other side of it, i.e., smart contracts can be used in a destructive manner. In particular, smart contracts can be utilized for bribery to affect existing consensus mechanisms. Bribery attacks or bribery contracts are severe problems like the fact that it can manipulate or destroy the fundamental assumption of standard smart contract execution model which primarily relies on consensus or majority accepted outcome [5,6]. An arbitrary person participates in a game and accepts game's rules does not necessarily mean that this person will never be manipulated to change his/her mind when he/she is offered an appealing compensation for violating game's rules. This attack can be achieved easily by any wealthy adversary. Remarkably, tracing a briber in a blockchain system seems to be extremely hard since it is designed as a decentralized environment and to protect user anonymity [12]. Importantly, the fraudulence behavior favors both briber and bribees since they both achieve some goals after.

3.2   Influences from Outside of a Blockchain

A distributed blockchain is built on the platform of many algorithms, security protocols which aim at maintaining unity and fairness for all joining parties. While the algorithms, protocols, and other factors in the blockchain network are fixed and are not likely to change, the human behavior of users in the system is complicated and may be prone to change. Unlike a machine which operates exactly as it is programmed, many people may change their behavior based on the surrounding conditions (and thus deviate from the protocol), and this is mainly the case for those who are chasing economic benefits in a system of financial incentives like a blockchain.

The Fig. 2 shows the power hash rate of Bitcoin and Ethereum mining pools. Note that these mining pools are not operated by individual ones. Instead, these are groups of miners who join a mining pool to get a better profit. In other words, these can be rational miners who intentionally chase the profit in mining. If they are offered a better amount, there is no doubt that they can easily switch.

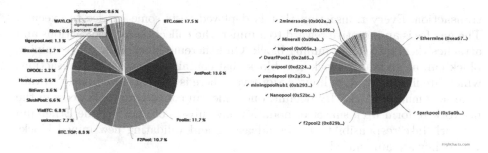

Fig. 2. Bitcoin and Ethereum mining pool hash rate power (https://btc.com/stats/pool, https://www.etherchain.org/charts/topMiners)

"Why buy when you can rent?" [4] since there always exist rational miners in a distributed-public blockchain. Note that our paper is aimed to discuss on possibility of cross-chain bribery attack. A briber or a group of briber targets and attacks a public blockchain on purpose. They are whales and have enough fund to perform an attack on another blockchain in favor of controlling block generation or disgracing another blockchain. Remarkably, the briber does not require to have a majority of hashing power nor to participate in mining. They can create a cross-chain contract to fascinate those rational miners in a targeted blockchain network.

4   Case Study and Analysis

In this section, we provide an example scenario of cross-chain bribery contract using decentralized-base platform Ethereum as a model architecture and victim chain. Note that the scenario can be applied on any public blockchain platform.

4.1   Ethereum Platform

Ethereum [9], a second largest decentralized cryptocurrency platform by market capitalization [1], allows for the execution of smart contracts on the blockchain. To create a protocol for smart contracts which offer beneficial and efficient interactions between participants in the network, Ethereum builds a Turing-complete machine, called as Ethereum Virtual Machine or EVM, as the heart of its blockchain platform. Developers can create their application, run on EVM using any friendly programming languages, to create their own arbitrary rules of ownership, transaction formats, and state transition functions. Thus, in term of a smart contract, Ethereum can sometimes be considered as a "world computer".

   In Ethereum, a user is called a client. A client that runs mining on Ethereum blockchain is called a miner/a node. A client can send ETH, which is the cryptocurrency of Ethereum, to a smart contract or to other clients by issuing a

---

[1] Available from: https://coinmarketcap.com/all/views/all/.

transaction. Every transaction that is deployed costs some gas fee to execute. The gas fee is an incentive reward to a miner who collects those transactions and attaches them into a new mining block. On Ethereum blockchain, a new mining block can be an empty block or a block that contains a number of transactions which are limited by "gas limit". Moreover, there is no centralized party to validate new mining blocks. By default, one node can connect up to 25 peers in the network to form up a subset of nodes. Many subsets of nodes in the Ethereum network take responsibility for broadcasting and validating new mined blocks when they are announced.

4.2   Ethereum Blockchain Structure

In Ethereum, there are two types of blocks - an uncle block and a main block. A main block is a valid block and is appended to a longest chain. Unlike Bitcoin platform which does not accept a late broadcasting block as an uncle block, Ethreum offers this feature to maintain the security of the chain, which allows for faster block generation time ($\approx$15 s in Ethereum, and $\approx$10 min in Bitcoin). A standard Ethereum's block structure consists of three components: a block header (contains parent's block hash, account's address, Merkle Tree root hash, a time stamp, block's difficulty, and a nonce,...), list of references to uncle blocks (max uncle reference is 2), and a set of transactions. While a main block contains three components as above, an uncle block only contains a block header. To be considered as an uncle block, this block requires to be referenced by another next main block within 7 rounds (see Fig. 3). Otherwise, it will be considered as "block lost".

4.3   Mining Reward

In Bitcoin blockchain, because block generation time is high ($\approx$10 min) which overcomes block propagation delay, an orphan block-a block is broadcast after a main block- is discarded and is not given any reward. Unlike Bitcoin, Ethereum aims to increase transaction's throughput by decreasing a block generation time ($\approx$15 s). Thus, to maintain the security of its chain, a late broadcasting block is also accepted as an uncle block and is given a partial reward. Hence, there are three types of block rewards: a main block reward, an uncle block reward, and a nephew block reward [10,17]. The main block reward is being used in both Bitcoin and Ethereum, which gives a reward to encourage those miners to solve a computational puzzle as fast as possible. The uncle and nephew block rewards are exclusive rewards by Ethereum. Because uncle blocks are submitted later than the main block, they are only given a partial reward which depends on when another main block references them. And the main block which references the uncle block is also given an additional reward, which is a nephew reward, to encourage miners attaching uncle blocks to maintain the chain's security (Table 1).

Each miner who successfully mines a main block can receive a reward of 2.0 ETH (not include nephew rewards, transactions fee reward). The uncle block

Table 1. Mining reward

	Ethereum	Bitcoin	Usage
Main reward	Yes	Yes	Incentive mining block
Uncle reward	Yes	No	Maintain chain's security
Nephew reward	Yes	No	Encourage to reference uncle block
Bribe uncle reward	No	No	Special reward in our theory giving to miner who mines on fork chain
Bribe accepted reward	No	No	Special reward in our theory giving to nodes who accept blocks on fork chain

reward is not a fixed number. The amount of reward is various since an uncle block is required to be referenced by a later main block. The sooner it is referenced, the higher the reward it is given. An equation to calculate an uncle block reward as:

$$U_R = (U_n + 8 - B_n) * R/8$$

U_R: uncle reward U_n: Uncle block height $R = 2.0$ ETH
B_n: referenced by main block's height

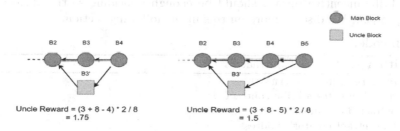

Uncle Reward = (3 + 8 - 4) * 2 / 8
            = 1.75

Uncle Reward = (3 + 8 - 5) * 2 / 8
            = 1.5

Fig. 3. Uncle block reward varies by time

In our theory scheme, we propose two more additional rewards to achieve a bribery attack: a bribe uncle reward and a bribe acceptance reward. The bribe uncle reward is given to those miners who accept to mine a block on a fork-chain instead of a longest chain. The bribe accepted reward is a reward giving to those clients/nodes which accept and insert a block on a fork-chain into their blockchain. The amount of each reward is discussed later in the following section.

4.4   Bribery Contract and Pseudocode

In our scheme of cross-chain bribery attack, we use the Ethereum blockchain platform as a model architecture to provide an example scenario. Note that this scheme can be applied on any public blockchain which is targeted by the briber. To set up our scheme, we consider the case of one briber who targets Ethereum to perform the bribery cross-chain attack. The briber has an account with his/her crypto-coins on another blockchain platform and also has enough money to perform this attack. Remarkably, a briber can be any individual-wealthy person or a group of people. They do not necessarily have a majority or even own any of Ethereum's computational power to do this bribery cross-chain attack. Their goal is to manipulate miners/nodes in the Ethereum network to control the generation of blocks or to disgrace Ethereum blockchain.

Miners run the mining process to find a block in getting an incentive reward. They can be an individual miner or can join a mining pool to pursue a more beneficial reward. Notably, they all share a common concept - maximizing the efficiency and profit of their mining process. More importantly, even if a miner is honest in the classical case, it does not necessarily mean they remain to be honest when they are offered a better compensation [3,5,11,18]. Thus, a bribery cross-chain contract is feasible when both a briber and bribees can achieve their goals.

In our scenario, we propose a *BribeContract* that rewards miners who intentionally mine blocks on a fork-chain, and also rewards bribees who accept and insert this new mining block into their chain. These pre-defined rules are created by the briber. Furthermore, a transaction reward is automatically issued when bribees prove that they meet the requirements. Our proposed approach requires one briber to pay a full cost to perform this cross-chain attack. The amount of the bribe incentive reward should be enough appealing so that bribees are willing to join. We discuss more on this in the following section.

Pseudocode:

Algorithm 1. Propose Contract

1: **procedure** BRIBE CONTRACT
2: - Briber B creates a bribe contract β
3: - Contract β contains:
4: + α_a: contract creator's address
5: + μ_m: amount incentive for mining block on fork-chain
6: + μ_a: amount incentive for accepting mining block on fork-chain
7: + γ: total side-chain token deposits into the contract
8: + $f(b)$: a context to identify arbitrary bribee (b)
9: + $f(c)$: a context function of condition (c) is met
10: + $f(t)$: a context to terminate contract when a fork-chain becomes a main chain.
11: + S_b: starting block on fork chain.
12: **end procedure**

Algorithm 2. Prove and Commit

---

    procedure PROVE
2:    - Bribee (b) proves contract's condition (c) is met
        if $c = mining\ block\ on\ fork\ chain$ **then**
4:        b commits a fork-chain to contract β
        end if
6:    **if** $c = accepting\ block\ on\ fork\ chain$ **then**
        b commits a fork-chain to contract β
8:    **end if**
    end procedure

Algorithm 3. Verify

---

    procedure VERIFY
    - A block should stay within a range of required number blocks
3:    - For example: $S_b \dots \leftarrow U_v \leftarrow U_{v+1} \leftarrow U_{v+2} \dots \leftarrow U_{v+7}$
        if $c = mining\ block\ on\ fork\text{-}chain$ **then**
            if $U_v \in [S_b, U_{v+7}]$ **then**
6:            $b \leftarrow \mu_m$
            end if
        end if
9:    **if** $c = accepting\ block\ on\ fork\text{-}chain$ **then**
            if $U_v \in [S_b, U_{v+7}]$ **then**
            $b \leftarrow \mu_a$
12:        **end if**
        end if
    end procedure

Algorithm 1 presents the contract proposal. This contract includes all required variables, functions to detect, to verify and to give incentive reward to bribees when a contract's condition is qualified. Algorithm 2 shows the process of a bribee, proving how he/she is qualified to receive a reward. If a bribee mined a block on a fork-chain, he/she should send its chain which is started from block S_b up to the latest block on a fork-chain. The similar request is also required in case of the bribees accepting and inserting a mined block on a fork-chain. Due to that Ethereum's chain structure design is tamper-free, a verifying block to be submitted must stay within a range of multiple blocks on the fork-chain. Algorithm 3 verifies this requirement to give a corresponding reward to bribees.

4.5 Incentive Discussion

The cross-chain bribery framework we described before needs to encourage both bribers and bribees to participate in such an attack. The incentive mechanism consists of two parts:

- Incentive reward that bribees receive when participating in a cross-chain bribery attack.
- The cost that a briber must pay so that they can achieve his/her goals.

Bribees: Although miners can be honest in the traditional mining process (without bribery), it does not necessarily mean they remain to be honest when they are offered a better compensation. The amount of Ethereum token that one miner receives can be described as:

$$\theta_h = \frac{\alpha}{\beta} \times R \times \frac{3600}{\phi},$$

where: (i) θ_h denotes a number of receiving tokens in one hour (ii) α denotes a hashing power of hardware using to solve a computational puzzle (iii) β denotes a network hash rate (iv) R denotes a main block reward ($R = 2$ ETH) (v) ϕ denotes a block generation time [1].

Unlike Bitcoin, it is less common to use ASIC to mine Ethereum. Most miners use GPU or CPU for mining. Thus, we set the value α in the range $[10, 400]$ MHash/s in our model.

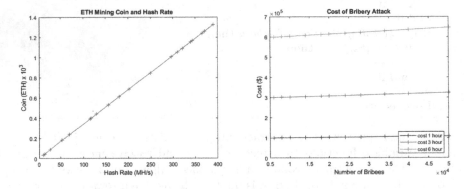

Fig. 4. Hourly reward and bribery contract cost

Table 2. Cost of cross-chain bribery attack

Number of bribees	1 h ($)	3 h ($)	6 h ($)
10,000	100,400	301,300	602,500
20,000	102,200	306,600	613,300
30,000	104,000	312,000	624,000
40,000	105,800	317,300	634,700
50,000	108,000	324,000	648,000

Figure 4 (left) shows the hourly reward that honest miners can receive by their contribution of a hash rate in mining a new block. The maximum ETH token that miners ($\alpha = 400$ MHash/s) can receive in one hour is around $\theta_h = 0.0014$ ETH/h. If a briber offers these rational miners a better incentive amount (i.e. $\tau_h = 0.002$ Token-worth(\$) in cross-chain for accepting new blocks, and $\gamma = 3.0$ Token-worth(\$) for mining on the fork-chain), rational miners have a high possibility to join our bribery cross-chain attack. The incentive bribe reward that bribees-rational miners in mining pool-can get if they join the attack as:

$$\Gamma = \tau_h + \frac{\alpha}{\beta} \times 3 \times \frac{3600}{\phi}.$$

Briber: A briber can be any wealthy-individual person or a group of people. They have enough fund to perform a cross-chain bribery attack. Their goal is to control blocks' generation or to disgrace Ethereum blockchain by bribing rational miners/nodes in the network. The major issue is how much it costs to perform such an attack. Figure 4 (right) and Table 2 show that the budget of cross-chain bribery attack is acceptable to bribers.

Consequences: In our model, a block generation time ϕ is around 15 s. Within six hours, the number of blocks can be generated by bribed miners is around 1440 blocks. If a briber targets one public blockchain to deploy cross-chain bribery attacks within a short time (i.e. 6 h of attack), their cost (see Table 2 and Fig. 4) to perform such an attack is lower than the potential damage caused to a victim blockchain. The attacker can potentially undermine a consensus mechanism of a victim chain or secretly shot a price of the victim chain currency while gaining financial benefits of dropped price or aim to disgrace the targeted chain.

5 Future Research and Open Problems

Our work points to a new direction of analyzing the security and stability of public blockchains and cryptocurrency systems. Distinguishing from prior efforts primarily focusing on analyzing selfish behaviors using incentives confined within a blockchain system (e.g., block reward), our approach applies a holistic view of of systems where a network of public blockchains and crypto-currencies are considered as inter-connected systems where external influences can happen in the form of cross-chain transactions and contracts. This may significantly change the selfish behaviors of users, and affect our understanding of sustainability and stability of public blockchain systems.

Our preliminary results suggest the necessity of additional research, in particular, detailed modeling of decisions and strategies that may be adopted by rational players in the existence of cross-chain incentives for selfish behaviors, risk posed by cross-chain bribery contracts to stability and well-being of victim chains, holistic analysis of strategy by rational players who maximize profit in multi-chain and multi-currency setting, and possible mitigation strategies and design options.

Holistic analysis under the agent perspective raises many open problems with respect to the nature of players in public blockchains. Although researchers are amenable to introduce rational players in analyzing public blockchains, there is a lack of consensus on proper assumptions of the players and implications of the assumptions to long term sustainability of public blockchain systems. In the presence of rational players with in-chain behaviors influenced by cross-chain rewards, how does it affect a theoretical analysis of blockchain consensus and security properties? In particular, an adversary can potentially gain profit from one chain by deliberately inducing disruptions to other chains. It means that selfish players who engage in bad behaviors within a blockchain may not necessarily look for rewards within the same blockchain.

6   Conclusion

Blockchain has found a variety of applications and it is critical to guarantee the correctness of the system. We study a new threat to the security of a blockchain, cross-chain bribery using smart contracts. Bribery is a perilous problem in the real world, especially in an economical aspect. It is unavoidable fraud and more importantly, difficult to find since it is utilized by cross-chain smart contracts on the distributed public blockchain. Recent studies have shown corrupted fraud utilizing smart contracts to conduct bribery. In our paper, we improve this idea by proposing a cross-chain bribery attack to undermine a victim's consensus mechanism. In this paper, we outline the possibility of a cross-chain bribery attack by bribing selfish, rational miners in a targeted network and discuss the potential example scenario. A cross-chain bribery attack is feasible to facilitate on public blockchains and cryptocurrency systems due to the fact that there always exist rational miners who are incentivized by beneficial rewards. The possibility of all miners avoid short term benefit to protect a long term one seems to be negligible. People might realize they did harmful things to others. However, in terms of getting a better beneficial reward, no one would even doubt trying to do such a thing. Remarkably, the cost of carrying out one cross-chain bribery attack can be acceptable while it can cause tremendous on a victim's chain such as dropping the price, or disgracing victim's blockchain.

References

1. Ethereum network status. https://ethstats.net
2. What are the most reliable smart contract platforms?, November 2018. https://www.cointelligence.com/content/smart-contract-platforms-guide/
3. Bai, Q., Zhou, X., Wang, X., Xu, Y., Wang, X., Kong, Q.: A deep dive into blockchain selfish mining. CoRR arXiv:abs/1811.08263 (2018)
4. Bonneau, J.: Why buy when you can rent? In: Clark, J., Meiklejohn, S., Ryan, P.Y.A., Wallach, D., Brenner, M., Rohloff, K. (eds.) FC 2016. LNCS, vol. 9604, pp. 19–26. Springer, Heidelberg (2016). https://doi.org/10.1007/978-3-662-53357-4_2

5. Chen, L., et al.: The game among bribers in a smart contract system. In: Zohar, A., et al. (eds.) FC 2018. LNCS, vol. 10958, pp. 294–307. Springer, Heidelberg (2019). https://doi.org/10.1007/978-3-662-58820-8_20

6. Chen, L., Xu, L., Gao, Z., Shah, N., Lu, Y., Shi, W.: Smart contract execution - the (+-)-biased ballot problem. In: ISAAC (2017)

7. Chen, L., Xu, L., Shah, N., Gao, Z., Lu, Y., Shi, W.: Decentralized execution of smart contracts: agent model perspective and its implications. In: Brenner, M., Rohloff, K., Bonneau, J., Miller, A., Ryan, P.Y.A., Teague, V., Bracciali, A., Sala, M., Pintore, F., Jakobsson, M. (eds.) FC 2017. LNCS, vol. 10323, pp. 468–477. Springer, Cham (2017). https://doi.org/10.1007/978-3-319-70278-0_29

8. Christidis, K., Devetsikiotis, M.: Blockchains and smart contracts for the internet of things. IEEE Access **4**, 2292–2303 (2016)

9. Ethereum: ethereum/wiki. https://github.com/ethereum/wiki/wiki/White-Paper

10. Ethereum: ethereum/wiki. https://github.com/ethereum/wiki/wiki/Mining

11. Eyal, I., Sirer, E.G.: Majority is not enough: bitcoin mining is vulnerable. In: Christin, N., Safavi-Naini, R. (eds.) FC 2014. LNCS, vol. 8437, pp. 436–454. Springer, Heidelberg (2014). https://doi.org/10.1007/978-3-662-45472-5_28

12. Heilman, E., Baldimtsi, F., Goldberg, S.: Blindly signed contracts: anonymous on-blockchain and off-blockchain bitcoin transactions. In: Clark, J., Meiklejohn, S., Ryan, P.Y.A., Wallach, D., Brenner, M., Rohloff, K. (eds.) FC 2016. LNCS, vol. 9604, pp. 43–60. Springer, Heidelberg (2016). https://doi.org/10.1007/978-3-662-53357-4_4

13. Karamitsos, I., Papadaki, M., Barghuthi, N.B.A.: Design of the blockchain smart contract: a use case for real estate. J. Inf. Secur. **09**(03), 177–190 (2018). https://doi.org/10.4236/jis.2018.93013

14. Kothapalli, A., Cordi, C.: A bribery framework using smartcontracts (2016)

15. McCorry, P., Hicks, A., Meiklejohn, S.: Smart contracts for bribing miners. In: Zohar, A., Eyal, I., Teague, V., Clark, J., Bracciali, A., Pintore, F., Sala, M. (eds.) FC 2018. LNCS, vol. 10958, pp. 3–18. Springer, Heidelberg (2019). https://doi.org/10.1007/978-3-662-58820-8_1

16. Nakamoto, S.: Bitcoin: a peer-to-peer electronic cash system (2008)

17. Nakamoto, W.S.: A next generation smart contract & decentralized application platform (2015)

18. Niu, J., Feng, C.: Selfish mining in ethereum. CoRR arXiv:abs/1901.04620 (2019)

19. Udokwu, C., Kormiltsyn, A., Thangalimodzi, K., Norta, A.: An exploration of blockchain enabled smart-contracts application in the enterprise (2018). https://doi.org/10.13140/RG.2.2.36464.97287

20. Xu, L., Chen, L., Gao, Z., Lu, Y., Shi, W.: CoC: secure supply chain management system based on public ledger. In: 2017 26th International Conference on Computer Communication and Networks (ICCCN), pp. 1–6 (2017). https://doi.org/10.1109/ICCCN.2017.8038514

21. Xu, L., Chen, L., Shah, N., Gao, Z., Lu, Y., Shi, W.: DL-BAC. In: Proceedings of the 26th International Conference on World Wide Web Companion - WWW 2017 Companion (2017). https://doi.org/10.1145/3041021.3053897

22. Xu, L., et al.: Enabling the sharing economy: privacy respecting contract based on public blockchain, pp. 15–21 (2017). https://doi.org/10.1145/3055518.3055527

Workshop on MAS for Complex Networks and Social Computation (CNSC)

Workshop on MAS for Complex Networks
and Social Computation (CNSC)

Many of the systems that can be found in our environment can be modeled as complex adaptive systems that consist of a dynamic network of agents (which may represent individuals, businesses, services, resources) that perform a set of activities in parallel and react to what other agents are doing. Multi-agent systems are considered a suitable tool for the study of complex adaptive systems and especially those that are distributed and dynamic. The Workshop on MAS for Complex Networks and Social Computation is focused on providing a forum in which researchers from many disciplines and methodological backgrounds discuss ideas, research questions, recent results, and future challenges in this emerging area of research and public interest.

Organization

Organizing Committee

Vicente Botti
Elena Del Val
Miguel Rebollo

Program Committee

Ludovico Boratto	Data Science and Big Data Analytics, EURECAT, Spain
Victor Sanchez Anguix	Coventry University, UK
Jaume Jordán	Universitat Politècnica de València, Spain
Carlos Carrascosa	Universitat Politècnica de València, Spain
Carmen Karina Vaca Ruiz	Escuela Superior Politécnica del Litoral, Ecuador
Francisco Grimaldo	Universitat de València, Spain
Alberto Palomares	Universitat Politècnica de València, Spain
Angelo Costa	Universidade do Minho, Portugal
Emilia Lopez Iñesta	Universitat de València, Spain
Miguel Rebollo	Universitat Politècnica de València, Spain

Decentralizing Decision Making Process of Simultaneous Bilateral Negotiations of Large Multiagent Systems in e-Commerce Applications Using Holonic Structures

Subha Fernando[1,2](✉)📵, Damith Premasiri[2]📵, Vishma Dias[2]📵,
Upali Kohomban[2]📵, Yohan Welikala[2]📵, and Harsha Subasinghe[2]📵

[1] University of Moratuwa, Moratuwa, Sri Lanka
subhaf@uom.lk
[2] Codegen International Pvt. Ltd., Colombo, Sri Lanka
{damith,vishma}@codgen.net, {upali,yohan,harsha}@codgen.co.uk

Abstract. Automated strategic negotiation is a key technology which facilitates to reach agreements between self-interested agents. Existing mechanisms mainly practice principles of auction mechanisms in which a single seller handles many buyers. The key advantage of that approach is the facility for the guarantee to reach the optimal deal because of global knowledge the seller has regarding the demand at hand. However, the main limitation of such an approach is the difficulty of exercising different negotiation strategies with different opponents. Although concurrent multiagent negotiation approaches resolve many of these limitations, the existing frameworks and protocols are too simplistic to handle dynamicity of larger multi-agent negotiation systems situated in very dynamic environments. The dynamicity of a large number of simultaneous bilateral negotiations can be appropriately coordinated through a topological structure that decentralises the autonomy of decision-making process under centralised supervision with the help of appropriate scheduling and planning mechanisms. This paper presents an application of a framework which coordinates the dynamicity of simultaneous bi-lateral negotiations by using Holonic structures. The framework possesses a top-down hierarchical structure with a decentralised control which takes the bottom-up perspective for effective decision making. The framework was simulated in an e-commerce application and showed how practically our approach could be utilised to model real-world scenarios to handle simultaneous bi-lateral negotiations of large multiagent systems.

Keywords: Holonic multiagent systems ·
Bilateral Concurrent Negotiations · e-Commerce applications

F. De la Prieta et al. (Eds.): PAAMS 2019 Workshops, CCIS 1047, pp. 137–151, 2019.
https://doi.org/10.1007/978-3-030-24299-2_12

1   Introduction

Multiagent systems consist of a collection of individual agents, each of which exhibits a certain degree of autonomy with respect to its actions and perception when they interact with the dynamic and uncertain environments. These autonomous agents can operate within flexible organisational structures by encapsulating the complexity of subsystems and by modularising its functionality [12].

Automated negotiation is a technology that facilitates an agreement between agents without revealing their utility spaces in agent systems. Both in multiagent negotiation and bilateral-agent negotiation, agent's utility may be changed due to the variations in the situated environment. As a result, the agent changes strategies and the associated utility space [6]. Auction mechanisms have mainly been used in one-to-many negotiation to obtain an agreement, where a single seller maintains bi-lateral negotiations simultaneously with multiple buyers. This way of negotiation with multiple buyers at a time allows the seller agent to compromise in one bilateral negotiation since he has a chance of winning another in a margin. Simultaneous negotiation among agents has been applied in various applications, such as agents seeking one side agreement or agreement among several agents independently with some inter-relations among specific issues in their goal [24]. This kind of approaches allows the system to reach strategically the best agreements under centralised supervision. However, in auctions, it is difficult to exercise different negotiation strategies with different opponents, and therefore, it needs greater flexibility.

Concurrent multiagent negotiation frameworks [17], protocols [7], strategies [1,21] and schemes [14] are trying to address these limitations of auction systems by facilitating concurrent bi-lateral many-to-many negotiation in different methods. In concurrent negotiation one agent negotiates simultaneously with several other agents to reach an agreement. A framework has been proposed in [17] to support one-to-many negotiations by coordinating concurrent many one-to-one bilateral negotiations. However, consistency and coordination are too difficult to handle as the number of agents involved increases. Coordinating the negotiation thread by performatives based protocol is discussed in [7] which has introduced two-phases of accept and reject into the alternating offers protocol. The protocol supports agents to use pre-accept or pre-reject performatives to deal with concurrent encounters. By doing so, the negotiation finishes the first phase and reaches the second phase, which calls for the final counter-offers to finalise the deal. The protocol mediates the negotiation process by coordinating the agents' negotiation threads to handle inconsistencies. However, as similar to other concurrent approaches, it is difficult to coordinate and handle larger concurrent multiagent negotiation systems using such a protocol especially when there are many overlapping options available for negotiation.

Automated negotiation is also an essential feature of e-marketplaces in which an individual seller handles a buyer. In such situations, where negotiation happens for limited resources, it requires extensive planning and sharing of activities to properly allocate the available resources for both the current and the future demand, while making individual oriented strategic responses. This paper presents a Holonic structure to support simultaneous bi-lateral negotiations among automated entities under proper planning and scheduling. The framework can be scaled up to handle a large number of agents and their concurrent negotiations due to its topological distribution of decision process and its attached scheduling and planning processes. The proposed approach has been practically tested on e-commerce application where a large number of agents simultaneously negotiate the price of hotel packages for bookings.

The rest of the paper is organized as follows: Sect. 2 presents brief overview of holonic multiagent systems. Section 3 outlines shared activity coordination mechanisms. Section 4 describes the application in e-commerce which uses the holonic framework and the experiential results. Finally 5 includes concluding remarks.

2   Holonic Multiagent Systems

The Holonic multiagent systems define agent-groups recursively by allowing dynamic organisation of the system during runtime. Agents in Holonic multiagent systems are called holonic agents if they compose of many sub-agents with the same inherent structure [19].

Agent-based Holonic Systems have been mainly applied into the process of scheduling in manufacturing systems because of its combinatorial aspects and dynamic nature [4] well support the inherent dynamicity in manufacturing systems. Holonic Multiagent approach has been implemented for scheduling in manufacturing systems as a distributed scheduling over a number of agents using local knowledge to improve the global performances of the system. Significant research findings principally adapted by many others in the manufacturing industry can be found in Paulo et al. [15]. They have assigned holon concepts to the entities: tasks, operations, and supervisors, in manufacturing systems which make decisions based on the available information. The communication channels between these holons have been established as economic exchanges to discourage unnecessary communication. The dynamic scheduling has been introduced to facilitate the dynamic interaction between the holon agents. These holons are organised in a hierarchy where supervisor holon coordinates operational holons or set of other supervisor holons. The chief supervisor generates a globally optimised schedule based on the information received from others. Further, to allocate the required resources among the operational holons, a multi-round contract net has been used which enables to call the contract net protocol iteratively until an agreement is reached.

Another useful perspective defines a holon as a whole and a part that consists of several holons as sub-structures. With this perspective, the Holonic systems in manufacturing have been proposed to combine a top-down hierarchical organisational structure with a decentralised control which takes the bottom-up perspective. In such multiagent systems, an agent appears as a single entity to the outside world may be composed of many sub-agents. These sub-agents decide whether to join into the coherent structure of the super-agent and act as a single entity based on the utility they receive. Agents consist of sub-agents with the same inherent structure are called holonic agents [11].

A holonic structure can be classified into main categories based on the degree of autonomy prossessed by sub-holons of the holon. If a model gives the full autonomy to all sub-holons, then head of the holon becomes a virtual entity only. In there, tasks are executed as a joint-intention with resource sharing through explicit communication. Another model of holonic multiagent systems is the creation of a single agent by merging the functionalities of sub-agents. In this case, sub-holons completely give-up their autonomy and merge into one agent. The decision of creating one agent by merging the sub-holons or terminating the agent to create sub-holons is taken based on the system requirements. These models are possible when a centralised agent allocates the same set of goals and the tasks for all the sub-holons. The other model which comes under the holonic multiagent systems enables each sub-holon to assign part of autonomy to the head of the holon. In there, the head-holon performs administrative tasks such as making the decisions and communicating them within, and outside the holon, adding new sub-holon or removing existing sub-holons from the holon, and planning and scheduling the tasks for sub-holon to execute [11,18].

A few significant researches are carried out in holonic multiagent systems in e-commerce applications [22,25]. A very few significant research can be found in facilitating negotiations in e-commerce applications using holonic multiagent systems [2,3]. These researches mainly targeted to develop learning based negotiation protocol between body holons and the head of holon.

3   Shared Activity Coordination

In simultaneous bi-lateral negotiation under constrained resources, reaching a consensus on their commitments is highly crucial before each entity starts a negotiation. Otherwise, it generates inconsistencies and invalid commitments during the process. Possible ways of implementing such coordination between agents have been critically analysed, and only the relevant literature is presented here.

Continuous Activity Scheduling, Planning Execution and Re-planning (CASPER [23]) has been developed as a distributed planning and scheduling environment for autonomous agents by extending the ASPEN. ASPEN is one of the important object-oriented systems primarily designed to provide a reusable set of components that can model the elements of intricate planning and scheduling systems [16]. CASPER consists of a modelling language to define the application domain precisely, constraint management systems for maintaining resource constraints and domain operability, and a temporal reasoning system for maintaining temporal constraints. CASPER was evaluated on autonomous rovers on Mars and has been successful in achieving the mission. The main characteristics of CASPER support the distributed planning by letting each rover maintain onboard planner and allowing them to do planning locally to face any slow communication channels between rovers. The central planner optimises the current plans at the rover level under a conflict resolution mechanism.

Bradley and Antony [5] have proposed a shared activity coordination mechanism which has been developed for autonomous agents in space application by extending CASPER. Their algorithm provides a platform for agents to coordinate their plans and it is composed of two windows: commitment window and shared window. Agents should setup values for the parameters of shared activities during the consensus window before committing. A shared activity has been defined as a tuple consisting of parameters: agent role, decomposition and constraints. These constraints mainly restrict the possible values for the parameters, but agents have been granted the permission to override these parameter values according to their privileges. The protocols specify communication channels, pathways and how to process the received information. Length of consensus window is determined by summing the expected execution time to reach consensus. This particular approach coordinates the shared activities by window functions and assigns a degree of autonomy to each agent-role according to their privileges. The constraints define possible values for parameters which guarantee the activities lie within feasible solution space.

4 Holonic Multiagent Systems in e-Commerce Applications

The proposed framework is explained here by considering an online hotel booking scenario of a seven-star hotel as an example. The hotel has at least 30 to 40 buyers come on-line to negotiate customizable hotel-packages for booking. These buyers are connected through chatbots. A chatbot is the interface of the seller of Holonic multiagent system. The facility of negotiating hotel-packages is the open-pricing concept of hotel industry which is in demand today. The scenario can be viewed as a simultaneous many one-to-one bilateral multi-issue negotiation. The process involves a large number of seller agents, and contains many options for negotiations such as change of room-type, shifting of check-in date, changing of auxiliary items, change of duration of stay, bargaining of the room price, alternating additional items, etc. In addition to those, the sellers need to exercise different strategic negotiations for different customers. More importantly, the negotiation process runs on limited resources because of the availability of a number of rooms, and other items. Seller's commitment to the buyer also plays a vital role here.

4.1 A Seller as a BGP Agent

Belief-Goal-Plan(BGP) is an extension of the Belief-Desire-Intention(BDI) Framework introduced under reactive agents [6]. A deep reinforcement learning is prevalent in Chatbot-applications as a key mechanism to support learning appropriate responses to user-queries [20]. Our seller agents are BGP agents connected with reinforcement learning to select the appropriate actions that are suited to a particular buyer. Among those actions, bi-lateral price bargaining is one of the important actions introduced to seller agents. The agent's action of price bargaining was adopted from the models proposed in Fatima et al. [8–10] which explore the possibility of selecting an optimal strategy based on the available but incomplete information. The proposed method defines optimal strategy as the best response to the opponent's actual strategy and reaches equilibrium within a bounded time interval.

However, in real-time chatbots based negotiation platforms, negotiation time is not the only critical parameter but there are other parameters such as efficiency (i.e. the number of agents satisfied with negotiation results), stability(i.e. sharing of experiences enhancing the efficiency of the system) [13] which are also key factors that determine the success of an automated strategic negotiation. Therefore, the model proposed by Fatima et al. [10] is further extended by facilitating the seller to practice strategies during the negotiation using behavioral-dependency and the time-dependency tactics based on the customer responses. The efficiency and time taken to reach an agreement are considered when updating the value function of the reinforcement learning algorithm.

4.2   Holon Structure and Information Flow

The framework follows the definition of holonic multiagent systems which enables each sub-holon to assign part of autonomy to the head of the holon. The head-holon performs administrative tasks such as making the decisions and communicating them within, and outside the holon, adding new sub-holon or removing existing sub-holons from the holon, and planning and scheduling the tasks for sub-holon to execute.

Agents in our framework are mainly classified into three levels based on the administrative privileges each agent-type possesses. Transaction agent is the supreme agent that has the control of the negotiation phase, called the head of the holon. Assistant agents are the body of the holon, which has the same sub-structure as head but with less administrative autonomy. Seller agents communicate to appropriate assistant agents based on a key (described later), and they have less administrative autonomy than assistant agents. Communication channels between these agents are specified using contract-net protocols. This particular structure allows top-down hierarchal organisational structure with a decentralised control which takes the bottom-up perspective in decision making as described next. Figure 1 shows initialisation of seller agents and assistant agent to the system.

Figure 2 shows the overall structure of the system and information stored at the individual level when negotiation takes place. A revenue agent is an external entity in the system which announces price margins - upper (UB) and lower(LB) boundaries per room-type per day based on a revenue optimisation algorithm. Accordingly, transaction agent releases lower and upper- price boundaries for each day for each room type. Head of the holon communicates price range to assistants, and then to the sellers. The price ranges released by the revenue agent are valid only within a window time interval. With the expiration of the time window, the revenue agent revises the price boundaries for the negotiation for the next window period. A buyer agent initiates the buying process by clicking on the Chatbot interface. A seller agent is created for each buyer. Based on the buyer-requirements, seller generates a key combining duration of stay, check-in date, room type, qty, an id of the buyer, etc. to identify each buyer uniquely. With the creation of sellers, assistants are also created based on the generated key if necessary. Moreover, these sellers are assigned to assistants based on the generated key. The main part of the key contains room-type, check-in date and length of stay. If there is no assistant created for the requested combination of the main part, a new assistant is created. The current demand for a given date range is available at the assistant level. Therefore, assistants could set up an artificial lower boundary within the price boundaries based on the on-site demand. The amount to be increased by the assistant agent for a given booking date is determined by linear regression function which was trained using historical data. Furthermore, since assistants have the current demand, request price ranges, available resources, etc., they inform these details to the seller so that this information can be utilised for marketing strategies. An assistant's lifetime is terminated when the number of sellers it handles is equal to zero. Knowledge accumulated at each agent level, tasks executed and administrative autonomy they possessed are described in Table 1.

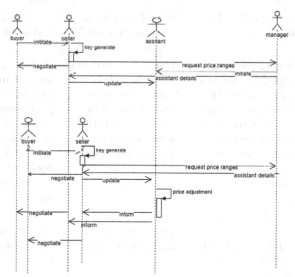

Fig. 1. Initialization of agents in the Holonic multiagent system

The overall process of negotiation happens under two phases to avoid conflicts in resource allocations and inconsistencies in price boundaries. Figure 3 shows the processes initiated and continued within the predeclared time window (w) by a revenue agent. At the start of each window, the revenue agent sends the lower- and upper boundaries for each day for each room type to transaction agent. These boundaries are sent to the assistant agents with the highest priority which overwrites all the existing price boundaries. Based on the available local knowledge about the current demand (see Table 1), assistant agents redefine lower boundary ALB, $UB \geq ALB \geq LB$. These ALB values are periodically (with substantial time interval) sent to the transaction agent. The global view of the on-site demand allows the transaction agent to redefine the lower boundary $M - ALB$, $UB \geq M - ALB \geq LB$. Before c time period to the end of w, $c < w$, the updated price boundaries are recorded at the revenue agent so that he could re-adjust the predicted price boundaries and initiate new w window. By following this process, prices are adjusted based on local knowledge at the assistant level and confirmed globally at higher levels. Proper coordination is the critical element for having successful joint task processes.

Figure 4 depicts the flow of information and authentication process associated with the negotiation before a booking is committed. Seller agents are allowed to start negotiation if the resources are available, and the query is valid only. Before confirming the booking, seller agents request permission to commit the booking being negotiated. They initiate a protocol with a topic called *IBC-*

Table 1. Distribution of autonomy and knowledge in Holon multiagent system

	Seller	Assistant	Transaction agent
Initialisation	Initialised with a new buyer	Initialised with a new non-repeated key generation	Initialised with the first seller
Task	Negotiates with buyer, Proposes a price within the given price range, Changes strategies and suggests to change booking requirements and conditions	Can setup artificial lower boundary within the issued price range, and contacts both the seller agents and transaction agent	Can setup artificial lower boundary within the issued price range by looking at the overall demand at onsite, and can communicate with both the assistant agents and revenue agent
Knowledge	Only buyer profile and his requirements, price proposed by the buyer	Onsite demand per room type for a given date-range	On-site demand for all the constrained resources available at hand
Autonomy	Determines the price reduction rate, strategies to play, and customised the booking	Revises the lower boundary of the price range under a particular key combination	Revises the lower boundary of the price range for all the resources based on artificial lower boundaries setup by assistants

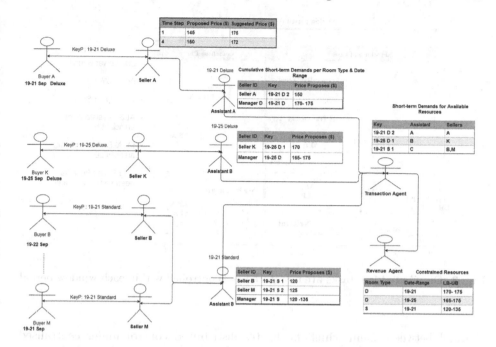

Fig. 2. Overall structure and Information stored at each agent level. For each buyer a seller is created, if there is no assistant to handle newly generated keyP (main key combination) a new assistant is created. Sellers have details about offers and counter-offers of a particular buyer. Assistants have details about all the counter-offers made by buyers of a particular room type for a given date range. On the other hand, the transaction agent has all the counter-offers made by all the buyers

Inform Before Confirmed, to receive the permission to book the room by the negotiated price from transaction agent. If it is confirmed only, seller agents are allowed to confirm the booking. Buyer is given a predefined time-interval to complete the booking; if he could not, the temporally booked resource reopens for negotiation. The role of assistants is essential because they provide a summary of the demand for a given date-range to the transaction agent, which is later used by the revenue agent to revise the price-boundaries. Moreover, until revenue agent revises the price-boundaries, assistants could revise the lower bound to suit the current demand. The role of assistants is crucial here to decentralise the decision process under centralised supervision of transaction agent.

4.3   Features of the Holonic Multiagent System

Here it is described the main characteristics of our holonic multi-agent system.

Holonic Structure and Distributed Autonomy. Holonic substructure of the transaction and the assistant agents, allows for a structured communication

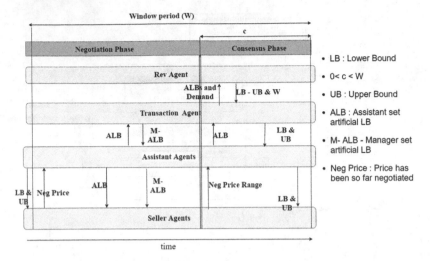

Fig. 3. Distributed join tasks are monitored and controlled within each window period

channel between them which facilitates distributed control under centralised supervision. As per the holon-definition, no communication channels between assistants have been established. Therefore, any information to assistant agents should be triggered from or passed through the head-holon. Seller agents are connected to each assistant agent at the higher levels of the hierarchy. From a transactional perspective, each assistant can be considered as an auctioneer for a given range of date period for a particular room type, which manifests global performance through centralised supervision. In order to avoid possible overlapping of bookings between assistants, the head-holon takes control of negotiated prices before a booking is confirmed to a buyer by requesting sub-holons to trigger *IBC* request as explained above.

Simultaneous Bi-Lateral Holon Agent Negotiation. The framework facilitates simultaneous bi-lateral multi-issue negotiations; here assistant agents play the role of auctioneer and transaction agent plays the role of an auctioneer of the set of auctions maintained by his assistants. However, from the perspective of a buyer, it is the buyer targeted well personalised strategic negotiation. Sellers can adjust negotiation strategies to suit the buyer's preference and customised the requirements to match the buyer's objective.

Decentralized Decision Making Under Centralized Supervision. Seller agent makes decisions for which strategy to play and the amount to be reduced which is based on the buyer's intent and negotiation style. However, before confirming the booking, the seller must request permission from the transaction agent through an assistant. Therefore, decisions are made and committed

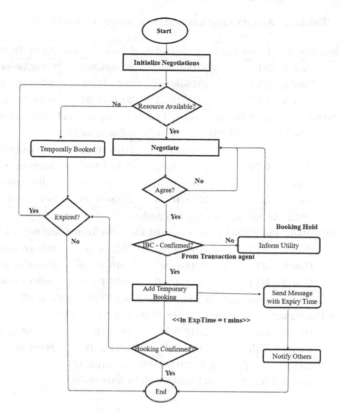

Fig. 4. Shared Activity coordination by transaction agent

under centralised supervision. The confirmation for booking makes the transaction agent call proposals from assistant agents to see whether there is a better offer than the requested (This is essential to manage prices of booking-requests with overlapping days which are handled by two different assistant agents). Such an approach encourages transaction agent to use local knowledge of seller to find the optimal deal for a given resource. Further, the top-down organisational structure in the Holonic structure eases the flow of decision to the lower-level while encouraging bottom-up reporting structure for the effective decision-making process.

4.4 Case Study: Holonic Multiagent System on e-Commerce Applications

The framework was evaluated by defining a use case. The creation of agents and associated assistant agents are shown in Table 2. As indicated in the table, when the number of buyers is increasing, the number of sellers also increases. The assistant agents are created only when no date-overlap could be found within the existing assistants. If there is a request that covers the date-range handled

Table 2. Agents creation and assignment to Assistants

Checkpoint No.	Buyer	Room type	Check-in date	Checkout date	Agents@Checkpoints
Check 0.	User 1	RT1	2018-9-27	2018-9-30	SellerAgent1
	User 2	RT1	2018-9-30	2018-10-02	SellerAgent2
	User 3	RT1	2018-10-03	2018-10-04	SellerAgent3

Assistant1 (2018-9-27 to 2018-10-02) is created for SellerAgent1 and SellerAgent2.
Assistant2 (2018-10-03 to 2018-10-04) is created for SellerAgent3

Check 1.	User 4	RT1	2018-10-03	2018-10-04	SellerAgent4
	User 5	RT1	2018-10-03	2018-10-04	SellerAgent5
	User 6	RT1	2018-10-07	2018-10-08	SellerAgent6
	User 7	RT1	2018-10-06	2018-10-08	SellerAgent7

SellerAgent4 and SellerAgent5 are assigned to Assistant2.
Assistant3 (2018-10-06 and 2018-10-08) is created for SellerAgent6 and SellerAgent7

Check 2.	User 8	RT1	2018-9-25	2018-9-30	SellerAgent8
	User 9	RT1	2018-9-28	2018-10-02	SellerAgent9
	User 10	RT1	2018-10-06	2018-10-10	SellerAgent10

SellerAgent8, and SellerAgent9 are assigned to Assistant1 (2018-9-25 to 2018-10-02)
SellerAgent10 is assigned for Assistant3 (2018-10-06 and 2018-10-10)

Check 3.	User 11	RT1	2018-9-29	2018-10-11	SellerAgent11
	User 12	RT1	2018-9-26	2018-9-27	SellerAgent12

SellerAgent11 is assigned to Assistant3 (2018-10-06 and 2018-10-11)
SellerAgent12 is assigned for Assistant1 (2018-9-25 to 2018-09-30)

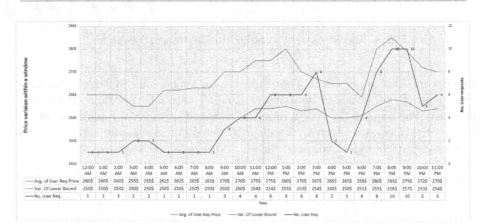

Fig. 5. Price variation within a window interval

by two different assistants, then the assistant who has the higher overlap handle the request.

Based on the predicted demand for September and for October, the revenue agent releases (250 − 290$) as the price boundary for the next window interval for room type *RT1*. The number of user requests made to book room type *RT1* on $2018 - 09 - 27$ is shown in Fig. 5. As depicted in the figure, as the number of user requests increases, the lower-boundary is set to a higher value within the released price boundary by assistant agents. So, therefore, the consensus prices of the buyers also go up as the lower boundary is raised to handle the high demand.

Thus delegating the administrative task of setting lower-boundary within the predefined price-boundary allows not only decentralises autonomy but also uses of local knowledge and short-term variations effectively at ground level before it reaches the higher level for decision making. This mechanism does not harm the hierarchical organisation because the confirmation is required from the centralised transaction agent to avoid resource conflicts. The holonic approach implemented in the system makes assistant agents work as a part of the head of the holon, and thus they are required to update the head-of holon before finalising price boundaries. This approach allows the centralised agent to be more efficient in decision making because decisions are made on the recommendations coming from the grassroots level.

5   Conclusions

Chatbot systems are very popular in e-commerce applications as Information bots. However, by integrating intelligent agents into these chatbots, they can be employed for more intelligent activities. Here, we introduced a multiagent platform for many one-to-one multi-issue negotiations using Holonic structures. The conventional approaches for bi-lateral negotiation are based on interactions between individual agents, or auctioneer agent. However, using these approaches, it is too difficult to handle the large automated multiagent systems in very dynamic environments where individual oriented strategic negotiations are required. Concurrent multiagent systems have answered this limitation for smaller agent-based systems, but their coordination and monitoring algorithms are too difficult to apply in larger negotiation systems. This paper presented an application of using a holonic agent framework that facilitates simultaneous bilateral multi-issue negotiation of multiagent systems using Holonic structure. The framework is scalable to handle large number of simultaneous bilateral multi-issue negotiations. The proposed framework can also be viewed as an extension to the concurrent multiagent framework proposed by [17] in which simultaneous bilateral negotiations are connected directly to an agent similar to the transaction agent. The introduction of assistant agents are crucial because they decentralise the decision-making process and respond vibrantly to the short-term demand. The transaction agent can easily handle conflicts in resource allocations and inconsistencies in the settled prices. The holonic structure of the system enables the proper distribution of autonomy under predefined obligations. The window functions help to coordinate the shared activity, the degree of autonomy assigned at holons define the ability to overwrite price boundaries. These features enable coordination of the dynamicity of simultaneous many one-to-one bilateral negotiations of larger systems more effectively as demonstrated by using hotel package-booking scenario.

References

1. Alrayes, B., Kafal, O., Stathis, K.: Concurrent bilateral negotiation for open e-markets: the Conan strategy. Knowl. Inf. Syst. **56**, 463–501 (2018)
2. Beheshti, R., Barmaki, R., Mozayani, N.: Negotiations in holonic multi-agent systems. In: Fukuta, N., Ito, T., Zhang, M., Fujita, K., Robu, V. (eds.) Recent Advances in Agent-based Complex Automated Negotiation. SCI, vol. 638, pp. 107–118. Springer, Cham (2016). https://doi.org/10.1007/978-3-319-30307-9_7
3. Beheshti, R., Mozayani, N.: Homan, a learning based negotiation method for holonic multi-agent systems. J. Intell. Fuzzy Syst. **26**, 655–666 (2014)
4. Botti, V., Giret, A.: A multi-agent Methodology for Holonic Manufacturing Systems, vol. XVI, Hardcover (2008)
5. Bradley, C., Anthony, B.: Activity coordination. Technical report, Jet Propulsion Laboratory, California Institute of Technology, USA (2003)
6. Cao, M., Luo, X., Luo, X., Dai, X.: Automated negotiation for e-commerce decision making: a goal deliberated agent architecture for multi-startegy selection. Decis. Support Syst. **73**, 1–14 (2015)
7. Dang, J., Huhns, M.N.: Concurrent multiple-issue negotiation for internet based services. IEEE Internet Comput. **10**, 42–49 (2006)
8. Fatima, S.S., Wooldridge, M., Jennings, N.R.: Optimal negotiation strategies for agents with incomplete information. In: Meyer, J.-J.C., Tambe, M. (eds.) ATAL 2001. LNCS (LNAI), vol. 2333, pp. 377–392. Springer, Heidelberg (2002). https://doi.org/10.1007/3-540-45448-9_28
9. Fatima, S., Wooldridge, M., Jennings, N.R.: A comparative study of game theoretic and evolutionary models for bargaining for software agents. Artif. Intell. Rev. **23**, 185–203 (2005)
10. Fatima, S., Wooldridge, M., Jennings, N.R.: Comparing equilibria for game-theoretic and evolutionary bargaining models. Artif. Intell. Rev. **23**(2), 187–205 (2005)
11. Fischer, K., Schillo, M., Siekmann, J.: Holonic multiagent systems: a foundation for the organisation of multiagent systems. In: Mařík, V., McFarlane, D., Valckenaers, P. (eds.) HoloMAS 2003. LNCS (LNAI), vol. 2744, pp. 71–80. Springer, Heidelberg (2003). https://doi.org/10.1007/978-3-540-45185-3_7
12. Jennings, N.: Agent based computing: promise and perils. In: Proceedings of the 16th International Joint Conference on Artificial Intelligence, vol. 3, pp. 1429–1436 (1999)
13. Kraus, S.: Automated negotiation and decision making in multiagent environments. In: Luck, M., Mařík, V., Štěpánková, O., Trappl, R. (eds.) ACAI 2001. LNCS (LNAI), vol. 2086, pp. 150–172. Springer, Heidelberg (2001). https://doi.org/10.1007/3-540-47745-4_7
14. Panagidi, K., Kolomvatsos, K., Hadjiefthymiades, S.: An intelligent scheme for concurrent multi-issue negotiations. Int. J. Artif. Intell. **12**, 129–149 (2014)
15. Paulo, L., Restivo, F.: A holonic approach to dynamic manufacturing scheduling. Robot. Comput.-Integr. Manuf. **24**(5), 625–634 (2007)
16. Powell, G.M.: Using continuous-planning techniques to achieve autonomy and coordination among multiple unmanned aerial vehicles, Technical report. U.S Army Communications-Electronics Command, Software Engineering Center, Fort Monmouth, NJ, USA(2001)
17. Rahwan, I.: Intelligent agents for automated one-to-many e-commerce negotiation. In: Twenty-Fifth Australian Computer Science Conference: Conference in Research and Practice in Information Technology (2001)

18. Schillo, M.: Self-organizing and adjustable autonomy: Two sides of the same medal. Technical Report WS-02-03, American Association for Artificial Intelligence (2002)
19. Schillo, M., Fischer, K.: Holonic multiagent systems. Technical report (2003)
20. Serban, I.V., Sankar, C., Germain, M., Zhang, S.: A deep reinforcement learning chatbot. In: Proceedings of the 31st Conference on Neural Information Processing Systems (2017)
21. Sim, K.M.: Complex and concurrent negotiations for multiple interrelated e-markets. IEEE Trans. Cybern. **43**, 230–245 (2013)
22. Tao, L., Gao, J.G., Mo, Z.: Study on the holonic agent-based integrated electronic commerce system of the tourism destination. In: The International Conference on E-Business and E-Government, ICEE (2010)
23. Estlin, T., Rabideau, G., Mutz, D., Chien, S.: Using continuous planning techniques to coordinate multiple rovers. Comput. Inf. Sci. **5** (2000)
24. Tsuruhashi, Y., Fukuta, N.: Next Frontier in Agent-Based Complex Automated Negotiation, Chap. 1. Studies in Computational Intelligence, vol. 596, 1st edn, pp. 3–18. Springer, Japan (2007)
25. Ulieru, M., Walker, S.S., Brennan, R.W.: Holonic enterprise as a collaborative information ecosystem. In: The Workshop on Holons: Autonomous and Cooperating Agents for Industry (2001)

Collective Behavior of Large Teams of Multi-agent Systems

Franciszek Seredyński and Jakub Gąsior[✉]

Department of Mathematics and Natural Sciences,
Cardinal Stefan Wyszyński University, Warsaw, Poland
{f.seredynski,j.gasior}@uksw.edu.pl

Abstract. In this paper, we study conditions of emergence of the phenomenon of collective behavior of agents in large multi-agent systems. Agents act in the two-dimensional (2D) Cellular Automata (CA) space, where each of them takes part in spatial Prisoner's Dilemma (PD) game. The system modeled by 2D CA evolves in discrete moments of time, where each cell-agent changes its state according to a currently assigned to its rule. Rules are initially assigned randomly to cells-agents, but during iterated game agents may replace their current rules by rules used by their neighbors. While each agent is oriented on a maximization of its own profit in the game, we are interested in answering the question if and when a phenomenon of global cooperation in a large set of agents is possible. We present results of the experimental study showing conditions and degree of emerging such cooperation.

Keywords: Agent-based modeling · Bounded rationality ·
Information in financial markets

1 Introduction

Recent advances in the development of computer-communication technologies require the application of new large scale multi-agent systems to provide effective distributed management. In an e.g., Internet of Things (IoT) hundreds of tiny sensors monitoring some area fully depend on their limited capacity batteries and sensors should locally cooperate to spare their energy to maximize a lifetime of the whole sensor network (see, [4]). In e.g. cloud computing thousands of human users and also devises of IoT will automatically require access to computing resources demanding computing resources with a predefined efficiency and level of security (see, [5]). These demands can be potentially fulfilled by solving in a centralized way a huge optimization problem with a request of full information about the system resources and users demands, what is intractable for realistic problems. Therefore we propose a large scale multi-agent approach, where agents are capable to solve these kinds of problems. The main requested ability of such multi-agent systems is the ability of collective behavior. The proposed system is

© Springer Nature Switzerland AG 2019
F. De la Prieta et al. (Eds.): PAAMS 2019 Workshops, CCIS 1047, pp. 152–163, 2019.
https://doi.org/10.1007/978-3-030-24299-2_13

based on a model of non-cooperative game theory and works in the framework of Cellular Automata (CA).

Prisoner's Dilemma (PD) game [8] is one of the most accepted game-theoretical models where both *cooperation* and *defection* of humans can be observed. A. Tucker formalized the game as the 2-person game and in 1980's Axelrod organized the first tournament [1] to recognize competitive strategies in the game. The winner was a strategy Tit-For-Tat (TFT) which assumes cooperation of a player on the first move and subsequent repeating actions of the opponent player used in the previous move. Next, Axelrod proposed [2] to apply Genetic Algorithms (GAs) to discover strategies enabling cooperation in the 2-person PD game. GAs were able to discover TFT strategy and a number of other interesting strategies specific for humans.

Discovering strategies of cooperation in N-person PD games ($N > 2$) is more complex problem. Therefore Yao and Darwen proposed in [12] another approach where GAs are still applied but the payoff function of the game was simplified. The main idea of the simplified payoff function was that a payoff of a given player in the game depends on a number of cooperating players among the remaining $N - 1$ participants of the game. Under these assumptions, GA was able to find strategies of players enabling global cooperation for a number of players equal to around 10. For more players, such strategies were not discovered by GA. One of the main reasons for that is the form of the payoff function which in fact assumes participation of a player in a game with a "crowd" - a large number of anonymous persons.

A concept of spatial games in 2D space with a neighbor relation between players helps to solve the crowd problem. Among the first concepts related to spatial Prisoner's Dilemma (IPD) was a game on the ring considered by Tsetlin [10] in the context of games of Learning Automata (LA), where a payoff of a given player depends on its action and actions of two immediate neighbors. A number of spatial IPD games on 2D grids has been studied recently. Nowak and May proposed [7] an original spatial IPD game on a 2D grid with two types of players - players who always cooperate (*all-C*) and players who always defect (*all-D*). Players occupy cells of 2D space and each of them plays PD game with all neighbors and depending on the total score is replaced by the best performing player in the neighborhood. They show that both types of players persist indefinitely in chaotically changing local structures.

Katsumata and Ishida in [6] extended the model of spatial IPD games proposed by [7] by considering 2D space as the 2D CA and introducing an additional strategy called k-D, which tolerates at most k defections in local neighborhood. They showed the emergence of specific spatial structures called membranes created by players using k-D strategies, which separate cooperating and defecting players.

In this paper we consider the model proposed in [6] but we focus on the study of conditions of emerging collective behavior in large CA-based teams of players. In the literature related to multi-agent collective behavior the term collective behavior concerns three classes of systems [3, 9] with specific characteristic of behavior: (a) spatially-organizing behaviors, where agents have a little interaction with an environment but they coordinate themselves to achieve a desired spatial formation, (b) collective exploration, where agents a little interact between themselves but interact with an environment to achieve some goal and (c) cooperative decision making, where agents both coordinate their actions and interact with an environment to accomplish some complex tasks. While CA belongs to the first class according to this classification, LA belongs to the second class. The distinctive feature of this paper is that we combine these two approaches in such way that we use CA-based multi-agent model but we want to inspect a degree of its global collective behavior measured by a total number of cooperating players, i.e. an ability to maximize the average total payoff of all agents of the system like it is expected from LA-based systems.

The structure of the paper is the following. In the next Section some background concerning CA is given. Section 3 contains details of the studied spatial IPD game. Section 4 contains results of the experimental study of the model from point of view of the ability of collective behavior, and the last Section contains Conclusions.

2   Cellular Automata

CA are spatially and temporally discrete computational systems (see, e.g. [11]) originally proposed by S. Ulam and J. von Neumann and today they are powerful tools used in computer science, mathematics and natural science to model different phenomena. One-dimensional (1D) CA is in the simplest case a collection of two-state elementary cells arranged in a lattice of the length n, which locally interact and evolve in a discrete time t.

For each cell i ($0 \leq i \leq n - 1$) called a central cell, a neighborhood of a radius r is defined. The neighborhood consists of $n_i = 2r + 1$ cells, including the cell i. A cyclic boundary condition is applied to a finite size of CA, which results is in a circle grid.

It is assumed that a state q_i^{t+1} of the i-th cell at the time $t + 1$ depends only on states of its neighborhood at the time t, and a transition function f called also a rule defines the way of updating the cell i. If CA updates states of its cells according to a single rule assigned to all cells, such CA is called a uniform CA. If two or more different rules are assigned to update cells, such CA is called a non-uniform CA.

Two dimensional (2D) CA is 2D lattice consisting of $n \times n$ elementary cells. For each cell a local 2D neighborhood of a radius r is defined. At a given discrete moment of time t each cell (i, j) is in some state $q_{i,j}^t$, in the simplest case it is a binary number 0 or 1.

At discrete moments of time, all cells synchronously update their states according to assigned to the local rules (transition functions), which depend on states of their neighborhood. A cyclic boundary condition is also applied to the finite size of 2D CA. 2D CA can be also uniform or non-uniform. In classical CA rules assigned to cells are not changed during evolving CA cells.

3   Iterated Spatial Prisoner's Dilemma Game

We consider 2D CA of the size $n \times n$. Each cell of CA has a Moore neighborhood of radius r, and also a rule assigned to it which depends on the state of its neighborhood.

Each cell of 2D CA will be considered as an agent (player) participating in the iterated spatial Prisoner's Dilemma (ISPD) game [6]. Each player (a cell of CA) has two possible actions: C (cooperate) and D (defect). It means that at a given moment of time each cell is either in the state C or the state D. Payoff function of the game is given in Table 1.

Table 1. Payoff function of a row player participating in ISPD game.

Action	Cooperate (C)	Defect (D)
Cooperate (C)	$R = 1$	$S = 0$
Defect (D)	$T = b$	$P = 0$

Each player playing a game with an opponent player in a single round (iteration) receives a payoff equal to R, T, S or P, where $T > R > P = S$. Values of these payoffs used in this study are specified in Table 1, where $P = S = 0$, $R = 1$, and $T = b$ $(1.1 < b < 1.8)$. This relaxation of the model by assuming $P = S$ is done to focus on the study of the influence of the main parameter of the payoff function - the parameter b. If a player takes action C and the opponent player also takes action C than the player receives payoff equal to $R = 1$. However, if a player takes action D and the opponent player still takes action C, the defecting player receives payoff equal to $T = b$. In two remaining cases, a player receives a payoff equal to 0.

In fact, each player associated with a given cell plays in a single round a game with each of his 8 neighbors and this way collects some total score. After q number of rounds (iterations of CA) each cell (agent) of CA can change its rule (strategy). We assume that considered 2D CA is non-uniform CA, and to each cell one of the following rules can be assigned: *all-C* (always cooperate), *all-D* (always defect), and *k-D* (cooperate until not more than k $(0 \le k \le 7)$ neighbors defect). The strategy *k-D* is a generalized strategy TFT, and when $k = 0$ it is exactly the strategy TFT.

A player changes its current strategy into another one comparing collected during q rounds total score with scores collected by his neighbors. He selects as his new strategy the strategy of the best performing neighbor, i.e. the player whose the collected total score is the highest. This new strategy is used by a cell (player) to change its current state, and the value of the state is used in games during the next q rounds.

It is worth to notice that the considered 2D CA differs from a classical CA, where rules assigned to cells do not change during evolving CA in time. CA with a possibility of changing rules is called the second-order CA. In opposite to classical CA, the second-order CA has potentials to solve optimization problems.

The main research issue in [6] was to study conditions of appearing of specific structures called membranes created by cells using k-D rules which protected cooperated players from defected players. In this study, we are interested in the collective behavior of a large team of players, in particular in conditions of emerging global cooperation in such teams.

4   Experimental Results

4.1   Parameter Settings

The following settings were used in the experiments.

- 2D CA with a size of 100×100 was used, i.e. with a total number of agent-players equal to 10000.
- An initial state C or D (player action) of each cell (agent-player) was set with probability $p_1 = 0.5$.
- To each cell one of 3 rules (all-C, all-D, k-D) was assigned with probabilities $p_{21} = 0.2$, $p_{22} = 0.2$ and $p_{23} = 0.6$, respectively; for all runs a constant value of $k = 7$ for the strategy k-D was used, but for a cell to which rule k-D was assigned, the value of k was an integer number randomly generated from the range $[0, \ldots, k]$.
- A neighborhood of each cell was set to $r = 1$.
- For a given run the value of b was selected from the range $[1.1, \ldots, 1.8]$.
- Updating of rules assigned to cells was conducted after $q = 1$ rounds (iterations).
- During a single run of an experiment, depending on values of b, a number of rounds ranged from 200 to 1000.
- If averaging of results was applied it was done on the base of 50 single runs.

4.2   Experiment #1: Sample Runs of ISPD Game

The purpose of the first set of experiments was to observe the typical dynamics of the game under a constant value of the parameter b of the payoff function. For the value of $b = 1.4$ ten sample runs of the game are shown in Fig. 1.

One can see in Fig. 1 (upper) that in all ten runs the team of players achieves a level of global cooperation close to 90% after around 500 iterations (red color). Before reaching this level of cooperation we can observe how frequencies of applying by players strategies all-C (orange color), all-D (green color) and k-D (blue color) were changing. The dominating strategy used by near 80% of players becomes all-D strategy. The number of players using all-C is decreasing in time to reach eventually the stable value of around 20%. The number of players using the strategy all-D is also decreasing to reach the value close to 0.

Figure 1 (lower) shows details of k-D strategy used by players. One can see that in each run around 45%–70% of players use 3-D strategy (green color)

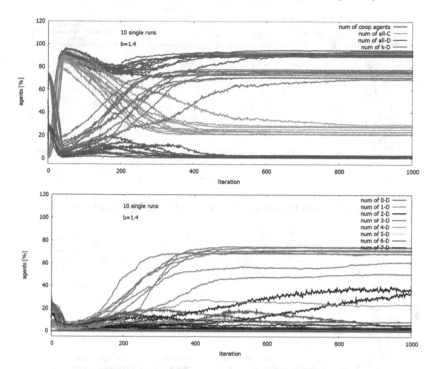

Fig. 1. Ten sample runs for $b = 1.4$: frequency of cooperation of agents and their strategies (upper) and frequencies of applied k-D strategies (lower). (Color figure online)

which assumes willing to cooperate until a number of defecting neighbors is less or equal to 3. The remaining around 30% of players use 2-D strategy (graphite color) and from around 5% to 20% uses 4-D strategy (orange color). Other k-D strategies like e.g. 0-D strategy corresponding to TFT strategy (red color) appears in the runs but finally is not accepted by players.

4.3 Experiment #2: Runs of ISPD Game Under Different Values of Parameters b

The purpose of the second set of experiments was to learn systematically a behavior of players in the game for different values of the parameter b under the same remaining setting parameters as shown above. Presented results were obtained on averaging of 50 runs.

Figure 2 shows results of runs for the value of parameter $b = 1.1$. One can see that after around 25 iterations of the game the players' team achieves the level of near 95% cooperation (red color). Near 90% of players use all-C strategy (orange color) and a few percentage of players use k-D strategy (green color).

The strategy k-D (blue color) is eliminated. One can see that the standard deviation of the observed parameters of the game is close to 0. One can see a similar behavior of the team of players in the games with values of $b = 1.2$

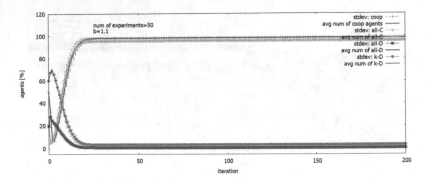

Fig. 2. Runs for values of $b = 1.1$. (Color figure online)

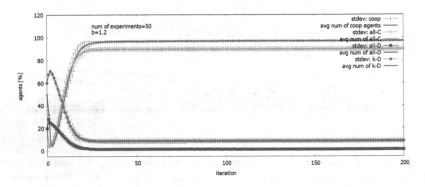

Fig. 3. Runs for values of $b = 1.2$. (Color figure online)

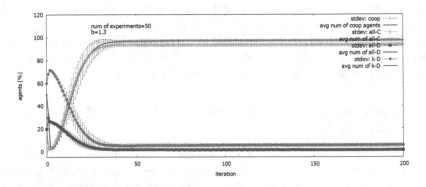

Fig. 4. Runs for values of $b = 1.3$. (Color figure online)

(see, Fig. 3) and $b = 1.3$ (see, Fig. 4). Players' team achieves still the level of near 95% cooperation but with an increasing value of the parameter b, increases the number of players using the strategy k-D assuming a tolerance to defecting neighbors and decreasing the number of players using the strategy all-C. This

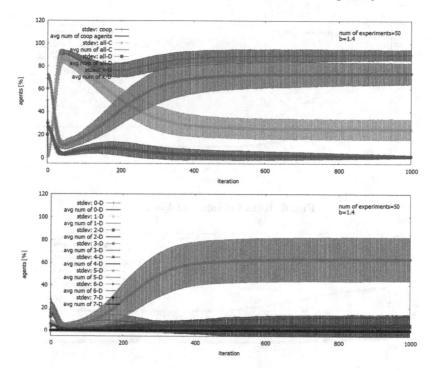

Fig. 5. Runs for $b = 1.4$: frequency of cooperation of agents and their strategies (upper) and frequencies of applied $k - D$ strategies (lower).

process of increasing the tolerance to defecting neighbors is accompanied by an increase of the standard deviation of the values of the parameters.

When $b = 1.4$ (see, Fig. 5(a)) a high level of cooperation in the team is still possible, as it was already signalized in Fig. 1 (upper). Around 90% of players still cooperate but now it is a result of applying by about 70% of players the k-D strategy and by about 25% of players all-C strategy. We can also notice an increasing number (about 5%) of players using strategy all-D. Reaching by players a stable equilibrium requires about 500 iterations and is much higher than for lower values of b. The whole process of shifting in a number of players applying a given strategy in the game is accompanied by a visible increase of the standard deviation of the parameters of the game.

Figure 5(b) shows details of k-D strategy used by players when $b = 1.4$. One can see that about 60% of players using k-D strategy apply 3-D strategy, and remaining 40% of players apply k-D strategies with other values of k.

When $b = 1.5$ the level of global cooperation drops to above 70% (see, Fig. 6) and is characterized by a relatively large standard deviation. This level of cooperation is maintained mainly by players using all-C strategy and in a limited degree by players using k-D strategy.

When $b = 1.6$ cooperation reaches only the level of about 25% and is provided by players which use all-C strategy. The same number of players (around 25%)

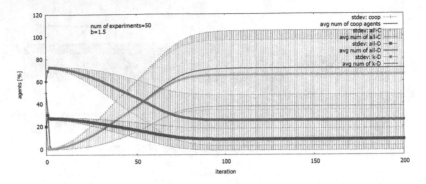

Fig. 6. Runs for values of $b = 1.5$.

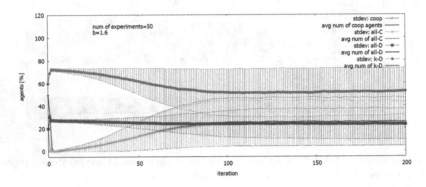

Fig. 7. Runs for values of $b = 1.6$.

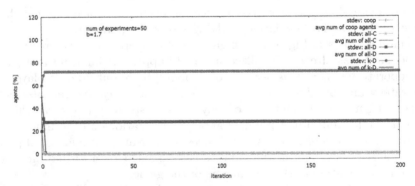

Fig. 8. Runs for values of $b = 1.7$.

use *all-D* strategy. Relatively large number of players (around 50%) uses *k-D* strategy (Fig. 7).

When $b = 1.7$ (see, Fig. 8) and also for values of $b \geq 1.7$ a global cooperation will not emerge in the team of players. Players use mostly (around 70%) *k-D* strategy or *all-D* strategy (around 30%).

4.4   Experiment #3: Patterns of Agents' Strategies

For presented above dependencies between the level of global cooperation and the parameter b accompany spatial patterns of strategies used by players.

Figure 9 (left) shows corresponding spatial pattern of players' strategies used by them in the game with the parameter $b = 1.1$. One can see that dominating strategy used by players is strategy all-C (white color) and some players use strategies all-D (black color) and k-D (tones of orange color which depends on the value of k). Strategies of players which use either all-D or k-D strategies create short, isolated, sometimes vertical or horizontal regular structures.

For games with values $b = 1.2$ (not shown) and $b = 1.3$ (see, Fig. 9 (right)) spatial structures of strategies are similar like for the game with $b = 1.1$, but we can observe an increasing length of regular vertical and horizontal structures, which are still isolated for $b = 1.2$, but more connected for $b = 1.3$. We can see also an increasing number of strategies k-D which replace the strategy all-C.

For $b = 1.4$ (see, Fig. 10 (left)) spatial structure of strategies are created by isolated small clusters of all-C strategies and rarely clusters of strategies all-D, both surrounded by strategies k-D.

When $b = 1.5$ (see, Fig. 10 (right)) spatial structures of strategies are created by long irregular isolated chains with two types of granularity of k-D strategies and all-D strategies.

When $b = 1.6$ (see, Fig. 11 (left)) the structure of spatial strategies is similar to that observed for $b = 1.4$. However, in this case we can see appearing new small clusters of all-D strategies.

Finally, when $b = 1.7$ (see, Fig. 11 (right)) we can notice that none of players uses all-C strategy but dominating strategy performed by them is strategy k-D with different values of k and some clusters of players use the strategy all-D.

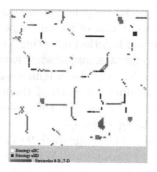 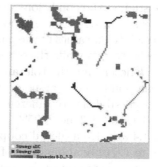

Fig. 9. Strategies distribution for: $b = 1.1$ (left) and $b = 1.3$ (right). (Color figure online)

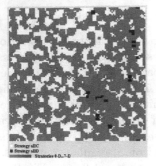 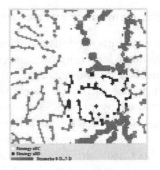

Fig. 10. Strategies distribution for: $b = 1.4$ (left) and $b = 1.5$ (right).

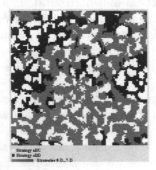 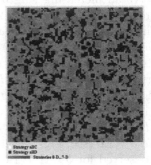

Fig. 11. Strategies distribution for: $b = 1.6$ (left) and $b = 1.7$ right).

5   Conclusions

We have studied the conditions of emergence of global cooperation in large CA-based agent teams. We have shown that the phenomenon of global cooperation depends mainly on values of the parameter b of payoff function reflecting a gain of a player who defects while the other players still cooperate, and to some extent on the value k describing the tolerance of players on defecting by neighbor-players.

We can point four regions of values of the parameter b, each of them characterizing possibilities of emergence of global cooperation. For the values of b between 1.1 and 1,3 near 95% of agents are willing to cooperate. When b is between 1.4 and 1.5 a global cooperation level is in the range 70%–90%. When b is close to 1.6 only about 25% of agents are able to cooperate. When b reaches 1.7 or more no cooperation is observed in the system.

If someone is planning an application of a game-theoretic approach to design a distributed management system he should be aware that more tight requirements concerning the payoff function parameters should be fulfilled.

References

1. Axelrod, R.: The Evolution of Cooperation. Basic Books Publishing, New York (1984)
2. Axelrod, R.: The evolution of strategies in the Iterated Prisoner's Dilemma. The Dynamics of Norms (1987)
3. Brambilla, M., Ferrante, E., Birattari, M., Dorigo, M.: Swarm robotics: a review from the swarm engineering perspective. Swarm Intell. **7**(1), 1–41 (2013)
4. Gąsior, J., Seredyński, F., Hoffmann, R.: Towards self-organizing sensor networks: game-theoretic ϵ-learning automata-based approach. In: Mauri, G., El Yacoubi, S., Dennunzio, A., Nishinari, K., Manzoni, L. (eds.) ACRI 2018. LNCS, vol. 11115, pp. 125–136. Springer, Cham (2018). https://doi.org/10.1007/978-3-319-99813-8_11
5. Gąsior, J., Seredyński, F., Tchernykh, A.: A security-driven approach to online job scheduling in IaaS cloud computing systems. In: Wyrzykowski, R., Dongarra, J., Deelman, E., Karczewski, K. (eds.) PPAM 2017. LNCS, vol. 10778, pp. 156–165. Springer, Cham (2018). https://doi.org/10.1007/978-3-319-78054-2_15
6. Katsumata, Y., Ishida, Y.: On a membrane formation in a spatio-temporally generalized Prisoner's Dilemma. In: Umeo, H., Morishita, S., Nishinari, K., Komatsuzaki, T., Bandini, S. (eds.) ACRI 2008. LNCS, vol. 5191, pp. 60–66. Springer, Heidelberg (2008). https://doi.org/10.1007/978-3-540-79992-4_8
7. Nowak, M.A., May, R.M.: Evolutionary games and spatial chaos. Nature **359**, 826 (1992)
8. Osborne, M.: An Introduction to Game Theory. Oxford University Press, New York (2009)
9. Rossi, F., Bandyopadhyay, S., Wolf, M., Pavone, M.: Review of multi-agent algorithms for collective behavior: a structural taxonomy. IFAC-PapersOnLine **51**(12), 112–117 (2018)
10. Tsetlin, M.: Automaton Theory and Modeling of Biological Systems. Academic Press, Cambridge (1973)
11. Wolfram, S.: A New Kind of Science. Wolfram Media, Champaign (2002)
12. Yao, X., Darwen, P.J.: An experimental study of N-Person Iterated Prisoner's Dilemma games. In: Yao, X. (ed.) EvoWorkshops 1993–1994. LNCS, vol. 956, pp. 90–108. Springer, Heidelberg (1995). https://doi.org/10.1007/3-540-60154-6_50

Asymmetric Information and Learning by Imitation in Agent-Based Financial Markets

Luca Gerotto[1], Paolo Pellizzari[1(✉)], and Marco Tolotti[2]

[1] Department of Economics, Ca' Foscari University,
Cannaregio 873, 30121 Venice, Italy
{luca.gerotto,paolop}@unive.it
[2] Department of Management, Ca' Foscari University,
Cannaregio 873, 30121 Venice, Italy
tolotti@unive.it

Abstract. We describe an agent-based model of a market where traders exchange a risky asset whose returns can be partly predicted purchasing a costly signal. The decision to be informed (at a cost) or uninformed is taken by means of a simple learning by imitation mechanism that periodically occurs.

The equilibrium is characterized describing the stationary distribution of the price and the fraction of the informed traders. We find that the number of agents who acquire the signal decreases with its cost and with agents' risk aversion and, conversely, it increases with the signal-to-noise ratio and when learning is slow, as opposed to frequent. Moreover, price volatility appears to directly depend on the fraction of informed traders and, hence, some heteroskedasticity is observed when this fraction fluctuates.

Keywords: Agent-based modeling · Bounded rationality · Information in financial markets

1 Introduction

Information is of paramount importance in competitive financial markets and one of the most sought-after properties of a market is its ability to spread information in a timely manner. However, some of the paradoxical implications of information are well known and have been widely analyzed in the last decades (see, for example, Schredelseker [1], Kurlat and Veldkamp [2], Veldkamp [3], and the evergreen Grossman and Stiglitz [4], hereafter referred to as GS). One of the celebrated achievements in GS is to show that, in exchange economies, a trading equilibrium among informed traders cannot exist, as a perfectly informative price system would not compensate arbitrageurs for their (costly) activity of information gathering and processing.

© Springer Nature Switzerland AG 2019
F. De la Prieta et al. (Eds.): PAAMS 2019 Workshops, CCIS 1047, pp. 164–175, 2019.
https://doi.org/10.1007/978-3-030-24299-2_14

In the standard treatment, fully rational agents *ex-ante* solve for the equilibrium, trading (only) at the equilibrium price given the fraction λ of informed traders and computing the unique λ that makes the expected utility of any informed agent equal to that of the uninformed one. This is a grueling task involving sophisticated cognitive and technical abilities that may belong to an abstract *Homo Economicus* but are likely to be scant in more realistic depictions of human behavior.

In this paper, we present an agent-based model of a dynamic market where the risky return depends on a random component as well as on an informative signal, which can be purchased for a constant cost. Informed agents can exploit the reduction in uncertainty provided by the signal and increase their profit by making educated bids on the future payoff. Uninformed agents do not bear any information cost and face greater risks but, intuitively, there is an equilibrium share of informed traders in which the benefits of purchasing the signal exactly offsets the cost, thus making expected profits equal for informed and uninformed traders.

In our model, agents are boundedly rational and noisily attempt to maximize their cumulated wealth over some span of time, deciding whether to acquire the signal (paying the required cost) or not. We do not assume the existence of an utility function, nor the ability to solve sophisticated maximization schemes or understand the complex endogenous structure of the stochastic equilibrium that should materialize (prices depends on the fraction of informed traders which, in turn, depends on the profit that are driven by the individual decisions ultimately responsible for the price dynamics).

Instead, we assume that traders evolve using a simple learning by imitation device: after a predetermined number of trading periods, some agents are randomly paired, compare their performance (namely, cumulated wealth) and the poorer trader ends up in copying the strategy of the richer; i.e., if the pair is formed by an informed and an uninformed agent, after learning, both will adopt the same (more favorable) strategy.[1]

We obtain three main results. First, for all the values of the parameters, the model converges to some equilibrium expressed in terms of the fraction of informed and the price of the risky asset. Second, the outcome is affected, as expected, by the informativeness of the signal, but also by a set of "learning" parameters of the model, and there are situations in which heteroskedasticity of prices is observed. Finally, the length of the period used to cumulate profits has a remarkable role and, say, short-term traders prefer not to use weakly informative signals whereas the same knowledge is purchased and exploited if more periods are allowed to average profits.

1.1   Related Literature

We depart from the seminal GS setup in that the "game" is no longer static but dynamically develops in a series of periods through an explicit learning

---

[1] To preserve diversity in the population, we add also a minimal degree of random "mutation" in every period, see the details below.

mechanism. Agents learn in a very simple and robust way, by checking whether another trader makes larger profits. By contrast, Routledge [5,6] uses full-blown genetic algorithms to equip agents with sophisticated learning skills. We enrich this extant literature showing that market outcomes are affected by learning in important ways and this holds even when learning takes place in extremely simple ways (or, if you like, also when the "genetic algorithm" has no proper selection or mutation operator and crossover is replaced by sheer imitation).

Perhaps more importantly, the agents of the model do not play a sequence of repeated but otherwise identical trading games, as done previously. We introduce a market maker in charge of adjusting the future price based on the excess demand produced by the traders in the current time. Hence, in a somewhat realistic fashion, price fluctuates because of random shocks, the changing fraction of informed/uninformed traders, as well as due to price adjustments stickily incorporating imbalances in demand for the risky asset.

Our paper can be related to the vast amount of work dealing with asymmetric information in financial markets. Several scholars have explored different setups and definition of *information*: Chen et al. [7], for instance, develop a model where returns are affected by the volume of Google searches of the asset ticker (the "driving force") and propose a simple three-bodies approximation of the resulting price dynamics. Billett et al. [8] examine how the reduction in analysts' coverage of one stock predict worse industry-adjusted performance, due to the reduction of the information available to investors.

Recently, Krichene and El-Aroui [9] presents a model in which, among other features, "information" is assumed to be essentially equivalent to traders' sentiment, which can spread and has the potential to trigger herds, bubbles and crashes. We feel that the previous and non-exhaustive list of models appears to depict *knowledge* (on a specific stock), more than *information* on the returns, that is expressed through economic analysis, extent of web coverage and perceptions/sentiment of investors. In our model, the signal directly refers to the future yield and may be thought as a simplified (or, if you wish, distilled) form of the just mentioned sources of knowledge.

The article is organized as follows. Next section describes the model and provides details both on the structure of the market and on the features of the agents. Section 3 presents the results of a NetLogo implementation of the model and relates the findings to the literature. We then have some concluding remarks and point out paths for future work.

2   The Model

Our model basically consists of two parts: a simple financial market where two assets are available and a staggered learning mechanism involving, at selected calendar dates, a random set of traders.

The Financial Market
We assume there are two assets in the market: a riskless asset with unit price and a risky asset, whose price p_t is determined by a market maker. While the safe

asset yields as return the risk-free rate $R \geq 1$, the risky asset has an uncertain return u_t that can be decomposed in three components:

$$u_t = d + \theta_t + \epsilon_t, \tag{1}$$

where $d \geq 1$ is a constant; $\theta_t \sim N(0, \sigma_\theta^2)$ is a signal observable at the beginning of the period by paying an amount c; and $\epsilon_t \sim N(0, \sigma_\epsilon^2)$ is an ex-ante unforecastable zero-mean shock.

The market is populated by N traders who can be either informed or uninformed. At the beginning of each period t, a fraction λ_t of traders spends c to be *informed* and learn θ_t, whereas the remaining traders are *uninformed*.

The information set Ω_t^j of agent j at time t can be either θ_t or the empty set, depending on whether he is informed. Accordingly, his demand for the risky asset is determined by the following heuristic:[2]

$$X_t(\Omega_t^j) = \frac{E(u_t|\Omega_t^j) - p_t R}{\alpha Var(u_t|\Omega_t^j)} = \begin{cases} \frac{d + \theta_t - p_t R}{\alpha \sigma_\epsilon^2} = X_t^I & \text{if } \Omega_t^j = \theta_t \\ \frac{d - p_t R}{\alpha(\sigma_\theta^2 + \sigma_\epsilon^2)} = X_t^U & \text{if } \Omega_t^j = \emptyset \end{cases} . \tag{2}$$

Intuitively, the higher the expected excess return $E(u_t|\Omega_t^j)$ with respect to the riskless asset, the higher the quantity demanded. Hence, the demand increases in d and, for informed traders, in θ_t, whereas it decreases in the price p_t and R, *ceteris paribus*. Under the assumption that agents are risk averse, their demand is negatively related to their degree of risk aversion α and to the perceived volatility of returns $Var(u_t|\Omega_t^j)$. The informed agents know the signal θ_t concerning u_t, which leads them to sell the risky asset when $d + \theta_t - p_t R$ is negative and buy the risky asset otherwise. They do so facing a residual risk that depends on the shock ϵ_t alone (being θ_t known). In contrast, the uninformed trader takes a short (long) position in the risky asset if $d - p_t R$ is negative (positive). The demand of the uninformed is typically lower than the one of the informed as the lack of knowledge of θ_t inflates the denominator to $\alpha(\sigma_\theta^2 + \sigma_\epsilon^2)$. As a consequence, the trading volume of the informed is most often much bigger than the one produced by the uninformed agents. Observe that all informed agents demand the identical amount X_t^I. The same holds for uninformed quantity X_t^U that is the same for any uninformed trader.

At the end of the period, the wealths of the informed and uninformed agents are, respectively:

$$w_t^I = (u_t - p_t R)X_t^I + (w_{t-1}^I - c)R \tag{3}$$

$$= \left(d + \theta_t + \epsilon_t\right)\left(\frac{d + \theta_t - p_t R}{\alpha \sigma_\epsilon^2}\right) + (w_{t-1}^I - c)R, \tag{4}$$

---

[2] This result corresponds to a simplified version of equations (8) and (8′) of Grossman and Stiglitz [4]. Note, in particular, that our agents are not able to exploit entirely the information revealed by the price p_t on the signal θ_t (hence, on u_t) as for the fully rational agents in GS.

and

$$w_t^U = (u_t - p_t R)X_t^U + w_{t-1}^U R \tag{5}$$

$$= \left(d + \theta_t + \epsilon_t \right) \left(\frac{d - p_t R}{\alpha(\sigma_\theta^2 + \sigma_\epsilon^2)} \right) + w_{t-1}^U R. \tag{6}$$

Once trading has occurred, the market maker reacts to any excess demand (supply) of the risky asset by proportionally increasing (decreasing) the price that will be available in the next trading period. As customarily done (see Cont and Bouchaud [10]), this is a simple device to introduce a reasonable price dynamics in the model, by means of adjustments of the current price based on the magnitude and sign of the current demand imbalance.

Given the average per-trader total excess demand $Q_t = \lambda_t X_t^I + (1 - \lambda_t)X_t^U$ at the end of the period, the market maker determines next price

$$p_{t+1} = p_t + k(Q_t - \eta_t), \tag{7}$$

where $\eta_t \sim N(0, \sigma_\eta^2)$ is an exogenous supply shock. The value of the parameter $k > 0$ determines the strength of the reaction of the market maker.

The Learning Mechanism
Staggered learning in the model is introduced assuming that from time to time agents assess their performance comparing their wealth to the one of other peers. We have two parameters in the learning mechanism: T is the horizon over which profits are cumulated before a learning round by imitation begins, while h is the number of couples of agents who compare the respective performances and eventually copy the more profitable strategy. More formally, every T periods, $2h$ out of the N agents are randomly paired. Denote by $\mathcal{T} = \{zT, z \in \mathbb{N}\}$, the set of calendar dates at which random matchings happen. For large N, at dates $\tau \in \mathcal{T}$, approximately $h\lambda_\tau(1 - \lambda_\tau)$ out of the h pairs are composed by an informed and an uninformed trader.[3] They compare their performance (i.e., cumulated wealth) and the poorer trader ends up in copying the strategy of the richer. As a result, after learning, they both will be either in the set of the informed or uninformed agents for the next T periods.

When some traders modify their strategy at time $\tau \in \mathcal{T}$, a change in the proportion of informed at the aggregate level follows: $\lambda_{\tau+1}$ will be higher than λ_τ if the informed outperformed the uninformed over the previous T periods, and will be lower otherwise. To avoid trivial situations in which all agents are either informed or uninformed, thus making the learning procedure useless, we conclude the process assigning a random status (Informed or Uninformed) to one agent.

Finally, in order to study the effects of the parameter T (the duration of the accumulation period), after learning has taken place all agents start from the

---

[3] Clearly, if the pair is formed by two agents that were equally informed or uninformed in the last T periods, no change happens as both members in the couple have the same wealth.

same wealth level w_0, i.e. all the previous gains and losses are reset (or wealth is entirely consumed, if the reader prefers an equivalent interpretation).

It is worth pointing out that the previous learning mechanism is, basically, a crude learning by imitation procedure requiring very little sophistication on the part of the agents, who are only assumed to be able to know, every once in a while, the wealth of a peer and whether he has been paying to obtain information in the (recent) past. We believe this is a cognitive plausible representation of agents and does not require the precise understanding of the endogenous equilibrium possibly arising or, say, the skills needed to maximize a utility function. Even if there are technical and conceptual similarities with genetic algorithms (whose variety is, incidentally, sweeping), our setup is greatly simplified as selection is totally random and independent of fitness and the crossover operator is replaced by sheer imitation.

Summarizing, we can argue that the equilibrium (λ, p) emerging in our model, expressed in terms of proportion of informed traders and price of the risky asset, is surely reachable by boundedly rational agents supported by a credible and simple learning heuristic. In the remainder of this article, we will analyze by means of simulation the behavior of the model and the properties of the equilibrium for different configurations of the parameters.

3   Results

We present here the results of many simulations of the model that was coded in NetLogo, see Wilensky [11]. The parameters of the model belong to two main sets. The first one is related to structural features including d, R, the information cost c and the variances σ_ϵ^2 and σ_θ^2. The second group of parameters are associated to the learning procedure: the horizon T and the number of couples h. In what follows, we assume the individual parameter α, the risk aversion of the agents, to be constant across the population.

We run 27000 simulations for 10000 periods,[4] setting $N = 1000, d = 1.1, R = 1.01$ and systematically allowing $\sigma_\epsilon^2, \sigma_\theta^2$ to take all the values in $\{0.03, 0.06, ..., 0.30\}$, $c \in \{0.1, 0.2, ..., 0.5\}$, $T \in \{1, 4, 16\}$, $h \in \{15, 30\}$ and $\alpha \in \{1, 2, 3\}$. We check for the absence of transient effects in the simulations, running the experiments beginning with a fraction λ_0 of informed agents in $\{0.3, 0.5, 0.7\}$.

To ease exposition, we define a benchmark model in which $\alpha = 2, \sigma_\epsilon^2 = 0.06, \sigma_\theta^2 = 0.09, c = 0.3, T = 1, h = 15, \lambda_0 = 0.5, k = 0.05, \sigma_\eta^2 = 0.005$. Figure 1 depicts the time series of prices and the evolution of λ_t in a representative run of the benchmark case. The average price in this specific simulation is 1.091 and λ fluctuates around an average value of 0.57.

Table 1 shows the estimate of the mean and standard deviation of the stationary distribution of the random variables p^* (equilibrium price) and λ^*. We denote them, respectively, by μ_p and σ_p (for price) and μ_λ and σ_λ (for the

---

[4] For simulations involving $T = 16$, 12000 periods.

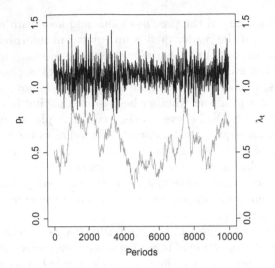

Fig. 1. Price p_t (black, left axis) and fraction of informed traders λ_t (red, right axis) in the benchmark configuration ($\alpha = 2, \sigma_\epsilon^2 = 0.06, \sigma_\theta^2 = 0.09, c = 0.3, T = 1, h = 15, \lambda_0 = 0.5$) (Color figure online)

fraction of informed). The table displays results obtained in the benchmark configuration, as well as in other situations in which one parameter alone is tilted with respect to the benchmark.

Table 1. Main outcomes of the model for the benchmark configuration and selected variations. Every entry in the table is the average of 6 independent simulations (3 values for $\lambda_0 \times 2$ values for h). Each row shows the sample mean and the standard deviation of the stationary distribution of price and of the share of informed traders

	μ_p	σ_p	μ_λ	σ_λ
Benchmark	1.089	0.091	0.557	0.168
$\alpha = 1$	1.089	0.239	0.958	0.015
$\sigma_\theta^2 = 0.12$	1.091	0.160	0.925	0.024
$c = 0.4$	1.089	0.038	0.111	0.039

The time-average of the price is remarkably close to $d/R = 1.089$ for all our simulations and all cases depicted in Table 1. Indeed, the mean aggregate demand in Eq. (2) is proportional to $d - Rp$ for all traders and any prolonged deviation of p from d/R is corrected by the market maker, who would detect and act on any sustained imbalance. In the benchmark case (first row), approximately 56% of traders are informed at each period, with the presence of oscillations that are visible in Fig. 1, as well as in the standard deviation σ_λ taking the value 0.17.

A further point is related to the heteroskedasticity in prices: it can be seen in Fig. 1 that the standard deviation of prices is high in every time interval featuring an high share of informed individuals, λ_t. The intuition is that if a large portion of traders acquires the information θ_t and acts accordingly, high pressure (either upward or downward) is put on prices. Conversely, if only a few individuals have superior information, they exploit the signal without heavily affecting the market.

Table 1 also exemplifies other general and sensible outcomes of the model. Other things being fixed, less risk-averse traders (with $\alpha = 1$) acquire the information in over 95% of cases. Raising σ_θ^2 to 0.12 (third row) makes the signal more informative and appealing, thus raising μ_λ from 0.56 to 0.93. As expected, if the cost is increased from 0.3 to 0.4 (fourth row), the fraction of informed traders drops to about 11%.

One of the most interesting features of the model is the relationship between μ_λ, the "informativeness" of the signal, σ_θ^2, and the baseline level of the idiosyncratic noise, σ_ϵ^2. In Fig. 2 we plot the average equilibrium fraction of informed agents as a function of σ_θ^2, for different values of σ_ϵ^2.

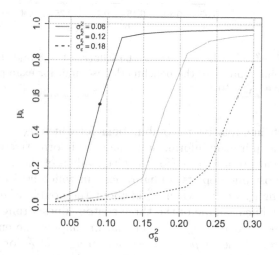

Fig. 2. Equilibrium fraction of the informed agents as a function of σ_θ^2, for $\sigma_\epsilon^2 = 0.06, 0.12, 0.18$. The thick point represents the benchmark configuration ($\alpha = 2, \sigma_\epsilon^2 = 0.06, \sigma_\theta^2 = 0.09, c = 0.3, T = 1$). (Color figure online)

Without doubt, scarcely informative signals lead to small values of μ_λ and, conversely, increasing σ_θ^2 to substantial levels (with respect to σ_ϵ^2) ultimately pushes the fraction of the informed ones to very high values approaching, but never reaching, 100%. Comparing the left solid line with the right dashed one, for instance, it can be seen that tripling σ_ϵ^2 for a given informativeness, greatly reduces the number of informed traders. This follows from the reduced utility of the signal embedded in a setup where the background noise is prevalent. In

Fig. 3, we further investigate how μ_λ depends on σ_ϵ^2 and σ_θ^2, plotting the set of couples of the parameters for which μ_λ takes the values 0.1, 0.5 and 0.9, respectively (i.e., we plot three contour levels of the function $\mu_\lambda(\sigma_\epsilon^2, \sigma_\theta^2)$, keeping fixed all the other parameters at the level taken in the benchmark case).

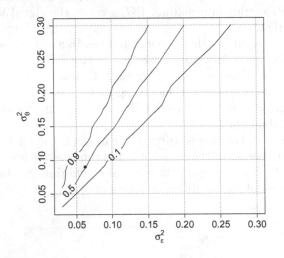

Fig. 3. The set of $(\sigma_\epsilon^2, \sigma_\theta^2)$ where μ_λ takes the values 0.1, 0.5 and 0.9 (from right to left). The thick point represents the benchmark case and, for example, when σ_ϵ^2 and σ_θ^2 are 0.10, we have $\mu_\lambda \sim 10\%$

The rightmost line, relative to combinations for which $\mu_\lambda = 10\%$, shows that very few traders acquire the information when the informativeness is about the same size of the background noise (for the given values of the other parameters). The steeper leftmost line depicts configurations in which 90% of the agents are informed: this roughly occurs when σ_θ^2 is about the double of σ_ϵ^2. More importantly, the almost linear shape of the three contour lines strongly suggests that the signal-to-noise ratio $\rho = \sigma_\theta^2/\sigma_\epsilon^2$ is crucial in shaping the emerging equilibrium. For instance, whenever $\rho = 3/2$, we obtain $\mu_\lambda \sim 50\%$ (or, put differently, one in two agents buys the signal). Essentially, and rather sensibly, it looks as if the important thing in a market where information is costly is the signal-to-noise ratio faced by the traders (and not the peculiar variances of the sources of noise determining the dividends paid by the risky asset).[5]

We turn then to another significant insight provided by the extended set of simulations we have run. An increase in the time T between two learning rounds has a deep effect on the outcomes. Recall that h traders are randomly paired with other agents every T periods and learn by imitation, copying the behavior

---

[5] It should be stressed that the result obviously depends also on the other parameters, say α and c, but the conclusion that the signal-to-noise ratio plays an important role robustly holds for all the combinations we have simulated (specific details are not discussed for brevity).

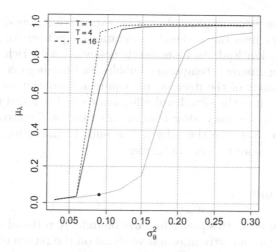

Fig. 4. Equilibrium fraction of the informed agents as a function of σ_θ^2, for $T = 1, 4, 16$. The thick point represents the benchmark configuration ($\alpha = 2, \sigma_\epsilon^2 = 0.12, \sigma_\theta^2 = 0.09, c = 0.3, T = 1$)

of the peer if the accumulated wealth over T periods proves to be higher. So far we have discussed the case $T = 1$, corresponding to a market populated by short-term traders, who revise their decision to buy (or not to buy) the signal based on the profits gained in a single period. Figure 4, resembling what was done in Fig. 2, depicts the average equilibrium fraction of informed agents as a function of σ_θ^2, for different values of T. For this analysis, we alter the benchmark configuration setting $\sigma_\epsilon^2 = 0.12$ (see the red line in Fig. 2) to help the reader spot the increase in μ_λ implied by an increase in T. Observe, for instance, the thick point in the figure where less than 10% of traders acquire the information when $T = 1$: keeping the other parameters fixed, it suffices to raise T from 1 to 4 to boost the number of the informed ones to over 60%. The effect is much stronger if $T = 16$, a situation in which λ abruptly increases to almost 100% as soon as the informativeness σ_θ^2 reaches 0.09.

Even though a greater T may be somewhat interpreted in terms of "stubbornness" on the part of the agents, who insist in using their strategy and less frequently try to learn from their peers, an alternative explanation is in order: if learning takes place less frequently, traders have more time to learn whether the signal is, on average, worth the cost. In the present setup, the second effect is clearly predominant over the first and the benefits of slower (and more accurate) learning outweigh what can be gained with frequent (but necessarily noisier) assessments of trading performances.

Our findings highlight that weakly informative signals, which will not be acquired if short-term gains are sought for, are nevertheless valuable in the long run (i.e., provided that multiple periods are considered and used to average the profits and adjust behaviour). A similar idea was presented in the seminal paper on the Santa Fe Artificial Stock Market, Arthur et al. [12], in which it is pointed out that "where investors explore alternative expectational models at a low rate, the market settles into the rational-expectations equilibrium", whereas high-frequency exploration leads to more hectic behavior, with rich psychology and "technical trading emerges, temporary bubbles and crashes occur". In a related fashion, fast revisions of the decision to acquire information in our model lead to episodic adoption of the signal, volatility bursts and reduced use of aggregate information; on the contrary, slow learning with larger T increases the fraction of traders who get and use the information and, in this sense, produces what can be deemed as more rational outcomes.

4   Conclusions

The model presented in this paper features boundedly rational agents who have the option to acquire a costly informative signal on the return of the risky asset. Paying for the information would make predictions more accurate and reduce the residual risk, increasing the traded volume. Uninformed agents, on the contrary, face greater uncertainty and typically buy or sell less but do not bear any additional cost. Some agents in the population learn by imitation whether their choice to get (or not to get) the information is convenient by comparing their profits every T periods with the ones of another peer.

We have shown that, similarly to Grossman and Stiglitz [4], the model converges to an equilibrium where stationary distributions for the price and the fraction of informed traders can be described. Numerical simulations demonstrate how the adoption of information increases with the informativeness of the signal or, more precisely, with the signal-to-noise ratio. Moreover, less information is used by more risk-averse agents and when the signal is more costly.

The volatility of the price, which is adjusted by a market maker based on the excess demand, is not constant and notably depends on the fluctuation of the fractions of informed, as a larger (smaller) magnitude of returns is observed on average when λ is big (small). The channel through which high values of λ cause large shocks is the larger volume of trades prompted by informed agents.

Finally, we have shown how the interval T between two learning rounds affects the equilibrium dynamics. An increase in T effectively results in slower learning, a situation where traders stick to the same strategy in a stubborn way for several periods, apparently renouncing the frequent opportunity to revise their strategy. However, slow learning also gives the chance to assess the value of the signal in a much more accurate (and less noisy) way. In our model, the latter effect prevails on the former and a larger T gives rise to markets where (many) more agents acquire the signal, suggesting that even weakly informative signals can be profitable if the trading gain they produce is assessed over a long horizon.

Further research would be needed to clarify how the market structure affects the results that, in the present framework, are mainly driven by the signal-to-noise ratio and by the frequency with which learning is activated. Indeed, the market maker used in the model adjusts the price only after demands are revealed and transactions are cleared. As such, he may delay or hamper the chance to infer the signal from the price and in principle a formal auction may disclose information in a more efficient and timely manner (even though it is difficult to ascertain under which dimensions this would be good or bad).

References

1. Schredelseker, K.: Is the usefulness approach useful? Some reflections on the utility of public information. In: McLeay, S., Riccaboni, A. (eds.) Contemporary Issues in Accounting Regulation, pp. 135–153. Springer, Boston (2001). https://doi.org/10.1007/978-1-4615-4589-7_8
2. Kurlat, P., Veldkamp, L.: Should we regulate financial information? J. Econ. Theory **158**, 697–720 (2015)
3. Veldkamp, L.L.: Media frenzies in markets for financial information. Am. Econ. Rev. **96**(3), 577–601 (2006)
4. Grossman, S.J., Stiglitz, J.E.: On the impossibility of informationally efficient markets. Am. Econ. Rev. **70**(3), 393–408 (1980)
5. Routledge, B.R.: Adaptive learning in financial markets. Rev. Financ. Stud. **12**(5), 1165–1202 (1999)
6. Routledge, B.R.: Genetic algorithm learning to choose and use information. Macroecon. Dyn. **5**(02), 303–325 (2001)
7. Chen, T.T., Zheng, B., Li, Y., Jiang, X.F.: Information driving force and its application in agent-based modeling. Phys. A: Stat. Mech. Its Appl. **496**, 593–601 (2018)
8. Billett, M.T., Garfinkel, J.A., Yu, M.: The effect of asymmetric information on product market outcomes. J. Financ. Econ. **123**(2), 357–376 (2017)
9. Krichene, H., El-Aroui, M.A.: Artificial stock markets with different maturity levels: simulation of information asymmetry and herd behavior using agent-based and network models. J. Econ. Interact. Coord. **13**(3), 511–535 (2018)
10. Cont, R., Bouchaud, J.P.: Herd behavior and aggregate fluctuations in financial markets. Macroecon. Dyn. **4**(2), 170–196 (2000)
11. Wilensky, U.: NetLogo. Center for Connected Learning and Computer-Based Modeling, Northwestern University, Evanston, IL (1999). http://ccl.northwestern.edu/netlogo/
12. Arthur, W.B., Holland, J.H., LeBaron, B., Palmer, R., Tayler, P.: Asset pricing under endogenous expectations in an artificial stock market. In: Arthur, W., Lane, D., Durlauf, S. (eds.) The Economy as an Evolving, Complex System II, pp. 15–44. Addison Wesley, Redwood City (1997)

A Preliminary Ontology
for Human-Agent Collectives

Pablo Pico-Valencia[1,2]($\boxtimes$), Juan A. Holgado-Terriza[2]($\boxtimes$),
and Luz M. Sierra Martínez[3]

[1] Pontifical Catholic University of Ecuador, Esmeraldas 080150, Ecuador
ppico@pucese.edu.ec
[2] University of Granada, 18015 Granada, Spain
jholgado@ugr.es
[3] University of Cauca, Popayán 190003, Colombia
lsierra@unicauca.edu.co

Abstract. Human-Agent Collectives (HAC) is an approach involving coalitions of humans and agents working together to exploit their intelligence capabilities to optimize tasks in systems with inherent uncertainty. This paper presents a review of the main features of the HAC approach as well as the possible interactions between the entities that take place in the coalitions of a HAC system. An ontology called ONT4HAC is defined to facilitate the management of actions in HAC scenarios.

Keywords: Collectives · Ontology · Humans · Agents · Coalitions

1 Introduction

The concept of ontology has recently been spreading in technological systems. Its aim is to facilitate the integration of heterogeneous systems and encourage semantic interoperability between them [21]. This is achieved because systems can employ a common vocabulary (described by means of ontologies) that describes the domain in which they are categorized (i.e., multi-agent systems (MASs) [11], networks of Internet of Things (IoT) [24]).

In Computer Science an ontology constitutes an explicit specification of a conceptualization of a part of the real world [11, 21]. Therefore, an ontology is a computational model that integrates the description of concepts and relationships that may exist in a particular domain of knowledge. For example, for agent-based systems an ontology can describe concepts and relationships for a MAS. However, these systems applied to specific areas require an extension of general ontologies to cover particular specifications used in specific areas. Some real cases are ontologies for MASs applied in manufacturing [21] and IoT [24].

Ontologies play an important role in sharing and reusing knowledge, making assumptions about a domain by applying semantic reasoning processes [21]. Additionally, using ontologies to describe the elements of a system contributes

© Springer Nature Switzerland AG 2019
F. De la Prieta et al. (Eds.): PAAMS 2019 Workshops, CCIS 1047, pp. 176–187, 2019.
https://doi.org/10.1007/978-3-030-24299-2_15

to disambiguate the information communicated in the information systems and especially in the MASs where the level of interaction between the agents is high and the decisions and actions executed depend on these interactions [11,22]. This is why ontologies have been integrated into MASs.

Because ontologies have supported control actions in MASs, this paper proposes extending their use for systems based on Human-Agent Collectives (HAC)—an emerging concept that models large groups of humans and software agents which interact and collaborate each other to meet common targets [12]. A case of HAC use is a disaster response system where decisions are critical [26]. Therefore, an ontology for HAC can facilitate machines and people understanding the information—captured, processed, transmitted and stored—by its meaning and thus execute more accurate actions.

This paper is organized as follows. Section 2 describes the main ontologies related to the area of MAS, human relationships, and the area where human and agents interact. In Sect. 3 the theoretical concepts related to the HAC approach are introduced. The proposed ontology we called ONT4HAC is described in Sect. 4. Finally, Sect. 5 outlines conclusions and future works.

2   Related Works

HAC is a socio-technical approach that contemplates the modelling of a high degree of interaction between humans and agents. This requires therefore that, in the case of an ontology such as this paper proposes, we consider aspects related to the description of MASs as well as the possible agents interactions, the interrelations between humans and the interaction between both types of entities. In this section, the main ontologies proposed to describe these aspects have been analysed. The analysis demonstrates the lack of a complete ontology to describe HAC ecosystems.

Regarding ontologies for MASs we evidenced the existence of ontologies covering specific issues such as: communication and interaction (e.g., Lightweight Ontology-based Content Language, LOCL [22], JADE [30], agent interaction protocols ontology [6]), collaboration and planning tasks (e.g., AgentOWL [15], ontology for MAS collaborative tasks [27]), architecture description (e.g., Onto2MAS [8], SOUPA [3], ontology for Belief-Desire-Interaction (BDI) agents [17], ontology form agent mobility [25]), ontology-based development (e.g., MAS Ontology [5], Onto2MAS [8]) forming agents organizations (e.g.,MAMbO5 ontology [9]) and negotiation (e.g., ontology for MAS negotiation [29]). However, most of these ontologies were not online available to be reused.

Likewise, with respect to the description of humans and interpersonal relationships a standard conceptualization has been proposed. We evidenced that many of the semantic web-based applications that require describing aspects of people use the Friend Of A Friend (FOAF) [7] vocabulary (e.g., human activity recognition ontology [1,19], pervasive environments ontology [4]). Therefore, this popular conceptualization can be used to describe some aspects related to coalitions of humans. Even so, this vocabulary remains incomplete because it does not cover all the aspects that human interactions in HAC are required.

Finally, we also verified that few ontologies have conceptualized the relationships between humans and agents, that is, ontologies oriented to describe knowledge of human-agent teamwork [31]. Thus, ontologies for describing human-agent interaction [10], cognition for human-agents [16] and human-agent negotiation [28] were recovered. These ontologies describe specific issues between humans, and software and physical agents. But they only partially cover the aspects related to the HAC approach. Complementarily, FOAF also describes some aspects but it neither covers the complete conceptualization to describe all HAC features as is theoretically recommended in [12]. This is why we believe that a particular conceptualization for the description of the entities, elements, relationships and mechanisms modelled in HAC systems is necessary.

In short, it is clear that there are proposed ontologies to describe knowledge in MASs and human-computer interaction (HCI), including physical agents and software. However, the aspects that characterize HAC systems, described in Sect. 3, are not comprehensively included in any of the ontological models and vocabularies previously described. The majority of the proposed ontologies cover aspects associated with interactions between MAS agents and between agents and humans. This has provided the basis for the development of our ontology.

3   Human-Agent Collectives

HAC proposed the creation of complex systems that inherently model large-scale real-time networks in which multiple teams of humans and software agents work collaboratively with varying degrees of autonomy to meet individual and collaborative goals [12,18]. This implies on the one hand that agents can support humans when they cannot autonomously complete a task for which they are themselves responsible (e.g., big volume of data, limited personal processing skills, inaccessible areas). On the other hand, software agents may also require the supervision of a human prior executing unforeseen actions or decisions for which it is not trained or does not have sufficient knowledge (e.g., incomplete data, unexpected events, unavailability of services required).

HAC systems need modelling flexibility with respect to system planning [12]. Both humans and agents can have some limitations in regarding cognition or computing capabilities would obstruct them from accomplishing the tasks entrusted to them. In addition, the participation of people and agents needs certain degree of autonomy to carry out actions and decision in HAC systems.

Complementary to the flexibility of autonomy of humans and agents that allows them operating in an autonomous or supervised fashion to avoid risks in the scenario where they operate, three additional features define HAC. These features include the following: (i) the formation of agile and temporary teams that allow coalitions achieving their specific targets planned at any time, (ii) the application of incentive engineering techniques aimed at motivating entities that form coalitions to cooperate as efficiently as possible, and finally, (iii) the use of mechanisms that encourage the veracity of the information used in each process executed in HAC, that is, for each data captured, generated and processed it is necessary to know its origin to avoid inconsistent decisions [12].

Figure 1 illustrates the elements that compose an HAC-based system. In summary, the system is made of single agents and individual humans which can be grouped coherently to achieve real-time targets forming homogeneous (human or agent) and/or heterogeneous coalitions (human and agent).

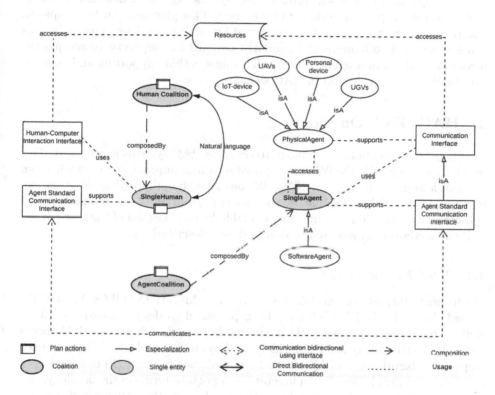

Fig. 1. Entities and interaction forms in Human-Agent Collectives.

For agent coalitions, tools such as JADE, Jadex can be employed to create them. However, it is mandatory that all agents of a HAC system must support a standard agent interface that allows them to establish communication with external entities such as human, machines and software agents. For agent interaction the communication interface (e.g., FIPA communication language) allows agents accessing authorized resources (e.g., cloud, databases, services) and establishing interaction and collaboration with software agents running over MASs or embedded devices. Therefore, the agentification of devices [23] takes significance when implementing HAC systems.

With respect to human coalitions, they are composed of a set of humans who communicate with each other through natural language. Furthermore, humans must rely on a HCI interface that can be used to access the resources of the HAC system or establish communication with software agents. For communication with agents all actions developed using the HCI interface (e.g., tactile, gestural, multi-modal) must be mapped to the language understandable by agents. Thus, communication in HAC is enabled at machine-machine, human-human and human-machine levels.

We emphasize that both humans and agents organized individually or as coalitions have a plan of actions to be carried. This planning can be completed autonomously as was planned or supported by external entities. That is, agents can give support to humans and similarly, humans can supervise or accepts the recommendations that agents suggest. This means that supporting and supervision tasks are very common in HAC systems.

4   HAC-OWL Ontology

In this paper a preliminary ontology to describe HAC systems is proposed. This ontology we called HAC-OWL is proposed as a first approximation of what can become a formal ontology for HAC. We describe the proposed ontology in two parts as proposed in [21], that is, the conceptualization of the domain and its respective specification in a machine readable format. Details of the first part as well the methodology selected to design it, are described.

4.1   Used Methodology

Traditional formal methodologies such as METHONTOLOGY, On-To-Knowledge and KBSI IDEF5 have been proposed to design ontologies [13] as well as more recently ones such as the methodology of Noy and McGuinness [20]. This methodology has been widely used to create ontologies following seven steps: (i) determining the domain and scope of the ontology, (ii) considering to reuse existing ontologies, (iii) enumerating important terms in the ontology, (iv) defining the classes and the class hierarchy, (v) defining the properties of classesslots, (vi) defining the facets of the slots, and finally, (vii) creating instances. All these steps were systematically applied for creating the conceptualization of the proposed ontology.

4.2   Conceptualization of HAC

Based on the current conceptualization of software agents and humans, the implications of the HAC approach were analysed in detail taking as a basis the definitions and the four features that normalize a HAC system. All this information was described in Sect. 2. However, considering HAC models interactions between large groups of humans and agents, we also took into account for the design of the conceptualization a set of consent patterns that allow us to describe how humans and agents participate in the establishment of collaboration, sharing and exchange of information. These patterns are proposed conceptually in [18].

The conceptualization of the HAC domain integrates four sub-ontologies such as: Flexible Autonomous Policy (`applies`), Agile Teaming (`conforms`), Incentive Engineering Method (`adopts`) and Accountability Information Infrastructure (`manages`). These sub-ontologies have been integrated with the purpose of defining the HAC-OWL upper ontology. Next, both the methodology selected for the ontology design as well the conceptualization of each of the sub-ontologies were defined. We describe each sub-ontology in terms of their purpose, main concepts and relationships. The resulting conceptualization is briefly described below.

Flexible-Autonomy-Policy. This sub-ontology, shown in Fig. 2, describes interactions that a single human (e.g., `operational`, `tactical`, `strategical`) and a software agent (e.g., `mobile`, `recommender`, `agent-of-things`, `gatherer`, `filtering`, `fusioner`, `predictor`) as well a coalition of a HAC system can form. For physical agents (`physical`) such as UAVs, UGVs or IoT-devices, we have considered them as agentified entities using a software agent [23]. In short, the adopted patterns for modelling interactions within HAC systems include basic modes of interaction such as `proxy`, `advisory` and `remote`, and more complex mode on interaction such as `consolidate intermediary`, `consolidate advisory` and `common pool` [18].

In addition, aspects related to responsibilities in coalitions (`leader`, `observer`, `coordinator` and `controller`) and the planning of actions (`action list`) to be carried out by `humans`, `agents` and/or `coalitions` are also described in terms of `missions` and `plans` (formulated and evaluated by strategical humans), `actions` (performed by operational humans), and `action list` and `workflow` (defined and modified by tactical humans). It is important to note that we have employed the concept of `workflow` as an element that implements plans for HAC in our view. In this way, we can define which specific `resources` must be used to execute each action in a HAC scenario regardless of whether it is a `temporal`, `cognitive` or `physical` action.

Agile-Teaming. This sub-ontology, illustrated in Fig. 3, describes agile teams or `coalitions` that are created by `tactical` humans in order to achieve an objective needed within a HAC system at a specific time period. This means therefore that each `agile team`, formed by `humans` or/and `agents`, has a specific `deadline` to be finished. This deadline depends on the complexity of the `mission` to be achieved and is determined by the `strategical` human who schedules the action list taking into account the available `resources` (existing resources of the HAC system or new resources that are external to the modelled HAC system) that can be used to execute the actions defined by the workflow that implements the `plan`.

Once the `mission` has been achieved by the agile team, it is completely disarticulated and the participants can keep working normally. In addition, the

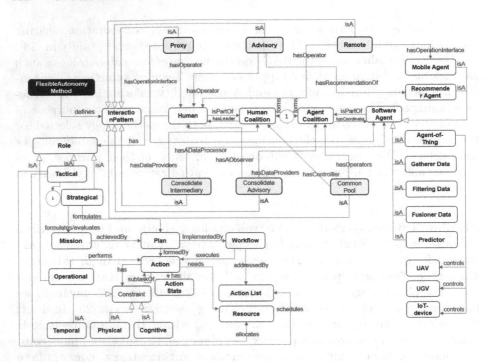

Fig. 2. Flexible-Autonomy-Policy sub-ontology.

employed **resources** can be used to achieve new objectives. It is important to highlight that the management of human and agent interactions in agile teams follows the same interaction patterns proposed in [18], that is, **proxy**, **advisory**, **remote**, **consolidate intermediary**, **consolidate advisory** and **common pool**. Furthermore, regarding **missions** and **plans** achieved by agile teams, they are scheduled in the same way as was described in Flexible Autonomy Sub-ontology (Fig. 2) but taking care the **deadline** (**temporary constraint**) all the time.

Deadline of **actions** involved into a **plan** help both **tactical** and strategic humans to evaluate the efficiency achieved for the achievement of each objective by each team formed and begin to quantitatively assess the capabilities of both **humans** and **agents** who worked to achieve specific **actions**. In addition, at the strategic level, decision makers may have supporting information to evaluate the degree of efficiency with which each **human** and **agent** works collaboratively and in response to **temporary constraints** and critical situations.

Incentive-Engineering-Method. This sub-ontology, illustrated in Fig. 4, describes concepts associated with a gamification system oriented to reward collaboration processes where humans and agents participate. In this way, an incentive mechanism from which humans and agents can be influenced for the

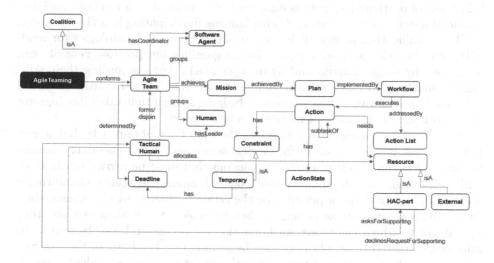

Fig. 3. Agile-Teaming sub-ontology.

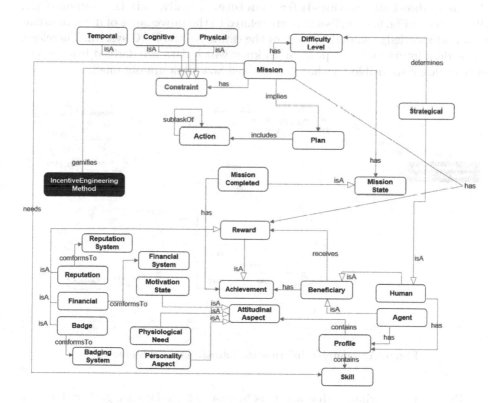

Fig. 4. Incentive Engineering Method sub-ontology.

fulfilment of particular targets is described. We emphasize in intrinsic, social or financial incentives to be coherent with humans participating in a HAC context.

The gamification process is based on already proposed ontologies for modelling collaboration scenarios [2,14]. In the gamification process, `rewards` can be gained by single `humans` and `agents`, or `coalitions` according their skills and personality aspects used to accomplish `missions`. These rewards are gained conform to a reputation, financial and a badging system that takes into account the `level of difficulty` of missions to be assigned.

Based on the information related to the incentives obtained by humans in HAC systems, it serves as input for tactical personnel to more effectively manage human and technological resources in missions that must be carried out individually or through multidisciplinary coalitions of humans and agents. Gamification has not been considered a priority for the actions achieved by the agents, since they will always operate according to their technological capabilities where they operate or to which they have authorization for access and use. However, the missions entrusted to agents may also be gamified on the basis of their proven efficiency in the execution of missions with respect to other equivalent agents.

Accountable-Information-Infrastructure. Finally, this last sub-ontology, illustrated in Fig. 5, describes aspects related to the provenance of data, information and knowledge shared by each of the entities of the HAC system. Therefore, these descriptors makes it possible to know which data are derived from, which entities are responsible for shared data, and how data are obtained.

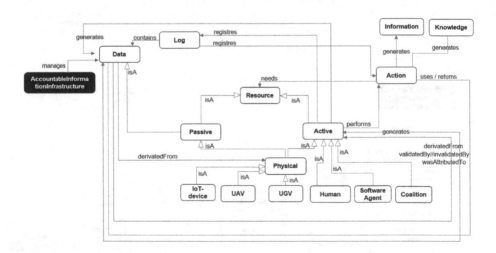

Fig. 5. Accountable Information Infrastructure sub-ontology.

Regarding descriptors that allow us to know which data are gathered or generated, we can see in Fig. 5 that data is `generated` by `resources` of `active` type belonging to the HAC system such as: `human`, `agent`, `coalitions` and `physical` devices (e.g., UAVs, UGVs and IoT-devices). Data is a passive resource normally used as input of actions such as: sensing, fusion, prediction, decision making, filtering, and among others. Thereby, once these actions are executed, such data can provide in information and knowledge which are contained and stored into a Log. Then, a Log can be employed by tactical and strategical humans in order to audit performed plans and evaluate the performance of any achieved mission defined in the HAC system.

In this case humans and intelligent agents can realize actions of validation (validatedBy) and invalidation (invalidatedBy) of the data generated and shared in the system. Thereby, the responsibility for the consistency of each data, information and knowledge in HAC is attributed to (isAttributedTo) both humans and agents.

5   Conclusions and Future Works

The use of an ontology that describes the domain of HAC can contribute to establish a common vocabulary allowing the integration of heterogeneous HAC systems. Additionally, the use of semantic labels describing the elements, entities, data, actions and interrelations of HAC systems can help to make automatic assumptions that lead to recommending preventive and corrective control actions based on semantic reasoning at both prior and post the execution of decisions.

The approach we have presented in this paper is still at an early stage, and there are a number of issues that need to be further investigated. Then, the next step, after obtaining feedback and refining this conceptualization, is to create the HAC-OWL ontology specification and publishing it to be reused as recommended by the semantic web.

References

1. Abdalla, A., Hu, Y., Carral, D., Li, N., Janowicz, K.: An ontology design pattern for activity reasoning. In: WOP, pp. 78–81 (2014)
2. Challco, G.C., Mizoguchi, R., Bittencourt, I.I., Isotani, S.: Gamification of collaborative learning scenarios: structuring persuasive strategies using game elements and ontologies. In: Koch, F., Koster, A., Primo, T. (eds.) SOCIALEDU 2015. CCIS, vol. 606, pp. 12–28. Springer, Cham (2016). https://doi.org/10.1007/978-3-319-39672-9_2
3. Chen, H., Finin, T., Joshi, A.: The SOUPA ontology for pervasive computing. In: Tamma, V., Cranefield, S., Finin, T.W., Willmott, S. (eds.) Ontologies for Agents: Theory and Experiences. WSSAT, pp. 233–258. Birkhäuser Basel, Basel (2005)
4. Chen, H., Perich, F., Finin, T., Joshi, A.: SOUPA: standard ontology for ubiquitous and pervasive applications. In: The First Annual International Conference on Mobile and Ubiquitous Systems: Networking and Services, MOBIQUITOUS 2004, pp. 258–267. IEEE (2004)
5. Cordeiro, F., Werneck, V., Santos, N., Cysneiros, L.: MAS ontology: ontology for multiagent systems. In: Proceedings of the 18th International Conference on Enterprise Information Systems, vol. 1, pp. 536–546. ACM, Rome (2016)

6. Cranefield, S., Purvis, M., Nowostawski, M., Hwang, P.: Ontologies for interaction protocols. In: Tamma, V., Cranefield, S., Finin, T.W., Willmott, S. (eds.) Ontologies for Agents: Theory and Experiences. WSSAT, pp. 1–17. Birkhäuser Basel, Basel (2005)

7. Dan, B., Libby, M.: FOAF vocabulary specification 0.99 (2014). http://xmlns.com/foaf/spec/. Accessed 4 Jan 2019

8. Donzelli, C., Kidanu, S.A., Chbeir, R., Cardinale, Y.: Onto2MAS: an ontology-based framework for automatic multi-agent system generation. In: 2016 12th International Conference on Signal-Image Technology and Internet-Based Systems (SITIS), pp. 381–388. IEEE, Naples (2016)

9. Durić, B.O., Rincon, J., Carrascosa, C., Schatten, M., Julian, V.: MAMbO5: a new ontology approach for modelling and managing intelligent virtual environments based on multi-agent systems. J. Ambient. Intell. Hum. Comput. 1–13 (2018)

10. Guzzoni, D., Baur, C., Cheyer, A.: Modeling human-agent interaction with active ontologies. In: Artificial Intelligence, pp. 52–59 (2007)

11. Huhns, M.N., Singh, M.P.: Ontologies for agents. IEEE Internet Comput. 1(6), 81–83 (1997)

12. Jennings, N.R., et al.: Human-agent collectives. Commun. ACM 57(12), 80–88 (2014)

13. Jones, D., Bench-Capon, T., Visser, P.: Methodologies for ontology development. In: 5th IFIP World Computer Congress, pp. 62–75. Chapman and Hall, London (1998)

14. Khemaja, M., Buendia, F.: Building context-aware gamified apps by using ontologies as unified representation and reasoning-based models. In: Ma, M., Oikonomou, A. (eds.) Serious Games and Edutainment Applications, pp. 675–702. Springer, Cham (2017). https://doi.org/10.1007/978-3-319-51645-5_29

15. Laclavik, M., Balogh, Z., Babik, M., Hluchỳ, L.: AgentOWL: semantic knowledge model and agent architecture. Comput. Inform. 25(5), 421–439 (2012)

16. Lemaignan, S., Warnier, M., Sisbot, E.A., Clodic, A., Alami, R.: Artificial cognition for social human robot interaction: an implementation. Artif. Intell. 247, 45–69 (2017). Special Issue on AI and Robotics

17. Liu, C.H., Chen, J.J.Y.: Using ontology-based BDI agent to dynamically customize workflow and bind semantic web service. J. Softw. 7(14), 884–894 (2012)

18. Moran, S., Luger, E., Rodden, T.: Exploring patterns as a framework for embedding consent mechanisms in human-agent collectives. In: Ślęzak, D., Schaefer, G., Vuong, S.T., Kim, Y.-S. (eds.) AMT 2014. LNCS, vol. 8610, pp. 475–486. Springer, Cham (2014). https://doi.org/10.1007/978-3-319-09912-5_40

19. Ni, Q., Pau de la Cruz, I., García Hernando, A.B.: A foundational ontology-based model for human activity representation in smart homes. J. Ambient Intell. Smart Environ. 8(1), 47–61 (2016)

20. Noy, N.F., McGuinness, D.L., et al.: Ontology development 101: a guide to creating your first ontology. Technical report, University of Stanford (2001). https://protege.stanford.edu/publications/ontology_development/ontology101.pdf

21. Obitko, M., Marík, V.: Ontologies for multi-agent systems in manufacturing domain. In: 13th International Workshop on Database and Expert Systems Applications, pp. 597–602. IEEE, Aix-en-Provence (2002)

22. Pai, F.P., Hsu, I.C., Chung, Y.C.: Semantic web technology for agent interoperability: a proposed infrastructure. Appl. Intell. 44(1), 1–16 (2016)

23. Pico-Valencia, P., Holgado-Terriza, J.A.: Agentification of the internet of things: a systematic review. Int. J. Distrib. Sens. Netw. 14(10) (2018)

24. Pico-Valencia, P., Holgado-Terriza, J.A., Senso, J.: Towards an internet of agents model based on linked open data approach. J. Auton. Agents Multi-Agent Syst. **33**(1–2), 84–131 (2019)
25. Price, R., Krishnaswamy, S., Loke, S.W., Chhetri, M.B.: Towards an ontology for agent mobility. In: Wang, S., et al. (eds.) ER 2004. LNCS, vol. 3289, pp. 484–495. Springer, Heidelberg (2004). https://doi.org/10.1007/978-3-540-30466-1_44
26. Ramchurn, S.D., et al.: HAC-ER: a disaster response system based on human-agent collectives. In: AAMAS 2015: 14th International Conference on Autonomous Agents and Multi-Agent Systems, Istanbul, Turkey, pp. 533–541 (2015)
27. Schmidt, D., Bordini, R.H., Meneguzzi, F., Vieira, R.: An ontology for collaborative tasks in multi-agent systems. In: Proceedings of the Brazilian Seminar on Ontologies (ONTOBRAS 2015), pp. 1–12 (2015)
28. Shahid, W., ur Rehman, M.: Negotiation content ontology for human-agent negotiation. In: 2012 1st International Conference on Future Trends in Computing and Communication Technologies, pp. 30–35 (2012)
29. Tamma, V., Wooldridge, M., Blacoe, I., Dickinson, I.: An ontology based approach to automated negotiation. In: Padget, J., Shehory, O., Parkes, D., Sadeh, N., Walsh, W.E. (eds.) AMEC 2002. LNCS (LNAI), vol. 2531, pp. 219–237. Springer, Heidelberg (2002). https://doi.org/10.1007/3-540-36378-5_14
30. Tomaiuolo, M., Turci, P., Bergenti, F., Poggi, A.: An ontology support for semantic aware agents. In: Kolp, M., Bresciani, P., Henderson-Sellers, B., Winikoff, M. (eds.) AOIS - 2005. LNCS (LNAI), vol. 3529, pp. 140–153. Springer, Heidelberg (2006). https://doi.org/10.1007/11916291_10
31. Van Diggelen, J., Neerincx, M., Peeters, M., Schraagen, J.M.: Developing effective and resilient human-agent teamwork using team design patterns. IEEE Intell. Syst. **34**(2), 1 (2018)

Workshop on Multi-agent-Based Applications for Energy Markets, Smart Grids, and Sustainable Energy Systems (MASGES)

Workshop on Multi-agent-Based Applications for Energy Markets, Smart Grids, and Sustainable Energy Systems (MASGES)

The electrical power industry has evolved into a distributed and competitive industry in which market forces drive the price of energy. Deregulation led to the establishment of wholesale markets, where competing generators can offer their electricity output to retailers, and retail markets, where end-use customers can choose their suppliers. Electricity markets are indeed a complex and evolving reality, meaning that researchers lack insight into numerous open problems that are being raised. Chief among these is the need for new market designs to manage the variability and uncertainty of the increasing levels of renewable generation.

Also, future power systems will integrate a large number of distributed energy resources and new players. Smart grids are intrinsically linked to the challenges raised by new power systems and are expected to improve their efficiency and effectiveness, while ensuring reliability and a secure delivery of electricity to end-users. They should be capable of autonomously and intelligently configuring themselves to make the most efficient use of the available resources, to be robust to different kinds of failures and energy production deviations, and to be extendable and adaptable in the face of the rapidly changing technologies and requirements.

The distributed nature of all these systems, and the autonomous behavior expected for them, points toward software agents and multi-agent systems as a foundation for their realization and deployment. Accordingly, the focus of this workshop is on the application of software agents and multi-agent systems to electricity markets for integrating variable renewable energy and emerging technologies, such as smart grids, distributed generation, demand response, storage, smart homes, and electrical vehicles.

Organization

Organizing Committee

Fernando Lopes	LNEG - National Laboratory of Energy and Geology, Portugal
Roozbeh Morsali	Swinburne University - Melbourne, Australia
Rainer Unland	University of Duisburg-Essen, Germany

Program Committee

Christian Derksen	Universität Duisburg-Essen, Germany
Costin Badica	University of Craiova, Romania

Fernando Lezama	Polytechnic Institute of Porto, Portugal
Fernando Lopes	LNEG National Research Institute, Portugal
Frank Allgower	University of Stuttgart, Germany
Helder Coelho	University of Lisbon, Portugal
Hugo Algarvio	Technical University of Lisbon, Portugal
Ingo Timm	University of Trier, Germany
Lars Monch	University of Hagen, Germany
Marcin Paprzycki	Polish Academy of Sciences, Poland
Nick Bassiliades	Aristotle University of Thessaloniki, Greece
Olivier Boissier	ENS Mines Saint-Etienne, France
Peter Palensky	TU Delft, The Netherlands
Rainer Unland	University of Duisburg-Essen, Germany
Ryszard Kowalczyk	Swinburne University of Technology, Australia
Tiago Pinto	University of Salamanca, Spain
Zita Vale	Polytechnic Institute of Porto, Portugal
Bo Nørregaard Jørgensen	University of Southern Denmark, Denmark
Matthias Klusch	Research Center for AI, DFKI, Germany
Miguel Lopez	University of Alcala, Spain
Georg Frey	Saarland University, Germany
Zheng Ma	University of Southern Denmark, Denmark
João Santana	University of Lisbon, Portugal

Hydro-Wind Balance in Daily Electricity Markets: A Case-Study

Hugo Algarvio[1,2(✉)], Fernando Lopes[1], and João Santana[2,3]

[1] LNEG–National Research Institute, Est. Paço do Lumiar 22, Lisbon, Portugal
fernando.lopes@lneg.pt
[2] Instituto Superior Técnico, Universidade de Lisboa, Lisbon, Portugal
{hugo.algarvio,jsantana}@tecnico.ulisboa.pt
[3] INESC-ID, Rua Alves Redol 9, 1000-029 Lisbon, Portugal

Abstract. The European Union has been one of the major drivers of the development of renewable energy. In Portugal, renewable generation is subject to specific licensing requirements and benefits from a feed-in-tariff. This paper pays special attention to wind and hydroelectric technologies. Typically, wind farms produce more energy during the night (off-peak periods), when the demand is lower, contributing to a reduction of the market price. Hydroelectric power plants use off-peak periods to pump water, and produce energy in the periods of a 24 hour day where the prices of electricity are higher (peak periods). This paper presents a case study aiming at analyzing the behavior of hydroelectric power producers—that is, in power systems with large renewable generation, producers typically use the periods of the day with lower energy prices for pumping, and the other periods (with higher energy prices) to produce electricity. The simulations are performed using MATREM (for Multi-Agent Trading in Electricity Markets). The results confirm (and rebate) the typical behavior of hydroelectric power producers.

Keywords: Electricity markets · Day-ahead markets · Wind power · Hydroelectric power · The MATREM system

1 Introduction

The goals of the European Union (EU) include the global leadership of Europe in renewables, the integration of variable renewable energy (VRE) in electricity markets, and the increase of the general welfare of consumers. To comply with these goals, European countries have been incentivizing VRE investors, notably with feed-in-tariffs. However, the increasing levels of variable renewable energy, such as solar and wind power (WP), are raising some difficulties to energy markets (see, e.g., [1]). VRE depends on meteorological conditions, meaning that it is not dispatchable (but see [2]).

H. Algarvio and J. Santana—This work was supported by "Fundação para a Ciência e Tecnologia" with references UID/CEC/50021/2019 and PD/BD/105863/2014.

F. De la Prieta et al. (Eds.): PAAMS 2019 Workshops, CCIS 1047, pp. 193–201, 2019.
https://doi.org/10.1007/978-3-030-24299-2_16

The European day-ahead markets (DAMs) close at 12 noon (CET), 12–36 hours before real-time operation. Typically, the global forecast system updates the meteorological information every six hours, starting at 12 midnight (UTC). So, the forecasts for variable renewable energy use meteorological data from 17 to 41 hours before physical delivery [3]. The marginal cost of variable generation is zero, or near-zero.

The bids that VRE producers submit in the DAM are based on forecasts, which can result in substantial deviations in relation to real-time production. These deviations should be compensated with very fast responsive power plants, such as hydroelectric power plants (HPPs). Accordingly, in the periods of a 24 hour day where exist an excess of renewable production (in comparison with the demand), HPPs can use that excess for pumping water at very low prices, instead of curtailing the production of variable renewable energy. Following the pumping of water, HPPs can use that water to produce electricity during peak periods (when the prices of electricity are higher). In general, this procedure increases the efficiency of the power systems and decreases the waste of ("free-of-cost") variable renewable energy.

This paper is devoted to the study of wind power forecasts, wind power bidding, and the operation of hydroelectric power plants, notably the hydro-wind balance in day-ahead markets. Wind power is very variable and its penetration in some systems achieved such a value that it is really important to consider dispatchable power plants able to exhibit a fast response to ramps (see e.g., [3,4]). Nuclear power plants should have (by nature) a stable operation, coal power plants have a very slow response, and fuel oil power plants have high marginal costs. Accordingly, hydroelectric power plants with reservoir and cycle combined gas turbines (CCGT) are often considered the best solution to resolve some problems associated with the variability and uncertainty of renewable energy. Normally, such power plants are marginal and their production is dependent of the hydroelectricity. Basically, in a year with high hydroelectricity, cycle combined gas turbines plants have few working hours, and in a year with low hydroelectricity, they have similar working hours in relation to hydroelectric power plants with reservoir.

The paper presents a case study involving a power system with relevant penetration of hydro and wind power (more than 50%). It aims at analysing (and confirming) the typical behaviour of hydroelectric power plants—that is, producers typically use the periods of the day with higher variable generation and/or lower prices for pumping, and the other periods (with higher prices) to produce energy. The simulations are performed with an agent-based tool, called MATREM (for Multi-Agent Trading in Electricity Markets).

The remainder of the paper is structured as follows. Section 2 addresses the key issues of wind power forecasts and the operation of hydroelectric power plants with storage, placing emphasis on bidding strategies. Section 3 presents a brief overview of the MATREM system. Section 4 presents a case study on hydro-wind balance in a day-ahead market and discusses the simulation results. Finally, Sect. 5 states the conclusions and outlines avenues for future work.

2   Energy Markets and Renewable Generation

In the Iberian market (MIBEL), the majority of the electricity is traded in the day-ahead market, which closes at 12 noon (CET). Producers submit bids according to their marginal costs. Energy prices are computed based on the marginal pricing theory. Following the operation of the DAM, market participants can submit bids to the intra-day market (involving six trading sessions), where players can adjust their schedules. Also, national balancing markets are used to minimize deviations between supply and demand, guaranteeing the security of the power system (see, e.g., [5]).

2.1   Wind Power Plants

In the past few years, numerous approaches to forecast wind power have been developed and detailed reviews of forecasting techniques can be found in the literature (see, e.g., [6,7]). The existing approaches may be classified into the following three categories: numerical weather prediction (NWP) models, statistical models, and approaches involving aspects of both models.

The NWP models are an indispensable tool for wind power producers participating in electricity markets. However, one of the main sources of errors in the wind/power forecasts, even when coupled with statistical approaches, is the data provided by such models. This drawback can be partially explained by: (i) the inadequate physics of most models, (ii) the inability of models to handle sub-grid scale phenomena, and (iii) the initial and boundary conditions (ICs).

The NWP models solve the equations that govern the status of the atmosphere using numerical methods. Therefore, ICs are necessary for the numerical calculations as well as digital maps of the terrain topography and roughness. These ICs are usually obtained from global models, such as the global forecast model system with 6 hours intervals (at 12 am (0), 6 am (6), 12 pm (12) and 6 pm (18) UTC), taking into account the assimilation of several different type of meteorological observations.

In this paper, we consider a K-nearest neighbor method in order to obtain the deterministic forecasts using the NWP outputs [3,8]. The importance of this technique (also known as analogous forecast) has been increasing due to: (i) its easy implementation and effectiveness [9], and (ii) the fact that it is a non-parametric approach, and as such no prior assumption needs to be taken regarding the distribution of the variables to predict.

Taking into account the current limitations associated with the periods to obtain the ICs, the actual bids to the DAM considered in this work are the forecasts themselves (as in the real-world, the point forecast of the aggregated wind farms are considered). Therefore, due to the limitations of the ICs and the operational time needed to manipulate data, the schedules resulting from the day-ahead market should be partially adjusted in the intra-day market, which in turn need to be adjusted in the balancing market (but see, e.g., [4]).

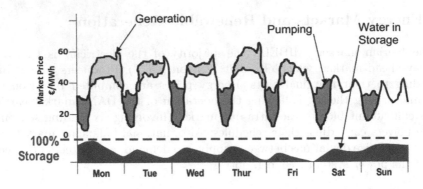

Fig. 1. Typical operation of HPPs with reservoir (adapted from [11])

2.2 Typical Operation of Hydroelectric Power Plants with Reservoir

In power systems with a high penetration of renewables (specially VRE), HPPs with reservoir typically consider the periods of a 24 hour day with the higher shares of VRE and/or lower prices for pumping, and the other periods (with higher prices) for producing energy (see Fig. 1).

HPPs with reservoir may act in the supply-side, as producers, and in the demand-side, as consumers (for pumping). Their bids are very important and should be defined as rigorously as possible. To this end, players should take into account the following: current storage, future outflow (production and other losses), future inflow (rain and pumping), and the rates of outflow and inflow of water. In this work, we consider the aggregation of all HPPs with reservoir and the bids of the resulting player are obtained by taking into account the nominal power, current storage and the social value of water.

The social value of water for electricity production can be considered the value that avoids (i.e., rules out) the production of the more expensive power plants [10]. This value depends of the seasonality of the production (time of operation), historical data for the inflow rate (rain), and also the hydroelectricity of the year (a low hydroelectricity refers to a dry year and a high hydroelectricity refers to a humid year). Normally, in a common hydroelectricity year (with a storage capacity filled more than 50%), the social value of water is the value that allows to rule out (of the market) the CCGT power plants. In the years with high hydroelectricity, the water value of hydropower may be lower than the values associated with coal power plants, but higher than the the common values for nuclear power plants. Otherwise, in the years with low hydroelectricity and a storage capacity filled bellow 50%, the water value of hydropower is higher than the common values for CCGT power plants, but lower than the values for fuel oil power plants. So, the social value of water for electricity production may be considered a value that rule out the more expensive power plants, in such a way that does not affect the future storage capacity [11].

Table 1. Key features of producer agents (software agents)

Agent	Technology	Power (MW)	Marginal price (€/MWh)	Bidding price (€/MWh)
GenCo WindPower	Wind	2000.00	0.00	0.00
GenCo Thermal	Coal	638.00	45.00	45.00
GenCo HydroPower	Hydro	2000.00	0.00	50.00
GenCo CCGT 1	Gas	830.00	54.50	54.50
GenCo CCGT 2	Gas	990.00	56.12	56.12
GenCo CCGT 3	Gas	1176.00	57.90	57.90

3   The MATREM System: An Overview

MATREM is an agent-based system composed by a power exchange and a derivatives exchange (see [12] for a detailed description of the system and [13] for its
classification according to a number of dimensions related to both competitive
energy markets and software agents).

In short, MATREM is able to simulate the day-ahead markets (see, e.g.,
[14]), the intra-day markets (based on auctions), the balancing markets (see,
e.g., [2]), the futures markets, and also the negotiation of bilateral agreements
(see, e.g., [15]). The pricing mechanism of the day-ahead and intra-day markets
is founded on the marginal pricing theory, specifically using the system marginal
pricing (typical of European markets) or the locational marginal pricing (typical
of North-American markets). The balancing markets consider an asymmetric
auction, also founded on the marginal pricing theory, where transmission system operators define the requirements for reserve control and market participants submit bids to buy or sell energy. The futures markets consider a direct
match (pay-as-bis scheme) between offers to sell and buy electricity. Bilateral
agreements can be negotiated privately between two parties, namely agreements
involving the details of tailored (or customized) long-term bilateral contracts.
The system is also able to simulate new elements of market design, giving suggestions for the design of (future) electricity markets with high penetrations of
VRE (see, e.g., [1]).

4   The Case-Study

This study involves a simplification of the Portuguese electric power system,
by considering six generation companies (GenCos) and five retail companies
(RetailCos). These eleven market players are modeled as software agents and
implemented in the MATREM system. Several key features of the GenCo agents
are shown in Table 1, including the generation technology, the maximum capacity and the production cost. The producer agent named "GenCo HydroPower"
makes bids to sell energy (3000 MW) in the DAM at 50 €/MWh (assumed to
be the water value of hydropower).

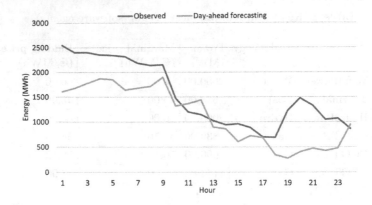

Fig. 2. GenCo WindPower agent: day-ahead forecast and real data

Figure 2 shows the hourly wind production data for the producer agent named "GenCo WindPower" in a typical day, together with the wind power forecast (the methodology employed was described in Sect. 2.1). The bids of this agent in the day-ahead market are assumed to be equal to the forecast. The figure also presents the difference between the forecast values at 6 a.m. (17 and 41 hours prior to real time production) offered in the DAM, and the (real) observed production.

The purpose of the case study is to analyse—and confirm—the typical behaviour of HPPs. Specifically, in power systems with high penetration of VRE, HPPs with reservoir often use the periods of a 24 hour day with high VRE penetration and/or lower prices for pumping, and the other periods (with higher prices) to produce electricity. Accordingly, the producer agent "GenCo HydroPower" considers both bids to sell and offers to buy energy. In this way, the demand-side is represented by five retailers and the producer agent ("GenCo HydroPower"). Table 2 shows the minimum and maximum energy quantities and prices of the six buyers (to offer in the DAM) in a particular day of operation. As shown in the Table, the agent "GenCo HydroPower" considers offers to buy 3000 MW at 10 €/MWh (assumed to be the pumping value).

Table 2. Retailer agents: day-ahead offers

Agent	Quantity (MWh)		Price (€/MWh)	
	Min.	Max.	Min.	Max.
Best Energy	191.92	530.07	51.59	60.34
SCO Corporation	440.45	1406.46	55.59	66.01
Electro Center	91.73	419.64	56.59	67.01
First Energy	351.89	1208.52	47.59	58.00
David Owen	505.54	1603.97	37.59	48.00
GenCo HydroPower	3000.00	3000.00	10.00	10.00

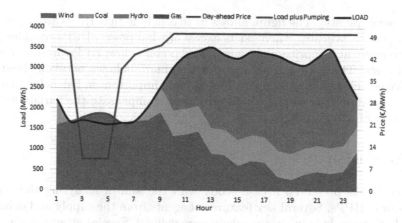

Fig. 3. Day-ahead load and prices (Color figure online)

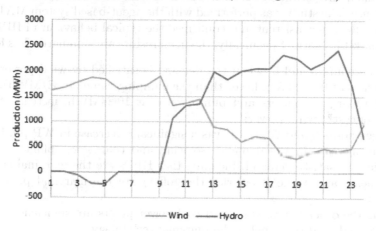

Fig. 4. Simulation results: part of hydro-wind balance

The results are presented in Fig. 3, namely the market-clearing prices and the power commitments. Clearly, between 3 a.m. and 5 a.m., when the demand is satisfied by wind power only (green color in the figure), and the market prices are low, there is the possibility to pump (specifically, 62.73 MWh at 3 a.m., 216.54 MWh at 4 a.m., and 240.78 MWh at 5 a.m.). Also, between 10 a.m. and midnight, the production of hydro energy is required (blue color in the figure). This occurs because of the reduction in wind power production (apart from the increase in demand). In this period, the production of the agent "GenCo HydroPower" ranges between 693.63 MWh and 2418.44 MWh.

Figure 4 shows part of the hydro-wind balance, namely the part that takes into account the pumping of HPPs from hour 3 to 5, where WP is enough to satisfy the load. Furthermore, between hours 9 and 24, the hydroelectric production increases (because the water value is lower than the marginal price of

CCGT power plants). The figure allows us to conclude that HPPs are dependent of wind power. Basically, when exists excess of wind power, HPPs consider such excess to pump at low prices, and when wind power is low, HPPs produce energy at high costs. Thus, we can assume an "informal" balance between these two technologies. This kind of "cooperation" is more important in balancing markets (during real-time operation), where HPPs can compensate the variability and uncertainty of wind generation.

5   Conclusion

This article has presented a case study with the aim of analysing the typical behaviour of HPPs. Several key features of agents from the supply and demand-side able to make bids in spot markets were defined. Special attention was paid to wind and hydro technologies, their bids in day-ahead markets, and the hydro-wind balance. The study was performed with the agent-based system MATREM.

The results are consistent and confirmed the typical behaviour of HPPs in a typical market scenario. Specifically, the main results are summarized as follows:

- Between hours 3 and 5, when the demand is satisfied by wind power (WP) with offers at 0 €/MWh, lower than the pumping value (10 €/MWh), HPPs are the marginal players and pump water at 10€/MWh, instead of waste ("free-of-cost") wind power;
- Between hours 9 and 24, there was a significant decrease in WP production, and an increase in the demand; so wind and coal power plants were not sufficient to satisfy demand, meaning that HPPs are the marginal suppliers and their water value (the price they offer) are the marginal price of the market;
- During the other hours, wind and coal power plants are sufficient to satisfy the demand, and thus coal is the marginal technology.

To conclude, HPPs are very important to compensate the wind power variability, since in cases of excess of wind power, HPPs can pump water (the alternatives are expensive storage technologies, such as batteries). And in cases of wind power decreases, HPPs can respond fast to compensate such decreases using a "free-of-cost" resource (water), receiving at least the social value of water without producing CO_2 emissions (the alternatives are fast CCGT or fuel-oil power plants, with high marginal costs and CO_2 emission).

References

1. Lopes, F., Coelho, H.: Electricity Markets with Increasing Levels of Renewable Generation: Structure, Operation, Agent-Based Simulation and Emerging Designs. Springer, Cham (2018). https://doi.org/10.1007/978-3-319-74263-2
2. Algarvio H., Lopes F., Couto A., Estanqueiro A.: Participation of wind power producers in day-ahead and balancing markets: an overview and a simulation-based study. WIREs Energy Environ. (2019). https://doi.org/10.1002/wene.343

3. Couto, A., Costa, P., Rodrigues, L., Lopes, V.V., Estanqueiro, A.: Impact of weather regimes on the wind power ramp forecast in Portugal. IEEE Trans. Sustain. Energy **6**(3), 934–942 (2015)
4. Skytte, K. Bobo, L.: Increasing the value of wind: from passive to active actors in multiple power markets. WIREs Energy Environ. (2018). https://doi.org/10.1002/wene.328
5. Algarvio, H., Couto, A., Lopes, F., Santana, S., Estanqueiro, A.: Effects of regulating the European internal market on the integration of variable renewable energy. WIREs Energy Environ. (2019). https://doi.org/10.1002/wene.346
6. Giebel, G., Brownsword, R., Kariniotakis, G., Denhard, M., Draxl, C.: The state-of-the-art in short-term prediction of wind power: a literature overview. Technical report, ANEMOS.plus Project, pp. 1–110 (2011)
7. Jung, J., Broadwater, R.P.: Current status and future advances for wind speed and power forecasting. Renew. Sustain. Energy Rev. **31**, 762–777 (2014)
8. Zorita, E., Von Storch, H.: The analog method as a simple statistical downscaling technique: comparison with more complicated methods. J. Clim. **12**(8), 2474–2489 (1999)
9. Taneja, S., Gupta, C., Goyal, K., Gureja, D.: An enhanced k-nearest neighbor algorithm using information gain and clustering. In: Fourth International Conference on Advanced Computing & Communication Technologies, pp. 325–329 (2014)
10. Wolfgang, O., Haugstad, A., Mo, B., Gjelsvik, A.: Hydro reservoir handling in Norway before and after deregulation. Energy **34**, 1642–1651 (2009)
11. MWH: Technical analysis of pumped storage and integration with wind power in the Pacific Northwest. Final Report Prepared for: U.S. Army Corps of Engineers Northwest Division Hydroelectric Design Center, August 2009
12. Lopes, F.: MATREM: an agent-based simulation tool for electricity markets. In: Lopes, F., Coelho, H. (eds.) Electricity Markets with Increasing Levels of Renewable Generation: Structure, Operation, Agent-based Simulation, and Emerging Designs. SSDC, vol. 144, pp. 189–225. Springer, Cham (2018). https://doi.org/10.1007/978-3-319-74263-2_8
13. Lopes, F., Coelho, H.: Electricity markets and intelligent agents part II: agent architectures and capabilities. In: Lopes, F., Coelho, H. (eds.) Electricity Markets with Increasing Levels of Renewable Generation: Structure, Operation, Agent-based Simulation, and Emerging Designs. SSDC, vol. 144, pp. 49–77. Springer, Cham (2018). https://doi.org/10.1007/978-3-319-74263-2_3
14. Lopes, F., Sá, J., Santana, J.: Renewable generation, support policies and the merit order effect: a comprehensive overview and the case of wind power in Portugal. In: Lopes, F., Coelho, H. (eds.) Electricity Markets with Increasing Levels of Renewable Generation: Structure, Operation, Agent-based Simulation, and Emerging Designs. SSDC, vol. 144, pp. 227–263. Springer, Cham (2018). https://doi.org/10.1007/978-3-319-74263-2_9
15. Lopes, F., Algarvio, H., Santana, J.: Agent-based simulation of electricity markets: risk management and contracts for difference. In: Alonso-Betanzos, A., Sánchez-Maroño, N., Fontenla-Romero, O., Polhill, J.G., Craig, T., Bajo, J., Corchado, J.M. (eds.) Agent-Based Modeling of Sustainable Behaviors. UCS, pp. 207–225. Springer, Cham (2017). https://doi.org/10.1007/978-3-319-46331-5_10

Collaborative Reinforcement Learning
of Energy Contracts Negotiation Strategies

Tiago Pinto[1(✉)], Isabel Praça[1], Zita Vale[2], and Carlos Santos[1]

[1] GECAD Research Group, Institute of Engineering,
Polytechnic of Porto (ISEP/IPP), Porto, Portugal
{tcp,icp}@isep.ipp.pt
[2] Polytechnic of Porto (ISEP/IPP), Porto, Portugal
zav@isep.ipp.pt

Abstract. This paper presents the application of collaborative reinforcement learning models to enable the distributed learning of energy contracts negotiation strategies. The learning model combines the learning process on the best negotiation strategies to apply against each opponent, in each context, from multiple learning sources. The diverse learning sources are the learning processes of several agents, which learn the same problem under different perspectives. By combining the different independent learning processes, it is possible to gather the diverse knowledge and reach a final decision on the most suitable negotiation strategy to be applied. The reinforcement learning process is based on the application of the Q-Learning algorithm; and the continuous combination of the different learning results applies and compares several collaborative learning algorithms, namely BEST-Q, Average (AVE)-Q; Particle Swarm Optimization (PSO)-Q, and Weighted Strategy Sharing (WSS)-Q. Results show that the collaborative learning process enables players' to correctly identify the negotiation strategy to apply in each moment, context and against each opponent.

Keywords: Collaborative reinforcement learning · Electricity markets ·
Energy contracts negotiation · Negotiation strategies · Q-Learning

1 Introduction

Electricity markets are evolving into a local trading setting [1], which makes it difficult for unexperienced players to achieve good agreements. One of the solutions to deal with this issue is to provide players with decision support solutions capable of aiding them in deciding which negotiation strategies to apply in each moment, context and against each specific opponent, in order to reach the best possible results from negotiations [2]. Different negotiation strategies have been proposed in the literature, e.g. exploring the game theoretic dimension of the market [3], assessing risk management in line with the portfolio theory [4], or by using forecasting approaches to predict prices and optimize the bidding process [5]. However, current models are not capable of adapting to different market circumstances and negotiating contexts, as they are limited to specific market scenarios and are not integrated in actual market simulation or

© Springer Nature Switzerland AG 2019
F. De la Prieta et al. (Eds.): PAAMS 2019 Workshops, CCIS 1047, pp. 202–210, 2019.
https://doi.org/10.1007/978-3-030-24299-2_17

decision support systems. Thereby current approaches are not able to provide market players with the means to change their behaviour in a real market environment, and therefore pursuit the achievement of the best possible outcomes.

This paper addresses this limitation by providing a contribution towards the adaptability of market players' actions in bilateral energy contracts negotiations. A collaborative reinforcement learning model is applied to enable combining the learning process on the best negotiation strategies to apply against each opponent, in each context, from multiple learning sources. The diverse learning sources are the learning processes of several agents, which learn the same problem under different perspectives (using different utility or results assessment functions). By combining the different independent learning processes, it is possible to gather the diverse knowledge and reach a final decision on the most suitable negotiation strategy to be applied. The reinforcement learning process is based on the application of the Q-Learning algorithm [6]; and the continuous combination of the different learning results applies and compares several collaborative learning algorithms, namely BEST-Q, Average (AVE)-Q; Particle Swarm Optimization (PSO)-Q, and Weighted Strategy Sharing (WSS)-Q [7]. Results show that the collaborative learning process enables players' to correctly identify the best (a-priori identified) negotiation strategy to apply in each moment, context and against each opponent. Moreover, the different algorithms enable the adaptation according to needs of each learning process, i.e. faster, yet not so solid, convergence; or slower convergence, but with higher guarantees of success.

After this introductory section, Sect. 2 presents the proposed methodology; Sect. 3 presents the experimental findings achieved when applying the proposed model, and Sect. 4 presents the most relevant conclusions of this work.

2 Proposed Methodology

The approach proposed in this paper concerns the combination of the learning process of different agents through collaborative learning. The different agents learn the same problem under different perspectives, using different utility or results assessment functions, which result from their own perspective when analysing the problem and the corresponding context. Despite the independent learning processes, all agents use Q-Learning as the reinforcement learning algorithm for this problem. The combination of the different learning process is then applied through several collaborative learning algorithms, namely BEST-Q, AVE-Q; PSO-Q, and WSS-Q [7].

2.1 Q-Learning

Q-Learning is a very popular reinforcement learning method. It is an algorithm that allows the autonomous establishment of an interactive action policy. It is demonstrated that the Q-Learning algorithm converges to the optimal proceeding when the learning state-action pairs Q is represented in a table containing the full information of each pair value [8]. The basic concept behind Q-Learning is that the learning algorithm is able to learn a function of optimal evaluation over the whole space of state-action pairs

$s \times a$. This evaluation thus defines the confidence value Q that each action a is able to represent the state s. The Q function performs the mapping as in Eq. (1).

$$Q : s \times a \rightarrow U \tag{1}$$

where U is the expected utility value when selecting action a in state s. As long as the state does not omit relevant information, nor introduce new information, once the optimal function Q is learned, the decision method will know precisely which action results on the higher future reward under each state. The reward r is attributed to each pair *action-state* in each iteration, representing the quality of this pair, and allows the confidence value Q to be updated after each observation. r is defined as in (2).

$$r_{a,s,t} = 1 - norm \left| RP_{a,s,t,o,p} - EP_{a,s,t,o,p} \right| \tag{2}$$

where $RP_{a,s,t,o,p}$ represents the real price that has been established in a contract with an opponent o, in state s, in time t, referring to an amount of power p; and $EP_{a,s,t,o,p}$ is the estimation price of scenario that corresponds to the same player, amount of power and state in time t. All r values are normalized in a scale from 0 to 1, in order to allow the Q (s, a) function to remain under these values, so that the confidence values Q can be easily assumed as probabilities of scenario occurrence under a context. $Q(s, a)$ is learned through by try an error, being updated every time a new observation (new contract establishment) becomes available, following Eq. (3).

$$Q_{t+1}(s_t, a_t) = Q_t(s_t, a_t) + \alpha \left[r_{s,a,t} + \gamma U_t(a_{t+1}) - Q_t(s_t, a_t) \right] \tag{3}$$

where α is the learning rate; γ is the discount factor; and U_t (4) is the utility resulting from action a under state s, obtained using the Q function learned so far.

$$U_t(s_{t+1}) = \max_a Q(s_{t+1}, a) \tag{4}$$

The Q Learning algorithm is executes as follows:

- For each a and s, initialize $Q(s, a) = 0$;
- Observe new event;
- Repeat until the stopping criterion is satisfied:
  - Select the action that presents the higher Q for the current state;
  - Receive reward $r_{a,s,t}$;
  - Update $Q(s, a)$;
  - Observe new state s';
  - $s \leftarrow s'$.

As the visiting of all action-state pairs tends to infinite, the method guarantees a generation of an estimative of Q_t which converges to the value of Q. In fact, the actions policy converges to the optimal policy in a finite time, however slowly. In order to accelerate the convergence process, not only the Q value of the chosen action is updated, but also that of all scenarios, since the r regarding all alternative scenarios can be computed by comparing the estimated prices by each action and the actual values that have been verified in a new contract agreement. After each updating process, all Q values are normalized, as in Eq. (5), so that they are always kept in a scale from 0 to 1, thus facilitating the interpretation as the probability of each action in correctly representing the negotiation reality.

$$Q'(s,a) = \frac{Q(s,a)}{\max[Q(s,a)]} \tag{5}$$

2.2   Collaborative Learning Approaches

2.2.1   BEST-Q

The BEST-Q algorithm selects, for each state-action pair, the best value (Q-value) from all tables (Q-tables) of all agents, as in (6). Then each agent updates its individual Q-table accordingly.

$$Q_i(s,a) \leftarrow Q^{best}(s,a), \forall i, s, a \tag{6}$$

where i is the agent.

The disadvantage of this approach is that optimum values (Q-values) are not found because the values (Q-values) become equal after each update. However, the BEST-Q algorithm can achieve good long-term simulation policy.

The BEST-Q algorithm uses as assumption the best confidence value for each state-action pair according to all the data of the agents present in the environment. Each agent updates its Q-table by updating the pairs with the best values obtained previously.

2.2.2   AVE-Q

The AVE-Q algorithm is similar to the BEST-Q except that each agent updates its Q-values with the average of its current value and the best value (Q-value) for each state-action from the tables (Q-tables) of all agents, as presented in (7)

$$Q_i(s,a) \leftarrow \frac{Q^{best}(s,a) + Q_i(s,a)}{2}, \quad \forall i, s, a \tag{7}$$

The main disadvantage of the AVE-Q algorithm is that it does not eliminate the bad values (Q-values) in the interaction stage. The AVE-Q algorithm is very similar to the BEST-Q algorithms except for updating the agent. It uses as assumption the best value of confidence for each state-action pair according to all the data of the agents present in the environment and its current value of learning, so the table of the agent is updated through the average of these two values. Each agent updates its Q-table by updating the pairs with the previously obtained values.

2.2.3   PSO-Q

Multi-agent optimization known as Particle Swarm Optimization (PSO), is part of the swarm intelligence methodologies and techniques. This algorithm was inspired by the rules of alignment and cohesion of the flocks of birds, and its particularity is represented by the transmission and sharing of information [9].

Each agent is initialized with a set of possible random solutions and the optimal solution is searched for in each generation. The movement of each agent is influenced by the global optimum and personal memory, with each agent having the ability to adapt its speed that directs its movement and remembers the best position found to date [10]. This movement follows the following four rules:

- Separation: there must be a separation between each agent, to avoid collisions.
- Alignment: it is necessary that each agent follows the same direction of neighboring particles.
- Cohesion: it is necessary that each agent follows the same position of neighboring particles.
- Deviation: in the encounter of an obstacle, it is necessary that the agent is able to deviate.

The PSO-Q algorithm uses PSO to find the near-optimal solution. PSO is an optimization method that repeatedly improves the candidate solution accordingly to with the qualitative measure. PSO solves decision problems that have multiple decision variables. In the PSO-Q algorithm the best values (Q-values) of each agent and the best global values (Q-values) of all agents are used by each agent to update its Q-table, as in (8) according to a velocity function V_i (9) that determines the movement of the particles involved in the search process.

$$Q_i(s,a) \leftarrow Q_i(s,a) + V_i(s,a), \quad \forall i, s, a \tag{8}$$

$$V_i(s,a) = WV_i(s,a) + C_1R_1[P_i(s,a) - Q_i(s,a)] \\ + C_2R_2[G(s,a) - Q_i(s,a)] \tag{9}$$

where W is the inertia component, which defines the degree in which the movement will stay closer to the previous position; $P_i(s,a)$ is the best Q-value of agent i for the pair $s \times a$, $G(s,a)$ is the best global solution for the $s \times a$ pair, C_1 and C_2 are weight components that determine the degree in which the new position will tend to the personal and global best, respectively; and R_1 and R_2 are random values ranging [0, 1].

In the PSO-Q, the reinforcement learning problem is modeled as an optimization problem in which the candidate solutions are the values (Q-values of the table), and the qualitative measure is the Q-function. In the PSO-Q algorithm, the best values (Q-values) of each agent and the best overall value of all agents are used for each agent to update its Q-table.

2.2.4 WSS-Q

In the WSS (Weighted Strategy-Sharing) method, it is assumed that homogeneous Q-Learning agents learn in some distinct environments, so their actions do not alter the environment of other agents and no hidden state is produced.

Agents learn in two ways: individual learning mode and cooperative learning mode. First, all agents are in the individual learning mode. The agent performs several learning attempts. Each learning attempt starts from a random state and ends when the agent reaches the goal. After a specified number of individual attempts, all agents switch to cooperative learning mode. In the collaborative mode, each agent delegates a weight to the other agents according to their expertise (trust value). Then, each agent updates through a weighted average with the values of the other tables resulting in a new table.

Using the WSS-Q algorithm, each agent assumes a weight for the tables of the other agents based on the relative skill of each agent. Subsequently, each agent uses the weighted average of all values of tables (Q-tables) to update its own table (10).

$$Q_i(s,a) \leftarrow \sum_{j=1}^{n} [W_{i,j} Q_j(s,a)], \quad \forall i, s, a \qquad (10)$$

where W_{ij} is the weight that agent i takes on the skill of agent j.

3   Case Study

3.1   Specifications

This case study considers 4 independent agents, which learn the same problem from different perspectives. In summary, each agent needs to learn which, from 10 distinct actions, is the best one; in which each action refers to the choice on a negotiation strategy to be applied against an opponent in a bilateral negotiation. Table 1 shows the a-priori defined best actions from each agent's perspective.

Table 1. Best a-priori actions for each agent

Agent id	1	2	3	4
Best actions #	10	10, 2	8, 2	8

From Table 1 it is visible that the best overall actions accordingly to the perspective of the 4 agents are actions 2, 8 and 10.

The number of Q-Learning episodes to perform has the value 200 being that each episode is composed of 1000 repetitions of the Q-Learning steps. The sharing of information between agents in done at every 10 episodes. All agents initially start in episode 1. The parameterization for Q-Learning is as follows: the discount factor is 0.9 for a slower exploration and a learning rate of 0.01 so that learning does not dispense with the desired value.

3.2   Results

Figures 1, 2, 3 and 4 present the evolution of the Q-values of each action, from each agent's perspective, throughout all the episodes, when using the BEST-Q, AVE-Q, PSO-Q and WSS-Q algorithms, respectively.

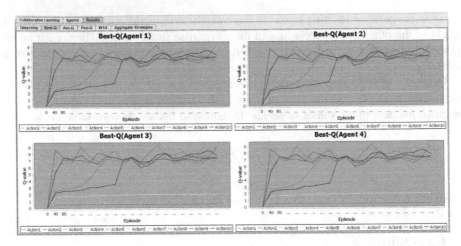

Fig. 1. Evolution Q-Values for BEST-Q

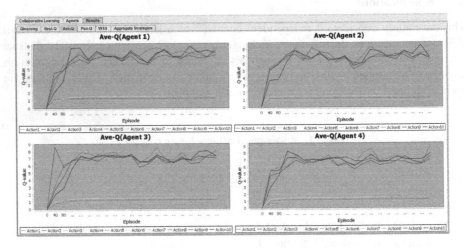

Fig. 2. Evolution Q-Values for AVE-Q

From Fig. 1 is can be seen that the agents present partially identical graphs because they use the best values of the other agents. The BEST-Q algorithm reaches a relative convergence at around 360 iterations. From Fig. 2 one can see that the AVE-Q algorithm in the first iterations presents a marked increase in values for the actions with greater reinforcement. The algorithm reaches a balance from the 160 iterations. It is concluded that AVE-Q reaches a quicker convergence that BEST-Q on the best actions.

From Fig. 3 it is visible that PSO-Q in the first iterations presents a marked increase in values for the actions with greater reinforcement. The algorithm reaches a balance from the 160 iterations. Although with the increase in the number of iterations another action stands out; *i.e.* the algorithm allows to explore other possibilities and make a management of learning with exploration and experience. In comparison with the previous algorithms this algorithm achieves a fast equilibrium allowing for the search of new emergent good actions. From Fig. 4, one can see that the WSS algorithm presents variations along the number of iterations. This algorithm limits the choice in only 3 actions for the proposed problem (2, 8 and 10 as a-priori identified). In comparison with the previous algorithms this one identifies the best actions, but it does not demonstrate a clear convergence, like the other algorithms.

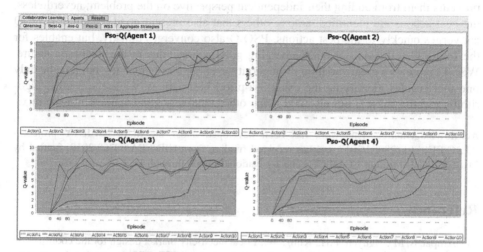

Fig. 3. Evolution Q-Values for PSO-Q

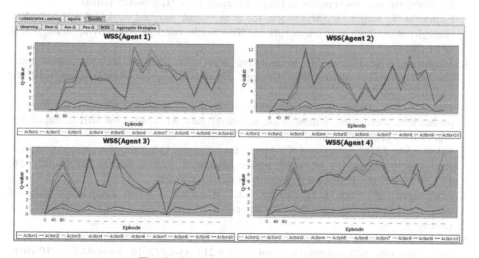

Fig. 4. Evolution Q-Values for WSS-Q

4 Conclusions

This paper has presented the application of four collaborative reinforcement learning algorithms (BEST-Q, AVE-Q, PSO-Q and WSS-Q) to the problem of identifying the best action (negotiation strategy) that is learned independently by several different agents, with different perspectives.

Results show that with BEST-Q all agents converge to the same Q-Tables, which prevents them from adding their independent perspective on the problem; nevertheless, the best actions are identified, among others that also present good potential. AVE-Q converges quickly to the best actions. PSO-Q also converges quickly, but enables for the future identification of other emerging good actions, due to the stochastic nature. WSS-Q presents a great variation throughout the entire set of episodes, but it is the only one that enables identifying the exact 3 a-priori best actions, while the 3 other algorithms identify these 3 but also add some other relatively good actions into the mix.

Acknowledgements. This work has been developed under the MAS-SOCIETY project - PTDC/EEI-EEE/28954/2017 and has received funding from UID/EEA/00760/2019, funded by FEDER Funds through COMPETE and by National Funds through FCT.

References

1. Ampatzis, M., Nguyen, P.H., Kling, W.: Local electricity market design for the coordination of distributed energy resources at district level. In: IEEE PES Innovative Smart Grid Technologies, Europe, pp. 1–6 (2014)
2. Pinto, T., Vale, Z., Sousa, T.M., et al.: Adaptive learning in agents behaviour: a framework for electricity markets simulation. Integr. Comput. Eng. **21**, 399–415 (2014)
3. Faqiry, M.N., Kundu, R., Mukherjee, R., et al.: Game theoretic model of energy trading strategies at equilibrium in microgrids. In: 2014 North American Power Symposium, NAPS 2014 (2014)
4. Meghwani, S.S., Thakur, M.: Multi-criteria algorithms for portfolio optimization under practical constraints. Swarm Evol. Comput. **37**, 104–125 (2017). https://doi.org/10.1016/j.swevo.2017.06.005
5. Nowotarski, J., Weron, R.: Recent advances in electricity price forecasting: a review of probabilistic forecasting. Renew. Sustain. Energy Rev. **81**, 1548–1568 (2018). https://doi.org/10.1016/j.rser.2017.05.234
6. Salehizadeh, M.R., Soltaniyan, S.: Application of fuzzy Q-learning for electricity market modeling by considering renewable power penetration. Renew. Sustain. Energy Rev. **56**, 1172–1181 (2016). https://doi.org/10.1016/j.rser.2015.12.020
7. Abed-alguni, B., Paul, D.J., Chalup, S.K., Henskens, F.A.: A comparison study of cooperative Q-learning algorithms for independent learners. Int. J. Artif. Intell. **14**, 71–93 (2016)
8. Kofinas, P., Dounis, A.I., Vouros, G.A.: Fuzzy Q-Learning for multi-agent decentralized energy management in microgrids. Appl. Energy **219**, 53–67 (2018). https://doi.org/10.1016/j.apenergy.2018.03.017
9. Kiran, M.S.: Particle swarm optimization with a new update mechanism (2017). https://doi.org/10.1016/j.asoc.2017.07.050
10. Kennedy, J., Eberhart, R.: Particle swarm optimization. In: 1995 Proceedings of International Conference on Neural Networks, vol. 4, pp. 1942–1948 (1995)

Potential Impact of Load Curtailment on the Day-Ahead Iberian Market: A Preliminary Analysis

Francisco Rodrigues[1], Hugo Algarvio[2,3]([✉]), Fernando Lopes[2],
Anabela Pronto[1], and João Santana[3,4]

[1] Faculdade de Ciências e Tecnologia, Universidade Nova de Lisboa, Lisbon, Portugal
fad.rodrigues@campus.fct.unl.pt, amg1@fct.unl.pt
[2] LNEG–National Research Institute, Est. do Paço do Lumiar 22, Lisbon, Portugal
fernando.lopes@lneg.pt
[3] Instituto Superior Técnico, Avenida Rovisco Pais 1, Lisbon, Portugal
{hugo.algarvio,jsantana}@tecnico.ulisboa.pt
[4] INESC-ID, Rua Alves Redol 9, Lisbon, Portugal

Abstract. Demand response (DR) in electricity markets may offer a variety of financial and operational benefits. Typically, customers respond to DR events by adopting curtailment and shifting strategies. This article focuses on the former strategy and assumes that consumers are encouraged to avoid consuming electricity during specific hours of a 24 h day, because the energy price is above a given threshold. It presents a study on the Iberian market, conducted with the help of an agent-based simulation tool, called MATREM. The results are very favorable to the adoption of the load curtailment strategy (as a consequence of the enrollment in different DR programs).

Keywords: Electricity markets · MIBEL · Demand response · Load curtailment · The MATREM system

1 Introduction

All over the world and especially in the European Union (EU), the restructuration of the electricity industry has contributed to the growth and development of many regional markets [1,2]. In particular, the Iberian Electricity market (MIBEL) has emerged from the cooperation between two member countries, Portugal and Spain, with the goal of integrating the electrical systems of both countries, reducing the problems associated with the process of interchanging electricity. One of the main goals of MIBEL is the free access and competition in the supply industry of electrical energy, requiring competitors to follow specific

H. Algarvio and J. Santana—This work was supported by "Fundação para a Ciência e Tecnologia" with references UID/CEC/50021/2019 and PD/BD/105863/2014.

F. De la Prieta et al. (Eds.): PAAMS 2019 Workshops, CCIS 1047, pp. 211–218, 2019.
https://doi.org/10.1007/978-3-030-24299-2_18

rules and behave in a transparent way regarding their objectives and market negotiations [3, 4].

With the implementation of MIBEL, a problem emerged, evidenced by the disconnection between the retail and wholesale markets, where consumers instead of "seeing" the price of electricity as something dynamic and changing on a hourly basis, "view" a static value, discouraging them from changing their consumption patterns (during periods of high market prices). Without such important changes that could happen in the demand side, the wholesale market is to some extent deprived of defenses against the high volatility of prices (inherent to the sale and purchase of electricity), giving market power to generating companies and benefiting them in the short-term to negotiate the electricity prices at high values. All of these could be avoided, at least in part, with the implementation of demand response programs [5, 6].

Demand response (DR) can be defined as a process where end-use customers of electricity, due to the changing prices, modify their usage values through changes in their daily energy consumption patterns. An interesting possibility to introduce this concept in the mind of energy consumers spins around some demand response programs that shift the market power to the hands of end-user customers, and most importantly, give them the choice to use the advantage of being part of an open market. DR programs can be divided into the following two categories [7]:

1. *Incentive-based programs:* rely on agreements between consumers and market entities, where it is expected that the first party responds to requests made by the second party, in critical hours, being rewarded economically when they do that, and suffering penalties when they fail to do that. Examples include direct load control and interruptible/curtailment agreements.
2. *Price-based programs:* rely on the implementation of time-varying tariffs involving a dynamic price for electricity, so that consumers can adjust their patterns of consumption. Examples include time-of-use (TOU) rates and Real-time pricing (RTP) rates.

In the EU, the inclusion of demand response in regional markets has been accomplished with the signing of various agreements, and consequently the drafting of a number of laws, the most important being the one celebrated in Paris, where it was decided that all the resources associated with DR should be used in order to obtain competitive prices, stimulating the markets to innovate, and encouraging consumers to participate.

Although some countries are proving that the implementation of DR programs is not impossible, the progress has been slow, in part due to a lack of "education" that consumers have towards this concept, and also because of the short and long-term investments that are needed in order to make these programs feasible. France is a country where the implementation of DR programs has been successful. At the time of writing, the concept of DR is implemented and fully operational—or pilot projects are ongoing—in all the sectors of the French electricity market, ranging from the wholesale market and the network services of distribution to the reserve and auxiliary mechanisms used in critical situations [8].

As for the Iberian electricity market, Spain has shown more progress than Portugal. Worthy to mention is the nationwide implementation of smart-meters, a form of consumers being informed of the real time-pricing of electricity and giving them more control of their household appliances [8,9].

Customers respond to DR events by adopting several basic load response strategies, notably shifting and curtailment [7]. This article focuses on the load curtailment strategy and considers that consumers are encouraged to avoid consuming electricity during specific hours of a 24 h day, because the energy price is above a given threshold. More specifically, the article considers different levels of demand response, modeled as load reductions between 1% and 5% when prices rise above a threshold between 80 and 100 €/MWh. The main goal of the article consists of analyzing the potential benefits of the load curtailment strategy for all participants of the Iberian market, namely to determine the price reductions in critical periods and to quantify the financial benefits. To this end, it presents a study on MIBEL, conducted with the help of an agent-based simulation tool, called MATREM (for Multi-agent TRading in Electricity Markets).

This article builds on our previous work in the area of demand response and energy markets. In particular, Lopes and Algarvio [9] investigated the impact of different levels of DR on the Iberian market prices, and analyzed the potential benefits for market participants and retail customers. Demand response was modeled as modest load reductions (between 1% and 5%) at times of high market prices (i.e., when prices rose above a threshold between 80 and 100 €/MWh). The period under consideration ranged between January 1, 2014 and June 30, 2017. This article extends our previous study by considering the following 18-month period: January 1, 2017 to June 30, 2018.

Now, there are other pieces of work that analyzed the potential effect of demand response on the Iberian market prices, notably Fernández et al. [10]. However, the authors did not consider price thresholds, meaning that all hours of the period of the study were considered (from April 2014 to March 2015)— that is, the study considers load reductions of 1.5%, 3% and 6% uniform for all hours of a 24-h day. In this way, and despite being a very detailed study, we believe that it does not represent very well practical situations (in terms of possible implementation in the real-world by end-use customers).

The remainder of this paper is structured as follows. Section 2 presents a brief overview of the MATREM system. Section 3 presents the case study and discusses the simulation results. Finally, Sect. 4 states the conclusions and outlines some avenues for future work.

2   Overview of the MATREM System

MATREM allows the user to conduct a wide range of simulations regarding the behaviour of electricity markets under a variety of conditions (see [11] for a detailed description of the system and [12] for its classification according to a number of dimensions related to both competitive energy markets and software agents).

MATREM supports a day-ahead market and a shorter-term market known as intraday market. Supply bids and demand offers are aggregated to find a clearing price at which supply and demand are equal (see, e.g., [13]). MATREM is also able to simulate a balancing market. The system operator defines the needs of this market and generating company agents may submit bids to buy or sell energy (see, e.g., [14]).

Furthermore, MATREM supports a derivatives exchange comprising a futures market for trading standardized bilateral contracts, and a marketplace for negotiating the details of tailored (or customized) long-term bilateral contracts (see, e.g., [15]). To this end, buyer and seller agents are equipped with a negotiation model that handles two-party and multi-issue negotiation (see, e.g., [16]). In short, the negotiation process involves three main phases or stages, namely pre-negotiation (focuses on preparation and planning for negotiation), actual negotiation (seeks a solution for a dispute and is characterized by movement toward a mutually acceptable agreement), and post-negotiation (centers on details and implementation of a final agreement).

Currently, MATREM considers six key types of market entities: generating companies, retailers, aggregators, consumers, market operators and system operators. Also, the tool considers two key types of software agents: market agents and assistant agents. Market agents represent the entities that take part in the various simulated markets. Assistant agents are categorized into interface managers (responsible for managing the interfaces of the simulated markets) and intelligent assistants (provide support to the user in making strategic decisions). The agents are being developed using the JAVA Agent Development Framework (JADE), an open source platform for peer-to-peer agent based applications [17]. The target platform for the system is a 32/64-bit computer running Microsoft Windows.

3   Case Study

The purpose of this study is to investigate the effects of different levels of demand response on the daily prices of the Iberian market and analyze the potential benefits that result to market participants and retail customers. The following sources of data are considered [18,19]: (i) day-ahead prices and energy quantities submitted to MIBEL, and (ii) market-clearing prices and energy quantities traded in MIBEL.[1]

The experimental method involves basically the following: (i) to simulate the day-ahead markets prices actually observed in MIBEL, (ii) to simulate the day-ahead market prices in the presence of specific levels of demand response, and

---

[1] This study extends our previous study about the impact of different levels of DR on the Iberian market prices [9], by considering the second half of 2017 and the first half of 2018. The software agents, method, and energy scenarios are essential identical in both studies, and details are therefore omitted.

Table 1. Average monthly price reductions

Scenario	Average price reduction (€/MWh) Year 2017	
	January	December
B1	1.11	1.09
B2	3.45	2.90
B3	6.06	4.43
C1	1.04	0.84
C2	3.57	1.77
C3	6.85	2.86
D1	0.39	—
D2	1.64	—
D3	2.76	—

(iii) to compute the effect on market price (estimated as the difference between the prices calculated in the two previous items).

The following ten scenarios for electricity consumption are considered:

- Scenario A (base-case scenario): the simulations are performed in order to reproduce the market prices reported by MIBEL;
- Scenarios B1–B3, C1–C3, D1–D3: to simulate what would have been the market prices in the presence of specific levels of DR, the values of the electricity demand are changed correspondingly (the letters indicate a specific threshold price, namely 80, 90 or 100 €/MWh respectively, and the numbers represent a particular level of DR, namely 1%, 3% or 5% respectively).

The time period of the study has the duration of 18 months: from January 1, 2017 to June 30, 2018.

The analysis is carried out using the MATREM system. The number of agents representing the electricity supply industry varies between 50 and 200. The demand for electrical energy is assumed to be perfectly inelastic, meaning that a single agent bids the entire demand at a price of 180 €/MWh. To represent the Iberian market in a realistic way, the study takes in account the hours where the phenomenon of market-splitting occurs. In such hours, MATREM simulates the Portuguese region only. In the remaining hours, MATREM simulates the market prices for both Portugal and Spain. There are 978 DR events in the period under consideration (interestingly, all events occurred in the year 2017).

Tables 1 and 2 summarize the results of the study. The values shown in Table 1 represent the average monthly price reductions. As expected, the price reductions increase with larger levels of DR, regardless of the threshold price. For scenario B3 (corresponding to a load reduction of 5% and a threshold price of 80 €/MWh), the price reduction in January reaches 6.06 €/MWh, decreasing to 4.43 €/MWh in December. For scenarios C1–C3, the largest price reduction

Table 2. Financial benefits of "demand response"

Scenario	Market value of energy (million €)	Load curtailment benefit (million €)
	2017	2017
B1	677.45	16.08
B2	646.02	47.51
B3	614.58	78.95
C1	298.85	6.51
C2	284.64	20.71
C3	268.49	36.87
D1	12.04	0.17
D2	11.65	0.56
D3	11.28	0.93

occurs in January (6.85 €/MWh in scenario C3, corresponding to a load reduction of 5% and a threshold price of 90 €/MWh). In December, the price reduction reaches 2.86 €/MWh only.

Table 2 shows the market value of energy during the time period of the study (considering the hours corresponding to DR events only). As expected, this value decreases with an increase of either the level of DR or the threshold price. For scenario B1, the market value of energy reaches the highest value (677.45 million €). And for scenario D3, it reaches the lowest value (11.28 million €). For scenarios B1 and B3, the difference between the corresponding market values of energy is 62.87 million €, decreasing to 30.36 million € for scenarios C1 and C3, and to 0.76 million € for scenarios D1 and D3. This can explained, at least in part, by the reduced occurrence of DR events in the scenarios corresponding to higher threshold prices.

Table 2 also shows the potential benefit of the load curtailment strategy. The results are very interesting, indicating that the adoption of this strategy (as a result of the enrollment in DR programs), is indeed beneficial to market participants and retail customers. For the particular case of scenario B3, the benefit of doing a small curtailment of load (5%) reaches the value of 78.95 million €, a considerable monetary value. Is also important to observe the result of scenario D3—involving 3 DR events only, occurring on 25 January 2017 (and corresponding to market prices ≥ 100 €/MWh)—where the financial benefit reaches almost 1 million €. Therefore, and in short, the adoption of the load curtailment strategy by end-use customers can be considered a very important aspect for the market sector, resulting in a win-win situation.

4   Conclusion

This paper has given an overview of the agent-based simulation tool for electricity markets, called MATREM, currently under development. It has also presented a study to investigate the impact of different levels of load curtailment on the daily prices of MIBEL and analyze the potential benefits that result to all participants.

The impacts of the load curtailment strategy on the Iberian market prices can be summarized as follows:

- In 2017, the annual price reduction ranged from 0.39 €/MWh to 6.76 €/MWh (a decline ranging from 0.39% to 7.22%). These values can be explained, at least in part, by the slope of the supply curve, especially in January (a month associated with more than 200 DR events, corresponding to scenarios B1–B3).
- In 2017, the financial benefits of the load curtailment strategy (or indirectly, the benefits of demand response) are very interesting, reaching the considerable value of 78.95 million €. This is probably due to the high number of DR events that occurred in this year.
- In the first half of 2018 (181 days), there were no DR events (since the market price was always below 80 €/MWh).

These results are very favorable to the adoption of the load curtailment strategy, as a consequence of the enrollment in different DR programs, since modest load curtailments (1% to 5%) led to substantial reductions of market prices and considerable financial benefits.

References

1. Stoft, S.: Power Systyem Economis - Designing Markets for Electricity. IEEE Press and Wiley, Hoboken (2002)
2. Lopes, F., Coelho, H.: Electricity Markets with Increasing Levels of Renewable Generation: Structure, Operation. Agent-based Simulation and Emerging Designs. Springer, Cham (2018). https://doi.org/10.1007/978-3-319-74263-2
3. OMIE: Day-ahead and Intraday Electricity Market Operating Rules, May 2018. http://www.omie.es/files/market_rules_2018.pdf. (Cited on 02 April, 2018)
4. OMIP: Trading RuleBook. MIBEL Derivatives Market, Lisbon, Portugal (2016)
5. Braithwait, S., Eakin, K. Inc, Laurits R. Christensen A.: The role of demand response in electric power market design. Technical report, Edison Electric Institute, Washington, D.C., October 2002
6. FERC: assessment of demand response and advance metering. Staff report of the federal energy regulatory commission, Washington, D.C., December 2015
7. DOE: Benefits of demand response in electricity markets and recommendations for achieving them. A report to the United States congress pursuant to Section 1252 of the energy policy act of 2005. US Department of Energy, February 2006
8. SEDC: Explicit demand response in Europe: mapping the markets 2017. Report of the smart energy demand coalition, Brussels, Belgium (2017)
9. Lopes, F., Algarvio, H.: Demand response in electricity markets: an overview and a study of the price-effect on the Iberian daily market. In: Lopes, F., Coelho, H. (eds.) Electricity Markets with Increasing Levels of Renewable Generation: Structure, Operation, Agent-based Simulation, and Emerging Designs. SSDC, vol. 144, pp. 265–303. Springer, Cham (2018). https://doi.org/10.1007/978-3-319-74263-2_10
10. Fernández, J., Payán, M., Santos, J., García, A.: The voluntary price for the small consumer: real-time pricing in Spain. Energy Policy 102, 41–51 (2017)

11. Lopes, F.: MATREM: an agent-based simulation tool for electricity markets. In: Lopes, F., Coelho, H. (eds.) Electricity Markets with Increasing Levels of Renewable Generation: Structure, Operation, Agent-based Simulation, and Emerging Designs. SSDC, vol. 144, pp. 189–225. Springer, Cham (2018). https://doi.org/10.1007/978-3-319-74263-2_8

12. Lopes, F., Coelho, H.: Electricity markets and intelligent agents part II: agent architectures and capabilities. In: Lopes, F., Coelho, H. (eds.) Electricity Markets with Increasing Levels of Renewable Generation: Structure, Operation, Agent-based Simulation, and Emerging Designs. SSDC, vol. 144, pp. 49–77. Springer, Cham (2018). https://doi.org/10.1007/978-3-319-74263-2_3

13. Lopes, F., Sá, J., Santana, J.: Renewable generation, support policies and the merit order effect: a comprehensive overview and the case of wind power in Portugal. In: Lopes, F., Coelho, H. (eds.) Electricity Markets with Increasing Levels of Renewable Generation: Structure, Operation, Agent-based Simulation, and Emerging Designs. SSDC, vol. 144, pp. 227–263. Springer, Cham (2018). https://doi.org/10.1007/978-3-319-74263-2_9

14. Algarvio H., Lopes F., Couto A., Estanqueiro A.: Participation of wind power producers in day-ahead and balancing markets: an overview and a simulation-based Study. WIREs Energy and Environment (2019). https://doi.org/10.1002/wene.343

15. Lopes, F., Algarvio, H., Santana, J.: Agent-based simulation of electricity markets: risk management and contracts for difference. In: Alonso-Betanzos, A., et al. (eds.) Agent-Based Modeling of Sustainable Behaviors. UCS, pp. 207–225. Springer, Cham (2017). https://doi.org/10.1007/978-3-319-46331-5_10

16. Lopes, F., Mamede, N., Novais, A.Q., Coelho, H.: A negotiation model for autonomous computational agents: formal description and empirical evaluation. J. Intell. Fuzzy Syst. **12**, 195–212 (2002)

17. Bellifemine, F., Caire, G., Greenwood, D.: Developing Multi-agent Systems with JADE. Wiley, Chichester (2007)

18. OMIE: "Operador del Mercado Ibérico de Energía (Spanish Electricity Market Operator)." Market Results (online data). http://www.omie.es/files/flash/ResultadosMercado.swf. Accessed 02 April 2019

19. REN: Redes Energéticas Nacionais, Preços Mercado Spot, Portugal e Espanha. http://www.mercado.ren.pt/PT/Electr/InfoMercado/InfOp/MercOmel/Paginas/Precos.aspx. Accessed 02 April 2019

Workshop on Smart Cities and Intelligent Agents (SCIA)

Workshop on Smart Cities and Intelligent Agents (SCIA)

Smart cities represent a new way of thinking about urban space by shaping a model that integrates aspects such as energy efficiency, sustainable mobility, protection of the environment, and economic sustainability. These aspects represent the goals for future software developments. Current cities provide potentially unlimited settings for intelligent agents to display their ability to react, act proactively, interact between themselves, or otherwise plan, learn, etc. in an intelligent, or rather human, manner.

Therefore, the objective of this workshop is to discuss the use of agent technology in the area of smart cities with the goal of providing intelligence to the cities. We welcome any paper about experiences in the use of agents in smart cities tackling issues related to smart architectures, urban simulations, intelligent infrastructure, smart transport, open data, etc. We also intend to address specific methodological and technological issues raised by the real deployment of agents in rich environments such as smart cities.

Organization

Organizing Committee

Vicente Julián	Universitat Politècnica de València, Spain
Adriana Giret	Universitat Politècnica de València, Spain
Juan Manuel Corchado	Universidad de Salamanca, Spain
Alberto Fernández	Universidad Rey Juan Carlos, Spain
Holger Billhardt	Universidad Rey Juan Carlos, Spain
Javier Bajo	Universidad Politécnica de iagent Agents

Program Committee

Adriana Giret	Universitat Politècnica de València, Spain
Alberto Fernandez	Universidad Rey Juan Carlos, Spain
Angelo Costa	University of Minho, Portugal
Carlos A. Iglesias	Universidad Politécnica de Madrid, Spain
Carlos Carrascosa	GTI-IA DSIC Universidad Politecnica de Valencia, Spain
Gabriel Villarrubia	University of Salamanca, Spain
Holger Billhardt	Universidad Rey Juan Carlos, Spain
Javier Bajo	Universidad Politécnica de Madrid, Spain
Javier Palanca	Universitat Politècnica de València, Spain
José Antonio Castellanos	University of Salamanca, Spain

Juan Francisco De Paz	University of Salamanca, Spain
María Navarro	University of Salamanca, Spain
Juan Manuel Corchado	University of Salamanca, Spain
Marin Lujak	IMT Lille Douai, France
Pablo Chamoso	University of Salamanca, Spain
Ramon Hermoso	University of Zaragoza, Spain
Roberto Centeno	Universidad Nacional de Educacion a Distancia, Spain
Sara Rodríguez	University of Salamanca, Spain
Sascha Ossowski	Universidad Rey Juan Carlos, Spain
Vicente Julian	Universitat Politècnica de València, Spain

Data Protection on Fintech Platforms

Elena Hernández[(⊠)], Mehmet Öztürk, Inés Sittón,
and Sara Rodríguez

IoT Digital Innovation HUB, University of Salamanca, Salamanca, Spain
{elenahn,mehmet,isittonc,srg}@usal.es

Abstract. The security of data has been challenged by the incorporation of new services into the digital world. Data protection has become essential to continue operating in the new financial environment, especially due to the advent of Financial Technology (Fintech). This article reviews how data protection is applied to financial recommendation platforms identifying current trends in this area. Moreover, it looks at the evolution of computer security in the field of Fintech due to the security level that it requires. In addition, it examines the solution techniques for data storage issues in cloud security and encryption methods that assure data protection. Also, the European Union's data protection regulation is considered; it not only affects the entities based in the European territory but also those that are outside of it but manage the data of European citizens.

Keywords: Data protection · Financial technology · Cloud computing · Big data

1 Introduction

Traditional banking has been changing dramatically during recent decade and this change has brought up new business models and ways for handling financial services. Although it does not have a common understanding and definition of Fintech in the research at the moment, it is one of the most used terms to define newly developed financial services and its related businesses. The term Fintech which is composed of the words "financial" and "technology" emerged as a result of the global economic-financial crisis that took place in 2008. At that time, companies known as Fintech began to expand by offering the services normally performed by banks. Fintech companies has brought new business models that offers more efficient and wider service than established financial services. Start-ups or IT companies entering the financial sector evolve at the point where IT and finance meet [16]. The term Fintech is also used to cover various aspects of security and privacy issues [15]. Also, Fintech can be seen as consequence of the emergence of Cloud Computing [13], of the spread of smart mobile devices, of Big Data processing, of the improvement of cybersecurity and other internet-related technologies [24]. This has made new emerging business models more efficient, secure, innovative and flexible than existing financial services [13].

Given that it is necessary to handle large volumes of data, the starting point for many researchers is understanding how to process them and correctly delimit the

F. De la Prieta et al. (Eds.): PAAMS 2019 Workshops, CCIS 1047, pp. 223–233, 2019.
https://doi.org/10.1007/978-3-030-24299-2_19

needed security level. Techniques focused on mass data analysis usually begin with a data extraction process that allows large volumes of data to be analyzed automatically. This automation is highly appreciated in the banking sector when dealing with financial data [16]. Obtaining and analyzing relevant data helps distinguish processes, impacts and results and to find solutions that improve the performance of financial services and ensure privacy [15].

There is a considerable amount of work being carried out in the field of data security. Some work focuses on data security in Fintech and others address the topic in general. Figure 1 shows a mapping graph which shows the principal techniques that address security and privacy solutions [38].

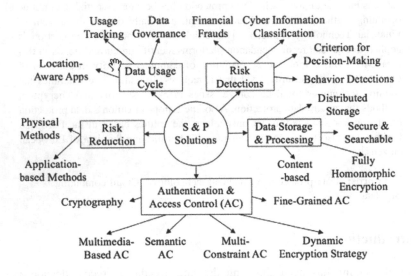

Fig. 1. Security and privacy solutions.

The research presented in this article attempts to define and identify the current data security techniques required on a Fintech platform. The aim of this research is to analyze Fintech's research on data security and to assess most relevant upcoming research. The paper reviews achievements in data protection in general, as well as in the financial sector. It also provides a proposal for data protection.

The article is structured as follows: Sect. 2 reviews current data analysis techniques and the current data protection situation. This is followed by a level tiered proposal for the protection of the Fintech environment. Finally, the research ends by concluding the proposal's security requirements.

2 Data Security

The protection and preservation of data privacy is considered one of the most significant aspects in the subject of financial security, it is a critical task in decision making when choosing a security strategy in organizations [33]. It is essential that the organizations in financial industry have the correct strategy to protect the data from the outset as it is well known that the consequences of a data breach could be catastrophic. With the emerge of cloud computing, integrity, confidentiality, privacy and availability of data have become more important than ever. Although cloud computing is making a significant contribution to Fintech platforms, it brings new risks to the scene. In general, the diverse and invisible infrastructure complicates data management and security. The use of virtualized environments allows the provider to share physical resources among users. This may lead to malicious infringements and attacks by someone on the inside. Table 1 gives a summary of various recently studied techniques, their authors and the research topic.

Table 1. Security techniques studied in the financial industry.

Authors	Research
Banu and Nagayeni (2013)	Used machine learning methods for data protection and privacy, applying clustering algorithms [6]
Chen and Weiss (2014); Zarandi et al. (2012)	Applied artificial intelligence techniques through virtual agent organizations to obtain financial risk predictions [9, 39]
Shim and Shim (2016); Gai and Li (2016)	Conducted their research on Web services models and Cloud Computing. They concluded that Cloud Computing is the most suitable in the financial industry because it allows users to stay connected to target markets, increase system performance, and develop collaborative work, for example, the Bank of America (BoA) collaborates with Microsoft Enterprise to improve their financial transactions using Blockchain technology [15, 31, 34]

The works described in Table 1 focus on the application of specific techniques, however, they provide universal solutions to security and privacy problems in computer systems. The objective of the present research work is to propose a set of techniques aimed at Fintech platforms, capable of facing the current security challenges.

2.1 Security Algorithms

From a security point of view, the biggest challenge for Fintech's services is the protection of users' data. Fintech organizations often store large amounts of personally identifiable information (PII) and therefore data privacy is a major concern. Because a large amount of data is stored, data breaches can have wider consequences than the data breaches we normally face. In this sense, a security breach of such a large amount of data will potentially affect a much larger number of users. Most of the solution techniques for data storage issues in cloud security employ several cryptography processes to assure data security and protection. Cryptography is a method of storing and transferring the data in a confidential way [4]. Encryption, for sure, is the main solution to ensuring that data remains protected. These algorithms can be used in providing data integrity, authentication and confidentiality. Security algorithms are mostly classified as private key/symmetric algorithms (RC6, 3DES, Blowfish), public key/asymmetric algorithms (RSA, Diffe Helman), signature algorithms (RSA, DH). Table 2 focuses on recent studies on data security in cloud computing environment.

Table 2. Security solutions studied in Cloud Computing

Authors	Research
Wei et al. (2014)	After modeling the security problems in Cloud Computing, the work proposed a protocol named SecCloud which aims to provide data storage security and computation auditing security. It uses encryption to store data in secure mode. It not only secures the stored data but also provides security on computational data It is also claimed that it is the first work that considers both of data storage security and computation auditing security in the cloud computing [15]
Tang et al. (2012)	This work presented an implementation of FADE (File Assured Deletion) protocol, a lightweight protocol using both asymmetric and symmetric encryption of data [37]
Liu et al. (2014)	A time-based proxy re-encryption (TimePRE) scheme to limit user's access right time automatically [32]
Zhe et al. (2017)	A summary of security policy that applied to cloud service providers. The paper pointed out that cloud security is not a technical issue but also involves the standardization, management, laws and regulation [11]
Hendre and Joshi (2015)	In this work, an ontology is developed which described the security controls, threads and compliances, and also an application aiming to classify threads has been developed [1]
Wang et al. (2013)	Proposed a secure cloud storage system supporting privacy-preserving public auditing [8]

Encryption is an effective way to protect data when it is on standby and also when it is being transmitted. However, with cloud IT infrastructures, data cannot be sent encrypted by users if operations will be applied to data in the cloud. In that case, the solution is to use Fully Homomorphic Encryption (FHE), which allows stored data in the cloud to perform operations on encrypted data. Table 3 outlines various researches on the encryption of the data in the cloud.

Table 3. Researches on data encryption for cloud computing

Authors	Research
Gai et al. (2016)	Proposed a data encryption approach called Dynamic Data Encryption Strategy (D2ES) which aims to selectively encrypt data using classification methods [19]
Gai et al. (2017)	Propose a new applicable Fully Homomorphic Encryption (FHE) scheme designed for operating real numbers with a good level of accuracy and efficiency [21]
Ateniese et al. (2008)	A Provable Data Possession (PDP) technique constructed entirely on the basis of symmetric key cryptography, without the need of bulk encryption [5]

The problems in the cloud mainly relate to the security and privacy of the stored data. The works shown in Table 3 are some of the works done in order to provide an efficient data encryption solution for cloud storage systems. These approaches provide significant data security benefits to Fintech platforms. Many techniques have been studied in the last decade, from cryptographic techniques to data anonymization techniques. The biggest challenge with encryption methods is that due to big amount of data stored in cloud, they might face performance issues.

2.2 Data Protection Regulation

The security in the cloud is not only a technical issue but also involves the standardization, management, laws and regulations. A new legislation on data protection has been declared across the European Union in May 2018. This new regulation affects to entities and subjects based in the EU and also those outside of the Union, managing EU citizens and resident's data. It strengthens the protection of individuals' personal data in the European Union and simplifies data legislation within the European Union. The GDPR regulates how technologies create and process all personal data [2].

The General Data Protection Regulation (GDPR) includes obligations for cloud consumers and cloud providers [23].

The following articles applied to consumers;

1. Article 5: Processing of personal data
2. Article 24: Responsibly of Consumer
3. Article 25: Data Protection by Design and by Default
4. Article 26: Joint Consumers
5. Article 27: Representatives of Consumers or Providers no established in Union
6. Article 34: Communication of Personal data breach

The following articles state the obligations of cloud providers

1. Article 28 (2-4) (10): Responsibility of Processor
2. Article 29: Processing under the consumer authority
3. Article 37: Designation of Data Protection Offices
4. Article 44: General Principles for Transfer

In GDPR, all the different types of cloud providers (IaaS, PaaS, SaaS) are named Processors and their obligations are defined. The following obligations show a selection of the obligations that cloud providers must meet.

1. Data destruction "...Processor must delete or return all the personal data to the controller after the end of the provision of services relating to processing, and deletes existing copies..." (Art 28.3.g).
2. Data Breaches, with processor to notify the Controller "without undue delay after becoming 'aware' of breach" (33.2).
3. Security of Processing (Art 32) and record of processing activities (Art. 30.2).

In addition to the specific Cloud Computing, the GDPR also sets basic standards. Provisions published in GDPR (such as Privacy by Design and by Default, Data

Protection Impact Assessment, right to be Forgotten, high sanctions), will have an impact on how emerging technologies will be utilized by Fintech organizations.

Laws protecting users' personal data are now more necessary than ever. The GDPR is an important milestone in this field. By having a broad intersection with the grinding technologies, Fintech platforms also benefit from these regulations. I understand that the GDPR is a complex legislative instrument and its importance has not yet been fully understood by many organizations. The first studies on the GDPR show that there is still a lack of awareness among consumers.

For Fintech platforms that outsource cloud services, another important issue is service level agreements (SLAs). It is a protocol that specifies a set of conditions and terms between the user and the cloud services provider. The SLA must contain actions that the cloud service provider will take when a data breach occurs, corrective actions and performance level at a minimum level [7].

3   Proposal for Protection

For the development of the data protection proposal for Fintech platforms, the research of Gai et al. [14, 15] was the main point of reference. The authors proposed the application of several data security techniques. This research presents a scheme of five data and risk management aspects which are shown in the Fig. 1. Each includes a safety-oriented technique of a Fintech platform. This ensure different levels of protection.

The safety components shown in Fig. 2, are described in the following order:

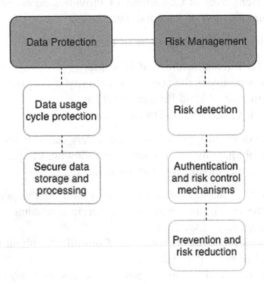

Fig. 2. Security on Fintech platforms

1. Data usage cycle protection: At this stage, the use of techniques for tracking the use, location and governance of data is contemplated. However, the latter becomes more complicated when the size of the platform increases and with it, the volume of data, functions, transactions and users. The data usage cycle is the most difficult to protect due to the activity of mobile device users whose locations are difficult to track. Therefore, risks in the data usage cycle come from unexpected third parties, unclear business processes, and distributed use of data [38].

2. Secure data storage and processing: Distributed storage techniques accompanied by appropriate encryption protect the stored data, reducing vulnerabilities in data processing during the execution of transactions. In other research, the use of primitive symmetric key encryption is suggested. Centralized as well as decentralized data storage/processing face several challenges, so all security threats that exist on a network must be taken into account on Fintech platforms. Many investigations have also validated the effectiveness of Cloud Computing techniques in protecting distributed data stores [12].

3. Risk detection: Research suggests that cloud computing techniques be used with clustering algorithms that will enable the classification of information and the analysis of patterns of suspicious transactions [15]. Additionally, the analysis of the correlation coefficient in clustering algorithms allows to detect behaviors indicative of abnormal financial operations [22]. The application of supervised learning algorithms combined with taxonomy, allows to classify cyber incidents and relate possible privacy leaks or attacks on the most vulnerable elements of the platform [14].

4. Authentication and risk control mechanisms: Financial information is protected through dynamic encryption, multiple constraint techniques and semantic analysis [10, 25]. Semantic accesses are associated with the characteristics of service applicants identified through ontology techniques for access control configurations [10]. Security and service performance are the key components that access control design in Fintech platform depends on.

5. Prevention and risk reduction: In general, there are two basic types of techniques for prevention and risk reduction on Fintech platforms: physical and application-based. Physical techniques refer to different methods of securing data during operations on the physical infrastructure, such as avoiding network damage. Application-based methods are based on cryptography, such as the configuration of access controls or the sequential logic access control rules currently used by social networks. In this field, research continues to be carried out to reduce the risk of cyber-attacks [17, 28].

The described components suggest the simultaneous application of safety methods or techniques on a Fintech platform. Significant security research has been conducted by increasing the ability to connect to the Internet from a wide variety of devices at any time or place, resulting in a large volume of transactions [22, 34].

In this research, it is proposed the use of hybrid security technologies in the design of Fintech platforms using artificial intelligence techniques at the different levels identified. Additional to the five aspects of security provided above, this hybrid scheme also includes the following methodologies:

- Storage encryption. The use of encryption algorithms is necessary in storage because it allows sensitive information such as personal identification, credit card numbers, accounting reports and financial information to be stored or transmitted on demand in an integral and confidential manner [15, 26]. The SecCloud [36] uses encryption to store data in secure mode. The File Assured Deletion (FADE) provides key management with data integrity and privacy [37].
- Clustering in risk detection. Identifying risk patterns is important because it allows you to detect fraudulent transactions. Clustering algorithms compare every new transaction with the customer's previous transactions, thus classifying unusual activities, they issue alerts when a transaction has been attempted, for the system to accept or reject it, depending on whether the pattern of behavior is normal or not [22, 27].
- Multi-agent systems control the system in a distributed way, managing resources (data, hardware, software, transactions) and solving problems related to attacks such as intrusion detection, spam, identify theft, among others, which affect the credibility of Web services of a Fintech platform.
- Access control via multimedia systems and reinforced biometric authentication systems to manage secure authentication, considering three important aspects of the protection strategy: security, privacy and trust.

4 Conclusions and Future Work

The analysis of the related work in the area of data security on Fintech platforms carried out in this research shows that there are many aspects that must be taken into account when designing a Fintech platform. Among the five main technical dimensions of Fintech's challenges (security and privacy, data techniques, hardware and infrastructure, applications and management and service models), the design and implementation of a correct security and privacy strategy is becoming more mandatory with the emergence of new technologies.

The protection of data on Fintech platforms requires multilayer security, starting with data transmission, transactions (data processing) and system outputs (user responses). To achieve security at several levels it is necessary to incorporate current techniques. In cloud computing, security mechanisms protect data from internal and external attacks. Industries demand the application of encryption techniques in cloud-based security solutions.

The implementation of a Fintech platform is based on the correct use of data at all times and it is crucial that developers take measures to avoid predictable threats and establish security mechanism that will allow to deal with unpredictable risks.

It is difficult to perceive all the possible cyber risks due to the large number of emerging technologies related to Fintech platforms, however, as discussed in the beginning of this proposal, security begins with understanding how the system works, and adopting proper risk management to reduce the possibility of cyberattacks.

This paper provides an analysis of recent studies on data protection in general and data protection specific to Fintech platforms. Although all the security and privacy studies that have been carried out or are being carried out under the terms of cloud computing, internet of things, fog computing are contributing directly to Fintech's platforms, as they are generally addressed more to them than to other services, data protection on Fintech's platforms is highly prioritized.

In this research, it is also suggested that data protection on Fintech platforms is not only a technical issue, but also requires a holistic approach such as compliance with GDPR legislation.

A future investigation is going to study the main vulnerabilities of Fintech platforms such as identity theft, access to private data, etc. Moreover, we plan to study trends in new data security methods for Fintech platforms.

Acknowledgements. This research has been partially supported by the European Regional Development Fund (FEDER) within the framework of the Interreg program V-A Spain-Portugal 2014-2020 (PocTep) under the IOTEC project grant 0123 IOTEC 3 E.

References

1. Hendre, A., Joshi, K.P.: A semantic approach to cloud security and compliance. In: 2015 IEEE 8th International Conference on Cloud Computing, New York, NY, pp. 1081–1084 (2015)
2. Addis, M.C., Kutar, M.: The general data protection regulation (GDPR), emerging technologies and UK organisations: awareness, implementation and readiness (2018)
3. Addis, M.C., Kutar, M.: The general data protection regulation (GDPR), emerging technologies and UK organisations: awareness, implementation and readiness. In: UK Academy for Information Systems Conference Proceedings 2018
4. Bhardwaj, A., Subrahmanyam, G.V.B., Avasthi, V., Sastry, H.: Security algorithms for cloud computing. Procedia Comput. Sci. **85**, 535–542 (2016)
5. Ateniese, G., Di Pietro, R., Mancini, L.V., Tsudik, G.: Scalable and efficient provable data possession. In: Proceedings of the 4th International Conference on Security and Privacy in Communication Networks, p. 9. ACM, September 2008
6. Banu, R.V., Nagaveni, N.: Evaluation of a perturbation-based technique for privacy preservation in a multi-party clustering scenario. Inf. Sci. **232**, 437–448 (2013)
7. Wang, C., Wang, Q., Ren, K., Cao, N., Lou, W.: Toward secure and dependable storage services in cloud computing. IEEE Trans. Serv. Comput. **5**(2), 220–232 (2012)
8. Wang, C., Chow, S.S.M., Wang, Q., Ren, K., Lou, W.: Privacy-preserving public auditing for secure cloud storage. IEEE Trans. Comput. **62**(2), 362–375 (2013)
9. Chen, S., Weiss, G.: An intelligent agent for bilateral negotiation with unknown opponents in continuous-time domains. In: ACM Transactions on Autonomous and Adaptive Systems (TAAS), vol. 9(3), p. 16 (2014)
10. Choi, C., Choi, J., Kim, P.: Ontology-based access control model for security policy reasoning in cloud computing. J. Supercomput. **67**(3), 711–722 (2014)
11. Zhe, D., Qinghong, W., Naizheng, S., Yuhan, Z.: Study on data security policy based on cloud storage. In: 2017 IEEE 3rd International Conference on Big Data Security on Cloud (Bigdatasecurity), IEEE International Conference on High Performance and Smart Computing (HPSC), and Ieee International Conference on Intelligent Data and Security (IDS), Beijing, pp. 145–149 (2017)

12. De la Prieta, F., Barriuso, A.L., Corchado, J.M., de Colsa, L.E.C.: Security services as cloud capabilities using MAS. In: Actas de las primeras Jornadas Nacionales de Investigación en Ciberseguridad: León, 14, 15, 16 de septiembre de 2015: I JNIC2015, pp. 82–83 (2015)
13. DeStefano, R.J., Tao, L., Gai, K.: Improving data governance in large organizations through ontology and linked data. In: IEEE 3rd International Conference on Cyber Security and Cloud Computing (CSCloud), pp. 279–284. IEEE (2016)
14. Gai, K., Du, Z., Qiu, M., Zhao, H.: Efficiency-aware workload optimizations of heterogeneous cloud computing for capacity planning in financial industry. In: 2015 IEEE 2nd International Conference on Cyber Security and Cloud Computing (CSCloud), pp. 1–6. IEEE (2015)
15. Gai, K., Qiu, M., Sun, X., Zhao, H.: Security and privacy issues: a survey on FinTech. In: Qiu, M. (ed.) SmartCom 2016. LNCS, vol. 10135, pp. 236–247. Springer, Cham (2017). https://doi.org/10.1007/978-3-319-52015-5_24
16. Gomber, P., Koch, J.A., Siering, M.: Digital Finance and FinTech: current research and future research directions. Bus. Econ. **87**, 537–580 (2017)
17. González Briones, A., Chamoso, P., Barriuso, A.L.: Review of the main security problems with multi-agent systems used in e-commerce applications. In: ADCAIJ: Advances in Distributed Computing and Artificial Intelligence, vol. 5, no. 3, pp. 55–61. Ediciones Universidad de Salamanca (2017)
18. Gonzalez, N., et al.: A quantitative analysis of current security concerns and solutions for cloud computing. J. Cloud Comput.: Adv. Syst. Appl. **1**(1), 11 (2012)
19. Gai, K., Qiu, M., Zhao, H., Xiong, J.: Privacy-aware adaptive data encryption strategy of big data in cloud computing. In: 2016 IEEE 3rd International Conference on Cyber Security and Cloud Computing (CSCloud), Beijing, pp. 273–278 (2016)
20. Gai, K., Qiu, M., Sun, X.: A survey on FinTech. J. Netw. Comput. Appl. **103**, 262–273 (2018)
21. Gai, K., Qiu, M., Li, Y., Liu, X.: Advanced fully homomorphic encryption scheme over real numbers. In: 2017 IEEE 4th International Conference on Cyber Security and Cloud Computing (CSCloud), New York, NY, pp. 64–69 (2017)
22. Kou, G., Peng, Y., Wang, G.: Evaluation of clustering algorithms for financial risk analysis using MCDM methods. Inf. Sci. **275**, 1–12 (2014)
23. Elluri, L., Joshi, K.P.: A knowledge representation of cloud data controls for EU GDPR compliance. In: 2018 IEEE World Congress on Services (SERVICES), San Francisco, CA, pp. 45–46 (2018)
24. Lazarova, D.: Fintech trends: the Internet of Things, January 2018. https://www.finleap.com/insights/fintech-trends-the-internet-of-things/
25. Li, B., Hoi, S.C.: Online portfolio selection: a survey. ACM Comput. Surv. (CSUR) **46**(3), 35 (2014)
26. Li, M., Yu, S., Ren, K., Lou, W., Hou, Y.T.: Toward privacy-assured and searchable cloud data storage services. IEEE Netw. **27**(4), 56–62 (2013)
27. Li, T., Corchado, J.M., Sun, S., Bajo, J.: Clustering for filtering: multi-object detection and estimation using multiple/massive sensors. Inf. Sci. **388**, 172–190 (2017)
28. Ma, J., Xu, W., Sun, Y., Turban, E., Wang, S., Liu, O.: An ontology-based textmining method to cluster proposals for research project selection. IEEE Trans. Syst. Man Cybern.-Part A: Syst. Hum. **42**(3), 784–790 (2012)
29. Vurukonda, N., Thirumala Rao, B.: A study on data storage security issues in cloud computing. Procedia Comput. Sci. **92**, 128–135 (2016)
30. Ravi Kumar, P., Herbert Raj, P., Jelciana, P.: Exploring data security issues and solutions in cloud computing. Procedia Comput. Sci. **125**, 691–697 (2018)

31. Prieto-Castrillo, F., Kushch, S., Corchado, J.M.: Distributed sequential consensus in networks: analysis of partially connected blockchains with uncertainty. Complexity **2017**, 1–11 (2017)
32. Liu, Q., Wang, G., Jie, W.: Time-based proxy re-encryption scheme for secure data sharing in a cloud environment. Inf. Sci. **258**, 355–370 (2014)
33. Sánchez, R., Almenares, F., Arias, P., Díaz-Sánchez, D., Marín, A.: Enhancing privacy and dynamic federation in IdM for consumer cloud computing. IEEE Trans. Consum. Electron. **58**(1), 95–103 (2012)
34. Shim, Y., Shin, D.H.: Analyzing China's fintech industry from the perspective of actor–network theory. Telecommun. Policy **40**(2–3), 168–181 (2016)
35. Aldossary, S., Allen, W.: Data security, privacy, availability and integrity in cloud computing: issues and current solutions. Int. J. Adv. Comput. Sci. Appl. (IJACSA) **7**(4), 485–598 (2016)
36. Wei, L., et al.: Security and privacy for storage and computation in cloud computing. Inf. Sci. **258**(371–386), 2014 (2014)
37. Tang, Y., Lee, P.P.C., Lui, J.C.S., Perlman, R.: Secure overlay cloud storage with access control and assured deletion. IEEE Trans. Dependable Secure Comput. **9**(6), 903–916 (2012)
38. Yu, K., Gao, Y., Zhang, P., Qiu, M.: Design and architecture of dell acceleration appliances for database (DAAD): a practical approach with high availability guaranteed. In: 2015 IEEE 17th International Conference on High Performance Computing and Communications (HPCC), 2015 IEEE 7th International Symposium on Cyberspace Safety and Security (CSS), 2015 IEEE 12th International Conference on Embedded Software and Systems (ICESS), pp. 430–435. IEEE (2015)
39. Zarandi, M.H., Hadavandi, E., Turksen, I.B.: A hybrid fuzzy intelligent agent - based system for stock price prediction. Int. J. Intell. Syst. **27**(11), 947–969 (2012)

A Two-Phase Context-Aware Approach to Emergency Evacuation in Smart Buildings

Qasim Khalid[1($\boxtimes$)], Alberto Fernández[1], Marin Lujak[2], and Arnaud Doniec[2]

[1] Universidad Rey Juan Carlos, Madrid, Spain
{qasim.khalid,alberto.fernandez}@urjc.es
[2] IMT Lille Douai, 59500 Douai, France
{marin.lujak,arnaud.doniec}@imt-lille-douai.fr

Abstract. Evacuation in buildings during emergency situations is crucial to the safety of people, therefore a pragmatic response plan is desirable. Due to the lack of awareness in buildings, either occupants have to wait for instructions from the administration or to start following each other to find the best evacuation route for them on the basis of hit and trial method. In this regard, we present a context-aware smart architecture for evacuation that provides real-time evacuation routes to occupants with respect to their characteristics. We also put forward a two-phase group evacuation technique in which people evacuate in the form of groups under the supervision of experts so-called group leaders. The first phase handles the assembly of evacuees at their allotted collection points and in the second phase evacuees follow their group leaders to safe points. Group leaders are equipped with hand-held devices having live information of building, routes and their group members. A use case is also discussed in the paper as an application of the proposed technique.

Keywords: Agent-based system · Evacuation · Semantic technology · Knowledge representation · Situation awareness · Smart buildings

1 Introduction

In case of any hazard or threat to the safety of the occupants of a building, evacuation is a first step to escape the building. The goal of this emergency evacuation is to exit a specific area or a building safely in a minimum possible time. Generally, static evacuation plans are followed, which are normally developed during the erection stage of a building. These plans are either not appropriate for all types of an emergency evacuation or not every occupant of the building is aware of them. In addition to this, the instantaneous state of the hazard is not known, and there is a lack of coordination between evacuees and administration as well. Due to this, several problems may occur, e.g., congestion at exit points or locations that are used frequently and, as a result, there are casualties. There are

© Springer Nature Switzerland AG 2019
F. De la Prieta et al. (Eds.): PAAMS 2019 Workshops, CCIS 1047, pp. 234–245, 2019.
https://doi.org/10.1007/978-3-030-24299-2_20

several factors that are associated with an emergency evacuation for example behavior and physical characteristics of occupants of the building, coordination of people with each other, type of emergency and relevant evacuation strategy.

Vermuyten et al. have conducted a literature survey in which they have discussed various evacuation strategies and its relevant topics such as crowd behavior, crowd flow, optimized paths, bottlenecks, etc. (see, e.g., [14]). These strategies have somehow improved the evacuation process, but most of the studies are static. Due to this reason, real-time status of building and evacuees is not known in case of an emergency and during the evacuation process. Therefore, there is still a need for an intelligent system that could detect hazardous situations and handle the evacuation problem on a real-time basis.

In this paper, we explain the architecture of a real-time agent-based system for mass evacuation in buildings. The novel concept for this study is that the information about events and evacuees is processed on a microscopic level while evacuation is done in the form of groups on a macroscopic level.

Some researchers have also observed that the evacuees prefer to evacuate in the form of group or rather to follow a group which is guided by a person (see, e.g., [7,8]). In the light of these studies, we propose a two-phase evacuation strategy in which the evacuees have to gather at specific points so-called collection points, to make groups. These collection points will be designed beforehand by the evacuation experts but the usable collection points during emergency evacuation will be chosen on the basis of the availability of group leaders, size of the crowd, type of the building spaces, and severity of the emergency. Later, these groups evacuate the building under the supervision of some experts known as group leaders. The selection of a group leader is also an interesting problem. Because the group leader should be a person, who has prior knowledge of a building as well as he/she will be physically and mentally fit. In this regard, the group leader could be either from the administration or a volunteer. The selection criteria could be different in each case. We are not discussing the selection criteria of a group leader in this work. We are assuming that group leaders are selected beforehand.

The rest of the paper is organized as follows. In Sect. 2, literature is briefly discussed which is followed by the motivation of using group evacuation technique. Later, we explain our proposed architecture with the whole evacuation process in Sect. 3. In Sect. 4, we look into the detail of having an efficient way of using the existing knowledge from a building and its occupants. In Sect. 5, we focus on the first phase of the evacuation strategy, i.e., assigning evacuees to the collection points according to their characteristics. In Sect. 6, a use case is presented as an application of the proposed strategy. Finally, the conclusion is drawn in Sect. 7 with some future directions.

2   Literature Review and Motivation

Various approaches have been proposed by researchers to evacuate buildings during emergencies (see, e.g., [9,15,18]). Crowd evacuation is a combination of various sub-problems such as detection of a hazard, taking relevant decisions, alarm people, analysis of possible actions that can be taken, escaping a particular area, etc. For this purpose, Talebi and Smith in [12] have explained that the whole evacuation process is taken in different phases.

On the other hand, Huges in [5] has explained two types of crowd evacuation; macroscopic and microscopic. He explained the significance and the applicability of both approaches for handling the crowd. Macroscopic model is used at a crowd level to implement the rules over a whole crowd while the microscopic model is used to model every individual participating in the evacuation process. Some authors have also proposed a hybrid approach to use both strategies as they complement each other (see, e.g., [16,17]).

In addition to this, Liu et al. in [7,8] have strengthened our motivation of performing an evacuation as a two-phase process and in the form of groups. They explained that the evacuation process is not only individual action, but it is a group activity where the efficiency of the whole process is dependent on everyone who is playing a role in that process. Hence, group coordination and cooperation between people is needed to make that evacuation process efficient. Similarly, Thomson et al. in [13] and Fruin et al. in [4] have emphasized that when people are located at a higher density, an individual movement is avoided. Consequently, individuals move in a group towards one direction like a fluid. Li et al. in [6] also observed this behavior in a crowd when people form small groups and evacuate in particular patterns which are different form the movement of individuals. These groups are formed on the basis of ties like friend or family. Hence, according to the authors, the crowd is a mixture of both individuals and groups which may also accelerate the speed of evacuation process. Shi et al. in [11] have found the existence of groups during an evacuation in a large public building where dense flow of crowd is observed.

On the other hand, when the crowd evacuates in the form of groups, synchronization and coordination issues arise. For example, Oxendine et al. in [10] have found that in case of any wrong decision by the group leadership, even worse disaster could happen as time is the most critical thing during that process. However, Li et al. in [6] have found that the evacuation time increases because of the presence of groups in the crowd.

From literature, we have come to know that there is a space to develop a strategy that could assist the evacuees in the formation of groups according to their characteristics as well as in choosing an optimal route for them. In the next sections, we will explain how we can develop an intelligent and real-time system for evacuation and later we will explain the group formation strategy from the information that we get from evacuees.

3 Agent-Based Architecture for Emergency Evacuation

In this section, we propose an architecture for emergency evacuation of people in buildings. We use an agent-based approach to handle the whole evacuation problem as a set of different sub-problems such as information of people and building, live status of hazard and evacuation, allocation of routes to people, management of groups according to and group leaders, and so on. The block diagram of the proposed architecture is shown in Fig. 1. There are three agents that are connected to each other as well as to hand-held devices. It means the output of all the agents are sent to this hand-held device. On the right side of the figure, there are groups of people. There are two roles that people play during an evacuation; group leaders and group members.

As we have mentioned earlier, group leaders use these hand-held devices, which have all the information coming from agents and lead their groups to safe points. Now, we explain how each agent works.

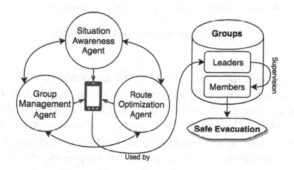

Fig. 1. Evacuation architecture

Group Management Agent manages occupants of the building and assigns collection points to them by their characteristics such as group leader, mobility impaired, family members or normal. The block diagram of this agent is shown in Fig. 2. In this figure, there are two types of inputs; static as well as dynamic knowledge of people. Static knowledge has information about physical characteristics, areas that can be accessed and family ties, whereas dynamic information consists of live locations of the people which is continuously detected and sent to the system. More information about representation of knowledge can be found in later sections. Every person in the building is equipped with radio-frequency identification (RFID) or iBeacon[1] transmitters and the location of each person is detected by iBeacon readers (which are installed in the building) in a real-time manner. Later, this static and dynamic knowledge is used by an algorithm as its input. The output of this agent is an assignment of collection points to each person to a nearest and feasible one. The assigned feasible collection point is calculated according to the characteristics and live location of each person. We will explain more about this agent in the later sections.

Situation Awareness Agent handles and processes the information of events coming from sensors in real-time and takes an appropriate action on the basis of

---

[1] https://developer.apple.com/ibeacon/ (accessed on May 31 2019).

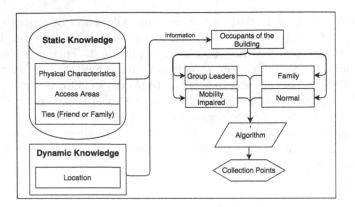

Fig. 2. Group management agent

these events. The block diagram of this agent is shown in Fig. 3. In this figure, we have an algorithm named Emergency Detection Algorithm in which there are two types of inputs; static and dynamic. The topology of the building is a static knowledge that holds all the information related to the building such as capacity and dimensions of each section, connectivity of sections with each other, distances between sections, locations of collection points, etc. Dynamic knowledge includes the real-time monitoring of activities such as fire, smoke, terrorist attack or threat, quarrel or any other emergency, being done in the building that could result in an emergency evacuation. It is done with the help of sensors (see, e.g., [1–3]). This agent also detects the status of the evacuation routes continuously. In case of any problem in the existing provided path, it communicates with other agents so that the relevant agents could assign another safe route to evacuees. It also handles the real-time information of each evacuee. For example, the location of each evacuee (or a group) is monitored and if any evacuee or a group takes a wrong direction then it either informs the administration or generates a message that can be read on a hand-held device used by a group leader. It also informs other agents in case of any abnormality in the building to take appropriate measures by the rest of the system.

Route Optimization Agent calculates the optimized path for each group of persons gathered at collection points with the help of an optimization algorithm. That is done by representing the building as a graph, where nodes are sections of the building and edges are connections between two sections. The block diagram is shown in Fig. 4. In this figure, the optimization algorithm takes dynamic knowledge of all members of each group such as their location as an input. Also, the video sensing of different locations of the building is done. The output results in the form of an optimized path that is calculated by considering the safety level, capacity of sections and paths with respect to evacuees, time required from a specific point to other points. Later, routes are created in which nodes and edges are connected to each other in the form of a connected route, e.g. starting points to ending points (exits in our scenario), and every group is

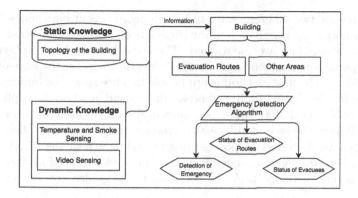

Fig. 3. Situation awareness agent

assigned a specific route according to their position and physical characteristics. Upon gathering on a collection point, the group leader and the group members have to follow the assigned route that is chosen by this agent.

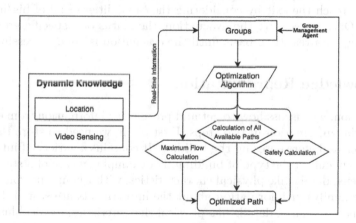

Fig. 4. Route optimization agent

Evacuation Process: As emergency evacuation is a multi-phase procedure [12], therefore we also propose a two-phase strategy of evacuating a building where evacuees have to gather at their relevant collection points and then they have to follow their respective group leaders up to the safest point or exit. We name them as Notification Phase and Evacuation phase.

Notification phase is further divided into two sub-phases. During the first sub-phase, occupants are informed about emergency and evacuation. Group leaders have to lead the group of evacuees to their exit points once they gather at collection points. Therefore it is important to inform people about their collection points. There are two different ways to inform people about emergency. The first method for informing people is sending them a text message or an email in which group collection points are mentioned. The second method is displaying their collection points on a screen w.r.t. people's location, e.g., in the case of general public building. The first method is applicable in office spaces or buildings where people are located individually whereas the second method is applicable for a general public building where people are already located in some random grouping. During the second sub-phase, evacuees have to move to their assigned collection points. As collection points are expected to be near the current location of each evacuee, and every evacuee knows about the location of his/her assigned collection point, therefore they do not need to be guided by someone at this stage.

Evacuation Phase starts when the evacuees gather at their collection points and they have to start to follow their relevant group leaders. These group leaders are selected beforehand and they use purpose-based hand-held devices. These hand-held devices have all the information which are calculated by the agents mentioned above. Group leaders use these devices to know about the current status of an evacuee, quantity of his/her group, physical characteristics of each group member, an optimal route from collection point to safest exit, and time required to reach the exit by considering the capabilities of all of his/her group members. Once, they start the evacuation, the status of a specific group keeps on updating on a real-time basis until the evacuation is done successfully.

4   Knowledge Representation

In this section, we discuss how to get and process the information from evacuees. We need this information in two steps. First of all, we need to store the details of every person before entering the building. It contains a variety of information that is dependent on the type of building. For example, in case of a stadium or a concert arena, details like physical characteristics, with whom a person has come (friends or family) or information about the impairments are stored. In case of an office space scenario, details like physical characteristics, medical history, the status of a person, job title, area of access are stored in the database. As this information is static, therefore it is either acquired as a pre-registration process, e.g. online or on the desk by the administration. Upon entering the details into the system, a special RFID tag or iBeacon tag is provided to each person so that all the movements and locations of people are traced using our proposed system.

We use an ontology to represent knowledge. In semantic web field, W3C recommends several languages for ontologies. We will use the Resource Description Framework (RDF), which represents knowledge as graphs where nodes are considered as concepts or instances and arcs are considered as properties or predicates. In RDF, we have used turtle syntax because of its simplicity. In turtle, an RDF graph is written as a set of triples, e.g.,$<subject><property><object>$. In Fig. 5, we show a fragment of the ontology we use for our architecture. In the figure, a reader can notice on the left side of the sample ontology that the persons are classified as group members or group leaders in terms of their role during an evacuation. Later, each person has personal details such as family, location and either whether he/she is mobility impaired or not. Similarly, on the right-hand side, details about the collection points are given. For example, there are details of each collection point about its location, capacity and with which section it is connected as this is important to generate a complete route. Also, the distance between all the sections and collection point is mentioned so that the system could find the path for evacuees which is nearest and feasible to them. In the next section, we will describe how we use these details to find the collection point for each person according to his/her characteristics.

```
:person3 rdf:type :GroupMember.              :cp_2 rdf:type :CollectionPoint.
:person2 rdf:type :GroupLeader.              :cp_2 :isLocatedIn :section6.
:GroupMember rdfs:SubClassOf :EvacueeRole.   :cp_2 :isConnectedTo :section5.
:GroupLeader rdfs:SubClassOf :EvacueeRole.   :cp_2 :hasCapacityOf "20".

                                             :section3 rdf:type :Section.
:person5 :isFamilyOf :person45.              :section3 :isConnectedTo :section8.
:person8 :isLocatedIn :section3.
:person8 :isMobilityImpaired "True".         :D3_8 rdf:type :Distance.
                                             :D3_8 :isConnectedTo :sectionID_3.
                                             :D3_8 :isConnectedTo :sectionID_8.
                                             :D3_8 :hasDistanceLength "5".
```

Fig. 5. Fragment of an ontology for our architecture. (On the left side and right side of the ontology, details about persons and building with its topology are given respectively.)

5   Group Formation

As we have mentioned in previous sections, in this paper, we focus on the group formation module of group management agent of the proposed architecture. Every person in the building has an RFID or iBeacon tag that is provided before entering into the building or during the registration process. These tags have a unique ID by which the data of every person can be accessed. If any hazard or risk is detected and evacuation is necessary, evacuees are provided by a location (known as collection points) where they have to gather and wait for next instructions from their group leaders. These collection points are assigned individually on the basis of the information we get from each evacuee.

Now we explain how evacuees are assigned to their nearest and feasible collection points with respect to their characteristics. Following is an algorithm that assigns collection points to each person located in the building. In Algorithm 1, as an input, we have a set of persons $\mathcal{P}$, collections points $\mathcal{C}$, and a vector $\mathcal{A}$ (which will be filled by the persons with their assigned collection points). Once the algorithm initializes, the nearest available collection point is chosen by calculating the distance from each collection point for each person i.e. $dist(p, c)$. The availability of collection point is checked with respect to its capacity i.e. $Capacity(c)$.

Algorithm 1. Assigning Collection Points to Each Person

    Input   : $\mathcal{P}$: set of persons
                 $\mathcal{C}$: set of collection points
                 $\mathcal{A}$: vector where $\mathcal{A}(c)$ is the set of persons allocated to $c \in \mathcal{C}$
    Output: $\mathcal{A}$ updated with people in $\mathcal{P}$ assigned to their nearest available
                 collection points

1 **foreach** $p \in \mathcal{P}$ **do**
2 | $minDist = \infty$;
3 | **foreach** $c \in \mathcal{C}$ **do**
4 | | **if** $| \mathcal{A}(c) | < Capacity(c) \wedge dist(p,c) < minDist$ **then**
5 | | | $minDist = dist(p,c)$;   /* find the nearest collection point */
                  | | | $nearestCP = c$;
6 | | **end**
7 | **end**
8 | $\mathcal{A}(nearestCP) = \mathcal{A}(nearestCP) \cup \{p\}$;
9 **end**
10 **return** $\mathcal{A}$;

In case, the nearest collection point is full, the second nearest collection point is assigned to that person. Due to this reason, we run this algorithm in order from highest to lowest priority. Firstly, this algorithm is run for the group leaders, secondly, for mobility impaired people, thirdly for family members and lastly for the rest of the people so-called normal ones. The output of the algorithm results in a vector $\mathcal{A}$ of persons with their assigned collection point.

On the other hand, in other proposed strategy, people who have family connections are supposed to evacuate together. For this reason, a different algorithm is given in Algorithm 2 that selects same collection point to each member of the family.

6 Use Case

In this section, we use an example as an application of our proposed algorithms. For this purpose, we have taken a map of a building that has ten sections (three of them are collection points) and 50 persons are located in the other seven sections randomly. Two out of those people are mobility impaired (P8, P43), two have family ties (P5, P45), and six of them are group leaders (P2, P11, P18, P36, P38, P41). As we have mentioned in previous sections that the group leaders have the highest priority. On the second, mobility people come, on third people with family ties and in the end, normal and healthy people are dealt. However, on the other hand, each collection point has a limit of holding group leaders as well as the maximum capacity of holding people as a whole. In our example, we have fixed a maximum of two for group leaders and maximum capacity of twenty, twenty and ten for collection point 1, collection point 2 and collection

---

Algorithm 2. Family assignment to collection point

Input : $\mathcal{F}$: set of members of a family, $\mathcal{F} \in \mathcal{P}$
$\mathcal{C}$: set of collection points
$\mathcal{A}$: vector where $\mathcal{A}(c)$ is the set of persons allocated to $c \in \mathcal{C}$
Output: $\mathcal{A}$ updated with all people in $\mathcal{F}$ assigned to the nearest and feasible available collection point to each member of the family

```
1  minDist = ∞;
2  foreach c ∈ C do
3  │   if | A(c) | +|F| < Capacity(c) then          /* the whole family fits in c */
4  │   │   maxDist = 0;
5  │   │   foreach p ∈ F do
6  │   │   │   maxDist = max(maxD, dist(p,c));       /* calculating max distance */
7  │   │   end
8  │   │   if maxDist < minDist then                 /* checks if c is the nearest */
9  │   │   │   minDist = maxDist;
10 │   │   │   nearestCP = c;
11 │   │   end
12 │   end
13 end
14 A(nearestCP)= A(nearestCP) ∪ F;
15 return A;
```

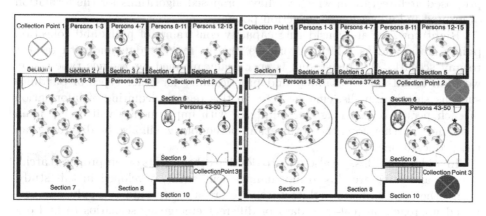

Fig. 6. Left Figure: Map of a building where 50 persons are located in random sections, Right Figure: Allocation of evacuees to their nearest and feasible collection points (Color figure online)

point 3 respectively. Therefore once the limit of collection point exceeds, remaining persons are allocated to their second nearest collection point. Once we run the algorithm, as a result, group leaders P2 and P18, P11 and P36, P38 and P41, are assigned to collection point 1, collection point 2 and collection point 3 respectively. Later, P8 and P43, who are mobility impaired are assigned to their nearest collection points; collection point 2 and collection point 3 respectively.

Persons who have family ties; P5 and P45, are assigned to the same collection point; collection point 2, because it is nearer to both of them. The rest of the persons are allocated to their nearest collection points.

The output of the algorithm can be seen in Fig. 6 visually. Collections points are colored in three different colors. Rings around the persons show that they have to gather at that specific collection point. Group leaders have a yellow ring around them whereas mobility impaired people have a bigger ring around them to represent their priority. Similarly, people who have family ties also have a bigger ring around them along with a star over them.

7   Conclusion

In this paper, we have proposed an intelligent evacuation architecture that can handle and manage the whole evacuation process from the detection of the hazard to the evacuation of people in the buildings. Our system is based on three different agents that perform their relevant actions. In our proposed strategy, evacuation is done in the form of small groups which are led by a group leader. The group leaders use special-purpose hand-held devices that are specifically designed and connected to the proposed system in a real-time manner. Due to the scope of this paper, we have only discussed group management agent of our proposed architecture in which we have proposed algorithms for the formation of groups and allocation of collection points.

Right now, we are considering capacity constraints of paths and collection points static and as a future work we plan to make it dynamic with respect to any scenario. As this system is specifically planned for a office type space, we plan to extend its usability and practicability for other types of buildings such as shopping malls, cinemas, etc. In this regard, acquiring of information of each person (either single or family or with impairments) will be the main challenge. Furthermore, the notification methodology will also be different than the proposed one.

In addition to this, we also plan to develop other agents of our proposed architecture and integrate this group management agent, developed in this study, with other parts of the architecture. We are also working to apply our proposed approach on real-time data of different emergency scenarios to find out the effectiveness and reliability of our system. Once we will have the results, we will compare them with other state-of-the-art techniques.

Acknowledgments. Work partially supported by the Autonomous Region of Madrid (grant "MOSI-AGIL-CM" (S2013/ICE-3019) co-funded by EU Structural Funds FSE and FEDER), project "SURF" (TIN2015-65515-C4-4-R (MINECO /FEDER)) funded by the Spanish Ministry of Economy and Competitiveness, and through the Excellence Research Group GES2ME (Ref. 30VCPIGI05) co-funded by URJC-Santander Bank.

References

1. Intelligent smoke detectors, kidde-fenwal systems. https://kidde-fenwal.com/ Public/System_Details/Kidde-Fire-Systems/SmartOne-Intelligent-Smoke-Detectors. Accessed 31 May 2019
2. Sentinel, accuware. https://www.sentinelcv.com/. Accessed 31 May 2019
3. Temperature sensors, texas instruments incorporated. http://www.ti.com/sensors/temperature-sensors/overview.html. Accessed 31 May 2019
4. Fruin, J.J.: Pedestrian planning and design. Technical report (1971)
5. Hughes, R.L.: A continuum theory for the flow of pedestrians. Transp. Res. Part B: Methodol. **36**(6), 507–535 (2002)
6. Li, Y., Liu, H., Liu, G.p., Li, L., Moore, P., Hu, B.: A grouping method based on grid density and relationship for crowd evacuation simulation. Phys. A: Stat. Mech. Appl. **473**, 319–336 (2017)
7. Liu, H.: Context-aware agents in cooperative design environment. Int. J. Comput. Appl. Technol. **39**(4), 187–198 (2010)
8. Liu, H., Sun, Y., Li, Y.: Modeling and path generation approaches for crowd simulation based on computational intelligence. Chinese J. Electron. **21**(4), 636–641 (2012)
9. Lujak, M., Billhardt, H., Dunkel, J., Fernández, A., Hermoso, R., Ossowski, S.: A distributed architecture for real-time evacuation guidance in large smart buildings. Comput. Sci. Inf. Syst. **14**(1), 257–282 (2017)
10. Oxendine, C., Sonwalkar, M., Waters, N.: A multi-objective, multi-criteria approach to improve situational awareness in emergency evacuation routing using mobile phone data. Trans. GIS **16**(3), 375–396 (2012)
11. Shi, J., Ren, A., Chen, C.: Agent-based evacuation model of large public buildings under fire conditions. Autom. Constr. **18**(3), 338–347 (2009)
12. Talebi, K., Smith, J.M.: Stochastic network evacuation models. Comput. Oper. Res. **12**(6), 559–577 (1985)
13. Thompson, P.A., Marchant, E.W.: Computer and fluid modelling of evacuation. Saf. Sci. **18**(4), 277–289 (1995)
14. Vermuyten, H., Beliën, J., De Boeck, L., Reniers, G., Wauters, T.: A review of optimisation models for pedestrian evacuation and design problems. Saf. Sci. **87**, 167–178 (2016)
15. Wagner, N., Agrawal, V.: An agent-based simulation system for concert venue crowd evacuation modeling in the presence of a fire disaster. Expert Syst. Appl. **41**(6), 2807–2815 (2014)
16. Xiong, M., Lees, M., Cai, W., Zhou, S., Low, M.Y.H.: Hybrid modelling of crowd simulation. Procedia Comput. Sci. **1**(1), 57–65 (2010)
17. Xiong, M., Tang, S., Zhao, D.: A hybrid model for simulating crowd evacuation. New Gen. Comput. **31**(3), 211–235 (2013)
18. Zheng, X., Zhong, T., Liu, M.: Modeling crowd evacuation of a building based on seven methodological approaches. Build. Environ. **44**(3), 437–445 (2009)

Robust Detection of Outdoor Urban Advertising Panels in Static Images

Ángel Morera[1], Ángel Sánchez[1(✉)], Ángel D. Sappa[2,3], and José F. Vélez[1]

[1] Universidad Rey Juan Carlos, 28933 Móstoles, Madrid, Spain
{angel.morera,angel.sanchez,jose.velez}@urjc.es
[2] Escuela Superior Politécnica del Litoral, ESPOL, Guayaquil, Ecuador
[3] Computer Vision Center, Bellaterra, Barcelona, Spain
sappa@ieee.org

Abstract. One interesting publicity application for Smart City environments is recognizing brand information contained in urban advertising panels. For such a purpose, a previous stage is to accurately detect and locate the position of these panels in images. This work presents an effective solution to this problem using a Single Shot Detector (SSD) based on a deep neural network architecture that minimizes the number of false detections under multiple variable conditions regarding the panels and the scene. Achieved experimental results using the Intersection over Union (IoU) accuracy metric make this proposal applicable in real complex urban images.

Keywords: Object detection · Urban ads panels ·
Deep learning · Single Shot Detector (SSD) architecture ·
Intersection over Union (IoU) metric · Augmented Reality

1 Introduction

The concept of *smart city* was coined twenty years ago [1] and it refers to a urban space that applies Information and Communication Technologies (ICT) to enhance the quality and performance of urban services such as energy, transportation and utilities in order to reduce resource consumption, wastage and overall costs. Urban space maintenance in smart cities is a challenging and time consuming task since this space is actually surrounded by or is embedded with smart IoT systems that can efficiently capture and process huge amount of data. Hence, in the smart city context, having an approach that allows a continuous monitoring of the urban space will help to envisage an efficient management of the public resources. The urban space monitoring problem has been recently tackled using frameworks based on citizens' sensing devices, under a crowdsourcing philosophy [10].

The outdoor advertising industry has experimented an important growth in recent years [2]. In streets of urban environments, ads panels and billboards are everywhere, and they are also the only media that drivers and pedestrians cannot

© Springer Nature Switzerland AG 2019
F. De la Prieta et al. (Eds.): PAAMS 2019 Workshops, CCIS 1047, pp. 246–256, 2019.
https://doi.org/10.1007/978-3-030-24299-2_21

escape (i.e., differently from other forms of publicity, outdoor advertising cannot be blocked by people). In consequence, this is one the most cost-effective forms of advertising available. Moreover, since current smartphones are equipped with a variety of embedded sensors like cameras, GPS or 3G/4G, it is possible to get closer the final user a variety of Augmented Reality (AR) applications [6]. This way, the citizens using their smartphones can better deepen and, perhaps, enjoy the contents associated to urban advertisements. Moreover, with the emergence of digital billboards/panels, the outdoor advertising industry is even more valuable since going digital gives advertisers the flexibility to schedule short and long-term publicity campaigns.

Advertising panels are a type of urban furniture that commonly presents a normalized shape and a more reduced size than billboards. Publicity panel detection in images presents important advantages both in the real world as well as in the virtual world. In the first case, after detection of panels, it is possible to recognize the product included in the publicity and get more information about it through AR applications. Moreover, it is possible to detect whether or not the advertised product information is currently updated. Regarding to the publicity in Internet urban images in applications like Google Street View, it would be possible, when detecting panels on these images, to replace the publicity that appears inside a panel by another one proposed by a financing company.

Automatic outdoor detection and localization in real urban outdoor images is a difficult task due to multiple variability conditions presenting images including those containing advertising elements like panels. For example, scene illumination conditions (solar daylight or artificial lights), panel perspective view, size ratio of present panels with respect to image size, complex scene background (i.e., presence of multiple elements surrounding the panels like buildings, vehicles and/or different infrastructures), among other factors. Figure 1 illustrates some of these involved difficulties in outdoor images containing advertising panels.

Visual detection and recognition problems, applied to specific elements, in outdoor images have been widely studied. For example, this is the case of vehicle localization [17], traffic sign detection [4] or car plates [11]. However, as far as we know, there are not published works on detecting outdoor ads panels. Related problems such as text and objects detection inside segmented billboard images [7] or the localization of billboards on streamed sport videos have been investigated [16]. Another related studied application is the insertion of virtual ads in street images based on localization of specific regions on them (e.g., buildings facades) [6].

Convolutional networks are deep artificial neural networks that are currently used in many Computer Vision tasks, such as classifying images into categories, detecting objects, clustering images by similarity or performing object recognition within scenes. The Single Shot Detector (SSD) [9] is based on a convolutional network that produces a fixed-size collection of bounding boxes and scores (related to the presence of object class elements in these boxes), followed by a non-maximum suppression stage to produce the final detections.

This paper proposes a robust method for the automatic detection of urban ads panels in outdoor images. The proposed solution is based on deep neural networks and it achieves a high accuracy in detection of panels under multiple and combined variabilites on illumination, position and size of detected targets. The number of false detections is reduced in order to allow a more practical application of the proposed approach.

The work is organized as follows. Section 2 describes a preprocessing stage applied to the given images, as well as the proposed deep architecture and its training. Section 3 offers some details on the dataset used and the experiments performed for detecting the panels in images. Finally, the last Section outlines the conclusions of this work.

2 Proposed Solution

This section summarizes the initial preprocessing applied to the images, the deep neural network used to detect outdoor panels and setup information on how this network was trained.

2.1 Image Preprocesing

Main preprocessing consists in rescaling the original images by preserving their aspect ratio. For such purpose the smaller side of an image was set to 512 pixels and the larger side was set to the proportional size in pixels, so that the aspect ratio is preserved. After that, the larger side is trimmed so that it would also be 512 pixels without losing any part of the panel. Therefore, all training, validation and test images were rescaled to 512×512.

2.2 Single Shot Detector (SSD) Architecture

Single Shot MultiBox Detector (SSD) networks were introduced by Liu and collaborators in 2016 [9]. A SSD network implements a method for detecting multiple object classes in images by generating confidence scores related to the presence of any object category in each default box. Moreover, it produces adjustments in boxes to better match the object shapes. This network model is suited for real-time applications since it does not resample features for bounding box hypotheses (like in models such as Faster R-CNN [13]). Additionally, SSD is as accurate as other single-shot approaches like YOLO [12]. The SSD architecture is based on a feed-forward convolutional network and its object detection approach has two steps: (1) extract feature maps, and (2) apply convolution filters to detect objects. SSD uses VGG16 [15] to extract feature maps. Then, it detects objects using the Conv4_3 layer. Each prediction is composed of a bounding box and 21 scores for each class (one extra class for no object); the class with highest score is selected as the one for the bounded object. Conv4_3 makes a total of $38 \times 38 \times 4$ predictions: four predictions per cell independently from depth of feature maps. Many predictions will contain no object as it is expected and uses the class '0' to indicate that none object was detected in the image. Figure 2 illustrates the typical layer structure of a SSD network.

Fig. 1. Some test images of panels including diverse variabilities: (a) night image; (b) panel rotated due to image perspective; (c) partial occlusion of panel; and (d) reduced size (and partial occlusion) of panel in the image.

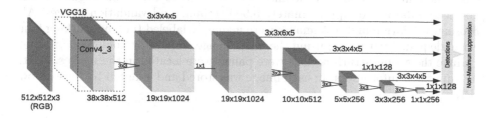

Fig. 2. Single Shot Detector (SSD) architecture model.

2.3 Training Details

SSD only needs an input image and the ground truth boxes for each object during training. In our approach, a SSD_MobileNet_v1, pretrained with Microsoft COCO dataset [8], was used. MobileNets [5] are a family of more efficient models including depth-wise separable convolutions, suitable for mobile and embedded vision applications.

The network input was adapted to the size of our preprocessed images. Then, it was finely tuned and trained using our own panel dataset (some details on the dataset are given in next section). In our problem, only one class was required (i.e. the 'panel' class) and the network itself can discriminate in images between what is a 'panel' and what is not. Experiments were performed on an standard computer and using an small batch size of 6–8 and different number of epochs so far of 180,000. Different values of learning rates varying from 0.004 to 0.001 were evaluated, with a momentum of 0.9. Approximately, a number of 5,800 panel images were used for training and 100 images for validation.

3 Results

This section describes the dataset used and the achieved experimental results. The influence of panels' sizes in images with respect to the accuracy on detections is also studied.

3.1 Dataset

As far as we know, there are not public datasets of outdoor urban panel images. In consequence, one of the first tasks in this project consisted in creating a dataset to train the SSD network. This dataset will be released to other researchers interested in the considered problem. We have firstly collected approximately 1,800 images which were separated into training and validation sets. Test images were collected separately, a number of 140 test images in total. Because the number of training images is small and the dataset was unbalanced with respect to variabilities in panels, a data augmentation stage was applied to balance this dataset and to increase the sample size. For such purpose, some geometric operations were applied to images; in particular, rotations from $-5°$ to $5°$, and different zooms on the images from -10% to 10%. This augmentation produced a dataset of approximately 5,900 training and validation images. All training, validation and test images were manually labeled (i.e., by marking four rectangle points per panel) using the VGG Image Annotator Tool [3] in order to produce the ground-truth regions were panels were located in the images. Next, the annotated information in each image was stored and adapted to TensorFlow API.

3.2 Global Results

Next, we show some qualitative and quantitative results regarding detection of panels in test images. Figure 3 illustrates several panel detections produced by our method on the same sample images shown in Fig. 1. Note that panels are accurately detected under different variable conditions like: night illumination, perspective, partial occlusions and reduced size in images. Moreover, our approach also worked well in presence of various combined variabilities in images (e.g., small and rotated urban panels).

(a)   (b)

(c)   (d)

Fig. 3. Detections achieved by proposed method on images of Fig. 1. Red and green rectangles respectively correspond to ground-truth and detected panels. (Color figure online)

Figure 4 illustrates a correct detection situation when more than one panels are present in the scene.

Fig. 4. Detection results of two panels in a sample image.

Regarding quantitative results, we used the Intersection over Union (IoU) metric [14] as accuracy measure in detections. With this metric, the accuracy of a panel detection is computed by dividing the intersection of respective hand-labeled ground-truth and model-predicted bounding boxes by the corresponding union of these two bounding boxes. The respective computed IoU values for the panels detected in images of Fig. 3 were: 0.93, 0.94, 0.88 and 0.93.

The output of the SSD network returns for each point of an input image the confidence to find a panel centered on that point. In the context of our model we are interested in the absence of False Positives (FP). We think it is preferable, in applications related to advertisements, to leave an old content inside the panel than to crush a wrong part of the image with an updated advertising publicity. Therefore, using the learning sample, we have set a threshold value of 0.7 for such a confidence in a correct panel detection. Thus, if the neuron in the output layer has a value greater than 0.7, we consider that the network decides that there is a panel at that point.

Using this threshold value, an IoU value greater than zero is obtained for all panels in the test images except in one case. Such a case could be considered a False Positive. Table 1 shows the number of posters detected with this threshold, and the IoU rate obtained in each case. This threshold leaves a False Rejection rate of 25% (35 of 140 panels). As can be seen in Table 2, many not detected panels correspond to very small ones (i.e., even much more smaller than 10% of the image size).

On the other hand, it must be determined which IoU threshold can be considered as a correct detection. Figure 5 shows the detection rate that would be obtained (on the y-axis) by setting detections that meet a minimum IoU (on the

x-axis) as correct. It can be seen that with IoU values below 40% the detection rate is 99%. Increasing the IoU threshold beyond 40% reduces the detection success. An interesting value is to consider the detection as correct when the IoU is 80%, in this case our system would also have an 80% success.

Table 1. Number of panels detected and their associated IoU values

IoU	Detected billboards
0.5	2
0.6	1
0.7	2
0.8	10
0.9	41
1	49

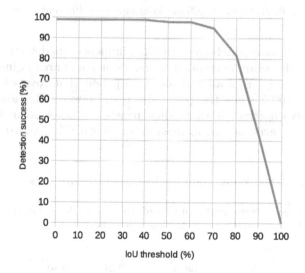

Fig. 5. Percentage of success in detections related to the IoU threshold value.

3.3   Influence of Panel Sizes in Detection Results

Figure 6 shows the distribution ratio of panel sizes with respect to image sizes (in percentages) for the test images. Note that most of panels in images are small (i.e., a 40% of them) and have a size ratio below or equal to 10%; a 81.5% of panels present a ratio size below or equal to 30%; and all panels are smaller or equal than half of the image. In our study, we have not considered very big panels (i.e., above 50% of image size) since their detection becomes easier even with a complex image background.

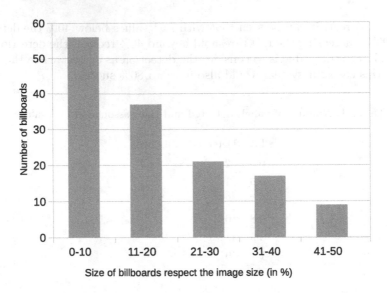

Fig. 6. Number of billboards grouped by different sizes.

With respect to how panel size variability influences its detection, we show in Table 2 that the detection percentage increases as panel area in image increases too. This value grows from around 53.5% in panels that covers less than 10% of the image to 100% when the panel size is in between 41% and 50% of the image. An interesting fact is that when panels are detected in images, their corresponding IoU accuracy is, in most cases, above 85%, regardless the panel size.

Table 2. Achieved detection results related to panel sizes in images.

Size ratio: panel vs image (in %)	Number of panels	Number of detections	Detections percentage	Mean IoU (in %)
0–10	56	30	53.57	86.80
11–20	37	31	83.78	88.54
21–30	21	20	95.24	84.14
31–40	17	15	88.24	87.79
41–50	9	9	100.00	89.74

4   Conclusion

This paper presents a method based on Single Shot MultiBox Detector (SSD) network to accurately locate the position of advertising panels in outdoor urban images. Our proposal is robust and produces good detections under multiple variabilities like panel sizes, illumination conditions, image perspective, partial occlusion of panels, complex background and multiple panels in scenes. The presented method reduces significantly the number of false detections in test images, which makes it useful in the smart city context. As future work, we aim to improve the detection of very small panels (i.e., those ones producing most false negatives). Another interesting future work consists in recognizing the elements contained inside the panels to determine the brand name of a given advertising or to use the panel detection to update the publicity in an Augmented Reality application.

Acknowledgments. The authors gratefully acknowledge the financial support of the CYTED Network "Ibero-American Thematic Network on ICT Applications for Smart Cities" (Ref: 518RT0559) and the Spanish MICINN RTI Project (Ref: RTI2018-098019-B-100). The third author acknowledge the support of the ESPOL project PRAIM (FIEC-09-2015), the Spanish MICINN Project TIN2017-89723-P and "CERCA Programme/Generalitat de Catalunya".

References

1. Anthopoulos, L.: Understanding Smart Cities: A Tool for Smart Government or an Industrial Trick? Springer, Heidelberg (2017). https://doi.org/10.1007/978-3-319-57015-0
2. Borisova, O., Martynova, A.: Comparing the effectiveness of outdoor advertising with internet advertising. Bachelor's thesis, JAMK University of Applied Sciences, Finland (2017)
3. Dutta, A., Gupta, A., Zissermann, A.: VGG Image Annotator (VIA) - Version: 1.0.6 (2016). http://www.robots.ox.ac.uk/~vgg/software/via. Accessed 19 Feb 2005
4. Garcia, M., Sotelo, M., Martin, E.: Traffic sign detection in static images using matlab. In: IEEE Conference on Emerging Technologies and Factory Automation (ETFA 2003) (2003)
5. Howard, A.G., et al.: Mobilenets: Efficient convolutional neural networks for mobile vision applications. CoRR abs/1704.04861 (2017)
6. Huang, Y., Hao, Q., Yu, H.: Virtual ads insertion in street building views for augmented reality. In: 18th IEEE International Conference on Image Processing (ICIP 2011), pp. 1117–1120 (2011)
7. Intasuwan, T., Kaewthong, J., Vittayakorn, S.: Text and object detection on billboards. In: 10th International Conference on Information Technology and Electrical Engineering (ICITEE 2018), pp. 6–11 (2018)
8. Lin, T.-Y., et al.: Microsoft COCO: common objects in context. In: Fleet, D., Pajdla, T., Schiele, B., Tuytelaars, T. (eds.) ECCV 2014. LNCS, vol. 8693, pp. 740–755. Springer, Cham (2014). https://doi.org/10.1007/978-3-319-10602-1_48
9. Liu, W., et al.: SSD: single shot multibox detector. In: Leibe, B., Matas, J., Sebe, N., Welling, M. (eds.) ECCV 2016. LNCS, vol. 9905, pp. 21–37. Springer, Cham (2016). https://doi.org/10.1007/978-3-319-46448-0_2
10. Murty, R., et al.: Citysense: an urban-scale wireless sensor network and testbed. In: 2008 IEEE International Conference on Technologies for Homeland Security (2008)

11. Panchal, T., Patel, H., Panchal, A.: License plate detection using harris corner and character segmentation by integrated approach from an image. Procedia Comput. Sci. **79**, 419–425 (2016). https://doi.org/10.1016/j.procs.2016.03.054

12. Redmon, J., Divvala, S., Girshick, R., Farhadi, A.: You only look once: unified, real-time object detection. In: Proceedings of the IEEE Conference on Computer Vision and Pattern Recognition, pp. 779–788 (2016)

13. Ren, S., He, K., Girshick, R., Sun, J.: Faster R-CNN: towards real-time object detection with region proposal networks. In: Advances in Neural Information Processing Systems, pp. 91–99 (2015)

14. Rosebrock, A.: Intersection over Union (IoU) for object detection (2016). https://www.pyimagesearch.com/2016/11/07/intersection-over-union-iou-for-object-detection/. Accessed 19 Feb 2005

15. Simonyan, K., Zisserman, A.: Very deep convolutional networks for large-scale image recognition. arXiv preprint arXiv:1409.1556 (2014)

16. Watve, A., Sural, S.: Soccer video processing for the detection of advertisement billboards. Pattern Recogn. Lett. **29**(7), 994–1006 (2008). https://doi.org/10.1016/j.patrec.2008.01.022

17. Wong, D., Deguchi, D., Ide, I., Murase, H.: Vision-based vehicle localization using a visual street map with embedded SURF scale. In: Agapito, L., Bronstein, M.M., Rother, C. (eds.) ECCV 2014. LNCS, vol. 8925, pp. 167–179. Springer, Cham (2015). https://doi.org/10.1007/978-3-319-16178-5_11

SimFleet: A New Transport Fleet Simulator Based on MAS

Javier Palanca[✉], Andrés Terrasa, Carlos Carrascosa, and Vicente Julián

Universitat Politècnica de València, Camí de Vera s/n, 46020 València, Spain
{jpalanca,aterrasa,carrasco,vinglada}@dsic.upv.es

Abstract. Mobility in the urban environment has undergone notable changes in recent years. The mobility of people or goods has been adapting to new technologies, emerging new mobility services for the potential users. In this sense, traditional vehicle fleets in a city are being transformed into more open fleets where their members can proactively decide whether or not to carry out certain services, with some of the centralized decisions disappearing. The management in terms of organization and strategies to follow of this type of open fleets is much more complex, which is why simulation tools that allow their analysis can be very useful. In this way, this paper presents an agent-based simulation tool for open fleets in open environments. The tool is instantiable in any type of fleet, in the paper presents an example of a fleet of taxis.

Keywords: Multi-agent systems · Coordination · Smart cities

1 Introduction

Nowadays, the increase of mobility and transportation in urban environments has become one of the challenges facing our todays society. Mobility is currently one of the causes of congestion problems, air pollution, inefficiencies in logistics and energy use in current cities. Over the last few years, innovative solutions for communication networks, information processing, and transport are being developed in order to approach this challenge, assuring a more efficient use of resources offering time flexible mobility solutions for citizens and businesses [1].

Current technology for public transport in urban environments can be used for improving the quality of service and therefore its attractiveness to passengers. Existing technology provides public transport managers with real-time information on the operational status of the public transport system. This allows service providers to manage their fleets in a more effectively way [2], and to take remedial measures against any unwanted event. Moreover, these systems can provide up-to-date information to passengers or users [3] anywhere (vehicles, stops, at home, etc.) and form the basis of a complete Smart Transport System [4,5].

The way to manage most transport and mobility services in today's cities has been transformed into a new concept called "open fleet" [1]. An open fleet differs from traditional fleets in the sense that individuals has complete autonomy and

© Springer Nature Switzerland AG 2019
F. De la Prieta et al. (Eds.): PAAMS 2019 Workshops, CCIS 1047, pp. 257–264, 2019.
https://doi.org/10.1007/978-3-030-24299-2_22

there is not a centralized entity that governs the fleet. In an open fleet, vehicles may interact with their environment in a Smart city, and join or leave the fleet at any time. In any case, similar to the traditional fleet concept, an open fleet requires a global regulatory entity that manages and coordinates the use of a limited set of resources in order to provide a specific transportation service. The efficiency of an open fleet depends on the use of appropriated coordination and regulation mechanisms that deal with the problem of balancing global and individual objectives. Regarding the coordination problem of urban fleet, this has traditionally been studied for more closed fleets in different areas, and its impact, especially in the field of emergency services [6] or, in recent years research, to the coordination of fleets for vehicles sharing [7].

Multi-agent systems technology perfectly fits with the concept of open fleets and, therefore, can be a good solution for the design and study of this kind of urban mobility. In a more specific way, we propose the use of agent-based simulation tools for the study and analysis of the more appropriated models, architectures or strategies for the management of systems of this kind. Agent-based simulation (ABS) offers a way to model social systems composed of agents that interact and influence each other, learning from their experiences and adapting their behaviour to achieve goals in the environment to which they have been destined, both individually and collectively [8]. Taking this into account, this paper presents an agent-based simulation for the management of open fleets in urban environments. The toolkit allows operators to analyze coordination and regulation strategies in order to assure an efficient operation of the fleet with regard to some globally desirable parameters.

The rest of the paper is structured as follows. Section 2 presents the proposed simulation tool; Sect. 3 illustrates a specific use of the tool for the management of a taxi fleet. Finally, Sect. 4 includes some conclusions.

2   SimFleet: A Simulation Tool for Open Fleets

SimFleet is a simulation tool which provides MAS researchers and learners with a convenient environment where to develop and test complex negotiation scenarios, in the context of a city containing one or more fleets of transportation vehicles. The tool can be used to simulate any kind of fleet where a group of vehicles transport *items* (goods or people) from one location to another, including among others, courier companies, taxi services, freight transport (by trucks), etc.

The tool has been built as a multi-agent system running on top of the SPADE platform [9], where the different actors in the fleet simulation (transportation vehicles and customers requesting items to be transported) are modeled as agents which can interact with each other by means of the SPADE communication facilities. The tool has been designed to hide most of the complexity of developing a multi-agent application by providing the user with three different interaction interfaces: the graphical user interface (GUI), the command-line execution interface and the Application Program Interface (API). The GUI is the part of the application that runs the simulator where the transportation vehicles and items to be transported are displayed within the city map of choice, and where the evolution of the simulation can be observed; this interface includes a limited set of interactions (starting and stopping the simulation, zooming, random placement of new vehicles and items, simulation statistics, etc.). The command-line interface is the way to start simulations offline and it features every possible configuration available in the simulation; this is a very convenient way to extend the functionality of the simulation tool (in general, or for a particular fleet environment) without having to modify the graphical interface. Among others, the command-line interface allows for the simulation of particular scenarios with fixed initial location for vehicles or items, as well as to set the negotiation strategies for the simulation agents; this way the simulation can consistently compare different negotiation schemes in equal terms. The third interface is the API for implementing custom negotiation strategies; some of the API functions are general, but many others are specific for particular fleet environments (package delivery, taxi service, etc.). The tool incorporates an abstract interface which can be easily extended in order to adapt the API to the fleet environment under study.

The following subsections explore the most relevant characteristics of *Sim-Fleet*, namely its underlying platform (SPADE), its internal architecture, and the way to use it in order to develop and test custom negotiation strategies, which is the tool's main objective.

2.1   The SPADE Platform

SPADE (Smart Python multi-Agent Development Environment) is a multi-agent system (MAS) platform based on two main technologies: the XMPP standard for messaging and presence [10] and the Python programming language. These technologies offer many features and facilities that assist in the construction of MAS, such as an existing communication channel, the concepts of users (agents) and servers (platforms) and an extensible communication protocol based on XML.

Extensible Messaging and Presence Protocol (XMPP) is an open, XML-inspired protocol for near-real-time, extensible instant messaging (IM) and presence information. The protocol is built to be open and free, asynchronous, decentralized, secure, extensible and flexible. The latter two features allow XMPP not only to be an instant messaging protocol, but also to be extended and used for many tasks and situations (IoT, WebRTC, social, ...). SPADE itself uses some XMPP extensions to provide extended features to its agents, such as remote procedure calls between agents (Jabber-RPC), file transfer (In-Band Bytestreams), an so on.

The internal components of the SPADE agents that provide their intelligence are the *behaviors*. A behavior is a task that an agent can run using some predefined repeating pattern. For example, the most basic behavior type (pattern) is the so-called cyclic behavior, which repeatedly executes the same method over and over again, indefinitely. This is the way to develop typical behaviors that wait for a perception, reason about it and finally execute an action, and then wait for the next perception.

2.2   SimFleet Architecture

Internally, *SimFleet* is structured in four layers, designed in order to separate the tool functionality and to make it easy to adapt it to particular fleet and negotiation scenarios. Figure 1 depicts this architecture, including the four layers (the simulator, the fleet, the agents and their respective strategies), which are now described.

The simulator is the agent controlling the simulation process and serving the GUI, and it is configured to locate the simulation display in a particular city, which can be modified. Besides the city map, the simulator mainly relies on a *Route Planner* agent which calculates valid routes through the city streets for the vehicles travelling from one point to another within the city. The simulator is also in charge of creating the rest of application agents in the simulation.

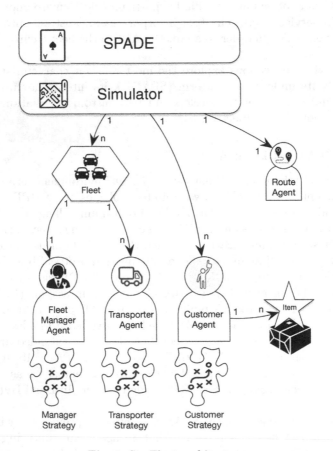

Fig. 1. SimFleet architecture.

A Fleet represents a company or institution which owns a group of vehicles which are capable of transporting goods or people from one point to another within the city. Each vehicle in the fleet has its own agent in the simulation, called the *Transporter*, described below in the agent layer. In addition to the transporter agents, each fleet includes another agent, called the *Fleet Manager*, which is in charge of receiving the requests from the customers and (potentially) making some decisions about how to organize the requests and coordinate the transport process of the fleet's vehicles. The amount of coordination and decision making of the manager depends on the strategies of both the manager and the transporter agents, allowing for the simulation of both centralized and decentralized fleets.

At the agent layer, the tool includes an agent for the Fleet Manager and all the Transporters of each fleet, and also an agent for every Customer which may issue transport requests in the simulation. A Transporter Agent represents both a vehicle and its driver, and it has some attributes which may be customized: maximum speed, cost per kilometer (or per delivery), fleet, name of the fleet manager, initial position, and its icon (in the simulator display). On the other hand, a Customer is an agent which may request transport services for any available fleet, and which includes some attributes such as amount of money available, list of items to be transported, and list of the names of all the available Fleet Managers. It is worth noting that the items to be transported are not represented as agents in *SimFleet* since all the negotiation processes are carried out by the item's owner, the Customer Agent. For this reason, items are here modeled as *artifacts*, including two main attributes, its location coordinates and its display icon. This model also allows for the case where the item to be transported is also the customer (for example, when a customer requests a taxi service), by linking the customer's location to the item's location.

The fourth layer is the set of negotiation strategies that the simulation agents apply in order to request, select, organize and coordinate the transport services. Each agent incorporates its own strategy according to its role in the simulation environment (Customer, Transporter or Fleet Manager) and its own particular goals. The *SimFleet* architecture provides a well-defined API in order to incorporate such strategies to agents. In particular, each agent incorporates a specific SPADE behavior (as defined above), which defines the negotiation goals and interactions with the relevant counterpart agents. Furthermore, this behavior is internally structured as a finite-state machine (inherited from the *SimFleet* FSMStrategyBehaviour class) where each state represents a possible situation in the agent's negotiation strategy (and implements the actions to be executed in that situation), and each transition represents a possible change from one situation to another within the strategy. This way, the tool offers a consistent framework for designing and developing negotiation strategies, where the actual code to be implemented is very little.

In addition to the above, this last layer has been designed by using the so-called *Strategy Pattern* [11], which is the best practice when an application incorporates different alternative versions of an algorithm and the user wants to be able to select for execution any of these versions at run time. *SimFleet* uses this design pattern in order to dynamically incorporate new negotiation behaviors to the simulation agents (customers, transporters, managers) at run time.

In particular, the files containing the code of those behaviors can be specified at the command-line when a simulation is released, and therefore there is no need to modify the tool's code files.

3   Case of Example: Taxi Simulator

This section presents the application of *SimFleet* to deal with taxi fleets. In this sense, the agent roles and interaction protocol have been adapted, along with the way agents behave and the different strategies used to assign Customer agents to Transporter agents. The rest of the section is going to show these changes.

Each Taxi Fleet will have a different Fleet Manager agent associated to it. Taxi agents are the agents inheriting from Transporter agents associated to the taxis in the fleet. Each Passenger agent inherits from Customer Agent taking into account that it is located in a position in the map, modelling each one to a client looking for a taxi. In this case, Passenger agents are not only Customer agents, but also their Item associated, as the taxi must carry the client itself, not any other item.

The main advantage of *SimFleet* is that, once the tool has been instantiated to a particular fleet environment (taxi fleets in this case), the implementation and testing of custom negotiation strategies is straightforward. As explained above, the internal architecture of *SimFleet* structures the code of each involved agent in a set of *behaviors* (as supported by the SPADE platform), and each agent has one particular behavior devoted to the negotiation interactions with the rest of agents (which are relevant to its strategy) in the simulation.

The negotiation strategy of the agents involved in a particular fleet environment is normally based on two aspects related to the negotiation process: its final goal and its interaction protocol. These two aspects are normally deeply influenced by the particular fleet environment that needs to be simulated. Nevertheless, the *Taxi Simulator* provides some abstractions (inherited from *SimFleet*) in order to allow for a reasonably easy customization of the tool to the intended environment, such as a Fleet Manager agent, a Route Planner agent to calculate routes by car through the city and some helpers that ease the use of the simulator (like a *pick up* function, a *deliver* function or a *move* function that taxi drivers may use inside their strategies).

One of the main features of *Taxi Simulator* is the ability to change the default negotiation strategy of the agents that interact in the simulation: the Fleet Manager agent, the Taxi agents and the Passenger agents. The overall goal of the negotiation strategy of these three agent types is to decide which taxi agent will transport each passenger agent to its destination, making sure that no passenger agent is left unattended. Additionally, the negotiation strategy may also try to optimize some metrics, such as the average time that passenger agents are waiting to be served, or the amount of gas spent by taxis in their movements. How taxis and passengers behave depends on the strategies injected into the simulator. Taxis may accept a passenger request, for example, depending on the distance to the passenger, the length of the trip, etc.

This negotiation strategy is built on two main elements. First, it is based on the internal logic of each agent type (Fleet Manager, Taxi and Passenger) and, in particular, on their respective strategy behavior, which includes the internal logic of each agent type regarding the negotiation process following a finite state machine. And second, it is also based on a protocol called CALL_FOR_TAXI which comprises the types of messages exchanged among the three agent types during the negotiation. The diagram in Fig. 2 presents the protocol in the typical FIPA[1] format, where agent types are depicted as vertical lines and the exchanged message types (or "performatives") in horizontal arrows. The CALL_FOR_TAXI protocol can be seen as an hybrid version of well-known REQUEST and MATCHMAKING protocols.

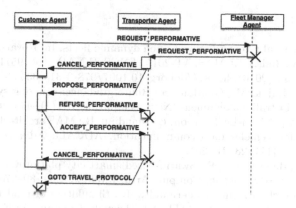

Fig. 2. The default CALL_FOR_TAXI protocol.

This case of example has illustrated how to build a simulation with a specific fleet type (in this case a taxi fleet) and what elements would be necessary to design in order to run a simulation of this type in SimFleet. With such a scenario you can perform as many simulations as you like in SimFleet to test different fleet management strategies in the context of a city.

4 Conclusions

This paper has presented a tool called *SimFleet* which can be used to simulate and analyze new mobility trends in current smart cities. In this context, the tool allows for the development and testing of new management policies regarding the mobility of vehicle fleets, as well as the study of different coordination strategies and regulations which may improve efficiency in the transport of goods or people in urban environments.

SimFleet is built as a multi-agent system running at the top of a real platform, called SPADE, where the different actors of the simulation are implemented as

---

[1] http://www.fipa.org/repository/ips.php3.

agents. The tool features clear interfaces at different levels which have been designed to easily incorporate new concepts and strategies to the simulation agents. In addition, the tool facilitates the definition of scenarios and metrics by which it is possible to compare the different policies under study in comparable terms.

Finally, the use of the tool has been illustrated with a case study which simulates the negotiation process between a taxi fleet and a group of customers which, individually, need to travel to certain destinations in a particular city.

Acknowledgments. This work was partially supported by MINECO/FEDER TIN2015-65515-C4-1-R of the Spanish government.

References

1. Billhardt, H., et al.: Towards smart open dynamic fleets. In: Rovatsos, M., Vouros, G., Julian, V. (eds.) EUMAS/AT-2015. LNCS (LNAI), vol. 9571, pp. 410–424. Springer, Cham (2016). https://doi.org/10.1007/978-3-319-33509-4_32
2. Ossowski, S., Lujak, M., Giordani, S.: Route guidance: bridging system and user optimization in traffic assignment. Neurocomputing **151**(1), 449–460 (2015)
3. Emmanuel, A., Grislin-Le Strugeon, E., Mandiau, R.: MAS architecture and knowledge model for vehicles data communication. ADCAIJ: Adv. Distrib. Comput. Artif. Intell. J. **1**(1), 23–31 (2012)
4. Chamoso, P., de la Prieta, F.: Swarm-based smart city platform: a traffic application. ADCAIJ: Adv. Distrib. Comput. Artif. Intell. J. **4**(2), 89–97 (2015)
5. Fernandez Isabel, A., Fuentes Fernandez, R.: Simulation of road traffic applying model-driven engineering. ADCAIJ: Adv. Distrib. Comput. Artif. Intell. J. **4**(2), 1–24 (2015)
6. Aboueljinane, L., Sahin, E., Jemai, Z.: A review on simulation models applied to emergency medical service operations. Comput. Ind. Eng. **66**(4), 734–750 (2013)
7. Nair, R., Miller-Hooks, E., Hampshire, R.C., Bušić, A.: Large-scale vehicle sharing systems: analysis of vélib'. Int. J. Sustainable Transp. **7**(1), 85–106 (2013)
8. Macal, C.M., North, M.J.: Tutorial on agent-based modelling and simulation. J. Simul. **4**(3), 151–162 (2010)
9. Gregori, M.E., Cámara, J.P., Bada, G.A.: A jabber-based multi-agent system platform. In: Proceedings of the Fifth International Joint Conference on Autonomous Agents and Multiagent Systems, pp. 1282–1284. ACM (2006)
10. Saint-Andre, P.: Extensible messaging and presence protocol (XMPP): Core. Technical report (2011)
11. Gamma, E., Helm, R., Johnson, R., Vlissides, J.: Design Patterns: Elements of Reusable Object-Oriented Software. Addison-Wesley Longman Publishing Co., Inc, Boston (1995)

Workshop on Swarm Intelligence and Swarm Robotics (SISR)

Workshop on Swarm Intelligence and Swarm Robotics (SISR)

Swarm intelligence (SI) refers to the complex collective behavior of self-organized and decentralized systems, typically composed of a (spatially distributed and often large) population of individuals or agents. These agents interact among themselves and with the environment using different, simple, and local rules for coordinating actions. Such swarm systems can be inherently robust, effective, and flexible. Put differently, SI can be regarded as a generic behavioral concept embracing a wide portfolio of decentralized algorithms for performing different tasks, such as signal and graph processing, inference, prediction, and optimization.

In this context, a myriad of application subfields of SI can be found in academia and industry, clear evidence of the momentum gained by this discipline. Specifically, swarm robotics (SR) refers to the application of SI methods and techniques to scenarios where the population of agents consists of physical or simulated robotic devices with motion, interaction, and communication capabilities. The focus of SR is to analyze how this swarm of relatively simple robots can be configured so as to coordinate in a distributed fashion and collectively accomplish different goals unaffordable for the capabilities of a single robot.

Organization

Organizing Committee

Eneko Osaba
Javier Del Ser
Andres Iglesias

Xin-She Yang

TECNALIA, Zamudio, Spain
University of the Basque Country, Spain
Toho University, Funabashi, Japan
  and University of Cantabria, Spain
School of Science and Technology, UK

Using Adaptive Novelty Search in Differential Evolution

Iztok Fister[1,3]([✉]), Andres Iglesias[2,3], Akemi Galvez[2,3], Javier Del Ser[4,5,6],
Eneko Osaba[4], and Iztok Fister Jr.[1]

[1] Faculty of Electrical Engineering and Computer Science, University of Maribor,
Koroška cesta 46, Maribor, Slovenia
{iztok.fister,iztok.fister1}@um.si
[2] Toho University, 2-2-1 Miyama, Funabashi 274-8510, Japan
[3] University of Cantabria, Avenida de los Castros, s/n, 39005 Santander, Spain
{iglesias,galveza}@unican.es
[4] TECNALIA, Derio, Spain
{javier.delser,eneko.osaba}@tecnalia.com
[5] University of the Basque Country (UPV/EHU), Bilbao, Spain
[6] Basque Center for Applied Mathematics (BCAM), Bilbao, Spain

Abstract. Novelty search ensures evaluation of solutions in stochastic population-based nature-inspired algorithms according to additional measure, where each solution is evaluated by a distance to its neighborhood beside the fitness function. Thus, the population diversity is preserved that is a prerequisite for the open-ended evolution in evolutionary robotics. Recently, the Novelty search was applied for solving the global optimization into differential evolution, where all Novelty search parameters remain unchanged during the run. The novelty area width parameter, that determines the diameter specifying the minimum change in each direction needed the solution for treating as the novelty, has a crucial influence on the optimization results. In this study, this parameter was adapted during the evolutionary process. The proposed self-adaptive differential evolution using the adaptive Novelty search were applied for solving the CEC 2014 Benchmark function suite, and the obtained results confirmed the usefulness of the adaptation.

Keywords: Adaptive Novelty search · Differential evolution ·
Evolutionary robotics · Open-ended evolution

1 Introduction

Two inspirations from the nature have been had the biggest influence on development of the stochastic nature-inspired population-based algorithms: (1) Darwinian evolution [1], and (2) behavior of some animals, or insects living in swarm [2]. The former has been led to emerging the Evolutionary Algorithms (EAs) [3], while the latter to Swarm Intelligence (SI) based algorithms [4]. Traditionally, these algorithms have been developed on disembodied computer systems, where there was no interaction between the system and the environment.

© Springer Nature Switzerland AG 2019
F. De la Prieta et al. (Eds.): PAAMS 2019 Workshops, CCIS 1047, pp. 267–275, 2019.
https://doi.org/10.1007/978-3-030-24299-2_23

Recently, both families of algorithms have been ported on the specific hardware, where act as autonomous agents devoted for solving the problems as delegated by their developers. These agents operate similar as human beings in society, where they need to cooperate, coordinate, and negotiate between each other in order to solve the problem [5]. This porting has been caused development of the so-called Evolutionary Robotics (ER), and Swarm Robotics (SR) [6].

New problems have been emerged by embedding the EAs and SI-based algorithms into hardware. Let us mentioned only two the most important ones: (1) selection pressure, and (2) fitness function evaluation. The selection pressure causes losing the population diversity that is a prerequisite for the open-ended evolution in ER and SR [13]. On the other hand, the fitness function in ER and SR cannot be evaluated in the traditional three-step evaluation chain genotype-phenotype-fitness. Due to the interaction of agent with environment, the fitness function must be evaluated according to the more suitable behavior that it has in the relation with the environment. Consequently, the fitness function is now calculated in a behavior space. As a result, the four-step evolution chain genotype-phenotype-behavior-fitness has replaced the three-step in ER and SR.

Indeed, two advantages in the Evolutionary Computation (EC) [19–22] enable ER and SR community to prevent the loosing of population diversity successfully [12]: (1) Multi-Objective Evolutionary Algorithms (MOEA) [14], and (2) Novelty Search (NS) [10]. The former technology allows to evaluate the same solution according to two or more criteria, while the latter to preserve the so-called novelty solution that will normally be eliminated by the fitness function. In more detail, the NS evaluate the solution in genotype space, where the distance from the neighborhood solutions is calculated. However, the solution is adopted as novelty one, when the distance is larger than those specified by the novelty area width parameter. In other words, the NS estimates the solutions according the two criteria (i.e., fitness function, and distance) and thus changes the traditional EA (or SI-based algorithm) into MOEA.

Interestingly, the operations of the NS are guided by two parameters: (1) the neighborhood size, and (2) the novelty area width needed for calculating the behavior distance metric. In NS for global optimization, these parameters remained unchanged during the evolutionary run until now [7,8]. According to Eiben [3], a fitness landscape of the particular problem is changed during the evolutionary search process. Therefore, changing the parameter setting during the run has potential of better adjusting the algorithm to the problem. Indeed, there are three types of parameter control in EC [3]: (1) deterministic, (2) adaptive, and (3) self-adaptive. Deterministic parameter control means that the parameters are changed according to some deterministic rule during the evolutionary search. In adaptive parameter control, a some feedback from the search process influences on the frequency and the magnitude of change of the problem variables, while the parameters are stored into representation of individuals together with problem variables and undergo the operations of variation operators during the self-adaptive parameter control. In our paper, the adaptive control of the novelty area width is applied, because the proper value of this parameter is not known in advance, in the one hand, and because it is the most crucial for performing of the NS on the other.

The adaptive NS (ANS) was implemented within the self-adaptive Differential Evolution (jDE) of Brest et al. [16] and applied for solving the CEC 2014 Benchmark function suite. The purpose of our experimental work was to show that the ANS into jDE (AnjDE) can improve the results of the nDE and njDE variants developed by Fister et al. [7,8]. Additionally, the achieved results can be comparable also with the state-of-the-art algorithms, like L-Shade [17] (the winner of the CEC-2014 Competition on Real-Parameter Single Objective) and MVMO [18].

The structure of the remainder of the paper is as follows. Section 2 refers to highlight the background information. A description of the adaptive AnjDE are presented in Sect. 3. The results of experiments are illustrated in Sect. 4. Summarizing of the performed work is the subject of the last section.

2   Background Information

This section presents a background information needed for understanding the subject that follows. In summary, this section captures the following topics: (1) differential evolution, (2) self-adaptive evolutionary evolution, and (3) Novelty search. In the remainder of the paper, the mentioned topics are illustrated in details.

2.1   Differential Evolution

DE belongs to the class of stochastic nature-inspired population-based algorithms that is appropriate for solving continuous as well as discrete optimization problems. DE was introduced by Storn and Price in 1995 [15] and since then many DE variants have been proposed. The original DE algorithm is represented by real-valued vectors that undergo operations of variation operators, such as mutation, crossover, and selection.

In the basic mutation, two solutions are selected randomly and their scaled difference is added to the third solution, as follows:

$$\mathbf{u}_i^{(t)} = \mathbf{x}_{r0}^{(t)} + F \cdot (\mathbf{x}_{r1}^{(t)} - \mathbf{x}_{r2}^{(t)}), \quad \text{for } i = 1 \dots Np, \tag{1}$$

where $F \in [0.1, 1.0]$ denotes the scaling factor that scales the rate of modification, while Np represents the population size and $r0$, $r1$, $r2$ are randomly selected values in the interval $1 \dots Np$. Note that the proposed interval of values for parameter F was enforced in the DE community.

DE employs a binomial (denoted as 'bin') or exponential (denoted as 'exp') crossover. The trial vector is built from parameter values copied from either the mutant vector generated by Eq. (1) or parent at the same index position laid i-th vector. Mathematically, this crossover can be expressed as follows:

$$w_{i,j}^{(t)} = u_{i,j}^{(t)} x_{i,j}^{(t)} \tag{2}$$

where $CR \in [0.0, 1.0]$ controls the fraction of parameters that are copied to the trial solution. The condition $j = j_{rand}$ ensures that the trial vector differs from the original solution $\mathbf{x}_i^{(t)}$ in at least one element. Mathematically, the selection can be expressed as follows:

$$\mathbf{x}_i^{(t+1)} = \begin{cases} \mathbf{w}_i^{(t)} & \text{if } f(\mathbf{w}_i^{(t)}) \leq f(\mathbf{x}_i^{(t)}), \\ \mathbf{x}_i^{(t)} & \text{otherwise}. \end{cases} \tag{3}$$

The selection is usually called 'one-to-one', because trial and corresponding vector laid on i-th position in the population compete for surviving in the next generation, where the better according to the fitness function will survive.

Mutation can be performed in several ways in DE. Consequently, a specific notation was introduced to describe the varieties of these methods (also mutation strategies), in general. For example, 'rand/1/bin' denotes that the base vector is randomly selected, 1 vector difference is added to it, and the number of modified parameters in the trial/offspring vector follows a binomial distribution.

2.2 jDE Algorithm

In 2006, Brest et al. [16] proposed an effective DE variant (jDE), where control parameters are self-adapted during the run. In this case, two parameters namely, scale factor F and crossover rate CR are added to the representation of every individual and undergo acting the variation operators. As a result, the individual in jDE is represented as follows:

$$\mathbf{x}_i^{(t)} = (x_{i,1}^{(t)}, x_{i,2}^{(t)}, ..., x_{i,D}^{(t)}, F_i^{(t)}, CR_i^{(t)}).$$

The jDE modifies parameters F and CR according to the following equations:

$$F_i^{(t+1)} = \begin{cases} F_l + \text{rand}_1 * (F_u - F_l) & \text{if } \text{rand}_2 < \tau_1, \\ F_i^{(t)} & \text{otherwise}, \end{cases} \tag{4}$$

$$CR_i^{(t+1)} = \begin{cases} \text{rand}_3 & \text{if } \text{rand}_4 < \tau_2, \\ CR_i^{(t)} & \text{otherwise}, \end{cases} \tag{5}$$

where: $\text{rand}_{i=1...4} \in [0, 1]$ are randomly generated values drawn from uniform distribution in interval $[0, 1]$, τ_1 and τ_2 are learning steps, F_l and F_u lower and upper bound for parameter F, respectively.

2.3 Novelty Search

NS measures the distance between each individual in a population and its k-th nearest neighbors in behavior space, in other words [10]:

$$\rho(\mathbf{x}) = \frac{1}{k} \sum_{i=1}^{k} dist(\mathbf{x}, \boldsymbol{\mu}_i), \tag{6}$$

where $\boldsymbol{\mu}_i$ is the i-th nearest neighbor of $\mathbf{x}$ with respect to the behavior distance metric $dist$.

Parameter k is a problem dependent, and must be determined by the developer experimentally. However, the same is also valid for selecting the distance metric. In general, the NS is weakly defined and the question, how to tailor the search so that the results are as good as possible, is left to the developer's criterium [11].

3   Adaptive Novelty Search into jDE

In our study, Adaptive NS (ANS) is applied into jDE. In line with this, two main modifications need to be performed: (1) implementation of the ANS, and (2) adjusting a jDE population scheme accordingly. Here, the same DE/jDE population scheme, as described in Fister et al. [7,8], was used. Therefore, the paper is focused on the description of the ANS. The pseudo-code of the ANS is illustrated in Algorithm 1.

Note that the function $\rho(\mathbf{x})$ in Algorithm 1 calculates the average value of the behavior distance metric in neighborhood. The behavior distance metric $dist$ in ANS is defined as follows:

$$dist(\mathbf{x}_i, \mathbf{x}_j) = \begin{cases} \frac{d(\mathbf{x}_i, \mathbf{x}_j)}{\sigma_{sh}^{(t)}}, & d(\mathbf{x}_i, \mathbf{x}_j) > \sigma_{sh}^{(t)}, \\ 0, & \text{otherwise}, \end{cases} \tag{7}$$

where $d(\mathbf{x}_i, \mathbf{x}_j)$ denotes a Euclidean distance between vectors $\mathbf{x}_i$ and $\mathbf{x}_j$ and $\sigma_{sh}^{(t)}$ determines the minimum distance needed for recognizing the novelty solution. Let us mention that the $\sigma_{sh}^{(t)}$ is not remained unchanged during the evolutionary search as proposed in previous studies, but this is modified according to the following equations:

$$\sigma_{sh}^{(t)} = K \cdot I_{\mathbf{c}}^{(t)}. \tag{8}$$

where K is a user-defined constant and $I_{\mathbf{c}}^{(t)}$ represents an inertia moment from mass center expressed as:

$$I_{\mathbf{c}}^{(t)} = \sum_{i=1}^{Np} \sum_{j=1}^{D} (x_{i.j} - c_j)^2. \tag{9}$$

In Eq. (9), vector $\mathbf{c} = \{c_j\}$ represents the mass center expressed as:

$$c_j^{(t)} = \frac{1}{Np} \sum_{i=1}^{Np} x_{i,j}, \quad \text{for } j = 1, \dots, D. \tag{10}$$

The constant K in Eq. (8) allows users to increase of decrease the value of novelty area width. The adaptation process is launched simultaneously with the ANS in the sense of the learning rate parameter $\tau_3 \in [0, 1]$. The ANS process is controlled with additional parameters replacement size $R \in [1, Np]$ that limits the number of novelty solutions.

Algorithm 1. Adaptive Novelty Search within the jDE algorithm

---

1: **procedure** NOVELTY SEARCH
2:　　$\mathcal{A} = \{\exists \boldsymbol{\mu}_i : f(\mathbf{w}_i) \leq f(\mathbf{x}_j) \wedge i \neq j\};$　// set of survivor solutions
3:　　$\mathcal{B} = \{\exists \mathbf{x}_i : f(\mathbf{w}_i) > f(\mathbf{x}_j) \wedge i \neq j\};$　// set of eliminated solutions
4:　　**if** $|\mathcal{A}| < k$ **then**　// number of survivor solutions less than the neighborhood?
5:　　　　$\mathcal{A} = \mathcal{A} \cup \mathcal{B};$　// increases the neighborhood set to the whole population
6:　　**end if**
7:　　$\forall \mathbf{x}_i \in \mathcal{B} : \exists \mathcal{N}(\mathbf{x}_i) : \boldsymbol{\mu}_j \in \mathcal{A} \wedge \mathbf{x}_i \neq \boldsymbol{\mu}_j \wedge |\mathcal{N}(\mathbf{x}_i)| \leq k;$ // select k-nearest
　　neighbors
8:　　$\forall \mathbf{x}_i \in \mathcal{B} : \rho(\mathbf{x}_i);$　　　　　// calculate their novelty values adaptively
9:　　$\mathcal{C} = \{\forall(\mathbf{x}_i, \mathbf{x}_j) \in \mathcal{B} : \max |\rho(\mathbf{x}_i) - \rho(\mathbf{x}_j| \wedge i \neq j \wedge |\mathcal{C}| \leq R\};$
10: **end procedure**

4　Experiments and Results

The purpose of our experimental work was to show that (1) the ANS improves the results of the original DE/jDE and the proposed nDE/njDE, as well as to indicate that (2) they are also comparable with those obtained by the MVMO and L-Shade, the winner of the CEC 2014 Competition on global optimization. In line with this, the CEC 2014 Benchmark function suite was used as a test bed. This suite consists of 30 shifted and rotated functions that present the big challenge for the majority of the optimization algorithms. Due to the paper length, this study was focused on the functions of dimension $D = 10$.

Table 1. Parameter setting of algorithms in tests.

Alg.	F	CR	$\tau_{1,2}$	σ_{sh}	$|\mathcal{N}|$	τ_3	R
DE	0.5	0.9	n/a	n/a	n/a	n/a	n/a
jDE	0.5	0.9	0.1	n/a	n/a	n/a	n/a
nDE	0.5	0.9	n/a	50	10	0.1	50
njDE	0.5	0.9	0.1	5	10	0.1	5

The parameter settings of the original DE/jDE and proposed nDE/njDE are presented in Table 1. All algorithms in tests were run with population size of $Np = 100$, while 25 independent runs were conducted per each algorithm. The results were measured according to five statistical measures: minimum, maximum, mean, median, and standard deviation. These values obtained by optimization of 30 particular functions were accumulated into statistical classifiers and entered into Friedman non-parametric tests [9].

To prove our hypotheses, two tests were conducted. The aim of the first was to show that the AnjDE improve the results of the traditional DE/jDE and proposed nDE/njDE. In line with this, the constant K was varied in the interval $[0.009, \ldots, 0.01]$ in steps of 0.001, in the interval $(0.01, \ldots, 0.1]$ in steps of 0.01, and in the interval $(0.1, \ldots, 0.6]$ in steps of 0.1. In line with this, 16 instances of the AnjDE algorithm were obtained for each of the six values of the neighborhood size $|\mathcal{N}| \in \{5, 10, 15, 20, 30, 50\}$ and the replacement size $R \in \{1, 2, 5, 10\}$. Thus, the $16 \times 6 \times 4 \times 25 = 9,600$ independent runs were conducted, from which the best AnjDE instance (i.e., AnjDE with $K = 0.3$, $|\mathcal{N}| = 30$, $\tau = 0.1$, and $R = 2$) according to the rank enters in Nemenyi post-hoc statistical test. The corresponding results according to average differences of ranks are depicted in Fig. 1.

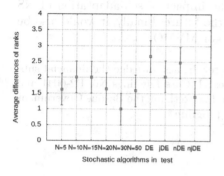
Fig. 1. Different AnjDE-variants

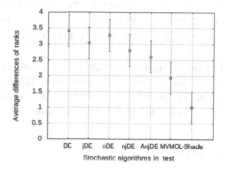
Fig. 2. State-of-the-art comparison

The second test was dedicated to show that the results of the AnjDE are comparable to the results obtained by the DE/jDE, and nDE/njDE as well as the winners of the CEC 2014 competition, i.e., L-Shade and MVMO. The results of mentioned algorithms are depicted according to average differences of ranks in Fig. 2, from which it can be seen that the AnjDE outperformed the results of the other DE algorithms in test substantially, while the results of the L-Shade and MVMO remains the hard problem for solving in the future.

5 Conclusion

Stochastic nature-inspired population-based algorithms have been achieved their maturity phase recently. In the past, they were developed on disembodied computer systems. With huge development of hardware, they have become a new application domain in ER and SR, where these algorithms were ported on specific hardware put into environment and play a role of autonomous agents. Throughout this process, two major problems have been emerged: (1) maintaining the population diversity as a prerequisite of open-ended evolution, and (2) evaluating the fitness function based on the behavior of the solution in environment.

In this paper, we were focused on solving of the first problem, where the NS was proposed as a tool for maintaining the population diversity. Actually, the paper is continuation of already published papers of Fister et al. [7,8], wherein the value of NS parameters remains unchanged during the search process. Indeed, the novelty area width, that is the crucial for the results of the optimization, was adapted and thus the proposed AnjDE algorithm is able to adjust to the problem during the search.

The proposed AnjDE was applied to CEC 2014 Benchmark function suite. The results of optimization showed that this improved the results of the traditional DE/nDE, and nDE/njDE substantially, when they are comparable with those obtained by the MVMO and L-Shade.

As the future work, finishing experiments on the higher dimensional functions remains in first place. Additionally, the impact of self-adaptation of NS parameters could become a big challenge in the future. Finally, it would also be interesting to incorporate the NS in L-Shade or MVMO.

Acknowledgments. Iztok Fister and Iztok Fister Jr. acknowledge the financial support from the Slovenian Research Agency (Research Core Fundings No. P2-0041 and P2-0057). Javier Del Ser and Eneko Osaba would like to thank the Basque Government for its funding support through the EMAITEK program.

References

1. Darwin, C.: On the Origin of Species. Harvard University Press, London (1852)
2. Beni, G., Wang, J.: Swarm intelligence in cellular robotic systems. In: Proceedings of NATO Advanced Workshop on Robots and Biological Systems, Tuscany, Italy, 26–30 June 1989
3. Eiben, A.E., Smith, J.E.: Introduction to Evolutionary Computing. Springer, Berlin (2003). https://doi.org/10.1007/978-3-662-05094-1
4. Blum, C., Merkle, D.: Swarm Intelligence: Introduction and Applications, 1st edn. Springer, Heidelberg (2008). https://doi.org/10.1007/978-3-540-74089-6
5. Wooldridge, M.: An Introduction to Multiagent Systems, 2nd edn. Wiley, Hoboken (2009)
6. Eiben, A.E., Smith, J.E.: From evolutionary computation to the evolution of things. Nature **521**(7553), 476–482 (2015)
7. Fister, I., Iglesias, A., Galvez, A., Del Ser, J., Osaba, E., Fister Jr., I.: Using novelty search in differential evolution. In: Bajo, J., et al. (eds.) PAAMS 2018. CCIS, vol. 887, pp. 534–542. Springer, Cham (2018). https://doi.org/10.1007/978-3-319-94779-2_46
8. Fister, I., et al.: Novelty search for global optimization. Appl. Math. Comput. **347**, 865–881 (2019)
9. Demšar, J.: Statistical comparisons of classifiers over multiple data sets. J. Mach. Learn. Res. **7**, 1–30 (2006). JMLR.org
10. Lehman, J., Stanley, K.O.: Exploiting open-endedness to solve problems through the search for novelty. In: Proceedings of the Eleventh International Conference on Artificial Life (ALIFE XI), pp. 329–336. MIT Press, Cambridge (2008)
11. Doncieux, S., Mouret, J.B.: Behavioral diversity measures for Evolutionary Robotics. In: IEEE Congress on Evolutionary Computation, Barcelona, pp. 1–8 (2010)
12. Doncieux, S., Mouret, J.B.: Beyond black-box optimization: a review of selective pressures for evolutionary robotics. Evol. Intell. **7**(2), 71–93 (2014)

13. Lynch, M.: The evolution of genetic networks by non-adaptive processes. Nat. Rev. Genet. **8**, 803–813 (2007)
14. Deb, K.: Multi-Objective Optimization Using Evolutionary Algorithms. Wiley, New York (2001)
15. Storn, R., Price, K.: Differential evolution-a simple and efficient heuristic for global optimization over continuous spaces. J. Global Optim. **11**(4), 341–359 (1997)
16. Brest, J., Greiner, S., Bošković, B., Mernik, M., Žumer, V.: Self-adapting control parameters in differential evolution: a comparative study on numerical benchmark problems. IEEE Trans. Evol. Comput. **10**(6), 646–657 (2006)
17. Tanabe, R., Fukunaga, A.S.: Improving the search performance of SHADE using linear population size reduction. In: 2014 IEEE Congress on Evolutionary Computation (CEC), Beijing, pp. 1658–1665 (2014)
18. Erlich, I., Rueda, J.L., Wildenhues, S., Shewarega, F.: Evaluating the mean-variance mapping optimization on the IEEE-CEC 2014 test suite. In: 2014 IEEE Congress on Evolutionary Computation (CEC), Beijing, pp. 1625–1632 (2014)
19. Valdez, F., Melin, P., Castillo, O.: An improved evolutionary method with fuzzy logic for combining particle swarm optimization and genetic algorithms. Appl. Soft Comput. **11**(2), 2625–2632 (2011)
20. Precup, R.-E., David, R.-C., Petriu, E.M., Preitl, S., Paul, A.S.: Gravitational search algorithm-based tuning of fuzzy control systems with a reduced parametric sensitivity. In: Gaspar-Cunha, A., Takahashi, R., Schaefer, G., Costa, L. (eds.) Soft Computing in Industrial Applications, vol. 96, pp. 141–150. Springer, Heidelberg (2011). https://doi.org/10.1007/978-3-642-20505-7_12
21. Saadat, J., Moallem, P., Koofigar, H.: Training echo state neural network using harmony search algorithm. Int. J. Artif. Intell. **15**(1), 163–179 (2017)
22. Vrkalovic, S., Lunca, E.-C., Borlea, I.-D.: Model-free sliding mode and fuzzy controllers for reverse osmosis desalination plants. Int. J. Artif. Intell. **16**(2), 208–222 (2018)

Swarm Intelligence Approach
for Parametric Learning of a Nonlinear
River Flood Routing Model

Rebeca Sánchez[1], Patricia Suárez[1], Akemi Gálvez[1,2], and Andrés Iglesias[1,2(✉)]

[1] Department of Applied Mathematics and Computational Sciences,
University of Cantabria, Avenida de los Castros s/n, 39005 Santander, Spain
iglesias@unican.es
[2] Department of Information Science, Faculty of Sciences,
Narashino Campus, Toho University, 2-2-1 Miyama, Funabashi 274-8510, Japan
http://personales.unican.es/iglesias

Abstract. Flood routing models are mathematical methods used to predict the changes over the time in variables such as the magnitude, speed and shape of a flood wave when water moves in a river, a stream or a reservoir. These techniques are widely used in water engineering for flood prediction and many other applications such as dam design, geographic and urban planning, disaster prevention, and so on. Flood routing models typically depend on some parameters that must be estimated from data. Several techniques have been described in the literature for this task. Among them, those based on swarm intelligence are getting increasing attention from the scientific community during the last few years. In this context, the present contribution applies a powerful swarm intelligence technique called bat algorithm to perform parametric learning of a hydrological model for nonlinear river flood routing. The method is applied to data of a real-world example of a river reach with very good results.

Keywords: Swarm intelligence · Bat algorithm · River flood routing ·
Nonlinear models · Parametric learning

1 Introduction

This paper concerns *flood routing*, a technique to determine the flood hydrograph (i.e., the plot of the rate of flow – or *discharge* – of water over the time) at a section of a river using the data of flood flow at one or several upstream sections. Flood routing is a very important issue in water engineering with many relevant applications, ranging from predicting landslides and urban flooding to structural and hydrological design of dams and spillways [18,19]. Other applications include flood prediction, geographic and urban planning, sewage system design, watershed simulations, and disaster prevention, to mention just a few.

© Springer Nature Switzerland AG 2019
F. De la Prieta et al. (Eds.): PAAMS 2019 Workshops, CCIS 1047, pp. 276–286, 2019.
https://doi.org/10.1007/978-3-030-24299-2_24

Flood routing methods can be roughly classified into two groups: hydraulic methods and hydrologic methods. The former are based on solutions of the conservation of mass and the conservation of momentum equations, while the latter are based on the solution of the conservation of mass equation and an equation for the storage and discharge in a river reach or a reservoir. Although hydraulic methods are generally more accurate, hydrologic methods are still widely used due to their higher simplicity and the fact that their solutions are acceptable in many practical situations. In any case, both families of methods consider the equation of continuity as their primary equation.

Suppose that we have a river reach, that is, a continuous section of a river between an upstream and downstream location and having similar hydrological conditions (e.g., discharge, slope, area) along the way, meaning that the flow measured at a point somewhere along the section is representative of conditions in that section of the river. In other words, the whole section can be hydrologically described by the same mathematical model and for the same parameters of the model all along the way [12]. Basically, equation of continuity states that the difference between the inflow rate at the upstream end of the river reach and the outflow rate at the downstream end is equal to the rate of change of the storage, that is:

$$\frac{dS_t}{dt} = I_t - O_t \tag{1}$$

where I is the inflow rate, O is the outflow rate, S is the storage (the volume of water stored). Alternatively, in a small time interval Δt, the difference between the total inflow volume and the total outflow volume in the reach is equal to the change in storage in that reach, so we have:

$$\bar{I}_{\Delta t}\Delta t - \bar{O}_{\Delta t}\Delta t = \Delta S_{\Delta t} \tag{2}$$

where $\bar{I}_{\Delta t}$ and $\bar{O}_{\Delta t}$ denote respectively the average inflow and outflow in time Δt, and $\Delta S_{\Delta t}$ is the change in storage during that span. Taking $\bar{I} = \dfrac{I_1 + I_2}{2}$, $\bar{O} = \dfrac{O_1 + O_2}{2}$, and $\Delta S = S_2 - S_1$, we have:

$$\frac{I_1 + I_2}{2} - \frac{O_1 + O_2}{2} = \frac{S_1 + S_2}{\Delta t}$$

where the subscripts 1 and 2 denote the values of those variables at the beginning and at the end of the time interval considered.

There are several models for flood routing of a river [18,19]. A very popular nonlinear model is given by:

$$\begin{cases} S_{t+1} = S_t + \Delta t \left[\left(\frac{1}{1-X}\right) \sqrt[m]{\frac{S_t}{K}} - \left(\frac{X}{1-X}\right) I_t \right] \\[4mm] O_{t+1} = \left(\frac{1}{1-X}\right) \sqrt[m]{\frac{S_{t+1}}{K}} - \left(\frac{X}{1-X}\right) I_{t+1} \end{cases} \tag{3}$$

where K is a storage time constant for the river reach that approximates the flow travel time through the river reach, χ is a weighting factor usually taken values between 0 and 0.3 for a river or stream channel and m is an exponent introduced to account for the effects of nonlinearity. Eqs. (1)–(3) allows us to compute the value of the storage and the outflow at time $t + 1$ using the inflow at time $t + 1$ and storage at time t.

This kind of mathematical models are widely used for prediction of flooding and other purposes. To this aim, parametric learning is to be achieved in order to determine suitable values of all parameters. With this parametric learning, we can reproduce the observed values of hydrographical time series data. Among the methods applied to tackle this issue, those based on swarm intelligence are receiving increasing attention during the last few years because of their ability to cope with problems where little or no information at all is available about the problem. These methods are also very effective for optimization problems where the objective function is not differentiable, thus making gradient-based methods unsuitable, or for problems under difficult conditions (e.g., noisy data, irregular sampling) commonly found in real-world applications [20]. Swarm intelligence methods applied to the flood routing problem include harmony search [10], particle swarm optimization [3], and artificial bee colony [17]. A very recent method also considers particle swarm optimization for this problem and investigates the effect of using variable values for the parameters [2].

In this paper, we address the nonlinear parametric learning problem for river flood routing given by Eqs. (1)–(3) by applying a powerful nature-inspired swarm intelligence technique for global optimization called bat algorithm. The structure of this paper is as follows: the main ideas and rules and the pseudocode of the bat algorithm are described in Sect. 2. The algorithm is applied to a real-world problem, namely, the parametric learning of hydrograph data of the flow of a river, in Sect. 3. Our experimental results are briefly discussed in Sect. 4. The paper closes with the main conclusions and some ideas for future work in the field.

2   The Bat Algorithm

The *bat algorithm* is a bio-inspired swarm intelligence algorithm originally proposed by Xin-She Yang in 2010 to solve optimization problems [21–23]. The algorithm is based on the echolocation behavior of bats. The author focused particularly on microbats, as they use a type of sonar called *echolocation*, with varying pulse rates of emission and loudness, to detect prey, avoid obstacles, and locate their roosting crevices in the dark.

2.1   Basic Rules

The idealization of the echolocation of microbats can be summarized as follows (see [21] for details):

1. Bats use echolocation to sense distance and distinguish between food, prey and background barriers.
2. Each virtual bat flies randomly with a velocity $\mathbf{v}_i$ at position (solution) $\mathbf{x}_i$ with a fixed frequency f_{min}, varying wavelength λ and loudness A_0 to search for prey. As it searches and finds its prey, it changes wavelength (or frequency) of their emitted pulses and adjust the rate of pulse emission r, depending on the proximity of the target.
3. It is assumed that the loudness will vary from an (initially large and positive) value A_0 to a minimum constant value A_{min}.

In order to apply the bat algorithm for optimization problems more efficiently, some additional assumptions are strongly advisable. In general, we assume that the frequency f evolves on a bounded interval $[f_{min}, f_{max}]$. This means that the wavelength λ is also bounded, because f and λ are related to each other by the fact that the product $\lambda.f$ is constant. For practical reasons, it is also convenient that the largest wavelength is chosen such that it is comparable to the size of the domain of interest (the search space, for optimization problems). For simplicity, we can assume that $f_{min} = 0$, so $f \in [0, f_{max}]$. The rate of pulse can simply be in the range $r \in [0, 1]$, where 0 means no pulses at all, and 1 means the maximum rate of pulse emission.

2.2 The Algorithm

With these idealized rules indicated above, the basic pseudo-code of the bat algorithm is shown in Algorithm 1. Basically, the algorithm considers an initial population of $\mathcal{P}$ individuals (bats). Each bat, representing a potential solution of the optimization problem, has a location $\mathbf{x}_i$ and velocity $\mathbf{v}_i$. The algorithm initializes these variables (lines 1–2) with random values within the search space. Then, the pulse frequency, pulse rate, and loudness are computed for each individual bat (lines 3–4). Then, the swarm evolves in a discrete way over generations (line 5), like time instances (line 19) until the maximum number of generations, $\mathcal{G}_{max}$, is reached (line 20). For each generation g and each bat (line 6), new frequency, location and velocity are computed (lines 7–8) according to the following evolution equations:

$$f_i^g = f_{min}^g + \beta(f_{max}^g - f_{min}^g) \tag{4}$$

$$\mathbf{v}_i^g = \mathbf{v}_i^{g-1} + [\mathbf{x}_i^{g-1} - \mathbf{x}^*] f_i^g \tag{5}$$

$$\mathbf{x}_i^g = \mathbf{x}_i^{g-1} + \mathbf{v}_i^g \tag{6}$$

where $\beta \in [0, 1]$ follows the random uniform distribution, and $\mathbf{x}^*$ represents the current global best location (solution), which is obtained through evaluation of the objective function at all bats and ranking of their fitness values. The superscript $(.)^g$ is used to denote the current generation g.

The best current solution and a local solution around it are probabilistically selected according to some given criteria (lines 8–11). Then, search is intensified by a local random walk (line 12). For this local search, once a solution is selected

Require: (Initial Parameters)
    Population size: $\mathcal{P}$
    Maximum number of generations: $\mathcal{G}_{max}$
    Loudness: $\mathcal{A}$
    Pulse rate: r
    Maximum frequency: f_{max}
    Dimension of the problem: d
    Objective function: $\phi(\mathbf{x})$, with $\mathbf{x} = (x_1, \ldots, x_d)^T$
    Random number: $\theta \in U(0, 1)$
1: $g \leftarrow 0$
2: Initialize the bat population $\mathbf{x}_i$ and $\mathbf{v}_i$, $(i = 1, \ldots, n)$
3: Define pulse frequency f_i at $\mathbf{x}_i$
4: Initialize pulse rates r_i and loudness $\mathcal{A}_i$
5: **while** $g < \mathcal{G}_{max}$ **do**
6:   **for** $i = 1$ **to** $\mathcal{P}$ **do**
7:     Generate new solutions by adjusting frequency,
8:     and updating velocities and locations //eqns. (4)-(6)
9:     **if** $\theta > r_i$ **then**
10:       $\mathbf{s}^{best} \leftarrow \mathbf{s}^g$ //select the best current solution
11:       $\mathbf{ls}^{best} \leftarrow \mathbf{ls}^g$ //generate a local solution around $\mathbf{s}^{best}$
12:     **end if**
13:     Generate a new solution by local random walk
14:     **if** $\theta < \mathcal{A}_i$ *and* $\phi(\mathbf{x_i}) < \phi(\mathbf{x}^*)$ **then**
15:       Accept new solutions
16:       Increase r_i and decrease $\mathcal{A}_i$
17:     **end if**
18:   **end for**
19:   $g \leftarrow g + 1$
20: **end while**
21: Rank the bats and find current best $\mathbf{x}^*$
22: **return** $\mathbf{x}^*$

Algorithm 1. Bat algorithm pseudocode

among the current best solutions, it is perturbed locally through a random walk of the form:

$$\mathbf{x}_{new} = \mathbf{x}_{old} + \epsilon \mathcal{A}^g \tag{7}$$

where ϵ is a random number with uniform distribution on the interval $[-1, 1]$ and $\mathcal{A}^g = <\mathcal{A}_i^g>$, is the average loudness of all the bats at generation g.

If the new solution achieved is better than the previous best one, it is probabilistically accepted depending on the value of the loudness. In that case, the algorithm increases the pulse rate and decreases the loudness (lines 13–16). This process is repeated for the given number of generations. In general, the loudness decreases once a bat finds its prey (in our analogy, once a new best solution is found), while the rate of pulse emission decreases. For simplicity, the following values are commonly used: $\mathcal{A}_0 = 1$ and $\mathcal{A}_{min} = 0$, assuming that this latter value means that a bat has found the prey and temporarily stop emitting any sound. The evolution rules for loudness and pulse rate are as follows:

$$\mathcal{A}_i^{g+1} = \alpha \mathcal{A}_i^g \tag{8}$$

$$r_i^{g+1} = r_i^0[1 - exp(-\gamma g)] \tag{9}$$

where α and γ are constants. Note that for any $0 < \alpha < 1$ an any $\gamma > 0$ we have:

$$\mathcal{A}_i^g \to 0, \quad r_i^g \to r_i^0, \quad \text{as} \quad g \to \infty \tag{10}$$

In general, each bat should have different values for loudness and pulse emission rate, which can be computationally achieved by randomization. To this aim, we can take an initial loudness $\mathcal{A}_i^0 \in (0, 2)$ while the initial emission rate r_i^0 can be any value in the interval $[0, 1]$. Loudness and emission rates will be updated only if the new solutions are improved, an indication that the bats are moving towards the optimal solution. As a result, the bat algorithm applies a parameter tuning technique to control the dynamic behavior of a swarm of bats. Similarly, the balance between exploration and exploitation can be controlled by tuning algorithm-dependent parameters.

Bat algorithm is a very promising method that has already been successfully applied to several problems, such as multilevel image thresholding [1], economic dispatch [11], curve and surface reconstruction [6,7] optimal design of structures in civil engineering [9], robotics [13–16], fuel arrangement optimization [8], planning of sport training sessions [4], medical applications [5], and many others. The interested reader is also referred to the general paper in [24] for a comprehensive review of the bat algorithm, its variants and other interesting applications

3 The Method

Suppose that we are provided with data of historical records of hydrograph variables for a given reach of a river (see Table 1 in Sect. 5 for an example). In particular, our input data is given by the numerical series for the observed time $\{T_i\}_i$, inflow rate $\{I_i\}_i$, outflow rate $\{O_i\}_i$, and storage rate $\{S_i\}_i$, $i = 1, \ldots, \mathcal{N}$. Our aim is to perform parametric learning to predict the storage and outflow based on the time series of inflow rate through our mathematical model given by Eqs. (1)–(3). We do it through the bat algorithm described above.

To apply the bat algorithm to our problem we need to define some important issues. Firstly, we need an adequate representation of the problem. Each bat $\mathcal{B}_j$, representing a potential solution, corresponds to a parametric vector of the free variables of the problem, of the form: $\mathcal{B}_j = (\mathcal{O}_j, \mathcal{S}_j, \mathcal{V}_j)$, where $\mathcal{O}_j$, $\mathcal{S}_j$ and $\mathcal{V}_j$ represent respectively the vector of predicted outflows, the vector of predicted storages, and the vector of parameters of the model. These parametric vectors are initialized with random values with a uniform distribution within their respective ranges, except the initial storage and the initial outflow, which are taken as:

$S_0 = KI_0^m$ and $O_0 = I_0$, respectively. Secondly, a fitness function is required for optimization. In our problem, the goal is to predict the outflow and storage rates given the inflow and then compare their predicted values with the observed ones. This can be properly done through least-squares minimization. Let O_t, $\bar{O}_t$, S_t, $\bar{S}_t$ be the observed and the predicted outflow and storage at time t, respectively. We consider the least-squares functional LSQ given by the weighted sum of the squares of the residuals:

$$LSQ = \phi_1 \sum_{t=1}^{\mathcal{N}} (O_t - \bar{O}_t)^2 + \phi_2 \sum_{t=1}^{\mathcal{N}} (S_t - \bar{S}_t)^2 \tag{11}$$

where $\mathcal{N}$ denotes the number of time instances of the inflow/outflow/storage time series. The values $\phi_1 = 2/3$ and $\phi_2 = 1/3$ have been taken in this paper to assign a larger weight to the outflow with respect to the storage, since that is the most important variable for the hydrograph. Finally, we need to address the important issue of parameter tuning. It is well-known that the performance of swarm intelligence techniques depends on a proper parameter tuning. This is also a problem-dependent issue. Due to this reason, our choice has been fully empirical, based on numerous computer simulations for different parameter values. In this paper, we consider a population size of $\mathcal{P} = 100$, as larger population sizes do increase the CPU times without improving our numerical results significantly. The initial and minimum loudness and parameter α are set to 0.5, 0, and 0.2, respectively. Regarding the stopping criterion, all executions are performed for 4500 iterations, which is more than enough to ensure convergence in all our simulations. Finally, all computational work has been carried out on a personal computer with Intel Core i7 processor and 8 GB of RAM. The source code has been implemented by the authors in the programming language C#.

4   Experimental Results

Our method has been applied to a real-world example of historical hydrographical data described in [18] and corresponding to a river flood routing problem. This example was previously used in the literature as a benchmark for different models in flood routing. Table 1 reports the values of the observed inflow, outflow, and storage (columns 2 to 4) for different time instances (column 1). All flow results are expressed in cubic meters per second (m^3/s). We also report the numerical results of the predicted outflow obtained using our method based on the bat algorithm (column 5). To avoid the spurious effects derived from the randomness of the process, we run 15 independent executions of our method and then consider the average value. This means that the results reported in the last column are not those of the best execution (which are even better) but the average of the 15 independent executions. Still, the numerical results obtained with our method are pretty good. A visual comparison between the columns 3 and 5 reveals that our method performs very well, as it is able to capture the real tendency of data for all times instances in the example. This means that our method has a good predictive capability.

Table 1. Observed inflow, outflow and storage and computed outflow (all in m^3/s) for the example in the paper

Time (d)	Observed inflow	Observed outflow	Observed storage	Computed outflow
0	166.2	118.4	47.8	118.4
1	263.6	197.4	66.2	197.2
2	365.3	214.1	151.2	214.4
3	580.5	402.1	178.4	402.3
4	594.7	518.2	76.5	518.2
5	662.6	523.9	138.7	524.0
6	920.3	603.1	317.2	602.9
7	1568.8	829.7	739.1	830.1
8	1775.5	1124.2	651.3	1124.1
9	1489.5	1379.0	110.5	1379.1
10	1223.3	1509.3	−286.0	1509.3
11	713.6	1379.0	−665.4	1378.8
12	645.6	1050.6	−405.0	1050.2
13	1166.7	1013.7	153.0	1013.8
14	1427.2	1013.7	413.5	1013.5
15	1282.8	1013.7	269.1	1013.5
16	1098.7	1209.1	−110.4	1209.1
17	764.6	1248.8	−484.2	1248.4
18	458.7	1002.4	−543.7	1002.3
19	351.1	713.6	−362.5	713.8
20	288.8	464.4	−175.6	464.7
21	228.8	325.6	−96.8	325.5
22	170.2	265.6	−95.4	265.8
23	143.0	222.6	−79.6	222.4

Our numerical results are confirmed visually in Fig. 1. The figure depicts the observed inflow and outflow hydrographs as well as the predicted outflow, computed with our bat algorithm-based method. Note the excellent visual matching between the observed outflow and the predicted outflow, as the latter becomes visually indistinguishable from the observed outflow and both hydrographs fully overlap each other. This is an excellent indicator of the good performance of our method for this real-world example.

Finally, Fig. 2 shows the convergence diagram of our method for the maximum, minimum and average values from the 15 independent executions. As shown, the method converges in all cases, and there is no large variation between the different executions, meaning that the method is quite robust, a valuable feature for real-world applications.

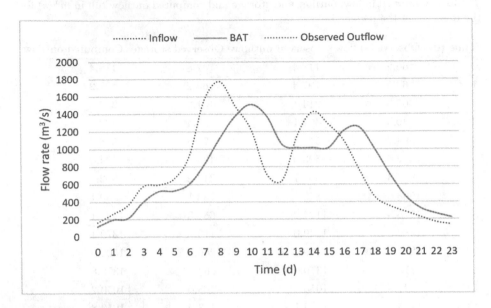

Fig. 1. Observed inflow and outflow and predicted outflow (computed with our bat algorithm-based method) hydrographs for the example in this paper.

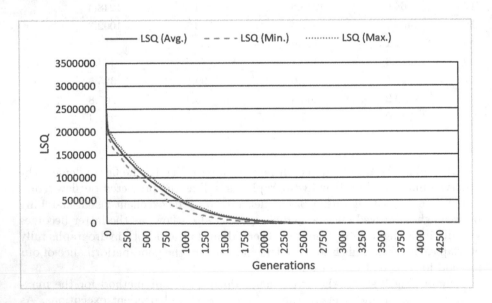

Fig. 2. Convergence diagram of the LSQ error function for the minimum, maximum and average values for 15 different executions.

5   Conclusions and Future Work

In this paper we presented a method for parametric learning of a nonlinear river flood routing model, a relevant problem in many areas of water engineering such as hydrology, flood forecasting, dam design, and other engineering fields. The method is based on the bat algorithm, a popular swarm intelligence metaheuristics for global optimization. The method has been applied to a real-world example of hydrological data of a river reach used as a benchmark in the field. Our computational experiments show that the method performs well, is robust and exhibits a good predictive ability. We conclude that this method is a promising approach for parametric learning in flood routing problems.

In spite of these good results, the method can still be improved in many different ways. Future work in the field includes the extension of this approach to other nonlinear models for flood routing having different parameters. Also, we will consider the extension of this approach to other interesting flood routing cases, such as the reservoir flood routing, where the parameters are expected to behave quite differently. Improving the accuracy of our method without increasing the computing times dramatically is also part of our future work in the field.

Acknowledgments. The authors acknowledge the financial support from the project PDE-GIR of the European Union's Horizon 2020 research and innovation programme under the Marie Sklodowska-Curie grant agreement No. 778035, the project from the Spanish Ministry of Science, Innovation and Universities (Computer Science National Program) under grant #TIN2017-89275-R of the Agencia Estatal de Investigación and European Funds FEDER (AEI/FEDER, UE), and the project #JU12, of SODER-CAN and EU Funds FEDER (SODERCAN/FEDER-UE). The last two authors are also grateful to the Department of Information Science of Toho University for all the facilities given to carry out this work.

References

1. Alihodzic, A., Tuba, M.: Improved bat algorithm applied to multilevel image thresholding. Sci. World J. **2014**, 16 (2014). Article ID 176718
2. Bazargan, J., Norouzi, H.: Investigation the effect of using variable values for the parameters of the linear Muskingum method using the particle swarm algorithm (PSO). Water Resour. Manag. **32**(14), 4763–4777 (2018)
3. Chu, H.J., Chang, L.C.: Applying particle swarm optimization to parameter estimation of the nonlinear Muskingum model. J. Hydrol. Eng. **14**(9), 1024–1027 (2009)
4. Fister, I., Rauter, S., Yang, X.-S., Ljubic, K., Fister Jr., I.: Planning the sports training sessions with the bat algorithm. Neurocomputing **149**(Part B), 993–1002 (2015)
5. Gálvez, A., Fister, I., Fister Jr., I., Osaba, E., Del Ser, J., Iglesias, A.: Automatic fitting of feature points for border detection of skin lesions in medical images with bat algorithm. In: Del Ser, J., Osaba, E., Bilbao, M.N., Sanchez-Medina, J.J., Vecchio, M., Yang, X.-S. (eds.) IDC 2018. SCI, vol. 798, pp. 357–368. Springer, Cham (2018). https://doi.org/10.1007/978-3-319-99626-4_31

6. Iglesias, A., Gálvez, A., Collantes, M.: Multilayer embedded bat algorithm for B-spline curve reconstruction. Integr. Comput.-Aided Eng. **24**(4), 385–399 (2017)
7. Iglesias, A., Gálvez, A., Collantes, M.: Iterative sequential bat algorithm for free-form rational Bézier surface reconstruction. Int. J. Bio-Inspired Comput. **11**(1), 1–15 (2018)
8. Kashi, S., Minuchehr, A., Poursalehi, N., Zolfaghari, A.: Bat algorithm for the fuel arrangement optimization of reactor core. Ann. Nucl. Energy **64**, 144–151 (2014)
9. Kaveh, A., Zakian, P.: Enhanced bat algorithm for optimal design of skeletal structures. Asian J. Civ. Eng. **15**(2), 179–212 (2014)
10. Kim, J.H., Geem, Z.W., Kim, E.S.: Parameter estimation of the nonlinear Muskingum model using harmony search. J. Am. Water Resour. Assoc. **375**, 1131–1138 (2001)
11. Latif, A., Palensky, P.: Economic dispatch using modified bat algorithm. Algorithms **7**(3), 328–338 (2014)
12. McCarthy G. T.: The unit hydrograph and flood routing. In: Conference North Atlantic Division. US Army Corps of Engineers, New London (1938)
13. Suárez, P., Iglesias, A.: Bat algorithm for coordinated exploration in swarm robotics. In: Del Ser, J. (ed.) ICHSA 2017. AISC, vol. 514, pp. 134–144. Springer, Singapore (2017). https://doi.org/10.1007/978-981-10-3728-3_14
14. Suárez, P., Gálvez, A., Iglesias, A.: Autonomous coordinated navigation of virtual swarm bots in dynamic indoor environments by bat algorithm. In: Tan, Y., Takagi, H., Shi, Y., Niu, B. (eds.) ICSI 2017. LNCS, vol. 10386, pp. 176–184. Springer, Cham (2017). https://doi.org/10.1007/978-3-319-61833-3_19
15. Suárez, P., et al.: Bat algorithm swarm robotics approach for dual non-cooperative search with self-centered mode. In: Yin, H., Camacho, D., Novais, P., Tallón-Ballesteros, A.J. (eds.) IDEAL 2018. LNCS, vol. 11315, pp. 201–209. Springer, Cham (2018). https://doi.org/10.1007/978-3-030-03496-2_23
16. Suárez, P., Iglesias, A., Gálvez, A.: Make robots be bats: specializing robotic swarms to the bat algorithm. Swarm Evol. Comput. **44**, 113–129 (2019)
17. Vafakhah, M., Dastorani, A., Moghaddam, A.: Optimal parameter estimation for nonlinear Muskingum model based on artificial bee Colony algorithm. EcoPersia **3**(1), 847–865 (2015)
18. Viessman Jr., W., Lewis, G.L.: Introduction to Hydrology. Pearson Education, Upper Saddle River (1974)
19. Wilson, E.M.: Engineering Hydrology. MacMillan, Hampshire (1974)
20. Yang, X.-S.: Nature-Inspired Metaheuristic Algorithms, 2nd edn. Luniver Press, Frome (2010)
21. Yang, X.S.: A new metaheuristic bat-inspired algorithm. In: González, J.R., Pelta, D.A., Cruz, C., Terrazas, G., Krasnogor, N. (eds.) Nature Inspired Cooperative Strategies for Optimization (NICSO 2010). Studies in Computational Intelligence, vol. 284, pp. 65–74. Springer, Berlin (2010). https://doi.org/10.1007/978-3-642-12538-6_6
22. Yang, X.S.: Bat algorithm for multiobjective optimization. Int. J. Bio-Inspired Comput. **3**(5), 267–274 (2011)
23. Yang, X.S., Gandomi, A.H.: Bat algorithm: a novel approach for global engineering optimization. Eng. Comput. **29**(5), 464–483 (2012)
24. Yang, X.S.: Bat algorithm: literature review and applications. Int. J. Bio-Inspired Comput. **5**(3), 141–149 (2013)

Special Session on Software Agents and Virtualizacion for Internet of Things (SAVIoTS)

Special Session on Software Agents and Virtualizacion for Internet of Things (SAVIoTS)

The dawn of the Internet of Things (IoT) paradigm has brought a series of novel services and applications never imagined a short time ago. Many buzzwords such as "smart cities," "smart homes," and "intelligent transportation systems (ITS)" show the democratization of the "things." However, things usually present notable limitations regarding both communication and processing capabilities. From this landscape, software agents as well as virtualization techniques arise with the aim of developing more complex IoT services based on users' needs. This synergy is evident in recent research advances integrated within the fog and edge computing paradigms in IoT scenarios. In a later stage, data collected from end-devices should be processed using a computing paradigm and taking advantage of big data algorithms. This with the aim of developing user-centric services or directly supporting the proper autonomous functioning of things.

This special session aims to exploit the momentum in these domains, by inviting researchers to contribute with original works on topics covering the development of software agents and virtualization techniques for IoT systems through analysis, simulation, and field trials.

Organization

Organizing Committee

Ramon Sanchez-Iborra	University of Murcia, Spain
Emilio Serrano	Technical University of Madrid, Spain

Program Committee

Diego Martín de Andrés	Technical University of Madrid, Spain
Antonio Guillén Pérez	Universidad Politécnica de Cartagena, Spain
Ramón Alcarria Garrido	Technical University of Madrid, Spain
Jose Manuel Martínez Caro	Universidad Politécnica de Cartagena, Spain
Javier Bajo Perez	Technical University of Madrid, Spain
Jose Santa	University of Murcia, Spain
Emilio Serrano	Technical University of Madrid, Spain
Ramon Sanchez-Iborra	University of Murcia, Spain

RETRACTED CHAPTER: A Survey on Software-Defined Networks and Edge Computing over IoT

Ricardo S. Alonso[(⊠)] [iD], Inés Sittón-Candanedo[iD], Sara Rodríguez-González[iD], Óscar García[iD], and Javier Prieto[iD]

IoT Digital Innovation HUB, University of Salamanca, Salamanca, Spain
{ralorin,isittonc,srg,oscgar,javierp}@usal.es
https://iotec.usal.es

Abstract. The Internet of Things (IoT) ceased to be a novel technology to become part of daily life through the millions of sensors, devices and tools that measure, collect, process and transfer data. The need to exchange, process, filter and store this huge volume of data has led to the emergence of Edge Computing (EC). The purpose of this new paradigm is to solve the challenges of IoT such as localized computing, reducing latency in information exchange, balancing data traffic on the network and providing responses in real-time. In order to reduce the complexity in the implementation of EC architectures, Software Defined Networks (SDNs) and the related concept Network Function Virtualization (NFV) are proposed by different approaches. This paper addresses the characteristics and capabilities of SDNs and NFV and why can be successful an innovative integration between SDNs and EC for IoT scenarios.

Keywords: Internet of Things · Software Defined Networks ·
Network Function Virtualization · Edge Computing · Cloud computing

1 Introduction

In 1999 Kevin Ashton was the first to use the term Internet of Things (IoT) with the aim of applying RFID in Procter & Gamble's (P&G) supply chain optimization processes [6]. The interest in the IoT increased in 2010 when Google began storing data related to its users' Wi-Fi networks. That same year, China established IoT as a priority topic for the development of its Five-Year Plan [50]. In 2011 the consulting firm Gartner included the Internet of Things as an emerging technology in its technological trends promotion catalogue. In 2012 important technology magazines such as *Forbes* or *Wired* began to use the IoT as their main trend theme [32]. Kethareswaran defines the Internet of Things as the connection of objects (buildings, vehicles) through a network infrastructure with electronic elements (sensors, actuators, radio frequency identification tags, etc.) to collect and exchange data [27].

The IoT is object of research and development in areas that allow objects to communicate with each other, send information they perceive from the environment to facilitate decision-making and improve the Quality of Service (QoS). The

---

The original version of this chapter was retracted: The retraction note to this chapter is available at https://doi.org/10.1007/978-3-030-24299-2_35

most important areas of research include transport and logistics [13], healthcare, smart homes [20], smart energy [11,18], smart cities [12], industry 4.0 [9,48] or personal domain [8,27], among others. The application of the IoT in the these areas results in the following challenges: need for real-time response; insufficient resources for data transmission, storage and processing; latency; security and privacy. Likewise the disruption of the Internet of Things causes the search for strategies to mitigate the processing of data generated and exchanged by millions of sensors and devices connected through complex networks to support this level of communications. One of these strategies is Edge Computing (EC) which aims to reduce congestion by the demand for computing resources, network or storage. With this trend, computational and service infrastructures approach the end user by migrating data filtering, processing or storage from the cloud to the edge of the network [46,60].

2   IoT, Heterogeneous WSNs and Cloud Computing

The Internet of Things can also be seen as an evolution of other concepts that are still part of the state of art of IoT technology [3, 61] and where innovative proposals are continuously being made nowadays such as Wireless Sensor Networks (WSNs) [4,15] and Real-Time Locating Systems (RTLS) [43,59].

Wireless Sensor Networks provide features aimed at gathering information about users and their environment in real time [28], which allow them to easily relate to Ambient Intelligence and those applications based on this paradigm [41]. On the one hand, there is currently a wide range of bio-metric sensors that allow collecting real-time information such as heart rate, temperature, activity (by means of MEMS – *Microelectromechanical Systems* [14]) or even more breakthrough proposals such as oximeters [17] and blood glucose levels [45]. In this sense, there are new trends in *wearable* devices, such as smart watches, activity wristbands or even smart fabrics [10] that allow monitoring real-time information about the health of people. Moreover, bio-metric sensors and Wireless Sensor Networks are also applied in animals such as livestock or even pets in order to monitor their health and prevent diseases [29]. On the other hand, Wireless Sensor Networks are widely applied for gathering information about the environment and even modifying this environment according to the users' needs by means of actuators. In this sense, there are a wide range of available sensors (temperature, humidity, light, rain, gases, wind, etc.) and applications (smart cities, home and building automation, healthcare and telecare, smart farming, hotels, etc.) [1,38]. There are different technologies and standards used to implement Wireless Sensor Networks, including IEEE 802.15.4 ZigBee or Wi-Fi, as well as newer proposals such as Bluetooth Low Energy, NB-IoT or LoRa, each of them providing advantages and drawbacks when applying to each scenario [2,4].

Real-Time Locating Systems [42] can be classified according to the type of its wireless infrastructure and by the locating techniques used to estimate the position of each user or asset in the environment (i.e., the locating algorithms or positioning engine) [43]. Likewise, there is a increasing range of wireless technologies aimed both at outdoor RTLS or global positioning, such as GPS, GLONASS,

Galileo and BeiDou [30], and at indoor location, such as ZigBee, Wi-Fi, UWB [53] and even Bluetooth Low Energy (BLE) [51], as well as multiple locating techniques that can be combined to determine the position of the devices tracking people, animals or objects [2]. Focused on each of them, locating systems based on Wi-Fi take advantage of Wi-Fi WLANs (Wireless Local Area Networks) working on the 2.4 and 5.8 GHz bands to estimate the positions of the mobile devices on people and assets [23]. Nonetheless, Wi-Fi based locating systems present some problems including interference with existing data transmissions and the elevated power consumption by the Wi-Fi devices [53]. ZigBee is another interesting technology that can be used to build RTLS [19].

The IEEE802.15.4 ZigBee standard is specially intended to implement Wireless Sensor Networks and, as Wi-Fi, can work in the 2.4 GHz ISM band, but also can work on the 868–915 MHz band. Ultra-Wide Band (UWB) is another technology aimed to develop high accuracy indoor locating system [37]. As it works at high frequencies (the band covers from 3.1 GHz to 10.6 GHz in the USA), it allows to achieve sub-meter location estimations. New Bluetooth Low Energy (BLE) standard provides a newly wide-spread and efficient way to implement indoor or event outdoor RTLS, which can take advantage of the existence of Bluetooth standard on almost every commercialized smart phone and which allow the use of a beacon-based schema in which reference points consume very low energy levels and have several years of battery life [51].

As can be seen, there is a challenge when building IoT scenarios gathering data from heterogeneous sources such as Wireless Sensor Networks and Real-Time Locating Systems implemented by means of different wireless technologies [4]. One way to deal with this issue is the deployment of intermediate IoT data ingestion layers [26] in order to gather data coming from different IoT sources and manage all of them in a homogeneous and normalized way in the Cloud. In fact, one of the most important features provided by IoT platforms is that they allow the collection of massive data from real scenarios. These massive data can be used for the construction of Big Data repositories [36] on which subsequently apply Data Analytics [31] or Machine Learning [5] techniques in order to extract added value from the data, detect anomalous patterns in them [49], as well as make real-time predictions from massive data coming from many different sources.

The following sections present a review of Edge Computing and another important trend that is the creation of Software-Defined Networks (SDN). In the opinion of Baktir et al., the integration of these technologies makes it possible to promote Edge Computing and its application in IoT scenarios [7].

3   Software Defined Networks and Network Virtualization

The continuous growth in the huge number of devices connected to the Internet, as well as the continuous arrival of new applications with ever greater demands on the quality of service they have to offer, in terms of bandwidth, latency and data integrity, foster the emerge of new approaches aimed to optimize the use of the resources of existing networks, as well as make profitable the investments associated with them. In this sense, and in order to provide a more efficient use of resources on IoT scenarios, which are usually made up of multiple and heterogeneous wireless sensor networks shared by different applications with distinct requirements, different solutions for the virtualization of computing, storage and network resources emerge. This is how, among other solutions, concepts such as Network Function Virtualization (NFV) arise, oriented to the virtualization of the different components of the network [21]. In a way closely related to the NFV, and often used complementing each other, Software-Defined Networks also emerge [44], as well as approaches specially focused on Software-Defined Wireless Networks (SDWNs) and Software-Defined Wireless Sensor Networks (SDWSNs) [16]. All of them are closely related to the use of Cloud over them [3].

3.1   Software Defined Networks (SDNs)

Software Defined Networks (SDNs) [25] are presented as a new option of approaching networking through a software application called a *controller*. In the SDN scheme, the network administrator uses a centralized control console to regulate traffic without resorting to switches [57]. In 2008, the OpenFlow protocol was introduced by the Open Networking Foundation, with its first version appearing in 2011 [44]. This protocol allows decoupling the *control plane* of the *data plane* of the networks. Thanks to the uncoupling of these two planes, the control and management of the network can be carried out remotely in the cloud (in a centralized or distributed way), while packet forwarding is carried out in the hardware devices that make up the network. The control plane commands hardware devices specifying how to forward these packets between their adjacent nodes. Therefore, it is no longer necessary to build different hardware devices with specific functions (ASIC circuits) [21], making it possible to use cheaper general-purpose hardware with a lower unit cost and that can evolve over time simply updating its functions and software remotely, reducing replacement and warehousing costs. Figure 1 depicts this architecture [57].

3.2   Network Function Virtualization

The concept of network virtualization is defined according to Granelli *et al.* as the process of combining hardware and software network resources, as well as the network own functionalities, into a single software-based entity that is called an entity [21]. Network virtualization improves the scheme of utilization and optimization of resources through the sharing of a set of physical resources in a virtual and stagnant way between the different virtual networks. That is, each of the virtual networks believes that they have their own dedicated hardware resources and is not aware that they are being shared by other virtual networks. Figure 2 shows this approach [57].

Nonetheless, to address Network Function Virtualization, it is necessary to provide a clear abstraction of the underlying hardware provided by the entity defined by software. In this way, multiple service and application providers can

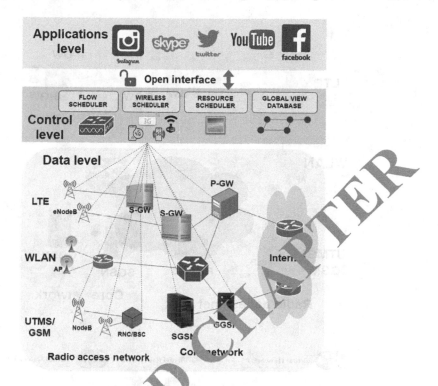

Fig. 1. Software Defined Network, based on the work of Yang *et al.* [57].

dynamically access the different resources of the physical network, configuring and controlling it from the control plane of the network defined by software [21].

4 Edge Computing

Edge computing emerge in the 90s with the content delivery networks (CDNs) concept introduced by Akamai Technologies. [40,54]. Shi *et al.*, defines Edge computing as computer and network resources located between data sources, such as IoT devices and cloud data centres [47].

Figure 3 shows a basic Edge Computing scheme in which technologies used at the edge of the network allow processes to be performed close to data sources. In this scheme an IoT device such as a Smartphone, a Tablet or a PDA collects the data closely to the source where end users are. Edge nodes perform compute tasks such as filtering, processing, caching, load balancing by reducing data sent or received from the cloud and requesting services and information. For these tasks to be performed efficiently and safely, the edge must be correctly defined because it has to withstand IoT requirements such as differentiation, reliability, extensibility, isolation and response time. Three levels can be seen in Fig. 3:

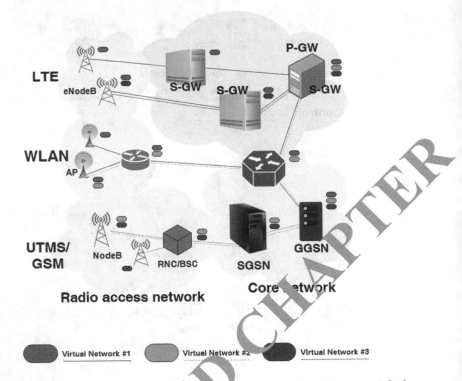

Fig. 2. Network Function Virtualization, based on the work of Yang *et al.* [57].

- *End users and IoT devices:* the group of IoT devices (sensors, actuators, smartphones, PDAs, tablets) that interact directly with the end user. Some offer services and answers in real time, however, due to their limited capacity, they send requests for services or resources to the computer equipment located in the Edge.
- *Edge Nodes:* These devices perform most of the processing, storage, support high data traffic, and because they are located closer to end users than cloud servers, they are able to process, cache and perform calculations for a larger volume of data. With this computing capacity, the reduction in data flow and cost for the use of cloud services is considerable in addition to the reduction in time and latency.
- *Cloud services:* in this scheme, cloud servers host applications for automatic learning, big data analysis and business intelligence.

In addition to Edge Computing as a trend that brings computer equipment and services closer to the end user, Software Defined Networks (SDNs) that integrate with the EC allow reducing its complexity to be implemented in IoT scenarios. The following sections present a review of models, architectures and benefits of SDN and Edge Computing integration.

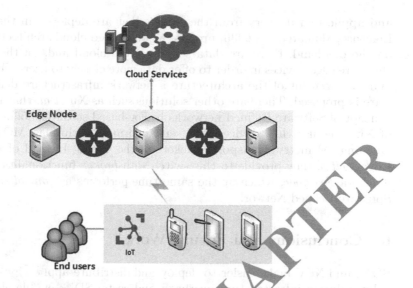

Fig. 3. Edge Computing Basic Architecture, based on the work of Yu *et al.* [60].

5   Combining SDNs and Edge Computing on IoT Scenarios

As can be seen in the previous sections, both software-defined networks and the use of Edge Computing techniques can optimize, separately, the computational, storage and network resources in the physical networks that make up the IoT scenarios.

We have seen how the different layers of the Edge Computing multi-layer paradigm (i.e., IoT, Edge and Cloud) allow reducing the data traffic exchanged between the IoT devices and the Cloud, reducing virtual infrastructure use costs and allowing preprocessing, applying Machine Learning techniques and showing valuable data in the Edge itself, without having to consume resources in the Cloud, where the information already processed arrive thanks to the Edge Computing paradigm [52]. On the one hand, there are several studies and solutions solely focused on the Cloud [55], or others that do take into account solutions based on Cloudlets [39] or Fog Computing [58]. On the other hand, there are studies in Software-Defined Networks [22], Wireless Software-Defined Networks [24] and Network Function Virtualization [34] as complementary technologies that could work together with Edge Computing architectures.

Furthermore, there are different solutions oriented to the combination of both paradigms in order to optimize even more the resources on IoT networks [7]. Within the different approaches, we find HomeCloud [39], a framework that combines the use of NFV and SDNs with the aim at allowing efficient orchestration and application delivery from the servers that are deployed in the Edge itself. Likewise, Monfared *et al.* [35] propose a two-layered cloud architecture in which, on the one hand, there are data servers in the cloud and, on the other hand, there are edge devices in order to offer data more closely to users. For the control and management of the architecture a network infrastructure defined by software is proposed. There are other solutions such as Xu *et al.* that introduce the concept of Software-Defined networks in Fog-based scenarios [56]. The proposal of Xu *el al.* uses IoT devices that send information through MQTT (Message Queuing Telemetry Transport) packets to the Cloud. Instead of using just an Edge *switch*, they provide to this switch with *broker* functionalities, converting it into a *Fog node*, which at the same time performs as *controller* node of the Software-Defined Network.

6   Conclusions and Future Work

SDNs and NFV make easier to deploy and distribute applications by dramatically reducing infrastructure overhead and costs. SDNs enable cloud architectures through automated and scalable application distribution and mobility. Moreover, VFN increase flexibility and resource utilization on SDNs by means of data center virtualization. Thanks to the application of SDNs on IoT scenarios, it is possible to separate the data plane from the network control plane and introduce a logically centralized control plane, called a controller, to abstract control functions from networking.

Programmable control mechanisms of software-defined networks make them an alternative for reducing the complexity of Edge Computing (EC) architectures by enabling more efficient use of available computing resources. By using SDNs the data traffic originating from Edge servers can be dynamically routed freeing Edge devices from the execution of complex network activities such as service detection, orchestration, and QoS (performance-delay) requirements.

Future work includes the proposal of a reference architecture for the creation of systems and applications based on the Edge Computing paradigm in IoT environments. This platform will also have a second iteration, with the possibility of implementing Software-Defined Networks, as well as Network Function Virtualization, including blockchain services integrated into the architecture in a native way for the creation of IoT platforms in different environments such as Industry 4.0, smart energy and smart farming.

Acknowledgments. This work has been supported by project "IOTEC: Development of Technological Capacities around the Industrial Application of Internet of Things (IoT)".0123-IOTEC-3-E. Project financed with FEDER funds, Interreg Spain-Portugal (PocTep). Inés Sittón has been supported by scholarship program: IFARHUSENACYT (Government of Panama).

References

1. Agrawal, H., Prieto, J., Ramos, C., Corchado, J.M.: Smart feeding in farming through IoT in silos. Intelligent Systems Technologies and Applications 2016. AISC, vol. 530, pp. 355–366. Springer, Cham (2016). https://doi.org/10.1007/978-3-319-47952-1_28

2. Ahmad, M., Ishtiaq, A., Habib, M.A., Ahmed, S.H.: A review of internet of things (IoT) connectivity techniques. In: Jan, M.A., Khan, F., Alam, M. (eds.) Recent Trends and Advances in Wireless and IoT-enabled Networks. EICC, pp. 25–36. Springer, Cham (2019). https://doi.org/10.1007/978-3-319-99966-1_3

3. Alenezi, M., Almustafa, K., Meerja, K.A.: Cloud based SDN and NFV architectures for IoT infrastructure. Egypt. Inform. J. (2018). https://doi.org/10.1016/j.eij.2018.03.004, http://www.sciencedirect.com/science/article/pii/S1110866518302523

4. Alonso, R.S., Tapia, D.I., Bajo, J., García, Ó., de Paz, J.F., Corchado, J.M.: Implementing a hardware-embedded reactive agents platform based on a service-oriented architecture over heterogeneous wireless sensor networks. Ad Hoc Netw. **11**(1), 151–166 (2013)

5. Alvarado-Pérez, J., Peluffo-Ordóñez, D.H., Therón, R.: Bridging the gap between human knowledge and machine learning. ADCAIJ: Adv. Distrib. Comput. Artif. Intell. J. **4**(1) (2015). http://revistas.usal.es/index.php/2255-2863/article/view/ADCAIJ2015415464

6. Ashton, K., et al.: That 'internet of things' thing. RFID J. **22**(7), 97–114 (2009)

7. Baktir, A.C., Ozgovde, A., Ersoy, C.: How can edge computing benefit from software-defined networking: a survey, use cases, and future directions. IEEE Commun. Surv. Tutor. **19**(4), 2359–2390 (2017). https://doi.org/10.1109/COMST.2017.2717482

8. Becerril, A.A.: The value of our personal data in the big data and the internet of all things era. ADCAIJ: Adv. Distrib. Comput. Artif. Intell. J. **7**(2), 71–80 (2018)

9. Bullon, J., Arrieta, A.G., Encinas, A.H., Dios, A.Q.: Manufacturing processes in the textile industry. Expert systems for fabrics production. ADCAIJ: Adv. Distrib. Comput. Artif. Intell. J. **6**(1) (2017). http://revistas.usal.es/index.php/2255-2863/article/view/ADCAIJ2017614150

10. Caldara, M., Colleoni, C., Guido, E., Re, V., Rosace, G.: Optical monitoring of sweat pH by a textile fabric wearable sensor based on covalently bonded litmus-3-glycidoxypropyltrimethoxysilane coating. Sens. Actuators B: Chem. **222**, 213–220 (2016). https://doi.org/10.1016/j.snb.2015.08.073, http://www.sciencedirect.com/science/article/pii/S0925400515302513

11. Casado-Vara, R., Vale, Z., Prieto, J., Corchado, J.: Fault-tolerant temperature control algorithm for IoT networks in smart buildings. Energies **11**(12), 3430 (2018)

12. Chamoso, P., González-Briones, A., Rodríguez, S., Corchado, J.M.: Tendencies of technologies and platforms in smart cities: a state-of-the-art review. Wirel. Commun. Mob. Comput. (2018). https://doi.org/10.1155/2018/3086854

13. Chamoso, P., Prieta, F.D.L.: Swarm-based smart city platform: a traffic application. ADCAIJ: Adv. Distrib. Comput. Artif. Intell. J. **4**(2), 89–98-98 (2015). https://doi.org/10.14201/ADCAIJ2015428998, http://revistas.usal.es/index.php/2255-2863/article/view/ADCAIJ2015428998

14. Fan, S., et al.: mm-scale and MEMS piezoelectric energy harvesters powering on-chip CMOS temperature sensing for IoT applications. In: 2017 19th International Conference on Solid-State Sensors, Actuators and Microsystems (TRANSDUCERS), pp. 1848–1850, June 2017. https://doi.org/10.1109/TRANSDUCERS.2017.7994430

15. Farash, M.S., Turkanović, M., Kumari, S., Hölbl, M.: An efficient user authentication and key agreement scheme for heterogeneous wireless sensor network tailored for the internet of things environment. Ad Hoc Netw. **36**, 152–176 (2016). https://doi.org/10.1016/j.adhoc.2015.05.014, http://www.sciencedirect.com/science/article/pii/S1570870515001195

16. Gante, A.D., Aslan, M., Matrawy, A.: Smart wireless sensor network management based on software-defined networking. In: 2014 27th Biennial Symposium on Communications (QBSC), pp. 71–75, June 2014. https://doi.org/10.1109/QBSC.2014.6841187

17. Garbhapu, V.V., Gopalan, S.: IoT based low cost single sensor node remote health monitoring system. Procedia Comput. Sci. **113**, 408–415 (2017). The 8 International Conference on Emerging Ubiquitous Systems and Pervasive Networks (EUSPN 2017)/The 7th International Conference on Current and future Trends of Information and Communication Technologies in Healthcare (ICTH-2017)/Affiliated Workshops. https://doi.org/10.1016/j.procs.2017.08.35, http://www.sciencedirect.com/science/article/pii/S1877050917317672

18. García, O., Alonso, R.S., Prieto, J., Corchado, J.M.: Energy efficiency in public buildings through context-aware social computing. Sensors **17**(4), 826 (2017). https://doi.org/10.3390/s17040826, https://www.mdpi.com/1424-8220/17/4/826

19. García, O., Chamoso, P., Prieto, J., Rodríguez, S., de la Prieta, F.: A serious game to reduce consumption in smart buildings. In: Bajo, J., et al. (eds.) PAAMS 201. Communications in Computer and Information Science, vol. 722, pp. 481–493. Springer, Cham (2017). https://doi.org/10.1007/978-3-319-60285-1_41

20. González-Briones, A., De La Prieta, F., Mohamad, M., Omatu, S., Corchado, J.: Multi-agent systems applications in energy optimization problems: a state-of-the-art review. Energies **11**(8), 1928 (2018)

21. Granelli, F., et al.: Software defined and virtualized wireless access in future wireless networks: scenarios and standards. IEEE Commun. Mag. **53**(6), 26–34 (2015). https://doi.org/10.1109/MCOM.2015.7120042

22. Hu, F., Hao, Q., Bao, K.: A survey on software-defined network and openflow: from concept to implementation. IEEE Commun. Surv. Tutor. **16**(4), 2181–2206 (2014). https://doi.org/10.1109/COMST.2014.2326417

23. Jachimczyk, B., Dziak, D., Kulesza, W.J.: Using the fingerprinting method to customize RTLS based on the AoA ranging technique. Sensors (Basel, Switzerland) **16**(6) (2016). https://doi.org/10.3390/s16060876

24. Jagadeesan, N.A., Krishnamachari, B.: Software-defined networking paradigms in wireless networks: a survey. ACM Comput. Surv. **47**(2), 27:1–27:11 (2014). https://doi.org/10.1145/2655690

25. Jammal, M., Singh, T., Shami, A., Asal, R., Li, Y.: Software defined networking: state of the art and research challenges (2014). https://doi.org/10.1016/j.comnet.2014.07.004

26. Kaed, C.E., Ponnouradjane, A., Shah, D.: A semantic based multi-platform IoT integration approach from sensors to chatbots. In: 2018 Global Internet of Things Summit (GIoTS), pp. 1–6, June 2018. https://doi.org/10.1109/GIOTS.2018.8534520

27. Kethareswaran, V., Ram, C.S.: An indian perspective on the adverse impact of internet of things (IoT). ADCAIJ: Adv. Distrib. Comput. Artif. Intell. J. **6**(4), 35–40 (2017)

28. Ko, H., Bae, K., Marreiros, G., Kim, H., Yoe, H., Ramos, C.: A study on the key management strategy for wireless sensor networks. ADCAIJ: Adv. Distrib. Comput. Artif. Intell. J. **3**(3) (2015). http://revistas.usal.es/index.php/2255-2863/article/view/ADCAIJ2014334353

29. Kumari, S., Yadav, S.K.: Development of IoT based smart animal health monitoring system using Raspberry Pi. SSRN Scholarly Paper ID 3315327, Social Science Research Network, Rochester, NY (2018). https://papers.ssrn.com/abstract=3315327

30. Li, X., Zhang, X., Ren, X., Fritsche, M., Wickert, J., Schuh, H.: Precise positioning with current multi-constellation Global Navigation Satellite Systems: GPS, GLONASS. Galileo and BeiDou. Sci. Rep. **5**, 8328 (2015). https://doi.org/10.1038/srep08328

31. Lima, A.C.E., de Castro, L.N., Corchado, J.M.: A polarity analysis framework for twitter messages. Appl. Math. Comput. **270**, 756–767 (2016). https://doi.org/10.1016/j.amc.2015.08.059, http://www.sciencedirect.com/science/article/pii/S0096300315011145

32. Lueth, K.L.: Why the internet of things is called internet of things: definition, history, disambiguation. IoT Anal. (2014). https://iot-analytics.com/internet-of-things-definition/

33. Mainetti, L., Patrono, L., Vilei, A.: Evolution of wireless sensor networks towards the Internet of Things: a survey. In: 19th International Conference on Software, Telecommunications and Computer Networks, SoftCOM 2011, pp. 1–6, September 2011

34. Mijumbi, R., Serrat, J., Gorricho, J., Bouten, N., Turck, F.D., Boutaba, R.: Network function virtualization: state-of-the-art and research challenges. IEEE Commun. Surv. Tutor. **18**(1), 236–262 (2016). https://doi.org/10.1109/COMST.2015.2477041

35. Monfared, S., Bannazadeh, H., Leon-Garcia, A.: Software defined wireless access for a two-tier cloud system. In: 2015 IFIP/IEEE International Symposium on Integrated Network Management (IM), pp. 566–571, May 2015. https://doi.org/10.1109/INM.2015.7140338

36. Monino, J.L., Sedkaoui, S.: The algorithm of the snail: an example to grasp the window of opportunity to boost big data. ADCAIJ: Adv. Distrib. Comput. Artif. Intell. J. **5**(3) (2016). http://revistas.usal.es/index.php/2255-2863/article/view/ADCAIJ201653671

37. Naghdi, S., Tjhai, C., O'Keefe, K.: Assessing a UWB RTLS as a means for rapid WLAN radio map generation. In: 2018 International Conference on Indoor Positioning and Indoor Navigation (IPIN), pp. 1–5, September 2018. https://doi.org/10.1109/IPIN.2018.8533819

38. Nawaz, N.A., Waqas, A., Yusof, Z.M., Shah, A.: A framework for smart estimation of demand-supply for crowdsource management using WSN. In: Proceedings of the Second International Conference on Internet of Things, Data and Cloud Computing, ICC 2017, Cambridge, United Kingdom, pp. 92:1–92:5. ACM, New York (2017). https://doi.org/10.1145/3018896.3025140

39. Pang, Z., Sun, L., Wang, Z., Tian, E., Yang, S.: A survey of cloudlet based mobile computing. In: 2015 International Conference on Cloud Computing and Big Data (CCBD), pp. 268–275, November 2015. https://doi.org/10.1109/CCBD.2015.54

40. Pathan, A.M.K., Buyya, R.: A taxonomy and survey of content delivery networks. Technical report 4, Grid Computing and Distributed Systems Laboratory, University of Melbourne (2007)

41. De la Prieta, F., Bajo, J., Rodríguez, S., Corchado, J.M.: MAS-based self-adaptive architecture for controlling and monitoring Cloud platforms. J. Ambient Intell. Human. Comput. **8**(2), 213–221 (2017). https://doi.org/10.1007/s12652-016-0434-8

42. Prieto, J., Chamoso, P., la Prieta, F.D., Corchado, J.M.: A generalized framework for wireless localization in gerontechnology. In: 2017 IEEE 17th International Conference on Ubiquitous Wireless Broadband (ICUWB), pp. 1–5, September 2017. https://doi.org/10.1109/ICUWB.2017.8250981

43. Prieto, J., Mazuelas, S., la Prieta, F.D., Corchado, J.M.: Feasibility of single-agent localization from sequential measurements. In: 2018 IEEE International Conference on Communications Workshops (ICC Workshops), pp. 1–6, May 2018. https://doi.org/10.1109/ICCW.2018.8403685

44. Puente Fernández, J.A., García Villalba, L.J., Kim, T.H.: Software defined networks in wireless sensor architectures. Entropy **20**(4), 225 (2018). https://doi.org/10.3390/e20040225, https://www.mdpi.com/1099-4300/20/4/225

45. Rahman, R.A., Aziz, N.S.A., Kassim, M., Yusof, M.I.: IoT-based personal health care monitoring device for diabetic patients. In: 2017 IEEE Symposium on Computer Applications Industrial Electronics (ISCAIE), pp. 168–173, April 2017. https://doi.org/10.1109/ISCAIE.2017.8074971

46. Sanchez-Iborra, R., Sanchez-Gomez, J., Skarmeta, A.: Evolving IoT networks by the confluence of MEC and LP-WAN paradigms. Future Gener. Comput. Syst. **88**, 199–208 (2018). https://doi.org/10.1016/j.future.2018.05.057, http://www.sciencedirect.com/science/article/pii/S0167739X17324159

47. Shi, W., Cao, J., Zhang, Q., Li, Y., Xu, L.: Edge computing: vision and challenges. IEEE Internet Things J. **3**(5), 637–646 (2016). https://doi.org/10.1109/JIOT.2016.2579198

48. Candanedo, I.S., Nieves, E.H., González, S.R., Martín, M.T.S., Briones, A.G.: Machine learning predictive model for industry 4.0. In: Uden, L., Hadzima, B., Ting, I.-H. (eds.) KMO 2018. CCIS, vol. 877, pp. 501–510. Springer, Cham (2018). https://doi.org/10.1007/978-3-319-95204-8_42

49. Sittón, I., Rodríguez, S.: Pattern extraction for the design of predictive models in industry 4.0. In: De la Prieta, F., et al. (eds.) PAAMS 2017. AISC, vol. 619, pp. 258–261. Springer, Cham (2018). https://doi.org/10.1007/978-3-319-61578-3_31

50. Srinidhi, N.N., Dilip Kumar, S.M., Venugopal, K.R.: Network optimizations in the Internet of Things: a review (2018). https://doi.org/10.1016/j.jestch.2018.09.003, https://www.sciencedirect.com/science/article/pii/S2215098618303379

51. Syafrudin, M., Lee, K., Alfian, G., Lee, J., Rhee, J.: Application of bluetooth low energy-based real-time location system for indoor environments. In: Proceedings of the 2018 2nd International Conference on Big Data and Internet of Things, BDIOT 2018, Beijing, China, pp. 167–171. ACM, New York (2018). https://doi.org/10.1145/3289430.3289470

52. Yanninada, V.R.: Software defined networking: redefining the future of internet in IoT and cloud era. In: 2014 International Conference on Future Internet of Things and Cloud, pp. 296–301, August 2014. https://doi.org/10.1109/FiCloud.2014.53

53. Tapia, D.I., et al.: Evaluating the n-core polaris real-time locating system in an indoor environment. In: Rodríguez, J.M.C., Pérez, J.B., Golinska, P., Giroux, S., Corchuelo, R. (eds.) Trends in Practical Applications of Agents and Multiagent Systems. Advances in Intelligent and Soft Computing, vol. 157, pp. 29–387. Springer, Heidelberg (2012). https://doi.org/10.1007/978-3-642-28795-4_4

54. Technologies, A.: Technical report (2007). https://www.akamaicom/es/es/. Accessed 5 Feb 2019

55. Toosi, A.N., Calheiros, R.N., Buyya, R.: Interconnected cloud computing environments: challenges, taxonomy, and survey. ACM Comput. Surv. **47**(1), 7:1–7:47 (2014). https://doi.org/10.1145/2593512
56. Xu, Y., Mahendran, V., Radhakrishnan, S.: Towards SDN-based fog computing: MQTT broker virtualization for effective and reliable delivery. In: 2016 8th International Conference on Communication Systems and Networks (COMSNETS), pp. 1–6, January 2016. https://doi.org/10.1109/COMSNETS.2016.7439974
57. Yang, M., Li, Y., Jin, D., Zeng, L., Wu, X., Vasilakos, A.V.: Software-defined and virtualized future mobile and wireless networks: a survey. Mob. Netw. Appl. **20**(1), 4–18 (2015). https://doi.org/10.1007/s11036-014-0533-8
58. Yi, S., Li, C., Li, Q.: A survey of fog computing: concepts, applications and issues. In: Proceedings of the 2015 Workshop on Mobile Big Data, Mobidata 2015, Hangzhou, China, pp. 37–42. ACM, New York (2015). https://doi.org/10.1145/2757384.2757397
59. Yin, Y., Zeng, Y., Chen, X., Fan, Y.: The internet of things in healthcare: an overview. J. Ind. Inf. Integr. **1**, 3–13 (2016). https://doi.org/10.1016/j.jii.2016.03.004. http://www.sciencedirect.com/science/article/pii/S2452414X16000066
60. Yu, W., et al.: A survey on the edge computing for the Internet of Things. IEEE Access **6**, 6900–6919 (2017). https://doi.org/10.1109/ACCESS.2017.2778504
61. Zorzi, M., Gluhak, A., Lange, S., Bassi, A.: From today's INTRAnet of things to a future INTERnet of things: a wireless- and mobility-related view. IEEE Wirel. Commun. **17**(6), 44–51 (2010). https://doi.org/10.1109/MWC.2010.5675777

An Intelligent and Autoadaptive System of Virtual Identities Based on Deep Learning for the Analysis of Online Advertising Networks

Elvira Amador-Domínguez[1] , Emilio Serrano[1(⊠)] ,
Juan David Mateos-Nobre[2], and Alfredo Ayala-Muñoz[2]

[1] Ontology Engineering Group, Department of Artificial Intelligence,
Universidad Politécnica de Madrid, Madrid, Spain
{eamador,emilioserra}@fi.upm.es
[2] Dooflow S.L.L. Madrid, Madrid, Spain
{david,alfredo}@semminer.com

Abstract. Marketing is one of the areas that benefits the most from web platforms. Several online marketing techniques have been developed throughout the years that focus on determining what is the most effective displayable content depending on the population target. In order to analyze the advertisements displayed to each population segment, a system based on Virtual Identities is proposed. In this system, each population target is represented by a virtual identity, that navigates the internet according to a scripted behavior. In each of the visited webpages, advertising content is displayed, that needs to be detected, located and subsequently analyzed to extract patterns. In this work, a Natural Language Processing model is presented, where advertising detection is treated as a binary classification problem, predicting for each block composing the webpage whether it is, or is not, commercial content. Two different approaches are considered for the input, depending on whether the HTML markup text is removed or not. Furthermore, several text embedding and predictive models are evaluated in order to select the best model according to the presented input.

Keywords: Natural Language Processing ·
Online advertising networks

This research work is supported by the "Comunidad de Madrid", under the programs "Ayudas para el fomento de la innovación tecnológica en sectores tecnológicos de la Comunidad de Madrid, en el marco de la Estrategia Regional de Investigación e Innovación para una Especialización Inteligente (RIS3)"; and, by the "Universidad Politécnica de Madrid" under the program "Ayudas Dirigidas a Jóvenes Investigadores para Fortalecer sus Planes de Investigación" and "Ayudas para Contratos Predoctorales para la Realización del Doctorado".

© Springer Nature Switzerland AG 2019
F. De la Prieta et al. (Eds.): PAAMS 2019 Workshops, CCIS 1047, pp. 302–309, 2019.
https://doi.org/10.1007/978-3-030-24299-2_26

1   Introduction

Online marketing comprises a considerable amount of the total content existing on the web, appearing in the form of videos, images and text. To be accepted by the target, commercial content should be ideally interesting for the user, adapted to their preferences and non-intrusive. In order to analyze the behaviour of current online advertising networks, an intelligent system based on *Virtual Identities* (VIs) is proposed. As shown in Fig. 1, different population groups are simulated using VIs. These VIs navigate the internet following a predefined behaviour, generating a set of visited webpages each. Gathered webpages contain both advertising and non-advertising content, that has to be subsequently separated by an advert detection system. Once the commercial content has been extracted, an in-depth study can be performed to identify different advertising trends. The contribution of this paper is the introduction of an online commercial content detector that is capable of accurately detecting commercial content independently of the nature of the input. Furthermore, this system can be easily updated to include newer types of advertising to fit the purpose of emerging VIs.

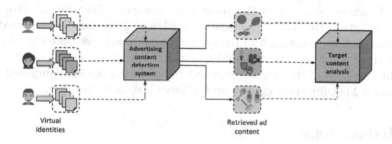

Fig. 1. An overview of the complete system

Although there are several existing applications for this task, most of them are based on filter comparison. This approach can be effective for detecting advertising content on a single web page, but can be very inefficient when processing bigger amounts of data. In filter-based systems, commercial content is detected by using regular expressions where the URLs embedded in the webpage are compared with a predefined list of filters. This approach is fairly limited, as the filter list needs to be constantly updated, and cannot detect more subtle forms of marketing. To tackle this issue, a *Natural Language Processing* (NLP) based system is proposed. In this approach, advert detection is contemplated as a binary text classification problem, where the different HTML blocks of each collected webpage are the input. The generated model, aside from being able to detect finer-grained textual advertising content, can be incrementally trained to detect emerging advertising patterns.

The paper is structured as follows. Section 2 presents an overview of the related works. Section 3 explains the employed methodology. Section 4 discusses the results obtained. Conclusions are drawn in Sect. 5.

2   Related Works

Most of the existing online advertising network analysis is based on sentiment analysis. The goal of these works is to determine whether certain content evokes a positive or a negative reaction in the user, by mining text information extracted from forums or customer reviews [3,8]. However, these approaches are oblivious to some of the most relevant marketing parameters, as age. Furthermore, they do not take into consideration existing advertising trends and their effectiveness.

Regarding advert detection, filter-based applications are currently the most spreadly-used ones. AdBlock [2] or UBlock [11] are two examples of applications of this kind, accounting more than 60 million users across the world. This proposals base their detection on a systematic comparison of all the existing URLs in the source code with a set of previously defined filters. This filters are obtained by subscription to both public [1] and private lists, which are regularly updated handcraftedly.

Opposite to this filtering approach, several machine learning methods have been proposed overtime. As noted in Oskuie et al. [9], these methods are constructed over the same principles, being the notation of spam detection as a binary classification problem the most representative. Prieto et al. [10] use a C4.5 classification tree as the predictive model, and subsequently enhanced with techniques such as boosting and bagging in order to achieve better predictions. Karimpour et al. [5] apply Principal Component Analysis to the input to generate the entrance of the semi-supervised classification model, composed by an Expectation Maximization cluster and a Naive Bayesian classifier.

3   Methodology

It is necessary to clearly specify the features of the input before designing the workflow of the system. Regarding webpages, two different inputs can be considered depending on whether the HTML markup text is removed or not. This information can also potentially enhance the predictions, although the size of the input increases when HTML markup text is not filtered out and consequently the processing time. In order to study up to what degree the predictive capability of the model is increased depending on whether or not this information is present, both approaches are considered in this work.

The presented approach is also capable of automatically detecting what kind of input has been presented, differentiating between single blocks and complete webpages. Furthermore, it can select the best existing model according to the input and the specified criteria. The final system is deployed both as an API Rest and as a webpage.

In Fig. 2, an overview of the designed predictive system is presented, specifying the order in which each stage is performed. The first two modules belong to the preprocessing stage, whereas the remaining three are responsible for the predictive stage. Both the text embedding and the predictive model modules require training, thus it is previously compulsory to split the existing data into

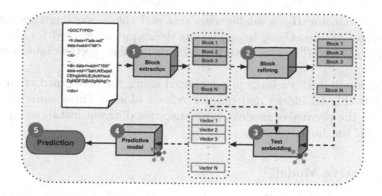

Fig. 2. Workflow of the commercial content detection module

training, validation and test sets. The proportion used is 60, 20 and 20%, respectively. All three partitions maintain an equal proportion of positive and negative examples.

3.1 Block Extraction

In order to make fine-grained predictions, the webpage is not considered as a whole, but as a composition multiple HTML blocks. This codification allows the model to predict more accurately not only if the webpage contains spam, but also where it is located. As HTML patterns vary from one type of page to another depending on its purpose, the defined method must be capable of dealing with all these heterogeneities.

As to extract these blocks, HTML markups are considered for block division. The block separators considered are: *ul-class*, *li-class* and *div data-hveid*. Once one of these opening separators is detected, the subsequent content is appended recursively to the block until the corresponding ending separator is found. Only non-empty blocks are considered.

3.2 Block Refining

Considering the filtered approach, a procedure for block refining is established. Considering the raw HTML block as the input, throughout these phase, the following elements are removed: (i) HTML markup text (ii) non-alphanumeric characters (iii) empty words (iv) JavaScript elements. Once this refinement is performed, the distinct content of the block is obtained.

3.3 Text Embedding

Given the incapability of machine learning techniques to deal with raw text, a text embedding step is necessary in order to convert the input text into fixed dimension vectors. Several text embedding techniques are considered for this purpose. Accounting the available resources and the processing time required for each candidate method, *bag of words* technique is selected for this work, although Doc2Vec [7] is also considered for evaluation. Vector dimension is set to 100.

Two different text vectorizers are trained using the predefined training set: one for raw HTML blocks and one for refined blocks. These same criteria is extended to the predictive models, generating two different instances for each of the potential methods.

3.4   Predictive Model

For this proposal, three different machine learning techniques are considered: a random forest, a multi-layer perceptron and FastText's text classification module [4]. The proposed random forest is composed by 50 estimators and the multi-layer perceptron is composed by two hidden layers, containing 30 and 50 neurons respectively. Adam [6] algorithm is employed for training. The training set is employed to train both versions of each model. FastText's text classification module is trained throughout 25 epochs with a fixed learning rate of 0.1.

In both previous models, text vectorization is performed strictly before prediction in an independent stage. On the contrary, FastText is self-contained, which implies that both steps are performed semi-simultaneously, decreasing the processing time needed.

4   Results and Discussion

In order to establish a fair comparison, different case scenarios are presented for each potential model. For each block criteria, two cases are studied. Firstly, an evaluation using the validation data set on each model is performed, followed by an evaluation of the winning model with the test set. Both sets are composed by predefined blocks, which have been manually extracted and labeled. A set of randomly selected web pages is considered as well to rank the performance of the proposed models in less favorable scenarios. These webpages are splitted into blocks using the methodology exposed in Sect. 3.1, and labeled using a filter approach using EasyList [1]. For comparison purposes, results obtained using bag of words and Doc2Vec are presented.

As shown in Table 1, FastText achieves the best results on all cases with the exception of web-extracted raw blocks, where it is slightly outperformed by the random forest in combination with bag of words vectorization. Its performance is particularly outstanding in the case of web-extracted filtered blocks, improving in nearly a 15% the second-best result, achieved by the multi-layer perceptron with bag of words.

It is relevant to note that, despite its higher complexity, Doc2Vec vectorization provides significantly lower results than the bag of words approach. This can be due to the nature of the blocks, where preserving high-level semantic

Table 1. Relation of *Area Under Receiver Operating Characteristic Curve* or AUC ROC per model. BoW refers to bag of words vectorization, whereas D2V refers to Doc2Vec vectorization. Elements in bold represents the best result for each presented case.

	Raw content		Filtered content	
	Predefined blocks	Web-extracted blocks	Predefined blocks	Web-extracted blocks
Random forest + BoW	0.99	**0.99**	0.99	0.54
Random forest + D2V	0.51	0.5	0.5	0.50
MLP + BoW	0.99	0.98	0.99	0.65
MLP + D2V	0.5	0.51	0.44	0.49
FastText	**0.99**	0.99	1.0	**0.81**

Table 2. Time (in seconds) needed per model to process 6,000 queries. Results obtained by using a filter-based approach are also presented

Method	Time needed for 6,000 queries
FastText	1202
Random forest + BoW	1276
Filter List	18214

context is not particularly relevant, but accounting the density of appearance of particular words is.

In order to assess the performance of the most accurate models a performance evaluation is conducted, whose results are shown in Table 2. To measure the efficiency of two of the best models, FastText and random forest with bag of words vectorization, the time needed for processing 6,000 queries is evaluated. The input of the query is a Google search result webpage composed by 23 blocks which are not subsequently filtered. For comparison purposes, the results obtained used the aforementioned filter-based approaches are also presented.

Although in the case of web-extracted blocks the best model is the random forest with bag of words vectorization, according to the efficiency results obtained, FastText would be a slightly better choice. Furthermore, it is demonstrated that the presented models severely outperform filter-based approaches in terms of efficiency, reducing the processing time in over 10 times.

The fact that raw content blocks achieve better performance in terms of accuracy than the filtered ones is also relevant, as it directly supports the idea that HTML markup text improves predictions. As shown in Fig. 3, in filtered HTML blocks there exists a high correlation between positive predictions and the appearance of the term 'anunciowww' amongst its terms, being this variable significantly more relevant than the others. On the other hand, in the case of raw HTML content, term relevance is more distributed, which allows for less rigid discrimination and encourages better predictions.

Finally, the selected models are evaluated over the corresponding test data sets. In the case of web-extracted blocks, a new set of randomly selected webpages is generated, and later divided into blocks and labeled as exposed previously

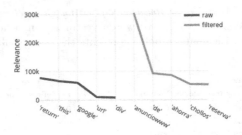

Fig. 3. Distribution of the relevance of the top-5 terms on both approaches. *Left:* Distribution of term relevance on raw HTML input. *Right:* Distribution of term relevance on filtered input.

on this section. These webpages come from very heterogeneous sources, ranging from newspaper's home webpages to search results from different search engines, such as Yahoo!, Google or Bing. The obtained areas under the ROC Curve for each model are presented in Fig. 4.

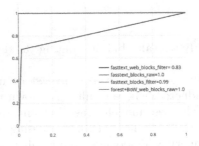

Fig. 4. AUC ROC of the selected models over the corresponding tests datasets.

According to the obtained results, the performances established previously for the different models are highly reliable, as no significant changes are noticed. Once the best models for each potential input are set, the system will automatically select the corresponding option according to the introduced data.

5   Conclusion and Future Works

In this work, a Natural Language Processing based module for commercial content detection in the context of Online Advertising Network analysis is presented. The proposed system comprises several agents, called Virtual Identities, which navigate the web following scripted behaviours in order to collect data from heterogeneous web sources. To extract advertising content from the gathered data, a binary text classification problem is formulated, where the blocks composing the web page serve as input and the objective is to determine whether they contain commercial content or not. Several text embedding and predictive models are studied in this work to solve the present problem. Furthermore, two different views are considered in regards of the input, depending on whether or not HTML markup text is removed.

As the input of the presented system are raw web pages, several preprocessing modules are introduced in order to split the content into blocks, cleaning and converting them into feature vectors that are later used to predict. After the evaluation procedure is conducted, FastText model is the best option, achieving a near perfect performance in most of the presented scenarios. Furthermore, the system has already been successfully with unseen data, efficiently retrieving commercial content from the presented web pages.

Our future works include improving block retrieval methodology in order to obtain optimal partitions and increase the current scope of detected commercial content as to integrate new potential marketing trends.

References

1. EasyList: Easylist. https://easylist.to/. Accessed 12 Feb 2018
2. Eyeo: Adblock. https://adblockplus.org/. Accessed 12 Feb 18
3. Glance, N., Hurst, M., Nigam, K., Siegler, M., Stockton, R., Tomokiyo, T.: Deriving marketing intelligence from online discussion. In: Proceedings of the Eleventh ACM SIGKDD International Conference on Knowledge Discovery in Data Mining, KDD 2005, pp. 419–428. ACM, New York (2005). https://doi.org/10.1145/1081870.1081919
4. Joulin, A., Grave, E., Bojanowski, P., Mikolov, T.: Bag of tricks for efficient text classification. arXiv preprint arXiv:1607.01759 (2016)
5. Karimpour, J., Noroozi, A.A., Alizadeh, S.: Web spam detection by learning from small labeled samples (2012)
6. Kingma, D.P., Ba, J.: Adam: a method for stochastic optimization. CoRR abs/1412.6980 (2014). http://arxiv.org/abs/1412.6980
7. Le, Q., Mikolov, T.: Distributed representations of sentences and documents. In: Proceedings of the 31st International Conference on International Conference on Machine Learning, ICML 2014, vol. 32, pp. II-1188-II-1196. JMLR.org (2014). http://dl.acm.org/citation.cfm?id=3044805.3045025
8. Li, N., Wu, D.D.: Using text mining and sentiment analysis for online forums hotspot detection and forecast. Decis. Support Syst. 48(2), 354–368 (2010). https://doi.org/10.1016/j.dss.2009.09.003. http://www.sciencedirect.com/science/article/pii/S0167923609002097
9. Oskuie, M.D., Razavi, S.N., et al.: A survey of web spam detection techniques. Int. J. Comput. Appl. Technol. Res. 3(3), 180–185
10. Prieto, V.M., Álvarez, M., Cacheda, F.: SAAD, a content based web Spam Analyzer and Detector. J. Syst. Softw. 86(11), 2906–2918 (2013). https://doi.org/10.1016/j.jss.2013.07.007
11. uBlock: ublock. https://www.ublock.org/. Accessed 12 Feb 18

Doctoral Consortium

Doctoral Consortium

The aim of the Doctoral Consortium is to provide a forum where students can present their ongoing research work and meet other students and researchers, and obtain feedback on future research directions.

The Doctoral Consortium is intended for students who have a specific research proposal and some preliminary results, but who are still far from completing their dissertation.

All proposals submitted to the Doctoral Consortium undergo a thorough re-viewing process with the aim of providing detailed and constructive feedback. Accepted submissions are presented at the Doctoral Consortium and published in the conference proceedings.

The submissions should identify:

Problem statement
Related work
Hypothesis
Proposal
Preliminary results and/or evaluation plan
Reflections

Organization

Doctoral Consortium Organizer

Fernando De la Prieta   University of Salamanca, Spain

Distributed Scheduling Based on Multi-agent Systems and Optimization Methods

Filipe Alves[1,2]([✉]), Ana Maria A. C. Rocha[2], Ana I. Pereira[1,2], and Paulo Leitao[1]

[1] Research Centre in Digitalization and Intelligent Robotics (CeDRI),
Instituto Politécnico de Bragança,
Campus de Santa Apolónia, 5300-253 Bragança, Portugal
{filipealves,apereira,pleitao}@ipb.pt
[2] ALGORITMI Center, University of Minho, 4710-057 Braga, Portugal
arocha@dps.uminho.pt

Abstract. The increasing relevance of complex systems in dynamic environments has received special attention during the last decade from the researchers. Such systems need to satisfy products or clients desires, which, after accomplished might change, becoming a very dynamic situation. Currently, decentralized approaches could assist in the automation of dynamic scheduling, based on the distribution of control functions over a swarm network of decision-making entities. Distributed scheduling, in an automatic manner, can be answered by a service coordination architecture of the different schedule components. However, it is necessary to introduce the control layer in the solution, encapsulating an intelligent service that merge agents with optimization methods. Multi-agent systems (MAS) can be combined with several optimization methods to extract the best of the two worlds: the intelligent control, cooperation and autonomy provided by MAS solutions and the optimum offered by optimization methods. The proposal intends to test the intelligent management of the schedule composition quality, in two case studies namely, manufacturing and home health care.

Keywords: Scheduling · Multi-agent system · Optimization methods

1 Problem Statement

Nowadays, sequencing, planning and scheduling are decision-making processes that play a crucial role in the manufacturing and service industries, economics and service operations management [8]. Moreover, the scheduling is a complex problem mainly due to its highly combinatorial aspect and its dynamic nature [4].

Traditionally, scheduling systems use centralized approaches, such as classical optimization methods, namely, heuristics, linear programming or metaheuristics. However, despite optimal solutions, they have high response times and consider

F. De la Prieta et al. (Eds.): PAAMS 2019 Workshops, CCIS 1047, pp. 313–317, 2019.
https://doi.org/10.1007/978-3-030-24299-2_27

the problems to be static and deterministic [6]. In contrast, multi-agent systems (MAS) offer an alternative way to design and control systems, differing from the conventional approaches due to fast and dynamic response and their inherent capabilities to adapt to emergence or disruptions [11]. However, the use of MAS, in turn, may not complement the search for optimized schedules provided by algorithms. Therefore, the lack of concrete solutions of distributed scheduling remains a problem, lacking validation on the design and implementation phase.

2   Related Work

Evolutions in Information and Communication Technologies (ICT) are based on the interaction of a multitude of different interconnected and even decision-capable smart objects (belonging to industrial and/or logistics and operational systems), with associated information counterparts (agents, swarms, holons) or purely digital [9]. These emerging ICT concepts provide powerful new solutions to challenges not yet addressed using decentralized approaches to operational and distributed scheduling (DS) [12]. The scheduling visions can be supported by the latest achievements in MAS and optimization methods, that are being employed for the design and development of the distributed scheduling [3, 7].

3   Hypothesis

Based on the stated problem, a research question emerges: "How to provide faster and more dynamic solutions in DS systems without losing optimum?"

The hypothesis will be, merging the better of two worlds (MAS and optimization methods) will allow to achieve innovative optimal solutions ensuring dynamic responsiveness and providing to the organizations minimal external intervention. In addition, a swarm approach can be studied. The challenge is facing the natural inspiration and self-organization concepts in the design of scheduling solutions. The hypotheses to cooperate with entities that can be regulated by simple rules, with reactive behavior and interactions in an environment without central authority, potentiates a DS architecture [5].

4   Proposal

This section outlines the vision of creating an architecture that facilitates an automatic search, selects, composes and provides DS solutions. Considering the problem, requirements and objectives, in this work a MAS approach is proposed taking into consideration recursive swarm design principles, that naturally matches the DS structure. Each agent is responsible to collect and analyze the data from its connected software, to support the control and monitoring actions. In addition, each agent has the ability to cooperate with other agents in order to achieve a balance between the optimums. The generic internal agent architecture illustrated in Fig. 1 comprises the intelligent management, the communication

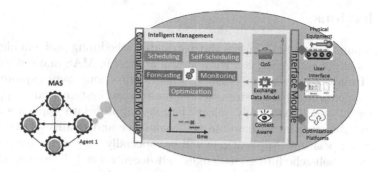

Fig. 1. Generic internal architecture of an agent.

module (inter-agent), the interface module (intra-agent) and the auxiliary modules, which the user can perform transparently.

Each agent is endowed with local autonomy and intelligence required to dynamically adapt to changes in the system. In this sense, the intelligent management module defines the several functions that are related to the acquisition and analysis of the distributed scheduling, comprising: scheduling, forecasting, self-scheduling, monitoring and optimization. The interface module provides, when needed, a connection to the physical devices, optimization platforms and/or displays information to the users using a friendly graphical user interface, which allows real-time monitoring of the scheduling state. These functions, as part of the intelligent management component, are complemented by the quality of service, exchange data model and context aware modules.

5 Preliminary Results and/or Evaluation Plan

The proposal will be applied to two different domains: in the manufacturing and in the Home Health Care (HHC). The manufacturing domain refers to the case study of a flexible manufacturing system production cell "AIP PRIMECA" [10]. In this sense, an approach and simulation has already been developed in this context, but using a simple dataset [1]. On the other hand, HHC services have significantly increased, namely in Portugal. The main idea is to find the schedule for home care visits for a certain day or days in a period horizon. A simulation has been carried out involving a real case study of a Health Unit in Bragança subject to unexpected events [2].

The simulations have benefited from a flexible architecture in obtaining optimized solutions providing an improvement in its usefulness. In turn, it was possible to offer, task effort distribution, reduced impact of broken resources and finally, fastest and most accurate reaction to changes or disruptions by agents. However, the scheduling comes from a centralized module, which in turn controls the simulation. The future goal will be to benefit from a distributed architecture for flexible scheduling solutions balancing the simple and fast reactions of the agents with the solutions by optimization methods to improve the utility.

6   Reflections

This paper points out and discusses the distributed scheduling problem highlighting the benefits of combining it with a swarm approach, MAS and optimization methods. To address such challenge, two major directions were explored. The first direction concerns the service-oriented multi-agent system swarm approach, to intelligently and dynamically select the most appropriate applications provided by reliable entities to increase the confidence and quality of the needed scheduling composition. Applications will be especially subject to reactive environments with self-scheduling challenges and decentralized decisions. The second direction consists of the combination of MAS with optimization methods for collaboration of optimized scheduling and thus obtain support for group decision-making.

In conclusion, the proposal can explore multidisciplinary domains. The applicability and optimization in different applications, such as manufacturing and home health care, can prove the dynamics in domains with emerging needs.

Acknowledgments. This work has been supported by FCT – Fundação para a Ciência e Tecnologia within the Projects Scope: UID/CEC/00319/2019.

References

1. Alves, F., Varela, M.L.R., Rocha, A.M.A.C., Pereira, A.I., Barbosa, J., Leitão, P.: Hybrid system for simultaneous job shop scheduling and layout optimization based on multi-agents and genetic algorithm. In: Madureira, A.M., Abraham, A., Gandhi, N., Varela, M.L. (eds.) HIS 2018. AISC, vol. 923, pp. 387–397. Springer, Cham (2020). https://doi.org/10.1007/978-3-030-14347-3_38
2. Alves, F., Pereira, A.I., Barbosa, J., Leitão, P.: Scheduling of home health care services based on multi-agent systems. In: Bajo, J., et al. (eds.) PAAMS 2018. CCIS, vol. 887, pp. 12–23. Springer, Cham (2018). https://doi.org/10.1007/978-3-319-94779-2_2
3. Çaliş, B., Bulkan, S.: A research survey: review of ai solution strategies of job shop scheduling problem. J. Intell. Manuf. **26**(5), 961–973 (2015)
4. Gen, M., Lin, L.: Multiobjective evolutionary algorithm for manufacturing scheduling problems: state-of-the-art survey. J. Intell. Manuf. **25**(5), 849–866 (2014). https://doi.org/10.1007/s10845-013-0804-4
5. Leitão, P., Barbosa, J.: Adaptive scheduling based on self-organized holonic swarm of schedulers. In: 2014 IEEE 23rd International Symposium on Industrial Electronics (ISIE), pp. 1706–1711, June 2014. https://doi.org/10.1109/ISIE.2014.6864872
6. Leitão, P., Restivo, F.: A holonic approach to dynamic manufacturing scheduling. Rob. Comput.-Integr. Manuf. **24**(5), 625–634 (2008)
7. Ouelhadj, D., Petrovic, S.: A survey of dynamic scheduling in manufacturing systems. J. Sched. **12**(4), 417 (2008)
8. Pinedo, M.L.: Scheduling: Theory, Algorithms, and Systems. Springer, Heidelberg (2016)
9. Trentesaux, D., Borangiu, T., Thomas, A.: Emerging ICT concepts for smart, safe and sustainable industrial systems. Comput. Ind. **81**, 1–10 (2016). https://doi.org/10.1016/j.compind.2016.05.001. http://www.sciencedirect.com/science/article/pii/S0166361516300665. ISSN 0166-3615

10. Trentesaux, D., et al.: Benchmarking flexible job-shop scheduling and control systems. Control Eng. Pract. **21**(9), 1204–1225 (2013)
11. Wooldridge, M.: An Introduction to MultiAgent Systems, 2nd edn. Wiley, Hoboken (2009)
12. Yang, Q., Yang, T., Li, W.: Smart Power Distribution Systems: Control, Communication, and Optimization. Elsevier Science, Amsterdam (2018)

GoOrg: Automated Organisational Chart Design for Open Multi-Agent Systems

Cleber Jorge Amaral[1,2]([✉]) [iD] and Jomi Fred Hübner[1] [iD]

[1] Federal University of Santa Catarina (UFSC), Florianópolis, SC, Brazil
jomi.hubner@ufsc.br
[2] Federal Institute of Santa Catarina (IFSC), São José, SC, Brazil
cleber.amaral@ifsc.edu.br
http://pgeas.ufsc.br/en/, http://www.ifsc.edu.br/

Abstract. The organisational structure is a key factor for open multi-agent systems. It is the way agents can enter into an organisation taking its position and cooperating to achieve mutual goals. In spite of its importance, there are few studies on automatic designers that generate explicit organisational structures. This paper introduces *GoOrg*, a proposal for automated design of organisations. Our designer uses as input a goals tree and other features such as necessary skills to achieve the goal, predicted workload and throughput. The output of *GoOrg* is an organisational chart. The generated structure, for instance, can be flatter or taller, accepting matrix connections of not, according to preferences and needing of more coordination levels.

Keywords: Automated organisational design · Organisational chart · Organisation's structure · Multi-Agent Systems

1 Introduction

The organisation structure is a way in which the activities of an organisation are split, organised and coordinated. It allows members to know where they fit relative to others and it reflects authority relations and responsibility for goals, providing a natural way to assign tasks [2]. An organisation structure is a key factor for large-scale Multi-Agent Systems (MAS) and open systems.

Currently, there are a few studies over automation of organisation design process that leads to explicit organisational structures [3,5]. Although seminal, these works still have limitations to overcome. This paper introduces *GoOrg*, an automated organisational designer that takes the organisational goals tree, looking for opportunities to gather goals into roles giving as output an organisation chart, an explicit organisational structure, according to preferences.

Supported by Petrobras project AG-BR, IFSC and UFSC.

2 Organisational Design

The organisation design is a process for choosing the best organisation class given necessary input such as goals, tasks and constraints to create aspects such as structure, strategy, leadership guidelines and so on [4]. In multi-agent systems, although there are few studies about automatic organisation designers, we have identified three classes of proposals.

The first class is *automated organisational structure designers* [3,5]. It considers as input organisation goals, available agents, resources and performance targets, and produces an explicit organisation, which may include roles, assignments of responsibilities, hierarchy and other relations. The main drawback of existing studies in this class is the requirement of several parameters including the modelling for each role, reducing its applicability when taking cost-benefit into account.

The second class is the *automated organisational design by task planning*. These designers create *problem-driven* organisations, for specific and generally temporal purposes. The organisational structure is not explicit and it usually is a casual result of a task distributing process. This class [1,6] creates organisations that are not suitable for open systems since the tasks were allocated to a particular MAS.

Finally, the third class is *self-organisational designers* [7]. These designers produce emergent organisations which are dynamic, may operate continuously, have overlapping tasks, have no external or central control, hierarchy and information flow in many directions. It usually overcome other classes in uncertainty scenarios. However, the structure is not carefully designed, and in open systems, entries and exits of agents make the system slower due to renegotiation processes.

3 Proposal

We have positioned our research on *automated organisational structure designer* class. The reasons for this choice are: (i) it is suitable to work in open systems; (ii) it helps to develop part of the organisation dimension; and (iii) its outcomes may be integrated into other planning techniques, reducing further efforts.

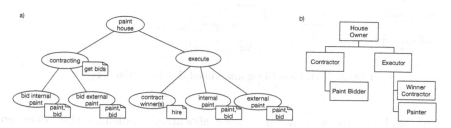

Fig. 1. Automated design for Paint a house example. (a) Inputs: goals tree and necessary skills. (b) Output: the less flat organisation chart

We propose the use of a state space search algorithm to apply in our designer, called *GoOrg*. It assigns goals to roles in a structured chart taking advantage of some characteristics of the goals such as the ones that have the same parent goal and requiring the same skills to be performed. Additionally, preferences can also determine whether to combine goals or not, e.g., if a *flatter* or *taller* organisation is preferred.

For example, in a goals tree for painting a house internally and externally it is necessary to contract agents to execute the tasks (Fig. 1). The *contracting* goal can be associated with the skill *get bids* and it may have as sub-goals: *bid internal paint* and *bid external paint*. Both sub-goals have the same necessary skills. The goal *execute* may have three sub-goals: *contract winner(s)*, *internal paint* and *external paint*. The first is associated with the skill *hire* and the others with skills *bid* and *paint*, similar to the sub-goals under *contracting* goal. In this example, the algorithm found that the sub-goals related to *contracting* could be gathered in the same role called *Paint Bidder*. The same has occurred in *execute* goal, where the *Painter* role was created.

For the next step of our research, the designing process is being split into two phases: the organisational chart designer and the binding phase. With this separation, it is expected that *GoOrg* becomes more suitable to deal with asynchronous changes on the system's resources availability and redesign requests. To enhance the first phase, we will add on each goal the predicted workload, necessary resources, communication topics, and predicted throughput (white shapes of Fig. 2). The expected workload can be used to determine how many agents should play the same role or if the same agent should perform more than one role. With communication topics and throughput, the hierarchy levels and departmentalisation can be set. In both phases, it is proposed to consider agents and artifacts availability as an input parameter.

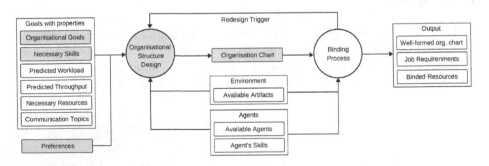

Fig. 2. Goal based Organisational designer (GoOrg).

The binding process can solve some allocation challenges that does not require a redesign. To illustrate it, consider that *external paint* goal also needs *scaffold use* skill. Consider that *agent A* and *agent B* play, respectively, the roles *internal paint* and *external paint* having all the necessary skills to play both.

Consider now that *agent B* left the system and *agent C* has joined it, but this agent has no *scaffold use* skill. The binding process can move *agent A* to *external paint* role, assigning *agent C* to *internal paint* role.

Finally, we will evaluate our solution using existing domains [1,3,5]. The goals tree and other aspects for these domains will be manually identified and we will firstly evaluate the amount of necessary input parameter needed for *GoOrg*. With these input, the ability of *GoOrg* to properly design organisations will be evaluated. These situations will be simulated to check if the organisations are able to fulfil the goals, in this sense, the evaluation will be qualitative. The preferences will be varied to evaluate different configurations and their impact on the output.

4   Conclusion

This paper has presented a proposal for an automated organisational designer based on goals and their properties as input. The current status of this research shows that it is feasible to draw an organisational chart only based on organisation's aspects, in other words, it is not necessary to build complex models as input. Besides the organisation chart, an extra outcome of *GoOrg* may be some decentralised task planning input since this study is also expecting to bind agents and roles. The previous allocation of resources is a guarantee that when running, this system will be able to have a well formed organisation. About evaluation criteria, we intended to consider the model of known domains and test if *GoOrg* is able to build suitable structures.

References

1. Cardoso, R.C., Bordini, R.H.: A modular framework for decentralised multi-agent planning. In: Proceedings of the 16th Conference on Autonomous Agents and MultiAgent Systems, pp. 1487–1489, São Paulo, Brazil (2017)
2. Hatch, M.: Organization Theory: Modern, Symbolic, and Postmodern Perspectives. Oxford University Press, Oxford (1997)
3. Horling, B., Lesser, V.: Using quantitative models to search for appropriate organizational designs. Auton. Agent. Multi-Agent Syst. **16**(2), 95–149 (2008)
4. Pattison, H.E., Corkill, D.D., Lesser, V.R.: Instantiating descriptions of organizational structures. In: Huhns, M.N. (ed.) Distributed Artificial Intelligence, pp. 59–96 (1987). Chap. 3
5. Sims, M., Corkill, D., Lesser, V.: Automated organization design for multi-agent systems. Auton. Agent. Multi-Agent Syst. **16**(2), 151–185 (2008)
6. Sleight, J., Durfee, E.H.: Organizational design principles and techniques for decision-theoretic agents. In: International Foundation for Autonomous Agents and Multiagent Systems, AAMAS 2013, pp. 463–470, Richland, SC (2013)
7. Ye, D., Zhang, M., Vasilakos, A.V.: A survey of self-organisation mechanisms in multi-agent systems. IEEE Trans. SMC Syst. **47**(3), 441–461 (2016)

Data Analysis Platform for the Optimization of Employability in Technological Profiles

Pablo Chamoso$^{(\boxtimes)}$, Alfonso González-Briones,
and Francisco José García-Peñalvo

Department of Computer Science and Automation, University of Salamanca,
Plaza de los Caídos s/n, Salamanca, Spain
{chamoso,alfonsogb,fgarcia}@usal.es

Abstract. The information technology (IT) sector has not only created the largest number of jobs but has also contributed to greater employability in other sectors. Thanks to major advances in computing, the analysis of large volumes of data for extraction of information unknown a priori, has become a trend in all sectors and its benefits and advantages are unquestionable. The aim of this research work is to extract knowledge from employability information for market trend analysis and use this knowledge to adapt the user's search for work to their profile and guide them accordingly. To this end, existing employability and training information will be retrieved, analysed and a platform will be created to allow the user to easily visualise the results, enabling users with no knowledge of data analysis to perform studies based on machine learning.

Keywords: Employability · Machine learning · Learning

1 Problem Statement

In our society, employability is a major concern [1]. One significant way in which a person's employability can increase is through training. Citizens are interested in receiving training because it will help increase their job opportunities and give them a give them a greater range of job options to choose from, being able to choose job positions with characteristics that best suit their profile [2]. Therefore, we can conclude that training is one of the main factors, although not the only one, that affect employability. So much so that, according to the University Employability and Employment Barometer, Master's edition, 2017, 90.58% of students who have earned their first master's degree would re-enrol in another master's programme [3]. These statistics reflect the desire to continue training and developing professionally in order to get better employment opportunities.

Furthermore, the technological advances that took place over the last decade have led to the availability of large amounts of information on the Internet [4], this information, which previously seemed to have no added value, can now provide valuable knowledge through information processing and extraction.

© Springer Nature Switzerland AG 2019
F. De la Prieta et al. (Eds.): PAAMS 2019 Workshops, CCIS 1047, pp. 322–325, 2019.
https://doi.org/10.1007/978-3-030-24299-2_29

The aim of this research work is to study possible forms of approaching the employability, training and technology sectors for knowledge extraction. The challenge lies in providing the extracted knowledge to users who are actively seeking employment, making it easy for them to understand market trends or the characteristics of the best paid jobs or get information about additional training they can receive to be able to find a job with their target salary.

There is a great variety of portals and social networks that aim to help users find employment, such as Infojobs, Tecnoempleo, Monster, XING, LinkedIn or beBee, but for the moment, none of them offer training guidance to the user to help them get the job they want.

The aim of this research is to design a platform capable of executing and evaluating a set of machine learning algorithms that allow for the extraction of all this information in a way that is simple for the user.

The most comprehensive example are IT professionals, as there is a high demand for such professionals and the range of possibilities and specializations is large enough (according to the data provided by the job search site, Infojobs), for this reason our research focuses on this specific case. To perform a market trend analysis, data are going to be obtained from external sources, such as different data repositories, job search websites for IT professionals or IT courses.

2 Hypothesis and Objectives

At present, there are no platforms that would autonomously analyze a user's profile and make suggestions or recommendations on the training that would help the user get a job with the characteristics specified by the user or with even better conditions. Unfortunately, current platforms are limited to making job recommendations on the basis of the user's current experience and skills [5].

People who choose to do some kind of training to increase their possibilities of getting a job, usually base their selection on personal recommendations or on a manual internet search, information they find on forums or specialized training portals [6]. However, these methods of selecting a training are limited and normally the choice of a training course is made before all the possibilities have been considered.

Thanks to computer tools such as crawlers or web scrapping, the compilation of the different possibilities can be carried out automatically [7] and this information can be analysed quickly by means of machine learning, providing users with a summary of the information or a series of recommendations that will guide them on a personalized basis [8].

In this way, the objectives to be achieved through the development of this doctoral thesis work are: (i) To perform an in-depth analysis of the state of art in terms of the key aspects related to the focus of this research work (of the employability and technological sectors, of recommender systems and of data analysis methodologies, mainly of those based on machine learning); (ii) To design a data analysis platform; (iii) To develop a methodology for the optimisation of employability in the technology sector; (iv) To implement the designed platform using the proposed methodology; (v) To design a case study; (vi) To evaluate, at different levels, the results obtained in the case study.

3   Proposal

The proposal (see Fig. 1) involves retrieving information on employability from different sources (existing portals or open data sets already existing in repositories) and from online training portals. These data will ideally be retrieved through official APIs or, if not available, we will consider the possibility of developing crawlers for the retrieval of information and information updates.

The recovered information will be stored in NoSQL (Not only Structured Query Language) databases and will be used by the machine learning layer for automatic learning, always using existing libraries (the development of new algorithms is not the goal of this work). Users will interact with the developed system through a dashboard, where they will state their professional profile information and pursued career objectives and where users will be able to visualize the results in an interactive way.

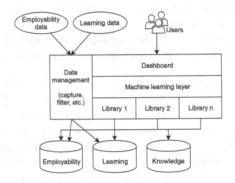

Fig. 1. Proposal schema.

4   Evaluation Plan

The main methodology followed in the evaluation of the research is Action-Research [9], which makes it possible to define a series of cycles that are evaluated and the obtained feedback is taken into account in the subsequent cycles. Thus, three main cycles have been planned:

1. First cycle - analysis of job vacancies for IT professionals
    - "Plan": Initially, the strategy will be to retrieve information on employability from technology profiles. The algorithms to be applied for knowledge extraction will be determined.
    - "Act": The necessary information will then be retrieved according to the plan and the algorithms will be applied.
    - "Observe": Preliminary results will then be analysed and the findings will be interpreted.

- "Reflect": Finally, possible changes are identified and the exact information to be from the profiles will be defined, since at this point we will have knowledge of the market trends.
2. Second cycle - analysis of technological profiles
   - "Plan": The strategy for retrieving technology profile information from the knowledge extracted in the first cycle is planned.
   - "Act": Retrieval of the profile information stated in the plan and application of machine learning methodologies to this information.
   - "Observe": Preliminary results will then be analysed and the findings will be interpreted.
   - "Reflect": Finally, technological trends will be identified and it will be analysed whether other types of information on technological job vacancies should be extracted to possibly improve the results.
3. Third cycle - recommendation of training to users.
   - "Plan": Strategy plan for the joint use the information extracted in previous cycles.
   - "Act": Cross-checking of previously collected data and application of methodologies according to the defined strategy.
   - "Observe": Analysis of the quality of results that are obtained on the basis of different adjustments.
   - "Reflect": Case study designed to validate the developed system.

References

1. Marx, P.: The effect of job insecurity and employability on preferences for redistribution in Western Europe. J. Eur. Soc. Policy **24**(4), 351–366 (2014)
2. Wheeler, A., Austin, S., Glass, J.: E-mentoring for employability. In: EE2012–Innovation, Practice and Research in Engineering Education, pp. 1–9 (2012)
3. Martínez, J.M., Vázquez-Ingelmo, A., García-Peñalvo, F.J., Michavila, F., Martín-González, M., Cruz-Benito, J.: Barómetro de empleabilidad y empleo universitarios. Edición Máster 2017. Observatorio de Empleabilidad y Empleo Universitarios (2018)
4. Chen, M., Mao, S., Liu, Y.: Big data: a survey. Mob. Netw. Appl. **19**(2), 171–209 (2014)
5. Chamoso, P., Rivas, A., Rodríguez, S., Bajo, J.: Relationship recommender system in a business and employment-oriented social network. Inf. Sci. **433**, 204–220 (2018)
6. Spink, A., Jansen, B.J.: A study of web search trends. Webology **1**(2), 4 (2004)
7. Slamet, C., Andrian, R., Maylawati, D.S.A., Darmalaksana, W., Ramdhani, M.A.: Web scraping and Naïve Bayes classification for job search engine. In: IOP Conference Series: Materials Science and Engineering, vol. 288, no. 1, p. 012038. IOP Publishing, January 2018
8. García-Peñalvo, F.J., Cruz-Benito, J., Martín-González, M., Vázquez-Ingelmo, A., Sánchez-Prieto, J.C., Therón, R.: Proposing a machine learning approach to analyze and predict employment and its factors. Int. J. Interact. Multimedia Artif. Intell. **5**(2), 39–45 (2018)
9. Schwaber, K.: Scrum development process. In: Sutherland, J., Casanave, C., Miller, J., Patel, P., Hollowell, G. (eds.) Business Object Design and Implementation, pp. 117–134. Springer, London (1997). https://doi.org/10.1007/978-1-4471-0947-1_11

Inclusive AI in Recruiting. Multi-agent Systems Architecture for Ethical and Legal Auditing

Carmen Fernández[(✉)] and Alberto Fernández

CETINIA, Universidad Rey Juan Carlos, Madrid, Spain
carmen.urjc@gmail.com, alberto.fernandez@urjc.es

Abstract. Artificial Intelligence (AI) domain-specific applications may have different ethical and legal implications depending on the domain. One of the current questions of the AI is the challenges behind the analysis of job video-interviews. There are pros and cons to using AI in recruitment processes, and potential ethical and legal consequences for candidates, companies and states. There is a deficit of regulation of these systems, and a need for external and neutral auditing of the types of analysis made in interviews. I propose a multi-agent system architecture for neutral auditing to guarantee a fair, inclusive and accurate AI and to reduce potential discrimination, for example on the basis of race or gender, in the job market.

Keywords: Domain specific AI · Ethics · Human Resources · Recruiting

1 Introduction to Research Question

Traditionally, Ai proved very valuable for resume and keywords scanning and for extraction of candidate skills devoid of bias. There has been a recent trend towards video-interview analysis in Human Resources. The survey by Personnel Today found that 38% of enterprises are already using AI in their workplace with 62% expecting to use it by 2018. In this research we address such a current issue of the AI.

Concerning video-interview systems, there are limitations, some are attributable to the very nature of the technology (incorrect or biased datasets) and other are related to the human bias or the specific agenda of the recruiting company. It is common measuring eye time or candidate response time. However, the state-of-the-art of image analysis may allow pre-selecting with respect to age or sexual orientation or other controversial characteristics. The analyses could lead to ethical and legal consequences (e.g. in some countries is forbidden to ask for age in processes). This is why fostering proper auditing of video-interview systems it is particularly important.

2 Problem Statement

There has been a recent trend towards video-interview analysis in HR depart-ments. Traditionally, AI played no more than an assistant role in HR, e.g. resume and CV

© Springer Nature Switzerland AG 2019
F. De la Prieta et al. (Eds.): PAAMS 2019 Workshops, CCIS 1047, pp. 326–329, 2019.
https://doi.org/10.1007/978-3-030-24299-2_30

scanning. But lately, apps and systems like HireVue[1], Montage[2], SparkHire[3] and WePow[4] have been changing how recruitment is carried out. An AI-based video interview system could be programmed to check, during an interview, features such as age, lighting, tone of voice, cadence, keywords used (substantial conversation), mood, behaviour (eccentric, movement or quite calm and not talkative), eye contact and, above all, emotions. AI targets the specific traits of a customer-oriented role that employers want in their teams.

AI has produced benefits for HR so far, including recruiting time and customised questions and answers. Attention to detail (eye contact time, emotions-intonation and body language) and lack of interviewer bias (physical appearance, tattoos, etc.) are other additional advantages.

But there are several problems that accompany the use of these technologies; for example, candidates are unfamiliar with video-interview analysis (for example, light-ing, settings), which could affect global performance. It is necessary to point out the Gender and racial bias and the imprecisions of technology. Traditionally, machine learning algorithms were trained with data from white people or biased datasets. For instance, Affectiva[5] dataset of human emotions was fed with data from Superbowl viewers, and could presumably have culture-bias.

We studied several potential controversial characteristics, among them, facial symmetry, race, gender, sexual orientations in voice and image recordings. The problem of racial-bias in AI is not new, just like the detection of mixed race in bad lighting conditions according to Siyao et al. [1]. As an illustration of the advances in sexual orientation recognition both in images and sound, one study [2] needed ethical supervision due to the opaque invasive nature of the research and the use of real user data from dating applications. Researchers argue that there is a relationship among homosexuality, morphological features e.g. jawline and exposure to particular con-centrations of hormones in the womb.

With reference to Ethical and legal aspects of AI, whilst the use of AI in this context may have its benefits, it also strips away aspects of humanity, reducing a human recruit to a set of descriptors. The automation of HR processes could lead to potential ethical and legal implications that cannot be ignored. In some countries, companies are not allowed to ask a candidate's age during recruitment. Traditionally, United States legislation has been particularly protective of racial discrimination in the workplace (the Civil Rights Act, 1964, for-bids "improperly classifying or segregating employees by race"). And yet, even while these regulations exist to reduce discrimi-nation, enterprises are given more and more freedom to customise their systems. We conclude it is risky to blindly follow the adoption of AI in recruiting.

---

[1] https://www.hirevue.com/.

[2] https://www.montagetalent.com.

[3] https://www.sparkhire.com.

[4] https://wwww.wepow.com/es.

[5] https://www.affectiva.com.

3   Related Work

Multi-agent systems pose similar challenges concerning information formats that traditional complex distributed systems and the problem is more acute in firms.

The **current approach** is the definition of agents tasks and implementations and the exploration of both MAS and ontologies and shared lexicons, which foster domain specification and interoperability, idea supported in previous works [3] so as to the introduction of MAS in complex corporate settings such as manufacturing industry. Additionally, we supported our research on previous works in legal formalization [4].

4   Hypothesis and Proposal

The Hypothesis behind our research is that automatization of tasks and the introduction of proper auditing could improve the business processes in Human Resources. To achieve this goal and solve the research problem of automatization and more ethical and legal auditing I am going to rely on the integration of ontologies into Multi-Agent Systems for Auditing in Human Resources.

The most relevant innovation of this proposed work will be the attempt to automatise part of this legal and ethical auditing as well as some analyses carried out by the different distributed agents. The **specific contribution** and progress made thus so far is mainly the proposal of a Multi-agent systems architecture for auditing HR (Fig. 1). Additionally, there has been prototyping of some parts - legal rules engine.

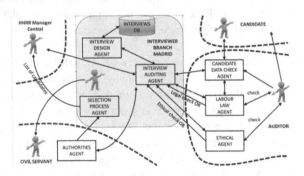

Fig. 1. Multi-agent systems architecture

The core of the architecture comprises three different parties that must collaborate: (i) a recruiter/company, (ii) external auditor, and (iii) government/authorities. An **Interview design agent**, based at the company central headquarters, is responsible for designing a general interview. The **Interview auditing agent** is based in company branches and applies the general interview format to a regional scenario of the country where the recruiting is taking place. The **Selection process agent** can cancel the process due to controversies or giveback a list of candidates to the central office if the process is fair. It is also capable of running checks with authorities and auditors. If the features analysed in the recruiting process break any law or if the process contravenes basic civil rights, the inter-view process agent would ask for the approval of the **Labour Law Agent** or **Ethical Agent** if necessary. If the recruiting process is dealing with a candidate's personal information, it would require the candidate's approval.

5 Preliminary Results and/or Evaluation Plan

Concerning limits, so far I am in the process of producing theoretical work and submitted automatization of legal auditing/prototyping of legal rules engine concerning Spanish and US Law. As the doctoral work advances, we will see if we could address in all detail the architecture or just the automatization of the legal auditing, if it involves hundreds of rules. There is an absence of affordable and limited testing opportunities of real corporate applications so we are counting on prototyping on simulated corporate scenario. The testing is very dependent on data availability, use of different ontologies and the real attributed measured by video-interview systems. Legal reasoning entails the correct formalization of laws and technical supervision of jurists.

6 Reflections

As a conclusion, we summarize the expected results. The **contribution of this PhD** is, therefore, the automatization. The benefits of our research, if successful, will be a step forward in the automatization of tasks in Human Resources and ethical and legal analyses of video-interview techniques. The trend is towards full automatization.

Acknowledgements. Work partially supported by the Spanish Ministry of Science, Innovation and Universities, co-funded by EU FEDER Funds, through grants TIN2015-65515-C4-4-R and RTI2018-095390-B-C33.

References

1. Siyao, F., Haibo, H., Zeng-Guang, H.: Learning from face: a survey. IEEE Trans. Pattern Anal. Mach. Intel **36**(12), 2483–2509 (2014)
2. Kosinski, M., Wang, Y.: Deep neural networks are more accurate than humans at detecting sexual orientation from images. J. Pers. Soc. Psychol. **114**(2), 246–257 (2018)
3. DiLeo, J., DeLoach, S.: Integrating ontologies into multiagent systems engineering. Air Univ Maxwell AFB AI Centre for Aerospace Doctrine Research and Educ. (2006)
4. Walker, V.R.: A default-logic framework for legal reasoning in multiagent systems. In: AAAI Fall Symposium. Technical report, pp. 88–95 (2006)

A Multi-agent System to Manage Users and Spaces in a Adaptive Environment System

Pedro Filipe Oliveira[1,2(✉)], Paulo Novais[1], and Paulo Matos[2]

[1] Department of Informatics, Algoritmi Centre/University of Minho, Braga, Portugal
pjon@di.uminho.pt
[2] Department of Informatics and Communications,
Institute Polytechnic of Bragança, Bragança, Portugal
{poliveira,pmatos}@ipb.pt

Abstract. This paper, deals with the actual problem of manage user preferences and local specifications on an IoT adaptive system, namely using a multi agent system to achieve a Smart Environment System. On a new era of interaction between persons and physical spaces, users want those spaces smartly adapt to their preferences in a transparent way. To achieve that, new approaches are needed. In this project we develop a multi agent system architecture with different layers to achieve a solution that entails all the proposed objectives.

Keywords: Adaptive-system · AmI · Multi-agent · IoT

1 Introduction

The Artificial Intelligence field continues with an exponential growth rate, especially in the different sectors applicability. Currently, multi-agent systems have been used to solve diverse situations.

Particularly in the AmI field, which is characterized by the creation of ubiquitous environments, interconnecting different technologies to perform common tasks of the user's daily life, autonomously, proactively and independently of the interaction of this [3].

This project proposes as well, a solution using a multi-agent system. Next, the problem will be detailed, as well as a solution proposal, which includes all the architecture developed, that later will be implemented and tested.

2 Materials and Methods

This work proposes an autonomous Smart Home model, controlled through cognitive agents, which get the final information to be applied by the actuators.

For do that, a house with five divisions was prototyped with different comfort features, namely temperature, luminosity, audio and video.

The considered parameters for performance evaluation are as follows:

© Springer Nature Switzerland AG 2019
F. De la Prieta et al. (Eds.): PAAMS 2019 Workshops, CCIS 1047, pp. 330–333, 2019.
https://doi.org/10.1007/978-3-030-24299-2_31

- Number of agents used;
- Agent speed reasoning;
- Information filtering;
- Environment perception time;

Figure 1, shows the scenario of an environment where it intends to develop this work. Explaining this figure, it can be seen the user who through its different devices (smartphone, wearable, and other compatible) communicates with the system, and for that can be used different technologies, like Near Field Communication (NFC) [7], Bluetooth Low Energy (BLE) [1] and Wi-Fi Direct [2]. Next, the system performs communication with the Cloud, to validate the information. And then the system will perform the management of the different components in the environment (climatization systems, security systems, other smart systems) (Fig. 2).

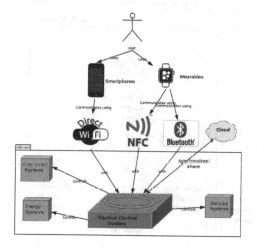

Fig. 1. Problem statement

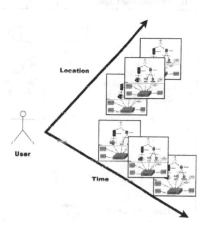

Fig. 2. Contextualization of time/ environment dimensions

To optimize the predictions of the solution proposed, an architecture for a multi-agent system was defined. The roles that each agent should represent, as well as the negotiation process to be taken, and the different scenarios in which this negotiation should take place and the way it should be processed were specified.

This work resulted in the complete specification of an architecture that supports the solution found, to solve the presented problem. It will now be implemented, tested and validated using real case studies, so as to gather statistical information to assess its effectiveness and performance in the context of application.

This work aims to give continuity and finalize the doctoral work presented in previous editions [4–6]. Thus the following Fig. 3 exemplifies in a global way the architecture of the system where this work has been carried out.

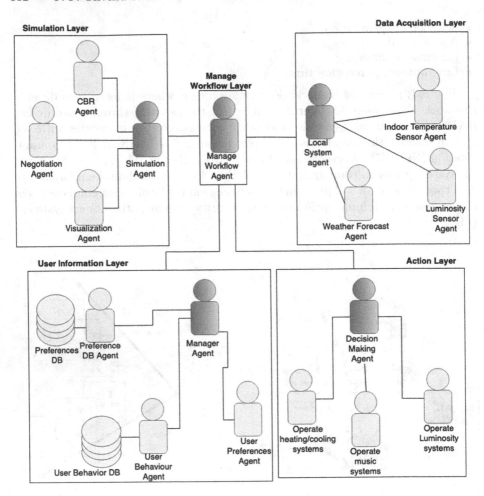

Fig. 3. Architecture of the multi-agent system

3   Results

Figure 3 represent the architecture separation into different layers, to be easily identified the purpose of each, and agents containing it.

The layers description is as follows:

- **Data acquisition layer**, which will import the necessary information for the agents operation, namely information of interior and exterior temperature and light sensors.
- **User layer**, in this layer we will have an agent that will represent each user and his preferences that must be taken into account in the negotiation process.
- **Local System layer,** here each local system will be represented by an agent, which contains all the information necessary to this location, either

the referred to user preferences, or local/users security (maximum/minimum temperature, safety values for CO2, etc.).

- **Simulation layer**, in this layer will be the negotiation between the different agents involved, namely the management of conflicts between the different users and local systems. After the negotiation process ends we will have as result the values to apply in the place.
- **Action layer**, after the process is executed in the simulation layer, and the values to be applied are obtained. These values are used in this layer and sent to the actuators that will apply them in the different automation systems present the local.

4   Discussion and Conclusions

The agent system modeling is fully developed. The whole structure of data acquisition, to feed the information acquisition layer, is also completed. At this stage the agent layer is being developed and will be subsequently implemented for testing in the testing environment developed for this project.

Acknowledgement. This work has been supported by FCT Fundação para a Ciência e Tecnologia within the Project Scope: UID/CEC/00319/2019.

References

1. Bluetooth Specification: Bluetooth core specification version 4.0. Specification of the Bluetooth System (2010)
2. Camps-Mur, D., Garcia-Saavedra, A., Serrano, P.: Device-to-device communications with Wi-Fi direct: overview and experimentation. Wirel. Commun. IEEE **20**(3), 96–104 (2013)
3. Chaouche, A.-C., El Fallah Seghrouchni, A., Ilié, J.-M., Saïdouni, D.E.: A higher-order agent model with contextual planning management for ambient systems. In: Kowalczyk, R., Nguyen, N.T. (eds.) Transactions on Computational Collective Intelligence XVI. LNCS, vol. 8780, pp. 146–169. Springer, Heidelberg (2014). https://doi.org/10.1007/978-3-662-44871-7_6
4. Oliveira, P., Matos, P., Novais, P.: Behaviour analysis in smart spaces. In: 2016 Intl IEEE Conferences on Ubiquitous Intelligence & Computing, Advanced and Trusted Computing, Scalable Computing and Communications, Cloud and Big Data Computing, Internet of People, and Smart World Congress (UIC/ATC/ScalCom/CBDCom/IoP/SmartWorld), pp. 880–887. IEEE (2016)
5. Oliveira, P., Novais, P., Matos, P.: Challenges in smart spaces: aware of users, preferences, behaviours and habits. In: De la Prieta, F., et al. (eds.) PAAMS 2017. AISC, vol. 619, pp. 268–271. Springer, Cham (2018). https://doi.org/10.1007/978-3-319-61578-3_34
6. Oliveira, P., Pedrosa, T., Novais, P., Matos, P.: Towards to secure an IoT adaptive environment system. In: Rodríguez, S., et al. (eds.) DCAI 2018. AISC, vol. 801, pp. 349–352. Springer, Cham (2019). https://doi.org/10.1007/978-3-319-99608-0_43
7. Want, R.: Near field communication. IEEE Pervasive Comput. **10**(3), 4–7 (2011)

Towards Self-managing Systems Through Decentralised Constraint Optimisation

Charles Harold[✉]

Swinburne University of Technology, Melbourne, Australia
charold@swin.edu.au

Abstract. With increases in cyber threats and network complexity the need for self-managing systems that can heal, optimise and coordinate themselves is becoming paramount. Self-managing systems encompass numerous properties, often referred to as self-* properties. This dissertation proposal hypothesises that using Distributed Constraint Optimisation (DisCO) to model each self-* properties yields a decentralised system whereby attacks on individual management nodes can be isolated. Consequently, the proposed dissertation seeks to address the challenges associated with realising self-* properties as DisCO problems.

Keywords: Self-managing systems · Self-adapting systems ·
Decentralised self-managing systems ·
Decentralised self-adapting systems

1 Motivation

In a world of persistent, pervasive and increasingly sophisticated cyber threats, focus from Government, Defence and Industry has been directed at creating *resilient* cyber systems. Cyber resilience refers to the ability of a system to *"[...] anticipate, withstand, recover from, and adapt to adverse conditions, stresses, attacks, or compromises on cyber resources"* [5]. As argued in [2,3,7] self-management is crucial in realising the goals of cyber resilience. Moreover, as interconnectivity between networks increases (e.g., cyber-physical systems, military information systems, IoT platforms), having systems that can validate and manage their behaviour autonomously is paramount [7,16]. Thus, it follows that realising self-managing systems is key in both modern resilient cyber systems [3] and in dealing with the growing uncertainty caused by large open computing ecosystems [16]. Yet, realising such systems in a concrete way presents a multitude of challenges, including problems related to: decentralisation [3,7], self-representation [2,3], establishing guarantees on run-time behaviour [12] and many others [16,17]. Recently proposed techniques realising self-management through Constraint Satisfaction (CS) (e.g., [2,3,14]) have shown promising progress in addressing many of the aforementioned issues. However, associated challenges require further investigation to yield efficient and robust solutions.

© Springer Nature Switzerland AG 2019
F. De la Prieta et al. (Eds.): PAAMS 2019 Workshops, CCIS 1047, pp. 334–338, 2019.
https://doi.org/10.1007/978-3-030-24299-2_32

Consequently, the proposed dissertation aims to address the challenges of applying constraint based techniques in the design of state-of-the-art decentralised self-managing systems.

2   Background

Driven by growing system complexity [1, 16] and cyber-security concerns [5, 7], an abundance of research has sought to classify the elements required to instantiate self-management, yielding a collection of self-* properties (e.g., self-healing, self-protecting, self-optimising, self-configuring, self-immunity, self-organising, self-scaling, self-containing and self-improving [4, 11]). Commonly, these managing components are separated from the main application and create a feedback control loop (typically each element requires its own loop, i.e., self-healing loop). These loops often use the MAPE-K model (a sequence of Monitoring, Analysing, Planing and Executing over the system, interconnected by a Knowledge base) [1]. Within large, complex and heterogeneous systems (such as modern resilient cyber systems) multiple MAPE-K loops are typically used to realise self-management. Numerous patterns for decentralisation of these loops have been suggested [17]. However, designing coordination patterns and interactions protocols between loops remains a crucial challenge [16, 17].

One defining feature of self-managing systems is that their behaviour is *adaptive*. A recurring problem in the design of self-adaptive systems pertains to putting assurances on their behaviour [12]. Numerous approaches have been proposed to create assurances on adaptive behaviour, including: adaptable requirements specifications [6, 18], constraint based approaches [2, 14] and control theory [8]. Of particular relevance to the proposed dissertation is the use of Distributed Constraint Satisfaction (DisCS) as a means of modelling *decentralised* Analysis in the self-healing loop [2, 3, 14]. In these examples the managed network state is mapped to a finite set of variable assignments. Subsequently, agents are given dominion over value assignments to particular variables; comparison of local value assignments with known constraints (CS) and unknown constraints held by other agents (DisCS) classifies the system state as: optimum, degraded or compromised.

A benefit of such approaches [2, 3, 14] is that guarantees on system behaviour can be made at design time. Conversely, a limitation is that design time constraints cannot be adapted to evolving run-time challenges. Engineering such flexibility is a key goal of adaptable requirements languages, such as the temporal requirements language RELAX [18]. Moreover, a method for adding flexibility to constraint problems that has seen little attention in the field of self-adaptive systems is DisCOptimization (DisCO)[1]. Subsequently, using temporal requirements languages to create DisCO Problems (DisCOP) that can yield both flexible and predictable adaptive behaviour is an important (unrealised) extension

---

[1] DisCO is an extension of DisCS, a formulation is where the satisfaction of individual constraints is weighted [13], i.e., satisfying a constraint yields some reward. Subsequently, satisfaction of constraints yielding the highest aggregated rewards corresponds to an optimal solution.

to the models proposed in [2,3,14]. An apparent limitation of such an approach relates to computational complexity of CSPs/COPs. Creating effectively solvable DisCOPs ultimately relates to how the original COP is decomposed into sub problems [19], which is a well studied problem [9].

3   Hypothesis, Proposal and Research Questions

Following on from results in the application of DisCS to analysis in self-healing [2,14] and planning [15], it seems apparent that self-healing (requiring both analysis and planning) may be modelled as a DisCSP [2,3]. Furthermore, if requirements languages such as RELAX can be translated into DisCOPs, it then seems plausible that other self-managing properties may be realised through solving DisCOPs. I hypothesise that using DisCOPs to model the analysis and planning components of each self-* property within a self-managing system has several advantages, including:

1. Each of these DisCOPs can be solved in a *concurrent* manner, eliminating the need for large or nested MAPE-K loops. Such an approach can be considered a type of coordinated control pattern. A notable benefit of such patterns is that the burden of self-management is spread over a variety of nodes [17].
2. Through obfuscation techniques [10] it may be possible to hide how individual agent behaviour influences others in the network. For example, by hashing variable names with different salts it may be intractable for any single agent to model other agents constraints. Thus, individuals cannot understand how their (detrimental) behaviour may influence the wider system, making sabotage from a small subset of nodes ineffective.

Subsequently, the primary goal of the proposed dissertation is to *address the challenges of applying DisCO in the design of state-of-the-art decentralised self-managing systems*. Based on the above hypothesis and goal, this research will be guided by the following key questions.

RQ1: How can temporal aspects of requirements languages be incorporated into existing constraint based frameworks and how can the subsequent local CO be guaranteed to reach the desired emergent (system level) behaviour?

RQ2: How can concurrent DisCOPs interact to share knowledge and/or adapt constraints and optimisation functions without adversely affecting real-time operations?

RQ3: How can tractability of both local COPs and global DisCOPs be assured? Furthermore, how can redundancy of agents be added without making the corresponding workload intractable?

4   Future Research Plan and Core Outcomes

Answering RQ1 and RQ2 will first require a review of the literature related to requirements languages, COPs, DisCOPs, concurrency and conflict resolution. Subsequent implementation will without-doubt provide ample motivation to extend upon our preliminary ideas. Subject to initial success, RQ3 will then require examination of the literature related to decomposition, specifically with a focus on, separation, parallelization, optimisation and simplification. At its conclusion, this dissertation will provide a re-usable software component that can bestow features of self-management (and subsequently resilience) upon heterogeneous system infrastructures.

References

1. Arcaini, P., Riccobene, E., Scandurra, P.: Modeling and analyzing MAPE-K feedback loops for self-adaptation. In: Proceedings of the 10th International Symposium on Software Engineering for Adaptive and Self-Managing Systems, pp. 13–23. IEEE Press (2015)
2. Chhetri, M.B., Luong, H., Uzunov, A.V., et al.: ADSL: an embedded domain-specific language for constraint-based distributed self-management. In: 2018 25th Australasian Software Engineering Conference (ASWEC), pp. 101–110. IEEE (2018)
3. Chhetri, M.B., Uzunov, A.V., Vo, Q.B., et al.: AWaRE - towards distributed self-management for resilient cyber systems. In: 2018 23rd International Conference on Engineering of Complex Computer Systems (ICECCS), pp. 101–110. IEEE (2018)
4. Berns, A., Ghosh, S.: Dissecting self-* properties. In: Third IEEE International Conference on Self-Adaptive and Self-Organizing System 2009, SASO 2009, pp. 10–19. IEEE (2009)
5. Bodeau, D., Graubart, R.: Cyber resiliency design principles. Technical report, The MITRE Corporation (2017). https://www.mitre
6. Cheng, B.H.C., Sawyer, P., Bencomo, N., Whittle, J.: A goal-based modeling approach to develop requirements of an adaptive system with environmental uncertainty. In: Schürr, A., Selic, B. (eds.) MODELS 2009. LNCS, vol. 5795, pp. 468–483. Springer, Heidelberg (2009). https://doi.org/10.1007/978-3-642-04425-0_36
7. Couture, M., Charpentier, R., Dagenais, M., Hamou-Lhadj, A., Gherbi, A.: Self-defence of information systems in cyber-space-a critical overview. Technical report, Defence Research And Development Canada Valcartier (QUEBEC) (2010)
8. Filieri, A., Hoffmann, H., Maggio, M.: Automated design of self-adaptive software with control-theoretical formal guarantees. In: Proceedings of the 36th International Conference on Software Engineering, pp. 299–310. ACM (2014)
9. Gottlob, G., Leone, N., Scarcello, F.: A comparison of structural CSP decomposition methods. Artif. Intell. **124**(2), 243–282 (2000)
10. Grinshpoun, T., Tassa, T.: P-SyncBB: a privacy preserving branch and bound DCOP algorithm. J. Artif. Intell. Res. **57**, 621–660 (2016)
11. Huebscher, M.C., McCann, J.A.: A survey of autonomic computing degrees, models, and applications. ACM Comput. Surv. (CSUR) **40**(3), 7 (2008)
12. de Lemos, R., et al.: Software engineering for self-adaptive systems: research challenges in the provision of assurances. In: de Lemos, R., Garlan, D., Ghezzi, C., Giese, H. (eds.) Software Engineering for Self-Adaptive Systems III. Assurances. LNCS, vol. 9640, pp. 3–30. Springer, Cham (2017). https://doi.org/10.1007/978-3-319-74183-3_1
13. Modi, P.J., Shen, W.M., et al.: An asynchronous complete method for distributed constraint optimization. In: AAMAS, vol. 3, pp. 161–168. Citeseer (2003)

14. Ramuhalli, P., Halappanavar, M., Coble, J., Dixit, M.: Towards a theory of autonomous reconstitution of compromised cyber-systems. In: 2013 IEEE International Conference on Technologies for Homeland Security (HST), pp. 577–583. IEEE (2013)
15. Van Beek, P., Chen, X.: CPlan: a constraint programming approach to planning. In: AAAI/IAAI, pp. 585–590 (1999)
16. Weyns, D.: Software engineering of self-adaptive systems: an organised tour and future challenges. In: Handbook of Software Engineering (2017)
17. Weyns, D., et al.: On patterns for decentralized control in self-adaptive systems. In: de Lemos, R., Giese, H., Müller, H.A., Shaw, M. (eds.) Software Engineering for Self-Adaptive Systems II. LNCS, vol. 7475, pp. 76–107. Springer, Heidelberg (2013). https://doi.org/10.1007/978-3-642-35813-5_4
18. Whittle, J., Sawyer, P., Bencomo, N., Cheng, B.H., Bruel, J.M.: Relax: incorporating uncertainty into the specification of self-adaptive systems. In: 17th IEEE International Requirements Engineering Conference 2009, RE 2009, pp. 79–88. IEEE (2009)
19. Yokoo, M.: Distributed Constraint Satisfaction: Foundations of Cooperation in Multi-agent Systems. Springer, Heidelberg (2012)

Intelligent Optimization and Machine Learning for 5G Network Control and Management

Carlos Hernández-Chulde[(✉)] and Cristina Cervelló-Pastor

Department of Network Engineering, Universitat Politècnica de Catalunya (UPC),
Barcelona, Spain
{carlos.hernandez,cristina}@entel.upc.edu

Abstract. The adoption of Software Define Networking (SDN), Network Function Virtualization (NFV) and Machine Learning (ML) will play a key role in the control and management of 5G network slices to fulfill the specific requirements of application/services and the new requirements of fifth generation (5G) networks. In this research, we propose a distributed architecture to perform network analytics applying ML techniques in the context of network operation and control of 5G networks.

Keywords: 5G · SDN · NFV · Network slicing · Machine learning

1 Introduction

The fifth generation (5G) of communication networks will bring with new requirements as high data rates, high traffic densities, low latency and high reliability; and use cases as Internet of Things (IoT) and critical communication applications. These requirements and use cases impose new challenges, which demand an efficient, intelligent and agile network management. In 5G, the network has to be flexible and able to adapt changing conditions to guarantee its performance and efficiency in energy and resource management. A flexible network implies a high degree of softwarization, virtualization and automation [3]. From the network perspective, Software Defined Networking (SDN) is considered as the materialization of softwarization concept, and Network Function Virtualization (NFV) of virtualization paradigm [6].

Additionally, 5G will create an ecosystem that boosts innovation opportunities for new applications involving vertical markets such as manufacturing, healthcare, media and entertainment, financial services, public safety, automotive, public transportation, energy utilities, food and agriculture, city management and many more. Each vertical has a specific set of requirements in latency, throughput, availability, reliability, coverage, mobility, etc. To efficiently satisfy these specific needs, tailored logical networks can be created on-demand for each use case. These logical networks are denoted as "network slices". A network slice

© Springer Nature Switzerland AG 2019
F. De la Prieta et al. (Eds.): PAAMS 2019 Workshops, CCIS 1047, pp. 339–342, 2019.
https://doi.org/10.1007/978-3-030-24299-2_33

involves a set of network functions and resources required to run these network functions. SDN and NFV can provide the programmability, flexibility, and modularity that is required to create network slices [8].

Since SDN and NFV allow network functions to run in software instead of being tightly coupled to the hardware, they provide flexibility and reconfigurability to the network. Thus, network functions can be modified, updated and placed at any location of the network. The dynamic behavior of network functions introduces complexities and makes the provisioning, management and control of network slices impractical in a manual way. In this dynamic environment, continuous monitoring and network analytics become compulsory to understand the network behavior. In the same way, providing automation capabilities to the network is essential for network operation and management. Network automation reduce operational costs, avoid human errors and accelerate the service time to market.

On the other hand, the application of ML on network analytics provides the network with learning and decision-making capabilities. ML techniques can extract relevant information from the network data, and then to leverage this knowledge for autonomic network control and management, as well as service provisioning. Based on historical and real time data, ML mechanisms can predict a network behavior and adapt it to the new network conditions by allocating the required amount of network resources without overprovisioning. ML can also be used for energy-saving optimization. If the current demand is low, it would be possible to switch off some elements or migrate services to locations with lower energy costs for optimizing energy consumption. ML may be well applicable for automatic network orchestration and network management, making self-organizing networks feasible. In other words, ML is a key enabler for automation and contributes to addressing the problem of deploying network intelligence. In this context, SDN and NFV combined with ML are key enablers of 5G networks [5].

The 3rd Generation Partnership Project 3GPP has introduced a Network Data Analytics Function (NWDAF) in the 5G System Architecture. In [2], NWDAF is defined as a operator managed network analytics logical function which could provide slice level network data analytics to a NF. The policy control function (PCF) and the network slice selection function (NSSF) are potential consumers of the NWDAF. PCF may use that data in its policy decisions whilst NSSF may use the load level information provided by NWDAF for slice selection. The European Telecommunications Standards Institute (ETSI) has created the Industry Specification Group (ISG) called Experimental Network Intelligence (ENI) that is defining a Cognitive Network Management architecture using artificial intelligence (AI) techniques and context-aware policies. ENI system is an innovative context-aware entity that enables intelligent service operation and management applying technologies, such as big data analysis and artificial intelligence mechanism to adjust offered services based on changes in user needs, environmental conditions and business goals [7].

A great number of related works deals with the application of AI and ML for traditional networking [4], and SDN [9]. These works present the adoption is diverse ML techniques to solve key problems in networking such as: traffic prediction, routing and classification, resource management QoS/QoE prediction and security.

2 Proposal

In 5G networks, it is expected that the number of devices connected to the 5G network will grow exponentially. Therefore, the amount of data collected for network control and management will also increase. It is not workable to run machine learning techniques in a centralized way, because we have to move all the data to be a central data center. As network analytics will assist in decision-making process to apply the adequate policies and configuration parameters in the network, this process must be fast enough in order to minimize the network response time to users' requests and fulfill the latency requirement of 5G. To this end, some decisions have to be made in a distributed way.

In this research, we propose a distributed network analytics architecture based on the 5G 3GPP system architecture, which will adopt machine learning for data analytics, see Fig. 1. In [2], the NWDAF is used for data collection and data analytics in centralized manner. An NWDAF may be used for analytics for one or more Network Slice. Nevertheless, certain analytics can be performed by a network function independently. In this case a NWDAF instance specific to that analytic maybe collocated with the network function.

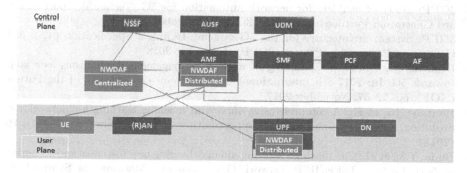

Fig. 1. Proposed distributed network analytics architecture

The main task of the proposed architecture is to provide the network of capabilities to autonomously and proactively execute the control and management of the network slices. For the purposes of this investigation we will also analyze:

- What network data must be analyzed in a centralized or distributed manner?
- What are the more suitable ML techniques in each use case, based on the complexity and accuracy of machine learning techniques? We will consider supervised, unsupervised and reinforce learning.
- Is it possible to apply existing machine learning distributed systems?

This architecture will be a general-purpose data-driven architecture for the use cases described in [1], They are, among others:

- NWDAF-Assisted QoS Provisioning and Adjustment
- NWDAF-Assisted Traffic Handling and Determination of Policy
- NWDAF assisting 5G edge computing
- NWDAF-assisted load balancing/re-balancing of network functions
- NWDAF-Assisted predictable network performance determination of areas with oscillation of network conditions
- How to ensure that slice SLA is guaranteed

3   Reflections

Many services and applications require high data rates, very low latency, higher density of connected devices, higher traffic volume density, and higher mobility. All of this has strong implications on the 5G network control layer design where ML has a great potential to accomplish 5G requirements. ML methods for networking can extract relevant information from the network data, and then to leverage this knowledge for autonomic network control and management, as well as service provisioning.

References

1. 3GPP: Study of enablers for network automation for 5G. Technical report (TR), 3rd Generation Partnership Project (3GPP), December 2018
2. 3GPP: System architecture for the 5G system. Technical Specification (TS), 3rd Generation Partnership Project (3GPP), December 2018
3. Bosneag, A., Wang, M.X.: Intelligent network management mechanisms as a step towards 5G. In: 2017 8th International Conference on the Network of the Future (NOF), pp. 52–57, November 2017
4. Boutaba, R., et al.: A comprehensive survey on machine learning for networking: evolution, applications and research opportunities. J. Internet Serv. Appl. 9(1), 16 (2018)
5. Buda, T.S., et al.: Can machine learning aid in delivering new use cases and scenarios in 5G?. In: 2016 IEEE/IFIP Network Operations and Management Symposium, NOMS 2016, pp. 1279–1284, April 2016
6. Condoluci, M., Mahmoodi, T.: Softwarization and virtualization in 5G mobile networks: benefits, trends and challenges. Comput. Netw. 146, 65–84 (2018)
7. ETSI: Experiential networked intelligence (ENI); ENI use cases. Group report, Experiential Networked Intelligence ETSI ISG, April 2018
8. Ordonez-Lucena, J., et al.: Network slicing for 5G with SDN/NFV: concepts, architectures, and challenges. IEEE Commun. Mag. 55(5), 80–87 (2017)
9. Xie, J., et al.: A survey of machine learning techniques applied to software defined networking (SDN): research issues and challenges. IEEE Commun. Surv. Tutor. 21(1), 393–430 (2018)

A Multi-agent System for Recommending Fire Evacuation Routes in Buildings, Based on Context and IoT

Joaquim Neto[1,2](✉), A. J. Morais[1,3], Ramiro Gonçalves[4], and A. Leça Coelho[2]

[1] Universidade Aberta, Lisbon, Portugal
jaqf.neto@gmail.com, jorge.Morais@uab.pt
[2] Laboratório Nacional de Engenharia Civil, Lisbon, Portugal
{jfn, alcoelho}@lnec.pt
[3] LIAAD - INESC TEC, Porto, Portugal
[4] INESC TEC, UTAD (Universidade de Trás-os-Montes e Alto Douro), Vila Real, Portugal
ramiro@utad.pt

Abstract. The herein proposed research project brings together the area of the multi-agent recommender systems and the IoT and aims to study the extent to which a context-based multi-agent recommender system can contribute to improving efficiency in the evacuation of buildings under a fire emergency, recommending the most adequate and efficient evacuation routes in real time.

Keywords: Recommender systems · Multi-agent systems · *Internet Of Things (IoT)* · Fire evacuation routes

1 Problem Statement and Related Work

The development of solutions capable of guiding the occupants of buildings in a fire emergency to a safe place is a pressing problem that deserves the attention of the academic community and society in general. Providing the building's occupants with real-time information on the most appropriate routes from the beginning of the fire emergency leads them to have more predictable behaviour, thus contributing to reducing the uncertainty that is typically associated with the people's behaviour in a fire situation. By integrating sensors, fire detection systems and other devices and interconnect them through Internet Of Things (IoT) conditions are created for obtaining the contextual information that can contribute to improving the people's well-being.

1.1 Multi-agent Systems and Recommender Systems

An intelligent agent may be defined as *"a computer system located in a given environment and capable of acting autonomously in that environment for the purpose of objectives that have been delegated to it"* [1, p. 21] and that have control over their behaviour and exhibit flexible behaviour in pursuit of their goals [2]. A multi-agent

© Springer Nature Switzerland AG 2019
F. De la Prieta et al. (Eds.): PAAMS 2019 Workshops, CCIS 1047, pp. 343–347, 2019.
https://doi.org/10.1007/978-3-030-24299-2_34

system can be defined as a system composed of multiple interacting intelligent agents [3], capable of working cooperatively to achieve objectives difficult to achieve by an individual agent or by a monolithic system [4, 5].

Recommender systems provide personalised information to users [6] allowing the adaptation to the environment. Although collaborative and content-based recommendation approaches continue to be the most used, they do not consider the context in which the recommendations occur. However, exploring the user's location and what nearby resources are available increases the quality of recommendations [6].

1.2   Related Work

The recommendation of things is a way of taking advantage of IoT for the benefit of people and society [7]. Recommender systems are used to suggest points of interest to tourists [8], to recommend the most efficient routes to motorists [9], help residents in a city [10] or suggest things to users [11]. Related to the area of optimisation of fire evacuation routes in buildings, [12] propose a multi-agent simulation model that assumes the occupants know the topology of the space and the alterations resulting from the fire. A solution supported on the information from different sensors interconnected by IoT is proposed by [13]. In their paper [14] present an architecture of a multi-agent system for evacuation route optimisation in large smart spaces where the best evacuation routes are displayed on smartphones. To provide the recommendation of real-time evacuation routes, [15] present an architecture for a multi-agent based solution, which considers the aspects related to the safety of the route and the influence of people's stress. In their study, [16] present an optimisation model that considers factors such as the length of the pathways, the density of people in the space and the risk factors such as temperature, thermal radiation, and toxic gas concentration.

2   Research Hypothesis and Research Questions

The integration of technology in our day-to-day life is the main objective in the development of applications for IoT [17], allowing, for example, the adaptability of spaces to occupants based on context information obtainable through IoT, such as the case of guiding the occupants of buildings under fire.

Thus, considering that combining multi-agent and recommender systems, supported on IoT, may contribute a solution capable of recommending the most adequate evacuation routes in real-time, our hypothesis can be stated as follows: *A multi-agent recommender system based on contextual information supported on IoT contributes to improving efficiency in the evacuation of buildings under fire, by recommending in real time the more efficient evacuation routes.*

Three research questions may be formulated: *How can a multi-agent approach ensure interoperability between things, people and systems, in a context of a fire building evacuation, supported by IoT? How can the context information supported in the IoT contribute to the evacuation of buildings under fire emergency? How can a multi-agent recommender system based on context improve the efficiency of the evacuation of buildings supported by IoT, by recommending real-time evacuation routes?*

3   Proposed Solution and Evaluation Plan

The herein proposed multi-agent system for the real-time route recommendation, as shown in Fig. 1, is supported on context information obtained from IoT devices installed in the buildings, namely sensors, fire detection systems, or the smartphones of the building's occupants. The recommendations produced by the system will consider contextual factors such as the location, the risk associated with fire or congestion of the evacuation routes. Considering the need to integrate information from the different sources referred above an ontological model will be developed to support the desired interoperability. The most appropriate fire evacuation routes will be made available through digital signage to be displayed on IoT devices as well as on smartphones.

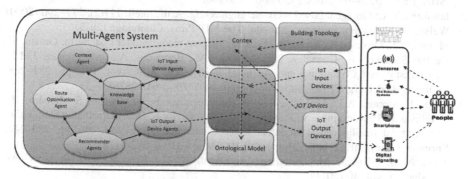

Fig. 1. Multi-agent recommender system global architecture

The prototype will be tested in a simulation environment with 2D plants of the spaces being the basis of the experimental scenarios. Several scenarios corresponding to different types of buildings will be considered and, for each scenario, two different hypotheses will be considered: first, the occupants do not have any information about the fire; second, they know in real time the most appropriate evacuation routes provided by the system proposed here. Thus, for each scenario, the evacuation times will be determined to evaluate the impact of our approach on occupant's safety.

4   Conclusion

Despite the vast study in the fire building evacuation area, we believe there is room for its deepening. The increasing installation of sensors and other IoT devices in buildings, combined with existing fire detection systems, transform these buildings into smart spaces more capable of supporting services to benefit people and society, such as the case of the real-time recommendation of fire evacuation routes herein proposed. By providing real-time information about the most appropriate routes from the beginning of the emergency, more predictable behaviour of the occupants is expected, thereby making it possible to reduce the evacuation time.

With the herein proposed solution some contributions to the state-of-the-art may be highlight: (i) the use of a multi-agent recommender system based on context, and on an ontological model; (ii) the use of contextual information to generate the recommendations; (iii) the creation of a solution that, with regard to routes' notification to the occupants, exempt the user to use any type of personal device which may not be available or even inconvenient to use under emergency; and (iv) the creation of the conditions to positively condition the reaction of the people to the fire.

References

1. Wooldridge, M.: An Introduction to Multiagent Systems, 2nd edn. Wiley, Hoboken (2009). ISBN-10: 0470519460 ISBN-13: 978-0470519462
2. Jennings, N.R.: On agent-based software engineering. Artif. Intell. **117**(2), 277–296 (2000)
3. Weiss, G.: Multiagent Systems, 2nd edn. The MIT Press, Cambridge (2013)
4. Morais, A.J., Oliveira, E., Jorge, A.M.: A multi-agent recommender system. In: Omatu, S., De Paz Santana, J.F., González, S.R., Molina, J.M., Bernardos, A.M., Rodríguez, J.M.C. (eds.) Distributed Computing and Artificial Intelligence. AISC, vol. 151, pp. 281–288. Springer, Heidelberg (2012). https://doi.org/10.1007/978-3-642-28765-7_33
5. Neto, J., Morais, A.J.: Multi-agent web recommendations. In: Omatu, S., Bersini, H., Corchado, J.M., Rodríguez, S., Pawlewski, P., Bucciarelli, E. (eds.) Distributed Computing and Artificial Intelligence, 11th International Conference. AISC, vol. 290, pp. 235–242. Springer, Cham (2014). https://doi.org/10.1007/978-3-319-07593-8_28
6. Jannach, D., Zanker, M., Felfernig, A., Friedrich, G.: Recommender Systems: An Introduction, vol. 40 (2011)
7. Yao, L., Sheng, Q.Z., Ngu, A.H.H., Ashman, H., Li, X.: Exploring recommendations in internet of things. In: Proceedings of 37th International ACM SIGIR Conference on Research and Development in Information Retrieval - SIGIR 2014, pp. 855–858 (2014)
8. García-Magariño, I.: Practical multi-agent system application for simulation of tourists in Madrid routes with INGENIAS. In: Demazeau, Y., Zambonelli, F., Corchado, J.M., Bajo, J. (eds.) PAAMS 2014. LNCS (LNAI), vol. 8473, pp. 122–133. Springer, Cham (2014). https://doi.org/10.1007/978-3-319-07551-8_11
9. Di Martino, S., Rossi, S.: An architecture for a mobility recommender system in smart cities. Procedia Comput. Sci. **98**, 425–430 (2016)
10. Tu, M., Chang, Y.-K., Chen, Y.-T.: A context-aware recommender system framework for IoT based interactive digital signage in urban space. In: Proceedings of the Second International Conference on IoT in Urban Space, pp. 39–42 (2016)
11. Cha, S., Ruiz, M.P., Wachowicz, M., Tran, L.H., Cao, H., Maduako, I.: The role of an IoT platform in the design of real-time recommender systems. In: 2016 IEEE 3rd World Forum Internet Things, WF-IoT 2016, pp. 448–453 (2017)
12. Tan, L., Hu, M., Lin, H.: Agent-based simulation of building evacuation: combining human behavior with predictable spatial accessibility in a fire emergency. Inf. Sci. (NY) **295**, 53–66 (2015)
13. Weifang, Z., Qiang, C.: Implementation of intelligent fire evacuation route based on internet of things. In: 2015 IEEE Advanced Information Technology, Electronic and Automation Control Conference (IAEAC), pp. 934–938 (2015)
14. Lujak, M., Giordani, S., Ossowski, S.: An architecture for safe evacuation route recommendation in smart spaces. In: CEUR Workshop Proceedings, vol. 1678 (2016)

15. Lujak, M., Ossowski, S.: Evacuation route optimization architecture considering human factor. AI Commun. **30**(1), 53–66 (2017)
16. Li, J.J., Zhu, H.Y.: A risk-based model of evacuation route optimization under fire. Procedia Eng. **211**, 365–371 (2018)
17. Miranda, J., et al.: From the internet of things to the internet of people. IEEE Internet Comput. **19**(2), 40–47 (2015)

Retraction Note to: A Survey on Software-Defined Networks and Edge Computing over IoT

Ricardo S. Alonso⑩, Inés Sittón-Candanedo⑩,
Sara Rodríguez-González⑩, Óscar García⑩, and Javier Prieto⑩

Retraction Note to:
Chapter 25 in: F. De la Prieta et al. (Eds.): *Highlights*
of Practical Applications of Survivable Agents
and Multi-Agent Systems, **CCIS 1047,**
https://doi.org/10.1007/978-3-030-24299-2_25

The Series Editor and the publisher have retracted this chapter. An investigation by the publisher found that a number of chapters, including this one, from multiple conference proceedings raise various concerns, including but not limited to compromised editorial handling, inappropriate or unusual citation behavior and undisclosed competing interests. Based on the findings of the investigation, the Series Editor and the publisher no longer have confidence in the results and conclusions of this chapter.

The authors disagree with this retraction.

The retracted version of this chapter can be found at
https://doi.org/10.1007/978-3-030-24299-2_25

F. De la Prieta et al. (Eds.): PAAMS 2019 Workshops, CCIS 1047, p. C1, 2024.
https://doi.org/10.1007/978-3-030-24299-2_35

Author Index

Printed in the United States
by Baker & Taylor Publisher Services

Printed in the United States
by Baker & Taylor Publisher Services